FROMMER'S

COMPREHENSIVE TRAVEL GUIDE

PUERTO RICO '95-'96

T3-BOJ-980

by Darwin Porter
Assisted by Danforth Prince

MACMILLAN • USA

MACMILLAN TRAVEL
A Simon & Schuster Macmillan Company
1633 Broadway
New York, NY 10019

Design by Robert Bull Design
Maps by Ortelius Design

ISBN 0-671-88379-8
ISSN 1062-4775

SPECIAL SALES
Bulk purchases (10 +) copies of Frommer's travel guides are
available to corporations at special discounts. The Special Sales
Department can produce custom editions to be used as premiums
and/or for sales promotion to suit individual needs. Existing
editions can be produced with custom cover imprints such as
corporate logos. For more information write to: Special Sales,
Macmillan General Reference, 15 Columbus Circle, New York,
NY 10023.

Manufactured in the United States of America.

CONTENTS

LIST OF MAPS

INVITATION TO THE READER

In researching this book, I have come across many fine establishments, the best of which I have included here. I'm sure that many of you will also come across appealing hotels, inns, restaurants, guesthouses, shops, and attractions. Please don't keep them to yourself. Share your experiences, especially if you want to comment on places that have been included in this edition that have changed for the worse. You can address your letters to:

Darwin Porter
Frommer's Puerto Rico '95–'96
c/o Macmillan Travel
15 Columbus Circle
New York, NY 10023

A DISCLAIMER

Readers are advised that prices fluctuate in the course of time, and travel information changes under the impact of the varied and volatile factors that affect the travel industry. Neither the author nor the publisher can be held responsible for the experiences of readers while traveling. Readers are invited to write to the publisher with ideas, comments, and suggestions for future editions.

SAFETY ADVISORY

Whenever you're traveling in an unfamiliar city or country, stay alert. Be aware of your immediate surroundings. Wear a moneybelt and keep a close eye on your possessions. Be particularly careful with cameras, purses, and wallets, all favorite targets of thieves and pickpockets.

CHAPTER 1

INTRODUCING PUERTO RICO

It was on Columbus's second voyage to the New World in 1493 that he sighted the island of San Juan (St. John the Baptist), later renamed Puerto Rico. Lush and verdant, Puerto Rico is only half the size of New Jersey, roughly speaking. It's located some 1,000 miles southeast of the tip of Florida. As such, it is at the hub of the Caribbean chain of islands, and you'll probably fly in and out of San Juan at least once if you're doing much touring in the area.

With 272 miles of Atlantic and Caribbean coastline and a culture dating back to the Taíno peoples 2,000 years ago, Puerto Rico is a formidable attraction. Today an American commonwealth, the island has experienced many political changes since the days of its first governor, Juan Ponce de León. Old San Juan is its greatest historic center, with nearly 500 years reflected in its restored Spanish colonial architecture.

The oldest city in the Caribbean under the U.S. flag, San Juan is the world's second-largest home port for cruise-ship passengers. The old port of San Juan faced a waterfront-renewal project, costing $100 million, and the paseo de la Princesa, dating from the 19th century, returned with royal palms and fountains after a two-year, $2.8-million restoration. However, the beauty and charm have remained since the first navigators set foot on Puerto Rican soil and called it the "island of enchantment."

You'll find some of the best golf and tennis in the Caribbean at such posh resorts as the Hyatt Dorado Beach and the Palmas del Mar. Accommodations have also greatly improved at out-on-the-island cities, such as Mayagüez with its Hilton. Paradores—government-sponsored inns—are sprinkled across the island for visitors who want a more personal experience than that provided by the posh hotels and gambling casinos of San Juan, with their Las Vegas–type shows.

1. GEOGRAPHY, LANGUAGE & PEOPLE

GEOGRAPHY

Puerto Rico is the most easterly and the smallest of the four major islands that form the Greater Antilles. (The other three land masses in this cluster include Cuba,

WHAT'S SPECIAL ABOUT PUERTO RICO

Beaches

- ☐ Luquillo, not far from San Juan, a crescent-shaped strip of white sand edged by a vast coconut grove.
- ☐ Punta Higuero, near the town of Rincón, one of the finest surfing beaches in the world.
- ☐ Boquerón Beach, a wide expanse of hard-packed sand ringed by coconut palms, south of Mayagüez.

Great Towns and Villages

- ☑ San Juan, the capital, cruise-ship favorite and international air hub, with a seven-square-block district of Spanish colonial architecture.
- ☐ San Germán, founded in 1512, a museum piece of Spanish colonial architecture, once the rival of San Juan.
- ☐ Ponce, the island's second-largest city, dating from 1692—named for Ponce de León and noted for its turn-of-the-century charm.

Ace Attractions

- ☑ El Yunque, 28,000-acre tropical rain forest, the only one in the U.S. National Forest system.
- ☐ Río Camuy Cave Park, a vast subterranean network of canyons, caverns, and sinkholes.

- ☐ Taíno Indian Ceremonial Ball Park, outside Utuado, where the early inhabitants celebrated rituals and practiced sports, two centuries before the European discovery of the New World.
- ☑ Arecibo Observatory, a radar/radiotelescope built inside a crater in the earth, the largest such facility in the world.

Museums

- ☑ The Museo de Arte de Ponce, Puerto Rico's most important art museum, with a historical collection donated by a wealthy former governor.

Historic Buildings

- ☑ Colonial-era structures such as El Morro, built by order of the King of Spain in 1540, the Caribbean's most outstanding example of military architecture.

Special Events

- ☐ The Casals Festival, a world-class music festival held every June since 1957—one of Puerto Rico's many outstanding religious and cultural celebrations.

Jamaica, and Hispaniola, which is home to two nations—Haiti and the Dominican Republic.) Surrounded by the Atlantic Ocean to the north and the Caribbean Sea to the south, Puerto Rico is flanked by a trio of smaller islands—Vieques and Culebra to the east and Mona to the west—that are considered its satellites by both politicians and geologists.

The island's most noteworthy geological feature is the Cordillera—the towering mountains that rise high above its central region. Geologists have identified the island's summits as the high parts of a chain of mountains whose mass is mostly buried beneath the sea. These mountains, probably the oldest of the many land masses of the West Indies, form a dramatic relief in Puerto Rico.

What makes their altitudes even more impressive is the existence, about 75 miles to the island's north, of one of the deepest depressions in the Atlantic, the Puerto Rico trough. Running more or less parallel to the island's northern shoreline, it reaches depths of up to 30,000 feet. Although not as obvious as the trench near the northern coastline, the sea floor a few miles from the island's southern coast also drops off, to nearly 17,000 feet below sea level. Geologists have calculated that if the base of this mountain chain were at sea level, the chain would be one of the highest land masses in the world. Puerto Rico's highest summit (Cerro de Punta at 4,389 feet) would exceed in altitude even the highest peaks of the Himalayas.

Most of Puerto Rico's geology, especially its mountain peaks, resulted from volcanic activity that deposited lava and igneous rock in consecutive layers. To a lesser degree, the island is also composed of quartz, diomites, and, along some of its edges, coral limestone.

REGIONS IN BRIEF

Although the many geological divisions of Puerto Rico might not be immediately apparent to the average visitor, its people take great pride in stressing the island's diversity. Its most important geological and political divisions are as follows:

SAN JUAN   One of the largest and best-preserved complexes of Spanish colonial architecture in the Caribbean, Old San Juan (founded in 1521) is the oldest capital city under the U.S. flag. Once a linchpin of Spanish dominance in the Caribbean, it has three major fortresses, miles of solidly built stone ramparts, a charming collection of antique buildings, and a modern business center. The city's economy is the most stable and solid in all of Latin America.

San Juan is the site of the official home and office of the governor of Puerto Rico (La Fortaleza), the 16th-century residence of Ponce de León's family, and several of the oldest places of Christian worship in the western hemisphere. Its bars, restaurants, shops, and nightclubs attract an animated group of patrons and fans as well. In recent years, the old city has become surrounded by acres of densely populated modern buildings, including an ultramodern airport, which makes San Juan one of the most dynamic cities in the West Indies.

THE NORTHEAST   The power and prestige of the capital city dominate Puerto Rico's northeast. Despite the region's congestion, there are still many remote areas, including some of the island's most important nature reserves. Among the region's most popular towns, parks, and attractions are the following:

El Yunque   In the Luquillo Mountains, 35 miles east of San Juan, El Yunque is a favorite escape from the capital. Teeming with plant and animal life, it is a sprawling tropical forest whose ecosystems are strictly protected by the U.S. Forest Service. Some 100 billion gallons of rainwater fall here each year, allowing about 250 species of trees and flowers to flourish.

Las Cabezas de San Juan Nature Reserve   About an hour's drive from San Juan, this is one of the island's newest ecological refuges. It was established in 1991 on 316 acres of forest, mangrove swamp, offshore cays, coral reefs, and freshwater lagoons—a representative sampling of virtually every ecosystem on Puerto Rico. There is a visitor's center, a 19th-century lighthouse ("El Faro") that still works, and ample opportunity to forget the pressures of urban life.

Loíza Aldea   Located about 12 miles east of San Juan, this coastal town is the center of an area whose population is largely composed of descendants of African, specifically Yoruba, slaves. During the 16th century, African slaves were imported to pan for gold in the nearby watercourse, the Río Grande de Loíza, and to work the sugarcane fields. Later, slaves from other Caribbean islands—either escapees who had been recaptured or spoils of war taken from rival British plantations—were added to the region's cultural mix. The town was founded in 1719; the foundations of one church were laid about 70 years before that. The town today is one of the three poorest municipalities on Puerto Rico. The region, with about 50,000 inhabitants, is considered the center of African-Hispanic culture on Puerto Rico.

Fajardo   Small and sleepy, this town was originally established as a supply depot for the many pirates who plied the nearby waters. Today, a host of private yachts bob at anchor in its harbor, and the many offshore cays provide naturalists with secluded beaches. From Fajardo, ferryboats make choppy but frequent runs to the offshore islands of Vieques and Culebra.

Caguas   Located 20 miles south of San Juan, Caguas is the largest city in the interior and the focal point of the broad and fertile Turabo Valley. Ringed by

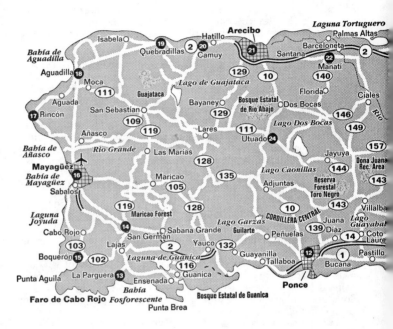

Aguadilla 18
Arecibo 21
Boquerón 15
Camuy 20
Caribbean
  National Forest 7
Cayey 10
Coamo 11
Culebra 25

Dorado 23
El Yunque 6
Fajardo 5
Guayama 9
Humacao 8
La Parguera 13
Loíza Aldea 2
Luquillo 4
Luquillo Beach 3

Ocean

SAN JUAN

Dorado 23
Vega Baja
Toa Baja
Bayamón
Cataño
Sabana Abajo
Punta Uvero
187 Loíza Aldea
2 Mediania Alta
3 Cabezas de San Juan
Luquillo Beach
(160)
Vega Alta
(155)
(164)
Corozal
Guaynabo
lorovis
167
Naranjito
1
52
Trujillo Alto
Carolina
Río Grande
3 Palmer
6 El Yunque
186
7
191
Caribbean Nat'l Forest
Fajardo 5
3
Las Croabas
Playa de Fajardo
Lago de Loíza
185
149
Aguas Buenas
Comerio
173 Caguas
El Cinco
Gurabo
Juncos
Río
Blanco
31
Las
Santa Maria
Ceiba
Roosevelt Roads U.S. Naval Res.
Quebrada Seca
Orocovis
156
Lago Cidra
Cidra
Piedras
San Lorenzo
Naguabo
30
Humacao 8
Playa de Naguabo
Playa de Humacao
Barranquitas
Aibonito
181
SIERRA DE CAYEY
155
14
Cayey 10
182
3
Yabucoa
Pasaje de Vieques
11 Coamo
153
1
52
15
Lago Carite
Guayama
Lago Patillas
Maunabo
Isla Vieques
see inset below
↓
52
elazquez
Salinas
Las Palmas
9 Palillas
Arroyo
anta Isabel
anta Isabel
Coqui
3
Jobás
Central Aguirre

Culebra
25
Puerto Rico

Sea

Vieques
26

Manatí 22
Mayagüez 16
Ponce 12
Quebradillas 19
Rincón 17
San Germán 14
San Juan 1
Utuado 24
Vieques 26

mountain peaks, the city has a population of around 120,000, many of whom commute to work in San Juan. The city was named after Caguax, the 16th-century Taíno chief who ruled the valley during the Spanish Conquest and whose peacemaking efforts eventually led, according to legend, to his conversion to Christianity. The town's central square, Plaza Palmer, with its 19th-century cathedral, is quite charming.

THE SOUTHEAST The southeastern quadrant has some of the most heavily developed as well as some of the least developed sections of the island.

Humacao Because of its easy access to San Juan, this small, verdant inland town has increasingly become one of the capital's residential suburbs.

Palmas del Mar This sprawling vacation and residential resort community is located near Humacao. A splendid golf course covers some of the 2,800-acre grounds, which once housed a sugarcane plantation.

The Reserva Forestal Carite This 6,000-acre nature reserve is known simply as Guavate. Its relatively cool temperatures (averaging 72°F) and frequent rainfall sustain acres of teak, mahogany, and sierra palm trees. The park's highest peak is the 3,000-foot Cerro La Santa, which has a radio/television tower on top.

Arroyo This village on Puerto Rico's southwestern coast was founded in 1855 and has slumbered ever since in quiet obscurity, a favorite retreat of escapists. It was visited in 1848 by Samuel Morse, the inventor of the Morse Code, who personally installed the local telegraph line. The town's main street, calle Morse, is named in his honor. Several of the town's most impressive houses were built by New England sea captains who—perhaps piqued by the calm, tropical beauty of the place—decided to settle there.

Barranquitas Set inland at an altitude of more than 1,800 feet, Barranquitas is considered one of the most photogenic towns on Puerto Rico. Capped with a dramatically situated Catholic church, the town's houses rise almost on top of one another, in a style similar to that of a fortified village in Spain. The town's most famous son was the statesman Luís Muñoz Rivera, who is honored by a small museum in the house where he was born in 1859. Near Barranquitas is one of Puerto Rico's deepest and most spectacular gorges, the nearly inaccessible canyon of San Cristobal. There, cliffs nearly 500 feet high overlook the raging waters of the Usabon River.

Coamo Although today Coamo is a bedroom community for the capital, originally it was the site of two different Taíno communities. Founded in 1579, it now has a charming main square draped with bougainvillea and one of the best-known Catholic churches on Puerto Rico. Even more famous, however, are the mineral springs whose therapeutic warm waters helped President Franklin D. Roosevelt during his recovery from polio. (Some historians claim that these springs inspired the legend of the Fountain of Youth, which Ponce de León had heard from the native peoples before heading off to Florida to search for it.)

THE SOUTHWEST One of Puerto Rico's most beautiful regions, the southwest is rich in local lore, civic pride, and natural wonders.

Ponce Puerto Rico's second-largest city, Ponce has always prided itself on its independence from the Spanish-derived laws and taxes that governed San Juan and the rest of the island. Long-ago home of some of the island's shrewdest traders, merchants, and smugglers, it is enjoying a renaissance as citizens and visitors rediscover its unique cultural and architectural charms. Located about 90 minutes by car from the capital on Puerto Rico's southern coast, Ponce contains a handful of superb museums, one of the most charming main squares in the Caribbean, an ancient cathedral, dozens of authentically restored colonial-era buildings, and a number of outlying mansions and villas that, at the time of their construction, were among the most opulent on the island.

Mayagüez The third-largest city on Puerto Rico, Mayagüez is named after the *majagua*, the Amerindian word for a tree that grows abundantly in the area. Because of an earthquake that destroyed almost everything in town in 1917, few old buildings remain. The town is known as the commercial and industrial capital of Puerto Rico's western sector. Its botanical garden is among the finest on the island.

San Germán   Located on the island's southwestern corner, small, sleepy, and charming San Germán was named after Ferdinand of Spain's second wife, Germaine de Foix, whom he married in 1503. San Germán's central church, Porta Coeli, was built in 1606. At one time much of the populace was engaged in piracy, pillaging the ships that sailed off the nearby coastline. The central area of this village is still sought out for its many reminders of the island's Spanish heritage and colonial charm.

Yauco   Established relatively late in the island's history (in 1756), Yauco immediately attracted a population of Corsicans and Haitian French, who grew a distinctive brand of coffee known for its low caffeine and mild flavor. By 1900, ravaged by hurricane damage and competition from other coffee-producing countries (such as Colombia), the town had declined into obscurity. Today it retains its steeply sloping streets, a handful of old houses, aromatic coffee, and a distinctive air of faded Spanish grandeur.

Cabo Rojo   Established in 1772, Cabo Rojo reached the peak of its prosperity during the 19th century, when immigrants from around the Mediterranean, fleeing revolutions in their own countries, arrived to establish sugarcane plantations. Today, cattle graze peacefully on land originally devoted almost exclusively to sugarcane, while the area's many varieties of exotic birds draw birdwatchers from throughout North America. Even the offshore waters are fertile: It's estimated that nearly half of all the fish consumed on Puerto Rico are caught in waters near Cabo Rojo.

Boquerón   Famous for the beauty of its beach and the abundant birds and wildlife in the nearby Boquerón Forest Reserve, this small and sleepy village is now ripe for large-scale tourism-related development. During the early 19th century, the island's most-feared pirate, Roberto Cofresi, terrorized the Puerto Rican coastline from a secret lair in a cave nearby.

La Parguera   Named after a breed of snapper (*pargos*) that abounds in the waters nearby, La Parguera is a quiet coastal town best known for the phosphorescent waters of La Bahía Fosforescente (Phosphorescent Bay). There, sheltered from the waves of the sea, billions of plankton (luminescent dinoflagellates) glow dimly when they are disturbed by movements of the water. The town comes alive on weekends, when crowds of young people from San Juan arrive to party the nights away. Filling modest rooming houses, they temporarily change the texture of the town as bands produce long and loud sessions of salsa music.

THE NORTHWEST   A fertile area with many rivers bringing valuable water for irrigation from the high mountains of the Cordillera, the northwest also offers abundant opportunities for sightseeing. The region's principal districts include the following:

Arecibo   Located on the northern coastline a two-hour drive west of San Juan, Arecibo was originally founded in 1556. Although little remains of its original architecture, the town is well known to physicists and astronomers around the world because of the radar/radiotelescope that fills a concave depression between six of the region's hills. Equal in size to 13 football fields and operated jointly by the National Science Foundation and Cornell University, it studies the shape and formation of the galaxies by accumulating and deciphering radio waves from space.

Río Camuy Cave Park   Located near Arecibo, this park's greatest attraction is underground, where a network of underground rivers and caves provide some of the most enjoyable spelunking in the world. At its heart lies one of the largest known underground rivers. Covering 300 acres above ground, the park is sought out by cave explorers the world over.

Rincón   Named after the 16th-century landowner Don Gonzalo Rincón, who donated its site to the poor of his district, the tiny town of Rincón is famous throughout Puerto Rico for its world-class surfing and beautiful beaches. The lighthouse that warns yachters away from dangerous offshore reefs is one of the most powerful on Puerto Rico.

Aguadilla   During his second voyage to the New World in 1493, Christopher

Columbus landed nearby. Today, the town has a busy airport, fine beaches, and a growing tourism-based infrastructure. It is also the center of Puerto Rico's tiny lace-making industry, a craft imported here many centuries ago by immigrants from Spain, Holland, and Belgium.

Utuado Small, sunny, and nestled amid the hills of the interior, Utuado is famous as the center of the *jíbaro* (hillbilly) culture of Puerto Rico. Some of Puerto Rico's finest mountain musicians have come from Utuado and mention the town in many of their ballads. The surrounding landscape is sculpted with caves and lushly covered with a variety of tropical plants and trees.

THE OFFSHORE ISLANDS Few *norteamericanos* realize that Puerto Rico has at least four well-known islands and a multitude of tiny cays lying offshore. The most famous of these include:

Cayo Santiago Lying off the southeastern coast is the small island of Cayo Santiago. Home to a group of about two dozen scientists and a community of rhesus monkeys originally imported from India, the island is a medical experimentation center run by the U.S. Public Health Service. Monkeys are studied in a "wild" but controlled environment both for insights into the behavioral sciences and for possible cures for such maladies as diabetes and arthritis. Apart from members of the scientific community, visitors are not permitted on Cayo Santiago.

Culebra and Vieques Located off the eastern coast, these two islands are among the most unsullied and untrammeled areas in the West Indies. Come here for sun, almost no scheduled activities, fresh seafood, clear waters, sandy beaches, and teeming coral reefs. Vieques is especially proud of its phosphorescent bay.

Mona Remote, uninhabited, and teeming with bird life, this barren island off the western coast is ringed by soaring cliffs and finely textured white beaches. Although overnight camping is permitted, the island has almost no facilities, so visitors seldom stay for more than a day of swimming and picnicking. The currents that surround Mona on all sides are legendary for their dangerous eddies, undertows, and sharks.

LANGUAGE

Spanish, of course, is the language of Puerto Rico, although English is widely spoken, especially in hotels, restaurants, shops, and nightclubs that attract tourists. In the hinterlands, however, Spanish prevails.

If you plan to travel extensively on Puerto Rico but don't speak Spanish, pick up a Spanish-language phrasebook. The most popular is *Berlitz Spanish for Travelers*, published by Collier Macmillan. The University of Chicago's *Pocketbook Dictionary* is equally helpful. If you already have a basic knowledge of Spanish and want to improve both your word usage and your sentence structure while in Puerto Rico, consider purchasing a copy of *Spanish Now*, published by Barron's.

Many Amerindian words from pre-Columbian times have been retained in the language. For example, the Puerto Rican national anthem, entitled "La Borinqueña," refers back to the Arawak name for the island, Borinquen, while Mayagüez, Yauco, Caguas, Guaynabo, and Arecibo are all pre-Columbian place names.

Many Amerindian words were borrowed to describe the new phenomena of the New World. The natives slept in *hamacas*, and today Puerto Ricans still lounge in hammocks. The god Huracan was feared by the Arawaks just as much as

---

IMPRESSIONS

A machete is the only instrument used in their work. With it, they cut the sticks, vines, and palm leaves to build their houses and also clear the ground and plant and cultivate their crops.
—FRAY INIGO ABBAD

contemporaries fear autumn hurricanes. African words were also added to the linguistic mix, and Castilian Spanish was significantly modified. For example, the Spanish *ll* and *y* sounds are pronounced as *J*s in English. This is best exemplified by the word *Luquillo,* the name of the island's most popular beach, which North American foreigners learn to pronounce by imitating the sounds evoked by the English-language phrase, "Look here, Joe." Words that end in *e* sounds are often truncated, such as *noche* in Spanish becoming *noch'. Café con leche* in Spain becomes *café co' lech'* in Puerto Rico. *S* sounds are often muted and perhaps will not appear at all. An example of this is in the Spanish word *gracias,* meaning "thank you," which will be pronounced in Puerto Rico as *graciah.*

With the American takeover in 1898, English became the first Germanic language to be introduced into Puerto Rico. This linguistic marriage led to what some scholars call Spanglish, a colloquial dialect blending English and Spanish into forms not considered classically correct in either linguistic tradition. An example of this is the borrowed English *el coat* (describing an outer garment).

The bilingual confusion was also greatly accelerated by the mass migration to the U.S. mainland of thousands of Puerto Ricans, who quickly altered their speech patterns to conform to the language used in the urban Puerto Rican communities of such cities as New York.

THE PEOPLE

Some 3.4 million people inhabit the island of Puerto Rico, making it one of the most densely populated islands in the world. There are about 1,000 people per square mile, a ratio higher than that within any of the 50 states. It is estimated that some 2 million Puerto Ricans have migrated to the United States. Had these people remained on Puerto Rico, the island would be so densely populated that there would be virtually no room for people to live. Because of the massive migration to the mainland, more Puerto Ricans are said to live in New York City than in San Juan. In recent years, many Puerto Ricans have returned to their island home, in large part because of inadequate economic opportunity in the United States.

On the island, one-third of the population is concentrated in the San Juan/Carolina/Bayamón metropolitan area. When the United States acquired the island in 1898, most Puerto Ricans worked in agriculture, but today, most jobs are industrial and are situated in the metropolitan areas.

The people of Puerto Rico represent a cultural and racial mix. When the Spanish forced the Taíno peoples into slavery, virtually the entire indigenous population was decimated, except for a few Amerindians who escaped into the remote mountains. Eventually they intermarried with the poor Spanish farmers and became known as *jíbaros.* Because of industrialization and migration to the cities, few jíbaros remain.

Besides the slaves imported from Africa to work on the plantations, other ethnic groups joined the island's racial mix. Fleeing Simón Bolívar's independence movements in South America, Spanish loyalists fled to Puerto Rico—a fiercely conservative Spanish colony during the early 1800s. French families also flocked here from both Louisiana and Haiti, as changing governments or violent revolutions turned their worlds upside down. Meanwhile, as word of the rich sugarcane economy reached economically depressed Scotland and Ireland, many farmers from those countries also journeyed to Puerto Rico in search of a better life.

During the mid-19th century, labor was needed to build roads; initially Chinese workers were imported for this task, followed by workers from such countries as Italy, France, Germany, and even Lebanon. American expatriates came to the island after 1898. Long after Spain had lost control of Puerto Rico, Spanish immigrants continued to arrive on the island. The most significant new immigrant population arrived in the

۞ Some 2 million Puerto Ricans have migrated to the United States.

1960s, when thousands of Cubans fled from Fidel Castro's Communist state. The latest arrivals in Puerto Rico have come from the economically depressed Dominican Republic.

2. HISTORY & POLITICS

DATELINE

- **1493** Christopher Columbus, the first European to visit Puerto Rico, lands near Aguadilla on November 19.
- **1508** Juan Ponce de León becomes the first governor of Puerto Rico.
- **1511** Amerindians (both Taínos and their traditional enemies, the Caribs) rebel against Spanish enslavement.
- **1521** The island Columbus named San Juan Bautista is renamed Puerto Rico ("rich port").
- **1595** English soldiers briefly conquer Puerto Rico.
- **1600** San Juan is enclosed by the most formidable ramparts in the Caribbean.
- **1625** Holland attacks San Juan, burning the city, but the Spanish repel the Dutch troops.
- **1868** Spanish governors repress a revolt in the mountain city of Lares.
- **1873** Slavery is abolished.

(continues)

HISTORY

PREHISTORY TO COLUMBUS

Although the Spanish occupation was probably the decisive factor defining Puerto Rico's current culture, the island was settled many thousands of years ago by Amerindians. The oldest archeological remains yet discovered were unearthed in 1948. Found in a limestone cave a few miles east of San Juan, in Loíza Aldea, the artifacts consisted of conch shells, stone implements, and crude hatchets deposited there by tribal peoples during the first century of the Christian Era. These people belonged to an archaic, seminomadic, cave-dwelling culture that had not developed either agriculture or pottery. Some ethnologists suggest that these early inhabitants originated in Florida, immigrated to Cuba, and from there began a steady migration along the West Indian archipelago.

Around A.D. 300, a different group of Amerindians, the Arawaks, migrated to Puerto Rico from the Orinoco Basin in what is now Venezuela. Known by ethnologists as the Saladoids, they were the first of Puerto Rico's inhabitants to make and use pottery, which they decorated with exotic geometric designs in red and white. Subsisting on fish, crabs, and whatever else they could catch, they populated the big island and the offshore island of Vieques as well.

By about A.D. 600, this culture had disappeared, bringing to an end the island's historic era of pottery making. Ethnologists' opinions differ as to whether the tribes were eradicated by new invasions from South America, succumbed to starvation or plague, or simply evolved into the next culture that dominated Puerto Rico—the Ostionoids.

Much less skilled at making pottery than their predecessors but more accomplished at polishing and grinding stones for jewelry and tools, the Ostionoids were the ethnic predecessors of the tribe that became the Taíno. The Taínos inhabited Puerto Rico when it was discovered and invaded by the Spanish beginning in 1493. The Taínos were spread throughout the West Indies but reached their greatest development in Puerto Rico and neighboring Hispaniola (the island shared by Haiti and the Dominican Republic).

Taíno culture impressed both the Spanish (who observed it) and modern sociologists; the Amerindians' achievements included construction of ceremonial ball parks whose boundaries were marked by upright stone dolmens, development of a universal language, and creation of a complicated religious cosmology. There was a hierarchy of deities who inhabited the sky; Yocahu was the supreme Creator. Another god, Jurancan, was perpetually angry and ruled the power of the hurricane. Myths and traditions were perpetuated through ceremonial dances (*areytos*), drumbeats, oral traditions, and a ceremonial ball game played between opposing teams (of 10 to 30 players per team) with a rubber ball; winning this game was thought to bring a good harvest and strong, healthy children.

Skilled at agriculture and hunting, the Taínos were also good sailors, canoe makers, and navigators.

About 100 years before the Spanish invasion, the Taínos were challenged by an invading South American tribe—the Caribs. Fierce, warlike, sadistic, and adept at using poison-tipped arrows, they raided Taíno settlements for slaves (especially female) and bodies for the completion of their rites of cannibalism. Some ethnologists argue that the preeminence of the Taínos, shaken by the attacks of the Caribs, was already jeopardized by the time of the Spanish occupation. In fact, it was the Caribs who fought the most effectively against the Europeans; their behavior probably led the Europeans to unfairly attribute warlike tendencies to all of the island's tribes. A dynamic tension between the Taínos and the Caribs certainly existed when Christopher Columbus landed on Puerto Rico.

In order to understand Puerto Rico's prehistoric era, it is important to know that the Taínos, far more than the Caribs, contributed greatly to the everyday life and language that evolved during the Spanish occupation. Taíno place names are still used for such towns as Utuado, Mayagüez, Caguas, and Humacao. Many Taíno implements and techniques were copied directly by the Europeans, including the *bohío* (straw hut) and the *hamaca* (hammock), the musical instrument known as the *maracas*, and the method of making cassava bread. Also, many Taíno superstitions and legends were adopted and adapted by the Spanish and still influence the Puerto Rican imagination.

THE SPANISH OCCUPATION

Christopher Columbus became the first European to land on the shores of Puerto Rico, on November 19, 1493, near what would become the town of Aguadilla, during his second voyage to the New World. Giving the island the name San Juan Bautista, he sailed on in search of shores with more obvious riches for the taking. A European foothold on the island was established in 1508 when Juan Ponce de León, the first governor of Puerto Rico, imported colonists from the nearby island of Hispaniola. They founded the town of Caparra, which lay close to the site of present-day San Juan. The town was almost immediately wracked with internal power struggles among the Spanish settlers, who pressed the native peoples into servitude, evangelized them, and frantically sought for gold, thus quickly changing the face of the island.

Meanwhile, the Amerindians began dying at an alarm-

DATELINE

• **1897** Spain grants Puerto Rico a measure of autonomy.
• **1898** U.S. army lands troops in Puerto Rico; at the end of the Spanish-American War, Spain cedes Puerto Rico to the United States.
• **1900** U.S. Congress recognizes Puerto Rico as an unincorporated territory, the governor appointed by the U.S. president.
• **1917** Puerto Ricans are granted U.S. citizenship, and islanders are given the right to elect their own legislature.
• **1935** FDR authorizes public works projects.
• **1940** Partida Popular Democratica takes control of the Puerto Rican Senate.
• **1944** U.S. Senate approves bill granting Puerto Ricans the right to elect their own governor, as Operation Bootstrap is launched.
• **1946** Truman designates native-born Jesús Piñero governor.
• **1947** U.S. Congress recognizes the right of Puerto Ricans to elect their own governor.
• **1948** Luís Muñoz Marín becomes the first
(continues)

DATELINE

elected governor of Puerto Rico.

1952 The Commonwealth of Puerto Rico is born.

1968 Luis A. Ferré, leader of a pro-statehood party, becomes governor of Puerto Rico.

1972 Partida Popular Democratica returns to power.

1979 Pan-American Games are held in San Juan.

1986 John Paul II's visit catalyzes a new interest in religion.

1991 In an islandwide vote, Puerto Ricans reject an amendment that would have "reviewed" their commonwealth status.

1993 Puerto Ricans vote in a nonbinding plebiscite to continue the island's commonwealth status.

ing rate, victims of imported diseases such as smallpox and whooping cough, against which they had no biologic immunity. The natives were not the only victims of diseases. The Spanish also contracted diseases against which their systems had little immunity. Both communities reeled, disoriented, from their contact with one another. In 1511, the Amerindians rebelled against attempts by the Spanish to enslave them. The rebellion was brutally suppressed by the Spanish forces of Ponce de León, whose muskets and firearms were vastly superior to the hatchets and arrows of the native peoples. In desperation, the remnants of the Taínos joined forces with their traditional enemies, the Caribs, but even that belated union did little to check the inexorable growth of European power.

Because the Amerindians languished in slavery, sometimes preferring mass suicide to imprisonment, their work in the fields and mines of Puerto Rico was soon taken over by Africans who were imported by Spanish, Danish, Portuguese, British, and American slavers.

By 1521 the island had been renamed Puerto Rico ("rich port") and was considered one of the most strategic islands in the Caribbean, which was increasingly viewed as a Spanish sea. Officials of the Spanish Crown dubbed the island "the strongest foothold of Spain in America" and hastened to strengthen the already-impressive bulwarks surrounding the city of San Juan.

Within a century, Puerto Rico's position at the easternmost edge of what would become Spanish America helped it play a major part in the Spanish expansion toward Florida, the South American coast, and Mexico. It was usually the first port of call for Spanish ships arriving in the Americas; recognizing that the island was a strategic keystone, the Spanish decided to strengthen its defenses. By 1540 La Fortaleza, the first of three massive fortresses built in San Juan, was completed. By 1600, San Juan was completely enclosed by some of the most formidable ramparts in the Caribbean while, ironically, the remainder of Puerto Rico was almost defenseless. In 1565 the King of Spain ordered the governor of Puerto Rico to provide men and materiel to strengthen the city of San Agustin (St. Augustine) in Florida.

By this time, the English (and, to a lesser extent, the French) were seriously harassing Spanish shipping in the Caribbean and North Atlantic. At least part of the French and English aggression was in retaliation for the 1493 Papal Bull dividing the New World between Portugal and Spain—an arrangement that eliminated all other nations from the spoils and colonization of the New World.

Queen Elizabeth I's most effective weapons against Spanish expansion in the Caribbean were John Hawkins and Sir Francis Drake, whose victories included the destruction of St. Augustine in Florida, Cartagena in Colombia, and Santo Domingo in what is now the Dominican Republic and the general harassment and pillaging of many Spanish ships and treasure convoys sailing from the New World to Europe with gold and silver from the Aztec and Inca empires. In 1588, Drake's destruction of the Spanish Armada marked the beginning of the rise of the English as a major maritime power and the beginning of an even more aggressive fortification of such islands as Puerto Rico.

In 1595, Drake and Hawkins persuaded an uncertain Queen Elizabeth to embark on a bold and daring plan to invade and conquer Puerto Rico. An English general, the

Earl of Cumberland, urged his men to bravery by "assuring your selves you have the maydenhead of Puerto Rico and so possesse the keyes of all the Indies." Confident that the island was "the very key of the West Indies which locketh and shutteth all the gold and silver in the continent of America and Brasilia," he brought into battle an English force of 4,500 soldiers and eventually captured La Fortaleza.

Although the occupation lasted a full 65 days, the English eventually abandoned Puerto Rico when their armies were decimated by tropical diseases and the local population, which began to engage in a kind of guerrilla warfare against the English. After pillaging and destroying much of the Puerto Rican countryside, the English left. Their short but abortive victory compelled the Spanish king, Philip III, to continue construction of the island's defenses. Despite these efforts, Puerto Rico retained a less-than-invincible aspect as Spanish soldiers in the forts often deserted or succumbed to tropical diseases.

In 1625, Puerto Rico was covetously eyed by Holland, whose traders and merchants desperately wanted a foothold in the West Indies. Spearheaded by the Dutch West India Company, which had received trading concessions from the Dutch Crown covering most of the West Indies, the Dutch armies besieged El Morro Fortress in San Juan in one of the bloodiest assaults the fortress ever sustained. Frustrated in their siege of the fortress and fearing the arrival of Spanish reinforcements from the western side of the island, the Dutch threatened to burn down every building in San Juan if the Spanish did not surrender. When the commanding officer of El Morro scorned the threat, the Dutch burned San Juan to the ground, including all church and civil archives and the bishop's library, by then the most famous and complete collection of books in America. Fueled by rage and courage, the Spanish rallied their forces and soon threw out the Dutch, who retreated in confusion, never again to assault the communities of Puerto Rico.

In response to the widespread destruction of the strongest link in the chain of Spanish defenses, Spain threw itself wholeheartedly into improving and reinforcing the defenses around San Juan. (Philip IV justified his expenditures by declaring Puerto Rico the "front and vanguard of the Western Indies and, consequently, the most important of them and most coveted by the enemies [of Spain].")

Within 150 years, after extravagant expenditures of time and money, the city's walls were considered almost impregnable. Military sophistication was added during the 1760s, when two Irishmen, Tomas O'Daly and Alejandro O'Reilly, surrounded the city with some of Europe's most technically up-to-date defenses. Despite the thick walls, the island's defenses remained precarious because of the frequent tropical epidemics that devastated the ranks of the soldiers; the chronically late pay, which weakened the soldiers' morale; and the belated and often wrong-minded priorities of the Spanish monarchy, which were decided upon thousands of miles away

THE COLONIAL CHURCH

From the earliest days of Spanish colonization, an army of priests and missionaries embarked on a vigorous crusade to convert Puerto Rico's Amerindians to Roman Catholicism. King Ferdinand himself paid for the construction of a Franciscan monastery and a series of chapels and required specific support of the church from the aristocrats who had been awarded land grants in the new territories. They were required to build churches, provide Christian burials, and grant religious instruction to both Amerindian and African slaves.

Among the church's most important activities were the Franciscan monks' efforts to teach the island's children how to read, count, and write. In 1688, Bishop Francisco Padilla, who is now included among the legends of Puerto Rico, established one of the island's most famous schools; when it became clear that local parents were too poor to provide their children with appropriate clothing, he succeeded in persuading the King of Spain to pay for the clothes.

Puerto Rico was declared by the pope as the first *see*—ecclesiastical headquarters—in the New World; in 1519 it became the general headquarters of the

Inquisition in the New World. (About 70 years later, the Inquisition's headquarters was transferred to the important and well-defended city of Cartagena, in Colombia.)

THE ECONOMY BETWEEN 1550 & 1700

The island's early development was shackled by Spain's insistence on a centrist economy. All goods exported from or imported to Puerto Rico had to pass through Spain itself (usually Seville). In effect, this policy prohibited any trade (at least, officially) between Puerto Rico and its island neighbors.

In response, a flourishing black market developed. Such cities as Ponce became smuggling centers. This black market was especially prevalent after the Spanish colonization of Mexico and Peru, when many Spanish goods, which once would have been sent to Puerto Rico, ended up in those more immediately lucrative colonies instead. Although smugglers were punished, nothing could curb this illegal (and untaxed) trade. Some historians estimate that almost everyone on the island—including priests, citizens, and military and civic authorities—were actively involved.

By the mid-1500s, the several hundred settlers who had immigrated to Puerto Rico from Spain heard (and sometimes believed) rumors of the fortunes to be made in the gold mines of Peru. When the island's population declined because of the ensuing mass exodus, the king enticed 500 families from the Canary Islands to settle on Puerto Rico between 1683 and 1691. Meanwhile, an active trade in slaves—imported as labor for fields that were increasingly used for sugarcane and tobacco production—swelled the island's ranks. This happened despite the Crown's imposition of strict controls on the number of slaves that could be brought in. Sugarcane earned profits for many islanders, but Spanish mismanagement, fraud within the government bureaucracy, and a lack of both labor and ships to transport the finished product to market discouraged the fledgling industry. Later, fortunes were made and lost in the production of ginger, an industry that died as soon as the Spanish government raised taxes on ginger imports to exorbitant levels. Despite the arrival of immigrants to Puerto Rico from many countries, diseases such as spotted fever, yellow fever, malaria, smallpox, and measles wiped out the population almost as fast as it grew.

THE 18TH CENTURY

As the philosophical and political movement known as the Enlightenment swept both Europe and North America during the late 1700s and the 1800s, Spain moved to improve Puerto Rico's economy through its local government. The island's defenses were beefed up, roads and bridges were built, and a public education program was launched. The island remained a major Spanish naval stronghold in the New World. Immigration from Europe and other places more than tripled the population. It was during this era that Puerto Rico began to develop a unique identity of its own, a native pride, and a consciousness of its importance within the Caribbean.

The heavily fortified city of San Juan, the island's civic centerpiece, remained under Spain's rigid control. The outlying countryside, without the benefit of encircling ramparts and victim occasionally of raids by both pirates and the forces of England and France, was usually left alone to develop its own local power centers. The city of Ponce, for example, flourished under the Spanish Crown's lax supervision and grew wealthy from the tons of contraband and the high-quality sugar that passed through its port. This trend was also encouraged by the unrealistic law that declared San Juan the island's only legal port. Contemporary sources, in fact, cite the fledgling United States as among the most active of Ponce's early contraband trading partners.

○ In the late 1700s and the 1800s, during the period known as the Enlightenment, Spain funneled resources into Puerto Rico, and the island began to develop a unique identity of its own.

IMPRESSIONS

The rest of this little lland (at least halfe a league in length) is for the most Woods complaining of the want of dressing and industrie, yet are they all youthfully greene, and none without some fruit or other, but so strange as would pose the professors of that skill in England: in these woods but Horses and Oxen grow fat, if they be suffered to rest.
—GEORGE, EARL OF CUMBERLAND, 1596

During the 18th century the number of towns on the island grew rapidly. There were five settlements in Puerto Rico in 1700; 100 years later there were almost 40 settlements, and the island's population had grown to more than 150,000.

Meanwhile, the waters of the Caribbean increasingly reflected the diplomatic wars unfolding in Europe. In 1797, the British, after easily capturing Trinidad (which was poorly defended by the Spanish), failed in a spectacular effort to conquer Puerto Rico. The *criollos*, or native Puerto Ricans, played a major role in the island's defense and later retained a growing sense of their own cultural identity.

Meanwhile, the islanders were becoming aware that Spain could not enforce the hundreds of laws it had previously imposed to support its centrist trade policies. Thousands of merchants, farmers, and civil authorities traded profitably with privateers from various nations, thereby deepening the tendency to evade or ignore the laws imposed by Spain and its colonial governors. The attacks by privateers on British shipping were especially severe, since pirates based in Puerto Rico ranged as far south as Trinidad, bringing dozens of captured British ships into Puerto Rican harbors. (Several decades earlier, British privateers operating out of Jamaica had endlessly harassed Spanish shipping; the tradition of government-sanctioned piracy was well established.)

It was during this period that coffee—which would later play an essential role in the island's economy—was introduced to the Puerto Rican highlands from the nearby Dominican Republic.

Despite the power of San Juan and its Spanish institutions, 18th-century Puerto Rico was predominantly rural. The report of a special emissary of the Spanish king, Marshal Alejandro O'Reilly, remains a remarkably complete analysis of 18th-century Puerto Rican society. It helped promote a more progressive series of fiscal and administrative policies that reflected the Enlightenment ideals found in many European countries.

Suddenly, Puerto Rico began to be viewed as a potential source of income for the Spanish Empire, rather than a drain on income. One of O'Reilly's most visible legacies was his recommendation that people live in towns rather than be scattered about the countryside. Shortly after this, seven new towns, some in the island's interior, were established.

Meanwhile, as the island prospered and its bourgeoisie became more numerous and affluent, daily life became more refined. New public buildings were erected; concerts were introduced; and the everyday aspects of life—such as furniture and social ritual—grew more ornate. Insights into Puerto Rico's changing life can be seen in the works of its most famous 18th-century painter, José Campeche, whose portraits, religious frescoes, and landscapes are among his era's most distinctive legacies.

18TH-CENTURY STRUGGLES FOR INDEPENDENCE

Much of the politics of 19th-century Latin America cannot be understood without reviewing Spain's problems at that time. Up until 1850 there was political and military turmoil in Spain, a combination that eventually led to the collapse of its empire. Since 1796, Spain had been a military satellite of postrevolutionary France, an alliance that brought it into conflict with England. In 1804, Admiral Horatio Lord Nelson's definitive victory for England over French and Spanish ships during the Battle of Trafalgar left England in supreme control of the international sea lanes and interrupted trade and communications between Spain and its colonies in the New World.

These events led to important changes for Spanish-speaking America. The revolutionary fervor of Simón Bolívar and his South American compatriots spilled over to the entire continent, embroiling Spain in a desperate attempt to hold onto the tattered remains of its empire at any cost. Recognizing that Puerto Rico and Cuba were probably the last bastions of Spanish Royalist sympathy in the Americas, Spain liberalized its trade policies, decreeing that goods no longer had to pass through Seville.

The sheer weight and volume of illegal Puerto Rican trade with such countries as Denmark, France, and—most important—the United States, forced Spain's hand in establishing a realistic set of trade reforms. A bloody revolution in Haiti, which had produced more sugarcane than almost any other West Indies island, spurred sugarcane and coffee production in Puerto Rico. Also important was the introduction of a new and more prolific species of sugarcane, the Otahiti, which helped increase production even more.

By the 1820s, the United States was providing ample supplies of such staples as lumber, salt, butter, fish, grain, and foodstuffs, while huge amounts of Puerto Rican sugar, molasses, coffee, and rum were consumed in the United States. Meanwhile, the United States was increasingly viewed as the keeper of the peace in the Caribbean, suppressing the piracy that flourished while Spain's navy was preoccupied with its European wars.

During Venezuela's separation from Spain, Venezualans loyal to the Spanish Crown fled en masse to the remaining Royalist bastions in the Americas—Puerto Rico and, to a lesser extent, Cuba. Although many arrived penniless, having forfeited their properties in South America in exchange for their lives, their excellent understanding of agriculture and commerce probably catalyzed much of the era's economic development in Puerto Rico. Simultaneously, many historians argue, their unflinching loyalty to the Spanish Crown contributed to one of the most conservative and reactionary social structures anywhere in the Spanish-speaking Caribbean. In any event, dozens of Spanish naval expeditions intended to suppress the revolutions in Venezuela were outfitted in Puerto Rican harbors during this period.

During the latter half of the 19th century, political divisions were drawn in Puerto Rico reflecting both the political instability in Spain and the increasing demands of Puerto Ricans for some form of self-rule. As governments and regimes in Spain rose and fell, Spanish policies toward its colonies in the New World changed, too.

In 1865, representatives from Puerto Rico, Cuba, and the Philippines were invited to Madrid to air their grievances as part of a process of liberalizing Spanish colonial policy. Reforms, however, did not follow as promised, and a much-publicized and very visible minirevolt (during which the mountain city of Lares was occupied) was suppressed by the Spanish governors in 1868. Some of the funds and much of the publicity for this revolt came from expatriate Puerto Ricans living in Chile, St. Thomas, and New York.

Slavery was abolished in March 1873, about 40 years after it had been abolished throughout the British Empire. About 32,000 slaves were freed following years of liberal agitation. Abolition was viewed as a major victory for liberal forces throughout Puerto Rico, although cynics claim that slavery was much less entrenched in Puerto

IMPRESSIONS

Puerto Ricans . . . your brothers in exile have conspired—and they ought to conspire—because the colonial regime must someday be ended in our island.
—R. EMETERIO BETANCES, PROCLAMATION SIGNED IN JULY 1867

Rico than in neighboring Cuba, where the sugar economy was far more dependent on slave labor.

The 1895 revolution in Cuba increased the Puerto Rican demand for greater self-rule; during the ensuing intellectual ferment, many political parties emerged. The Cuban revolution provided part of the spark that led to the Spanish-American War, Cuban independence, and U.S. control of Puerto Rico, the Philippines, and the Pacific island of Guam.

THE AMERICAN COLONIAL EXPERIMENT

In 1897, faced with intense pressure from sources within Puerto Rico, a weakened Spain granted its colony a measure of autonomy, but it came too late. Other events were taking place between Spain and the United States that would forever change the future of Puerto Rico.

On February 15, 1898, the U.S. battleship *Maine* was blown up in the harbor of Havana, killing 266 men. The so-called "yellow press" in the United States, especially the papers owned by the tycoon William Randolph Hearst, aroused Americans' emotions into a fever pitch for war, with the rallying cry "Remember the *Maine*."

On April 20th of that year, President William McKinley signed a resolution demanding Spanish withdrawal from Cuba. The president ordered a blockade of Cuba's ports, and on April 24th, Spain, in retaliation, declared a state of war with the United States. On April 25th the U.S. Congress declared war on Spain. In Cuba, the naval battle of Santiago was won by American forces, and in another part of the world, the Spanish colony of the Philippines was also captured by U.S. troops.

On July 17th Santiago surrendered to American forces, and on July 25th American troops landed at Guánica, Puerto Rico, and several days later at Ponce as well. U.S. Army Capt. Alfred T. Mahan later wrote that the United States viewed Puerto Rico, Spain's remaining colonial outpost in the Caribbean, as vital to American interests in the area. Puerto Rico could be used as a military base to help the United States maintain control of the isthmus and to keep communications and traffic flowing between the Atlantic and the Pacific.

Spain offered to trade other territory for Puerto Rico, but the United States refused and demanded Spain's ouster from the island. Left with little choice against superior U.S. forces, Spain capitulated. The Spanish-American War ended on August 31, 1898, with the surrender of Spain and the virtual collapse of the once-powerful Spanish Empire. Puerto Rico, in the words of McKinley, was to "become a territory of the United States."

Although the entire war lasted just over four months, the invasion of Puerto Rico took only two weeks. "It wasn't much of a war," remarked Theodore Roosevelt, who had led the Rough Riders cavalry outfit in their charge up San Juan Hill, "but it was all the war there was." The United States had suffered only four casualties while acquiring Puerto Rico, the Philippines, and the island of Guam. The Treaty of Paris, signed on December 10, 1898, settled the terms of Spain's surrender.

Some Americans looked on Puerto Rico as a "dubious prize." One-third of the population consisted of mulattoes and blacks, descended from slaves, who had no money or land. Only about 12% of the population could read or write. About 8% were enrolled in school. It is estimated that a powerful landed gentry—only about 2% of the population—owned more than two-thirds of the land.

Washington set up a military government in Puerto Rico, headed by the War Department. A series of governors-general were appointed to rule the island, with almost the authority of a dictator. Ruling over a rather unhappy populace, these governors-general brought about much-needed change, including tax and public health reforms. Most Puerto Ricans still wanted autonomy, and many leaders, including Luís Muñoz Rivera, tried to persuade Washington to compromise. However, their protests generally fell on deaf ears.

The island's beleaguered economy was further devastated by an 1899 hurricane that caused millions of dollars' worth of property damage and killed 3,000 people.

One out of four people was left homeless. Belatedly, Congress allocated the sum of $200,000, but this did little to relieve the suffering.

Tensions mounted between Puerto Ricans and their new American governors. In 1900, U.S. Secretary of War Elihu Root decided that military rule of the island was inadequate; he advocated a program of autonomy that won the endorsement of President McKinley.

Thus began a nearly 50-year colonial protectorate relationship as Puerto Rico was recognized as an unincorporated territory with its own governor, to be named by the president of the United States. Only the president had the right to override the veto of the island's governors. The legislative branch was composed of an 11-member executive committee appointed by the president, plus a 35-member chamber of delegates elected by popular vote. A resident commissioner, it was agreed, would represent Puerto Rico in Congress, "with voice but no vote."

As the United States prepared to enter World War I in 1917, Puerto Ricans were granted American citizenship and thus were subject to military service. The people of Puerto Rico were allowed to elect their legislature, which had been reorganized into a Senate and a House of Representatives. The president of the United States continued to appoint the governor of the island and retained the power to veto any of the governor's actions.

Many Puerto Ricans continued, at times rather violently, to agitate for independence. Requests for a plebiscite were constantly turned down. Meanwhile, economic conditions improved, as the island's population began to grow dramatically. Government revenues increased as large corporations from the U.S. mainland found Puerto Rico a profitable place in which to do business. There was much labor unrest and, by 1909, a labor movement demanding better working conditions and higher wages was gaining momentum.

The emerging labor movement showed its strength by organizing a cigar workers' strike in 1914 and a sugarcane workers' strike the following year. The 1930s proved to be disastrous for Puerto Rico, since it suffered greatly from the worldwide depression. To make matters worse, two devastating hurricanes—one in 1928 and another in 1932—destroyed millions of dollars' worth of crops and property. There was also an outbreak of disease that, along with starvation, demoralized the population. Some relief came in the form of food shipments authorized by Congress.

As tension between Puerto Rico and the United States intensified, there emerged Pedro Albizu Campos, a graduate of Harvard Law School and a former U.S. army officer. Leading a group of militant anti-American revolutionaries, he held that America's claim to Puerto Rico was illegal, since the island had already been granted autonomy by Spain. Terrorist acts by his followers, including assassinations, led to Albizu's imprisonment, but terrorist activities still continued.

In 1935 President Franklin D. Roosevelt launched the Puerto Rican Reconstruction Administration, which provided for agricultural development, public works, and electrification of the island. The following year, Sen. Millard E. Tidings of Maryland introduced a measure to grant independence to the island. His efforts were cheered by a local leader, Luís Muñoz Marín, son of the statesman Luís Muñoz Rivera. The young Muñoz founded the Partido Popular Democratica ("Popular Democratic Party") in 1938, which adopted the slogan "Bread, Land, and Liberty." By 1940 this new party had gained control of more than 50% of the seats of both the upper and the lower houses of government, and the young Muñoz was elected leader of the Senate.

IMPRESSIONS

I spent all of yesterday with the spyglass in my hands; from Desecheo to Ataud, from Punta Borinquen to Punta Ponce, I saw all of her, I looked and looked at her, I admired her, and blessed her, and grieved for her.
—EUGENIO MARIA DE HOSTOS, IN HIS DIARY, SEPTEMBER 13, 1898

Roosevelt appointed Rexford Guy Tugwell as governor of Puerto Rico; he spoke Spanish and seemed to have a genuine concern for the plight of the islanders. Muñoz met with Tugwell and convinced him that Puerto Rico was capable of electing its own governor. As a step in that direction, Roosevelt appointed Jesús Piñero as the first resident commissioner of the island.

OPERATION BOOTSTRAP

In 1944, the U.S. Senate unanimously approved a bill granting Puerto Rico the right to elect its own governor. This was the beginning of the famed Operation Bootstrap, a pump-priming fiscal and economic aid package designed to improve the island's standard of living.

In 1946, President Harry S Truman appointed native-born Piñero as governor of Puerto Rico, and the following year the U.S. Congress recognized the right of Puerto Ricans to elect their own governor. In 1948, Luís Muñoz Marín became the first elected governor and immediately recommended that Puerto Rico be transformed into an "associated free state." Endorsement of his plan was delayed by Washington, but President Truman approved the Puerto Rican Commonwealth Bill in 1950, providing for a plebiscite in which voters would decide whether they would remain a colony or become a U.S. commonwealth. In June 1951, Puerto Ricans voted three to one for commonwealth status, and on July 25, 1952, the Commonwealth of Puerto Rico was born.

○ **Amid much debate and a certain amount of turmoil, the Commonwealth of Puerto Rico was born on July 25, 1952.**

This event was marred by a group of nationalists who marched on the Governor's Mansion in San Juan, resulting in 27 deaths and hundreds of casualties. A month later, two Puerto Rican nationalists made an attempt on Truman's life in Washington, and in March 1954, four Puerto Rican nationalists fired into the House of Representatives from the Visitors' Gallery. Their gunfire wounded five congressmen.

In spite of this violence, during the 1950s Puerto Rico began to take pride in its own culture and traditions. In 1955, the Institute of Puerto Rican Culture was established in San Juan, and 1957 saw the inauguration of the Pablo Casals Festival, which launched a renaissance of classical music and a celebration of the arts, a tradition that continues to this day. In 1959, a wealthy industrialist, Luís A. Ferré, donated his personal art collection toward the establishment of the Museum of Fine Arts in Ponce.

Muñoz resigned from office in 1964, but his party continued to win subsequent elections. The independent party, which demanded complete autonomy, gradually lost power. An election on July 23, 1967, reconfirmed the desire of most Puerto Ricans to maintain commonwealth status. In 1968, Luís A. Ferré won a close race for governor, spearheading a pro-statehood party, the Partida Progressiva Nueva (New Progressive Party). It staunchly advocated statehood as an alternative to the island's commonwealth status, but in 1972, the Partida Popular Democratica returned to power; by then, the island's economy was based largely on tourism, rum, and industry. Operation Bootstrap had been successful in creating thousands of new jobs, although more than 100,000 Puerto Ricans moved to the U.S. mainland during the 1950s, seeking a better life. The island's economy continued to improve, although perhaps not as quickly as anticipated by Operation Bootstrap.

Puerto Rico has one of the most prosperous economies in Latin America, although personal income still lags behind that in the poorest U.S. state. The commonwealth still relies on direct subsidies from the United States, which amount to 25% of its gross domestic product. Unemployment sometimes runs as high as 20%.

Puerto Rico grabbed the world's attention in 1979 with the launching of the Pan-American Games. It is vigorously attempting to bring the Summer Olympics there in 2004. The island's culture received a boost in 1981 with the opening of the Center of the Performing Arts in San Juan, which attracted world-famous performers and virtuosos. The international spotlight again focused on Puerto Rico at the time of the first papal visit there in 1986. John Paul II (or Juan Pablo II, as he was called locally) kindled a renewed interest in religion, especially among the Catholic youth of the island.

As Puerto Rico moves further into the 1990s, it still faces troubling questions that have plagued it throughout the 20th century. Statehood, commonwealth, or independence is still an issue. In a nonbinding plebiscite held in November 1993, 48.4% of Puerto Rican voters indicated their preference for the status quo as a commonwealth, 46.2% preferred statehood, and 4.4% chose independence. Increasingly, Puerto Rico is adapting to its role as a vital link between the United States and the Spanish-speaking nations to the south, and tourism is becoming more important to its economy every year as millions of people visit the island.

POLITICS

Politics has been called the national sport of Puerto Rico. Classified as a "commonwealth," Puerto Rico has a constitution (proclaimed on July 25, 1952) that provides for an autonomous form of representative government. The rights of its citizens and guarantees of personal liberties are assured in a constitutional bill of rights. Puerto Ricans can modify their constitution so long as changes do not conflict with provisions of the U.S. Constitution.

Puerto Ricans are U.S. citizens and have the freedom to travel to and live in the United States, as millions of them have done. Puerto Ricans are also subject to the military draft, although they are not allowed to vote in U.S. elections unless they move to the mainland. The island's constitution provides for a government whose powers are split among three branches: executive, legislative, and judicial. Island governors are elected by the people for a term of four years. Governors have wide-ranging powers and the authority to appoint more than 500 executive and judicial officials. The bicameral legislature consists of a *Senado* (Senate) with 27 elected members and a *Camera de Representantes* (House of Representatives) with 51 members. Members of the legislature are elected for a four-year term. Both houses may be enlarged by "at large" seats, which are added when any one party gains more than two-thirds of the seats in an election. The official language of both houses is Spanish, of course. The Puerto Rican Supreme Court is the highest court within the judicial system, and contested decisions are subject to review by the U.S. Supreme Court.

Puerto Rico is divided into 76 municipalities. Each city or town is responsible for electing a mayor or an assembly whose job is to provide education, health centers, relief, and other services for its people. The Puerto Rican electorate sends a resident commissioner to the U.S. Congress for a four-year term; however, this individual has no vote.

The island has many *partidos* (political parties), but some have only limited support. Puerto Rican political parties often splinter into many factions. Each of the two major parties—the Partido Popular Democratica and the Partido Progressiva Nueva—has approximately half a million supporters (out of a total of 2 million registered voters). The Partido Popular Democratica wants to maintain the island's current commonwealth status, while hoping to achieve greater autonomy. The Partido Progressiva Nueva supports statehood for Puerto Rico and its members are often called *estadistas* (statehooders). Their bitterest critics claim that they are "enemies of Puerto Rican culture." There are also smaller political parties demanding total

---

IMPRESSIONS

It is a kind of lost love-child, born to the Spanish Empire, and fostered by the United States.
—Nicholas Wollaston, *Red Rumba*, 1962

independence from the United States. One of these, dating back to 1946, is the Puerto Rican Socialist Party, which advocates "independence by any means." One of the most dangerous parties is the FALN, which advocates terrorism on the U.S. mainland.

3. FAMOUS PUERTO RICANS

Pedro Albizu Campos (1891–1964) Terrorist to his enemies and critics, hero to the most fervent Puerto Rican nationalists, this dedicated anti-American was imprisoned several times for conspiring in armed revolts against the interests of the United States.

Ramón Baldorioty de Castro (1822–89) A delegate to the Spanish parliament, he is considered the father of Puerto Rican autonomy from Spain, although his achievement was superseded by the U.S. annexation. The statesman fought to abolish slavery and establish a constitution guaranteeing the rights of islanders. In 1887, he founded the Autonomist Party, whose platform advocated home government for Puerto Rico and representation in the Spanish parliament.

Tomás Blanco (1900–75) This author and essayist wrote one of the best histories of the island, *Prontuario historico de Puerto Rico* (1935).

Salvador Brau (1842–1912) A historian, journalist, and essayist, he wrote an earlier but equally definitive history of the island, *Historia de Puerto Rico* (1904).

José Campeche (1752–1809) Son of a freed slave and a Canary Islander, this Sanjuanero became one of Puerto Rico's most eminent painters. Trained by a court painter banished from Spain, Campeche produced approximately 400 paintings, thereby earning a reputation as "the most gifted of Latin American rococo artists." Devoutly religious, he often painted for churches but was also a noted portrait painter of subjects ranging from leading politicians to the local landed gentry.

José Celso Barbosa (1857–1921) A gifted mulatto medical doctor, Barbosa is better known as the father of the Statehood for Puerto Rico movement. He formed the pro-statehood Republican Party in the aftermath of the Spanish-American War. Until his death in 1921, he held a seat in the Puerto Rican Senate.

José De Diego (1866–1918) Considered a brilliant orator, De Diego was also a major poet, but his claim to fame today rests on his advocacy of independence for Puerto Rico. His dream was to see the establishment of a confederation of Spanish-speaking islands in the Caribbean, including the Dominican Republic. History considers him a father to both the modern Puerto Rican poetry movement and the island's modern independence movement.

Manuel Fernández Juncos (1846–1928) One of Puerto Rico's best-known journalists, Juncos launched the newspaper *El Buscapie* in 1876. An active member of the Autonomist Party (see Baldorioty de Castro), he also founded the Puerto Rican Red Cross.

Miguel Henríquez (ca. early 1700s) This hero, a mulatto who was once a shoemaker, eventually became a corsair and then experienced many adventures as captain of a Spanish warship. He may have participated in conquering the offshore island of Vieques.

René Marqués (1919–79) Marqués was a distinguished playwright, short-story writer, novelist, and essayist. His best-known play, *La carreta*, opened in 1951

IMPRESSIONS

Puerto Ricans are at the center of U.S. efforts to "stabilize" the Caribbean. Puerto Rico is the anchor of the Caribbean Basin Initiative and the prime line of defense for the United States in Latin America.
—CLARA E. RODRIGUEZ, *PUERTO RICANS BORN IN THE U.S.A.*, 1991

and helped secure his reputation as the leading literary figure in Puerto Rico during the 1950s.

Rita Moreno (b. 1931) This Puerto Rican actress has secured a distinct place in movies, notably because of her role in Robert Wise's 1961 film *West Side Story,* about Puerto Ricans in New York. She also appeared in such hits as *Singin' in the Rain* (1952), *The King and I* (1956), and Tennessee Williams's *Summer and Smoke* (1961), starring Geraldine Page.

Luís Muñoz Marín (1898–1980) Educated in the United States, Muñoz Marín was once known as the New Deal's Golden Boy. He wrote such works as *Pan, tierra y libertad* (Bread, land, and liberty), but he is best known as Puerto Rico's first elected governor (beginning in 1948). He had a rocky but distinguished career— always advocating the interests of Puerto Rico—but by 1964 he was retiring from the political scene.

Luís Muñoz Rivera (1859–1916) Father of Luís Muñoz Marín (above), Muñoz Rivera was president of Puerto Rico's Liberal Party and a leading spokesman for autonomy.

Francisco Oller (1833–1917) Greatly influenced by the European art world, Oller studied in Spain and Paris, although it meant abandoning his wife and children for 11 years. Following such painters as Pissarro and Cézanne, Oller became the first Latin American impressionist, adapting their obsession with light and color to tropical skies. He was also a realistic painter of landscapes and still lifes in Puerto Rico, brilliantly capturing the local flora.

Chita Rivera (b. 1933) Born Dolores Conchita Figueroa del Rivero, this Puerto Rican/American actress made her Broadway debut in *Call Me Madam* (1952) and won the Tony Award as best actress for her Broadway role in *Kiss of the Spider Woman.* "The ageless hoofer" once danced for choreographer George Balanchine with blood-soaked ballet shoes.

Lola Rodríguez de Tío (1843–1924) This was the first Puerto Rico–born poet to establish a reputation throughout the West Indies. She lived for many years in Cuba and eventually died there.

Alejandro Tapía y Rivera (1826–82) This playwright and journalist is today considered the father of Puerto Rican literature. His memoirs, *Mis memorias,* were first published in 1927, many years after his death.

Edwin Torres (b. 1931) This distinguished jurist and novelist was born to Puerto Rican immigrants in a New York tenement. After attending Brooklyn College, he was eventually appointed to the New York Supreme Court, where he made many tough decisions. His most celebrated case was in 1991—the Brian Watkins case—in which a young tourist from Utah was murdered on a New York subway platform. He also wrote such novels as *Carlito's Way, Q. & A.,* and *After Hours.*

Manuel Zeno Gandía (1885–1930) One of Puerto Rico's outstanding novelists, Zeno Gandía is known today primarily for the novel *La charca,* first published in 1894. His major works were published in a collection called *Cronicas de un mundo enfermo* (Chronicles of a sick world).

4. ARCHITECTURE, LITERATURE & MUSIC

ARCHITECTURE

The Columbus Quincentennial in 1992 sparked a major refurbishing of the colonial architecture of Puerto Rico. The island's architectural heritage is Spanish, of course, as seen in the narrow, winding cobblestone streets and the pastel-colored, tile-roofed buildings with ornate balconies and heavy wooden doors that open onto inner courtyards in the style of Andalusia in southern Spain.

Current restoration and renewal projects focus on Old San Juan and the city of Ponce. It is estimated that there are at least 400 structures of historic value in Old San Juan, including some of the finest examples of Spanish colonial architecture in the New World. Old San Juan was Spain's major center of commerce and military power in the West Indies for nearly four centuries.

Spain ordered that the city be protected by sandstone walls and massive fortresses, since the island was the first port of call for galleons entering the West Indies and the last safe harbor for ships, laden with treasures, making the return trip to Cádiz or Seville. Because Old San Juan had no space for expansion, new buildings had to be erected to the east of the old town, in what is known today as the modern city of San Juan. Thus, most of the old structures have survived more or less since the 16th century. The most notable of these include El Morro Fortress, the San Juan Cathedral, and the Dominican Convent. Casa Blanca, a mansion built for the island's first governor, Ponce de León, still stands.

On a walking tour of Old San Juan, you will see an architectural melange of buildings that range from the style popular during the Spanish Conquest to the neoclassical style of the 19th century. The most significant of all is El Morro Fortress, largest in the Caribbean, which has stood guard over San Juan Bay for more than four centuries. In 1973 it was declared a "World Heritage Site," putting it in the same class as Versailles, the Taj Mahal, and the Egyptian pyramids.

Other outstanding examples of Spanish colonial military architecture and engineering in San Juan include the old city walls and the nearby San Cristóbal fortress. La Fortaleza, dating from 1533, is another World Heritage Site. Built to protect Spanish settlers from attack by the cannibalistic Carib tribes, it was at first a small medieval-style fortress with two round towers. In time, it became the residence of the island's governors. Still in use today, it is the official residence of the governor of Puerto Rico and the oldest executive mansion in continuous use in the New World. Built around its 16th-century core is a 19th-century facade with neoclassical motifs and a richly furnished interior.

Those who restored La Fortaleza and other landmarks in Old San Juan tried whenever possible to use original materials such as native-grown *ausubo* (ironwood) beams, which had to be salvaged from elsewhere on the island. The Puerto Rican General Archives and the Archives of the Indies in Seville (Spain) were able to provide the original plans of many late 18th- and 19th-century buildings; they were used in the restoration of many of the island's structures. The greatest challenge was to restore 16th-century buildings, for

❂ **The massive El Morro Fortress has guarded San Juan Harbor for more than four centuries.**

which there were no original plans. One example of this is San José Church, the only true Gothic building under the U.S. flag. The walls of this church had to be scraped to uncover the original 16th-century features. Buried under layers of concrete, the restorers found one of the earliest murals painted in the Americas—the work of a friar whose identity will probably never be known.

The facade of San Juan Cathedral, added in the early 19th century, is baroque, but it shelters a vaulted tower and four rooms dating from 1540, which are rare examples of medieval architecture in the New World. In 1913 the body of Ponce de León was moved here and is now in a marble tomb near the cathedral's transept.

The Dominican Convent—another Old San Juan 16th-century structure—now houses the Institute of Culture. Friars began its construction in 1523; there are tall arcaded galleries set into its two stories, a large interior patio, and a chapel that now serves as a museum.

The waterfront area of San Juan, known as the paseo de La Princesa, is also being restored to its original 19th-century splendor as a broad esplanade graced with fountains and towering royal palms. The promenade sweeps from the cruise piers to La Princesa, a restored 19th-century prison, now the headquarters of the Puerto Rico Tourism Company. La Princesa sets a good example for future architectural restorations, with its huge mahogany doors, impressive arcades, polished floors, and elegant appointments.

A second major architectural renaissance and renovation is taking place in Ponce. At the turn of the century, Ponce rivaled San Juan as an affluent business and cultural center. When the Ponce revitalization plan—arguably the most extensive ever undertaken in the West Indies—is completed, visitors will be able to stroll along gaslit streets lined with period structures, as old-fashioned horse-drawn carriages clop by. Strollers will enjoy sidewalks edged with pink marble.

The commonwealth has allocated $440 million to restore a 66-block downtown area of 1,046 buildings ranging in style from old Spanish colonial to neoclassical, from "Ponce Créole" to art deco. Many of Ponce's central buildings were erected between the late 1890s and the 1930s, when the city was the hub of the island's rum, sugarcane, and shipping industries and was known as La Perla del Sur, the "Pearl of the South." It was home to many artists, politicians, and poets.

With funds provided by the Spanish government, the Institute of Ibero-American Cooperation designated which structures were worthy of preservation. Many of the buildings radiate outward from the stately main square, Plaza de Las Delicias (Plaza of Delights). Other streets with buildings of architectural interest include Cristina, Isabel, Luna, Reina, and Pabellones.

The Institute of Puerto Rican Culture restored the neoclassical Casa Armstrong-Poventud, a mansion with caryatid columns gracing its facade. Today, the restored building houses the Ponce Tourism Information Center, the regional office of the Institute of Puerto Rican Culture, and a museum. Another major 19th-century building, El Castillo, originally served as the Ponce Village Infantry Quarter. It later became the Ponce Jail, but is now the Ponce School of Fine Arts.

Yet another notable building, the Museum of Puerto Rican Music, was restored in 1990 by the Institute of Culture. It pays tribute to the works of Puerto Rican musicians, including native-born Ruth Fernández. The museum is housed in the old Museum of Art on Cristina Street, built in the 1850s as the home of a wealthy industrialist.

The institute is also responsible for restoring Casa Serrallés, the former home of the oldest rum-producing family on the island, the makers of Don Q rum. It also restored Casa Villaronga, the former home of Alfredo Wiechers, a famous Ponce architect. Casa Villaronga exemplifies the characteristic elegance and whimsy of Ponce architecture with its trellised roof garden, stucco garlands, colored glass, and Spanish tiles.

Overlooking Ponce from its perch on El Vigía Hill is one more recently restored landmark, the Castillo Serrallés, another home of the rum-producing Serrallés family. This is a multilevel Spanish-style hacienda, featuring an elegant open courtyard with fountains and a splendid carved wooden ceiling in the dining room.

Plaza del Mercado, the old marketplace, has been converted to an artisans' market, replete with typical food, fruits, and flowers. Converted from an art deco movie theater, it probably draws more sightseers and consumers than any other complex in the old town.

At Plaza de Las Delicias, Ponce has revived its traditional horse-drawn carriage service. Four carriages offer free rides to visitors. Standing on the square is the boldly painted, century-old Parque de Bombas (Firehouse), which reopened as a museum after a $140,000 restoration.

IMPRESSIONS

The new cultural pride can be seen increasingly in architectural restoration, environmental preservation, artistic expression, and no less than a culinary revolution.
—PATRICIA J. BELL, GOURMET, 1991

The architect Ilia Sánchez Arana, who coordinated many aspects of the restoration of Ponce, said, "The city has a type of architecture found nowhere else in Puerto Rico. For example, the neoclassical style of many of the city's public buildings reflect the local climate and taste, incorporating balconies and facades of the local pink marble. The typical Ponce Créole architecture includes elements such as columns on the balcony, an inside balcony with a wall of small windows to let in light from the patio, and a two- or four-sided roof."

LITERATURE

Puerto Rico's literature dates back to the era of conquest and colonization. The early settlers, along with friars and governors, began to describe the new land they had discovered and its Taíno inhabitants. Their letters and documents provide clues to what life was like in the Caribbean before the coming of Columbus.

Notable in this collection are letters written by Puerto Rico's first governor, Ponce de León, to both the rulers in Spain and the ecclesiastical hierarchies in Seville. Here are found the first descriptions of the island's luxuriant flora and fauna. Also in these letters and other accounts of the *conquistadores*, the vocabulary and descriptions of the mythological rites of the Taíno peoples appear for the first time. Many Puerto Rican towns and rivers still bear pre-Columbian names. Town names that have survived include Humacao, Coamo, Utuado, and Caguas. It is believed that the Taíno language became extinct by the mid-16th century, although pockets of Amerindian culture may have survived in the remote hinterlands.

◊ **Much of what the world knows about the pre-Columbian inhabitants of Puerto Rico, the Taíno peoples, comes from the letters and other records of the Spanish *conquistadores*.**

The new conquerors of Puerto Rico, writing verse, memoirs, diaries, and especially letters back home, also had a close affinity with New Spain, the territory that is now Mexico. The writings of two Puerto Ricans became known in Mexico because of these close bonds—the poet Francisco de Ayerra y Santa María, a noted Latin scholar, and Alonso Ramírez, a carpenter's son who authored a series of high adventures. After living for a time in Mexico, the Spanish author Bernardo de Balbuena arrived in Puerto Rico in 1620 with the largest known library in the West Indies. He housed his library in a church, which, regrettably, was destroyed and pillaged in 1625 when Dutch troops burned the city to the ground. Balbuena wrote some of his works on the island; they were highly praised in Spain, although Balbuena's portrait of an abundantly wealthy Puerto Rico was probably exaggerated.

In Madrid the first complete history of Puerto Rico was published in 1788. Titled *The Geographic, Civil, and Political History of the Island of Saint John the Baptist of Puerto Rico*, this work was a major achievement, both as a history and as a literary work. The writer, Fray Inigo Abbad y Lasierra, had been captivated especially by the flora, fauna, and folklore of Puerto Rico.

The last half of the 19th century was particularly fruitful in terms of literary works as the increasing numbers of new settlers tried to capture the rhythms and landscapes of their new world in prose and poetry. A trio of outstanding lyrical and romantic poets emerged from this period: Lola Rodríguez de Tío (1843–1924), José Gautier Benítez (1851–80), and El Caribe, the nom de plume of José Gualbierto Padilla (1829–96). Other distinguished writers of that era included Salvador Brau (1842–1912), Eugenio María de Hostas (1839–1903), and Alejandro Tapia y Rivera (1826–82).

Many foreign writers visited Puerto Rico during the 19th century and recorded their impressions. Their literary works provide some valuable clues to the life of those times. For example, in 1834 George Dawson Flinter published a report in London depicting the everyday life and social customs of *el jíbaro*, the "hillbilly" whose traditional homeland was the verdant mountains of central Puerto Rico. Many of these writers took an idealized view of peasant life of the times, describing it as relatively carefree and happy. A dissenting point of view emerged in Manuel Zeno Gandía's naturalistic novel *La charca* (The stagnant pool), first published in 1894. The novel presents a dismal view of social conditions in the Spanish colony at that time.

The Spanish-American War in 1898 significantly changed the literature of Puerto Rico. From the early years of the 20th century, many writers began to focus on the conflict between traditional Hispanic culture and the increasing Americanization of the island. One of the most notable writers to emerge from this period was José De Diego (1867–1918), a precursor of Puerto Rican modernist writers. His works kept alive the dream of independence for the island.

One of the leading 20th-century poets was Evaristo Ribera Chevremont (1896–1974), who wrote about both urban and rural life. His poems composed from 1924 to 1950 were brought together and published in *Antologia poetica* (Poetic anthology).

Antonio S. Pedreira (1899–1939), a professor of Hispanic studies, wrote a landmark work, *Insularismo,* which documented the unique phenomenon of Puerto Rican culture after some 3½ decades of U.S. political control. His work seems to have released a floodgate of works by other Puerto Ricans who in essays, novels, and poetry explored the cultural struggle faced by the island since 1898. Notable among these works were *La llamarada* (Flash of fire) and *Los amos benevolos* (The benevolent masters), by Enrique Laguerre (born 1906).

Another notable novelist was Pedro Juan Soto (born 1928), who lived in New York, taught English, and was a true bilingual writer. Among his best-known works were *Spiks,* which appeared in 1956, and *Usmail,* published in 1958.

The most distinguished Puerto Rican playwright was René Marqués, author of the three-act *La carreta* (The oxcart). This play depicts the poor economic conditions that led to the mass exodus of Puerto Ricans to the United States.

MUSIC

One of Puerto Rico's notable exports is its music, which is probably the predominant Caribbean music heard in the United States.

At least some of the instruments used in traditional Puerto Rican music originated with the Taíno peoples. Most noteworthy is the *güicharo,* or *güiro,* a notched, hollowed-out gourd, which was adapted from pre-Columbian days. The musical traditions of the Spanish and Africans can also be heard in Puerto Rico's music. At least four different instruments were adapted from the six-string Spanish classical guitar: the *requinto,* the *bordonua,* the *cuatro,* and the *tiple,* each of which produces a unique tone and pitch. The most popular of these, and the one for which the greatest number of adaptations and compositions have been written, is the cuatro, a guitarlike instrument with 10 strings (arranged in five different pairs) whose name (translated as "the fourth") is derived from the tradition of tuning its strings in variables of half-octaves (that is, fourths). Usually carved from solid blocks of laurel wood and known for resonances and pitches different from those produced by its Spanish counterpart, this instrument's graceful baroque body has been revered for decades as the national instrument of Puerto Rico.

Also prevalent on the island are such percussion instruments as *tambours* (hollowed tree trunks covered with stretched-out animal skin), *maracas* (gourds filled with pebbles or dried beans and mounted on handles), and a variety of drums whose original designs were brought from Africa by the island's slaves. All these instruments contribute to the rich variety of folk music with roots in the cultural melting pot of the island's Spanish, African, and Taíno traditions.

CLASSICAL MUSIC IN PUERTO RICO During the conversion of Puerto Rico's Amerindians and slaves to Christianity after its colonization by the early Spanish, the only formal music imported from Spain was chants and religious music. Later, however, as the fortunes of a handful of Puerto Rican planters increased during the 19th century, their social aspirations grew as well. Those whose children showed musical promise were often sent abroad—usually to Spain—for the further development of their talents.

One of these was Puerto Rican–born Manuel Tavares, a composer whose orchestral techniques matured within the musical traditions of 19th-century Spain and whose success encouraged other generations of Puerto Rican classicists to follow in his footsteps.

By 1850, another group of island composers, many only informally trained, had adapted a Puerto Rican interpretation of the most popular dance of that era—the minuet—into a musical form known as the *danza*. Based on a refined, somewhat rigid classical score, with an underlying lilt that is unmistakably Caribbean, its most popular early advocate was composer Juan-Morel Campos. Later, this dance style evolved into the dance rhythms still popular today. Also popular during the early and mid-1800s was a narrative tale set to music, sometimes embellished on the spot by a skilled storyteller known as a *decima;* the tales originated as rigidly metered 10-line stanzas of eight-syllable lines with a rhyme structure that could vary according to the inspiration of the composer. Their musical form—which might have been the closest thing to a troubadour tradition ever developed in Puerto Rico—was often used to convey moral lessons, love tragedies, and stories of other kinds.

One world-class operatic tenor was Antonio Paoli (1872–46). Also noteworthy was Jesús María Sanroma (1902–84), a pianist who performed both Puerto Rican danzas and works from the classical European repertoire.

Puerto Rico's classical and orchestral tradition reached its height with cellist Pablo Casals. Of partial Puerto Rican descent, he chose, at the age of 81, to spend the last years of his life on the island and brought musical fame to San Juan by making it home to the internationally acclaimed Casals Festival.

PUERTO RICAN FOLK MUSIC During Puerto Rico's colonial years, a series of musical traditions evolved that were based on the folk songs and romantic ballads of 18th- and 19th-century Spain. Eventually these became fused with music either imported or native to the Hispanic New World. Dealing with life, death, and everyday events of an agrarian society far removed from the royal courts of Europe, this music has been studiously collected and reorchestrated for modern audiences.

One collector of this music was Don Felo, whose 19th-century compositions were based on the melodic traditions of both Spain and the Spanish-speaking Caribbean. In the 20th century, Narciso Figueroa continued the tradition of collecting folk songs and reorchestrating them for chamber orchestras; his recordings have been sponsored by the Institute of Puerto Rican Culture.

Today, the most widely applauded—and, to many, most enjoyable—of the island's folk music are the hillbilly pieces created by the mountain-dwelling jíbaros. Using the full array of stringed and percussion instruments described above, they give lyrical performances whose live or recorded versions are popular at everything from island weddings to commencement exercises. Despite the appeal other island musical forms, such as salsa, it could be argued that the jíbaro tradition of cuatro with drums is the island's most notable—and the one most likely to evoke homesickness in the hearts of any expatriate Puerto Rican.

BOMBA Y PLENA Although usually grouped together, *bomba y plena* are actually two entirely different types of music that are coupled with dance. Bomba,

---

IMPRESSIONS

All the islands are very beautiful and possess a most luxuriant soil, but this last island appeared to exceed all others in beauty.
—DR. DIEGO ALVAREZ CHANCA, TRANSLATED FROM A LETTER WRITTEN DURING THE SECOND VOYAGE OF COLUMBUS TO THE NEW WORLD IN 1493

pure African, was brought over by black slaves who worked on the island's sugar plantations. It's a rhythmic music using barrel-shaped drums covered with tightly stretched animal skins and played by hand. This form of music is produced by one large drum plus a smaller drum called a *subidor*. The drums are accompanied by the rhythmical beating of sticks and maracas to create a swelling tide of drumbeats, in which aficionados can hear the drummers bang out a series of responses one to another.

Bomba is described as a dialogue between dancer and drummer. It's as if the drummer were challenging the dancer to a rhythmic duel. The dance can go on just as long as the dancer can continue. Although critics are uncertain about the exact origins of bomba, it is divided into different rhythmic backgrounds and variations, such as the Euba, Cocobale, and Sica. As the dance and the drummer's beat continue, the music grows more spirited and more complex. The best bomba, and the most purely African version of this music and dance, may come from the northeastern coast town of Loíza Aldea.

Whereas bomba is purely African in origin, plena blends elements from Puerto Ricans' wide cultural backgrounds, including music that the Taíno tribes may have used during their ceremonies. This type of music first appeared in Ponce, where performing the plena became a hallmark of Spanish tradition and coquetry.

Instruments used in plena include the güiro, a dried-out gourd whose surface is cut with parallel grooves and, when rubbed with a stick, produces a raspy and rhythmical percussive noise. The Taínos may have invented this instrument. From the guitars brought to the New World by the Spanish conquistadores emerged the 10-stringed cuatro. To the güiro and cuatro is added the tambourine, known as *panderos*, originally derived from Africa. Dancing plena became a kind of living newspaper. Singers recited the events of the day and often satirized local politicians or scandals. Sometimes plenas were filled with biting satire; at other times, they commented on major news events of the day, such as a devastating hurricane.

Bomba y plena remain the most popular forms of folk music on the island, and many cultural events highlight this music for entertainment. In a somewhat commercialized form, bomba y plena shows are often presented at resort hotels along San Juan's Condado beachfront strip.

SALSA   The major type of music coming out of Puerto Rico is salsa, the rhythm of the islands. Its name literally translates as the "sauce" that makes parties happen. Originally developed within the Puerto Rican community of New York, it draws heavily from the musical roots of the Cuban and the African-Caribbean experience. Highly danceable, its rhythms are hot, urban, rhythmically sophisticated, and compelling. Today, the center of salsa has probably shifted from New York back to Puerto Rico, where local musicians compete fiercely with those from Cuba for the most infectious melodies.

Cuban salsa tends to be less avant-garde than the constantly mutating versions produced in Puerto Rico. Even within the salsa tradition, different groups adhere more or less fervently to the traditions of mainstream jazz, popular Latin song, and African inspirations.

Salsa is not an old form of music at all. Music critics claim that it originated in New York City nightclubs in the years following World War II, an evolution of the era's Big Band tradition. The first great salsa musician was Tito Puente, who, after a stint with the U.S. Navy, studied percussion at New York's Juilliard School of Music. He went on to organize his own band, Puente's Latin Jazz Ensemble, which has been heard by audiences around the world. One critic said that the music is what results when the sounds of Big Band jazz meet African-Caribbean rhythms.

۞ Tito Puente, one of the kings of Puerto Rican salsa, studied percussion at New York's Juilliard School of Music.

Other critics say that salsa is a combination of fast Latin music that embraces the rumba, mambo, cha-cha, guaguancho, and merengue.

Salsa has definitely made Puerto Rico famous in the world of international music. Salsa bands require access to a huge array of percussion instruments, including güiros, the gourds on which the Taíno peoples may have played music. Other instruments include maracas, bongos, timbales, conga drums, and claves—and, to add the jíbaro (hillbilly) touch, a clanging cow bell. Of course, it also takes a bass, a horn section, a chorus, and a lead vocalist to get the combination right.

No one quite agrees about who is the king of salsa today, but Willie Colón, El Gran Combo de Puerto Rico, and Hector Lovoe are on everyone's list as the "Grand Masters of today's salsa beat." Hundreds of young *salseros* are waiting to take their thrones as the popularity (and income levels) of the emerging salsa stars continues to climb. Young Puerto Ricans would definitely give the vote to Menudo, the darling of fan magazines and screaming, teary-eyed girls throughout the island.

5. ARTS & CRAFTS

ARTS Serious students of Puerto Rican art always go to the Institute of Puerto Rican Culture in the Dominican Convent in Old San Juan. It's the best source of information on the island about Puerto Rican arts and crafts.

With its dozen or so museums and even more art galleries, Old San Juan is the greatest repository of Puerto Rican arts and crafts. Galleries sell everything from pre-Columbian artifacts to paintings by relatively contemporary artists such as Angel Botello, who died in 1986. The Galleria Botello, at calle del Cristo 208, was his former home. He restored the colonial mansion himself; now his paintings and sculptures are on display there.

Another good place to see Puerto Rican art is the Museum of the University of Puerto Rico in Río Piedras. Because of space limitations, the museum's galleries can exhibit only a fifth of their vast collection at one time, but the work is always of top-notch quality. The collection ranges from pre-Columbian artifacts to works by today's major painters.

The greatest art on the island is at the Museo de Arte de Ponce, avenida de las Americas, in Puerto Rico's second-largest city. The collection, donated by former governor Luís A. Ferré, ranges from Jan van Eyck's *Salvatore Mundi* to Rossetti's confrontational *Daughters of King Lear*. The museum building was designed by Edward Durell Stone, who also designed New York's Museum of Modern Art. Works are displayed here in a honeycomb of skylit hexagonal rooms. Puerto Rican artists who are represented include José Campeche and Francisco Oller (see below). In addition to such European masters as Reubens, van Dyck, and Murillo, the museum features works by Latin American artists, including some by the Mexican Diego Rivera.

The first major Puerto Rican artist of note was José Campeche, an 18th-century *Sanjuanero* who lived his entire life in and drew inspiration from the city of his birth. The son of a freed slave and an immigrant from the Canary Islands; Campeche was greatly influenced by a Spanish court painter who was banished to San Juan. Since Campeche was fascinated by religious paintings, many of his 400 works were for churches. He was also a distinguished portrait painter, whose subjects ranged from governors of the colony to local personalities to members of well-to-do families.

Francisco Oller, born in 1833, was also an eminent Puerto Rican painter. He was greatly influenced by European art, especially the works of Cézanne and Pissarro. Oller became the first Latin American artist to adapt the impressionists' interest in light and color to the tropical skies of Puerto Rico. Island scenes fascinated him, and he depicted everything from life on a sugarcane plantation to a funeral wake in the Puerto Rican countryside. His still lifes of local flora, including palm trees and bananas, are eagerly sought by collectors.

Many Puerto Rican artists have followed in Oller's footsteps, including Ramón Frade and Miguel Pou. Frade's painting of *The Jíbaro* pays homage to the country peasant farmer.

Funded by the government, a tradition of artistic posters became popular in the 1940s. Printmaking still flourishes, and the field has attracted such artists as Antonio Martorell and José Rosa.

Since the 1960s, nearly every major Puerto Rican artist has studied abroad, in both Europe and America. Some artists prefer to live abroad, returning to the island from time to time for inspiration. One of them, Rafael Ferrer, is perhaps better known in New York art galleries than in San Juan. Savvy collectors are also buying the works of such contemporary artists as Ivette Cabrera, Consuelo Gotay, and Juan Ramón Velázquez.

CRAFTS The most impressive of the island's crafts are the *santos,* carved religious figures that have been produced since the 1500s. Craftspeople who make these are called *santeiros;* using clay, gold, stone, or cedarwood, they carve figurines representing saints, usually from 8 to 20 inches tall. Before the Spanish colonization, small statues called *zemi* stood in native tribal villages and camps as objects of veneration, and Puerto Rico's santos may derive from that pre-Columbian tradition. Every town has its patron saint and every home has its santos to protect the family. For some families, worshiping the santos replaces a traditional mass.

Art historians view the carving of santos as Puerto Rico's greatest contribution to the plastic arts. The earliest figures were richly baroque, indicating a strong Spanish influence, but as the islanders began to assert their own identity, the carved figures often became simpler.

In carving santos, craftspeople often used handmade tools. Sometimes such natural materials as vegetable dyes and even human hair were used. The saints represented by most santos can be identified by their accompanying symbols; for example, Saint Anthony is usually depicted with the infant Jesus and a book. Perhaps the most popular group of santos are the Three Kings. The Trinity and the Nativity also are depicted frequently. Art experts claim that santos-making approached its zenith at the turn of the century, although hundreds of santeiros still practice their craft throughout the island.

Some of the best santos on the island can be seen at the Capilla del Cristo in Old San Juan. Perhaps at some future date a museum devoted entirely to santos will open on Puerto Rico.

Another Puerto Rican craft has undergone a big revival just as it seemed that it would disappear forever. Originating in Spain, *mundillos* (tatted fabrics) are the product of a type of bobbin lacemaking. This craft, five centuries old, exists today only in Puerto Rico and Spain.

The first lace made in Puerto Rico was called *torchon* ("beggar's lace"). Early examples of beggar's lace were considered of inferior quality, but artisans today have transformed this fabric into a delicate art form, eagerly sought by collectors. Lace bands called *entrados* have two straight borders, whereas the other traditional style, *puntilla,* has both a straight and a scalloped border. The best place to see the craft of the mundillo is the Folk Arts Center at the Dominican Convent in Old San Juan. This center has information on island shops that make and sell mundillos. You can also attend the Puerto Rican Weaving Festival, held annually at the end of April in the town of Isabela.

Perhaps the most popular of all Puerto Rican crafts are the frightening *caretas*— papier-mâché masks worn at island carnivals. Tangles of menacing horns, fang-toothed leering expressions, and bulging eyes of these half-demon, half-animal creations send children running screaming to their parents. At carnival time, they are worn by costumed revelers called *vejigantes.* Vejigantes often wear bat-winged jumpsuits and roam the streets either individually or in groups.

The origins of these masks and carnivals may go back to medieval Spain and/or tribal Africa. A processional tradition in Spain, dating from the early 17th century, was intended to terrify sinners with marching devils in the hope that they would return to church. Cervantes described it briefly in *Don Quijote*. Puerto Rico blended this Spanish procession with the masked tradition brought by slaves from Africa. Some historians believe that the Taínos also were accomplished mask makers, which would make this a very ancient tradition indeed.

○ Tangles of menacing horns, fang-toothed leering expressions, and bulging eyes characterize *caretas*, papier-mâché masks worn at island carnivals.

The predominant mask colors, at least traditionally, were black, red, and yellow, all symbols of hellfire and damnation. Today, pastels are more likely to be used. Each vejigante sports at least two or three horns, although some masks may have hundreds of horns in all shapes and sizes. Mask making in Ponce, the major center for this craft, and in Loíza Aldea, a palm-fringed town on the island's northeastern coast, has since led to a renaissance of Puerto Rican folk art.

You can purchase these masks year-round at various places, even in the homes of the mask makers, providing that you have their addresses. Although many masks are extremely elaborate and expensive, they typically range in price from $10 to $75. The premier store selling these masks is Puerto Rican Art and Crafts, at calle Fortaleza 204, in Old San Juan. Masks can be seen in action at the three big masquerade carnivals on the island: the Ponce Festival in February, the Festival of Loíza Aldea in July, and the Día de las Mascaras at Hatillo in December.

6. RELIGION & FOLKLORE

RELIGION The majority of Puerto Ricans are Roman Catholic, but religious freedom for all faiths is guaranteed by the Commonwealth Constitution. Catholic services are conducted throughout the island in both English and Spanish. There is a Jewish Community Center in Miramar, plus a Jewish Reformed Congregation in Santurce. There are English-speaking Protestant services for Baptists, Episcopalians, Lutherans, Presbyterians, and other interdenominational services.

Although predominantly Catholic, Puerto Rico does not follow Catholic dogma and rituals as assiduously as do the churches of Spain and Italy. Because the church supported slavery, there was a long-lasting resentment against the all-Spanish clergy of colonial days. Island-born men were excluded from the priesthood. When Puerto Ricans eventually took over the Catholic churches on the island, they followed some guidelines from Spain and Italy but modified or ignored others. For example, many Catholic couples in Puerto Rico practice birth control and are married outside the Catholic church.

Following the U.S. acquisition of the island in 1898, Protestantism grew in influence and popularity. There were Protestants on the island before the invasion, but their numbers increased after Puerto Rico became an American colony. Many islanders liked the idea of separation of church and state, as provided for in the U.S. Constitution. In recent years, a pentecostal fundamentalism has swept across the island. There are perhaps some 1,500 evangelical churches in Puerto Rico today.

As throughout the Latin American world, the practice of Catholicism in Puerto Rico blends certain native Taíno and African traditions with mainstream tenets of the faith. It has been said that the real religion of Puerto Rico is *espiritismo* (spiritualism), a quasi-magical belief in occult forces. Spanish colonial rulers outlawed spiritualism, but under the U.S. occupation it flourished in dozens of isolated pockets of the island.

Students of religion trace spiritualism to the Taínos, and their belief that *jípia* (the spirits of the dead—somewhat like the legendary vampire) slumbered by day and prowled the island by night. Instead of looking for bodies, the jípia were seeking wild fruit to eat. Thus arose the Puerto Rican tradition of putting out fruit on the kitchen table. Even in modern homes today, you'll often find a bowl of plastic, flamboyantly colored fruit resting atop a refrigerator.

Many islanders still believe in the "evil eye," or *mal de ojo*. To look on a person or a person's possessions covetously, according to believers, can lead to that individual's sickness or perhaps death. Little children are given bead charm bracelets to guard against the evil eye. Spiritualism also extends into healing, folk medicine, and food. Some spiritualists, for example, believe that cold food should never be eaten with hot food. Various island plants, herbs, and oils are believed to have certain healing properties, and spiritualist literature is available throughout the island.

FOLKLORE The Taíno tribespeople, the Spanish conquistadores, and the black slaves imported from Africa all contributed to the folklore heritage of Puerto Rico. The Taíno passed their legends down orally; they were first recorded by the Spanish colonialists. Some of the Taíno language was preserved by writers who used Taíno words to describe the alien aspects of their new surroundings, including *casabe* (a kind of bread) and *bohío* (a native thatched hut).

As for the tribe's mythology, Fray Damian Lopez de Haro (1581–1648) and Juan de Castellanos (1522–1607) both recorded some of the more frequently recited Taíno folktales. Today, Puerto Rican anthropologists, writers, and artists are once again examining Taíno folk culture to better understand their "roots."

Many of these legends are ghost tales about demons who roam the island after dark, pursuing food or people or else protecting gold and loot that pirates long ago stashed away for safekeeping. Much of the island's folklore also dealt with the forces of nature that would descend in the form of a "big blow" (hurricane), decimating local crops and settlements. Recently some Puerto Rican writers have made serious attempts to collect this body of written folktales. Cayetano Coll y Toste (1850–1930), for example, published his literary classic *Leyendas y tradiciones puertorriqueas* between 1924 and 1925.

In 1977, a medical academician, José Ramírez Rivera, translated and published in English 12 of these stories, simplifying the tales and language for the modern reader. Basically tales of adventure, they include "The Gold Nugget" (1530), which deals with Spanish greed in the New World, and "Carabali: The Rebellious Slave" (1830), which tells about a group of mistreated Africans who escaped from their masters and lived in a cave, venturing out at night to rob and pillage the countryside.

Some stories are about the Taíno peoples, including the legend of "Guanina" (1511), which tells of Don Cristóbal de Sotomayor, a young man from Valladolid, Spain, who was enchanted by a graceful Amerindian girl, Guanina. This is the famous *Romeo and Juliet* tale of Puerto Rico, comparable in some ways to the early Virginian legend of Capt. John Smith and his Native American bride, Pocohantas. At the end of the story, the Christian soldier is found dead along with the body of Guanina, her head resting on his bloody chest. It was said that a witch doctor buried their bodies under the roots of a towering ceiba tree and that white lilies and red poppies grew from their graves. Locals claimed to hear sweet songs of love rustling through the leaves of the giant ceiba, and some people assert that the lovers still come out on moonlit nights to renew their vows of devotion.

7. PERFORMING ARTS & EVENING ENTERTAINMENT

Since 1976, the Puerto Rico Tourism Company has sponsored a year-round program that is a virtual LeLoLai festival. LeLoLai is a musical expression derived from the songs of the mountain-dwelling Puerto Rican jíbaros. Various LeLoLai folkloric presentations showcase the island's Amerindian, Spanish, and African heritage, giving visitors a chance to experience island hospitality and learn about Puerto Rican culture—all at a discount. The folkloric shows alone are worth the card's membership price—only $10.

For further information about this program—now called LeLoLai VIP (Value in Puerto Rico)—see "Evening Entertainment," in Chapter 7.

The most prestigious cultural event in the Caribbean, and sufficient reason to go to Puerto Rico, is the Casals Festival in June. The festival was established by Pablo Casals, whose mother was Puerto Rican. This world-famed cellist died in Puerto Rico in 1973 at the age of 97. The festival attracts a glittering array of international guest conductors, orchestras, and soloists; it also features the Puerto Rico Symphony Orchestra. For more information on this event, see the "San Juan Calendar of Events," in Chapter 2.

Puerto Rico has the most extensive theater, music, and dance program in the Caribbean. The Puerto Rico Symphony Orchestra usually performs at the Fine Arts Center, at De Diego and Ponce de León Avenues in Santurce (tel. 809/725-7334). Besides hosting the Casals Festival, this center also schedules major opera and ballet performances by both regional and touring international companies, plays (in Spanish), and popular musical concerts.

○ The LeLoLai Festival features performances of La Danza, a uniquely Puerto Rican dance that evolved from European ballroom dances.

The Tapía Theater, Plaza de Colón (tel. 809/722-0407), is one of the oldest theaters in the western hemisphere. Restored in 1976 to its neoclassical elegance, the theater presents concerts, Spanish and Puerto Rican dramas, and ballets.

If you speak Spanish, the most interesting and experimental entertainment is presented at the University of Puerto Rico Theater, Ponce de León Avenue, Río Piedras (tel. 809/764-0000, ext. 2505). A lot of talent—Puerto Rican, American, and international, ranging from concert pianists to mimes—is presented here.

La Perla Theater, at calles Mayor and Cristina in Ponce (tel. 809/841-0105), also hosts plays and concerts; in Mayagüez, the island's westernmost city, the Yagüez Theater, at calles McKinley and D. R. Basora (tel. 809/834-0523), was founded in 1909. Originally the Yagüez was a theater for silent movies, accompanied by a six-piece chamber orchestra. Today, the recently restored and expanded theater is considered the cultural hub of Mayagüez and the surrounding region; Spanish-language plays and concerts are presented here.

Puerto Rico's casinos draw people to the island since it's one of the few places under U.S. jurisdiction where gambling is legal. More than a dozen major casinos in Puerto Rico offer games ranging from blackjack to baccarat. All are in large hotels, including the Caribe Hilton, Condado Plaza Hotel, El San Juan Hotel, and Sands Hotel. To the east, there's a casino at the Palmas Inn Hotel & Casino in Humacao.

Puerto Rico wants to maintain a dignified atmosphere at its casinos; drinking is not permitted at casino tables. You can, however, order free coffee or soft drinks. The dress code is somewhat relaxed during the afternoon, but at night men should wear suits and ties. You must be at least 18 years old to enter the casinos, and most are open daily from noon until 4am.

San Juan offers more nightlife than any place else in the Caribbean, with the emphasis on discos and hotel showrooms (spotlighting Latin revues). There are also numerous piano bars.

Most of the big resort hotels of the Condado and Isla Verde have lounges with combos for dancing. Often there is no cover charge. If you look around or ask at your hotel reception desk, you might also be directed to a flamenco show, but you would have to go to Spain to experience authentic flamenco.

San Juan, especially in the Condado neighborhood, is sometimes considered the gay capital of the Caribbean; there are many gay bars and discos, some of which are private clubs.

Once you leave San Juan and the Condado, you'll probably need a good book or companion to keep yourself occupied. The two Hyatt Hotels in Dorado, on the island's north coast, and the Mayagüez Hilton International on the island's west coast, offer evening entertainment. You can also find nightlife diversions at Palmas del Mar, the 2,800-acre Mediterranean-style resort in the east. Otherwise, except for some spontaneous salsa music that might be presented at a beachfront bar or at one of the island's little inns, the island can be sleepy and fairly quiet.

8. SPORTS & RECREATION

Puerto Rico offers a wide variety of participant and spectator sports, including golf, tennis, all kinds of water sports, boating, deep-sea and freshwater fishing, horseback riding and thoroughbred racing, baseball, and polo.

Many resorts offer a large choice of sports activities, and a variety of all-inclusive sports-vacation packages are available from hotels and airlines serving Puerto Rico.

Dorado Beach, Cerromar Beach, and Palmas del Mar are the chief centers for those seeking golf, tennis, and beach life. San Juan's hotels on the Condado/Isla Verde coast also generally offer a complete array of water sports.

BASEBALL   While the United States may claim baseball as its national pastime, the sport also has a long, illustrious history in Puerto Rico. Imported around the turn of the century by plantation owners as a leisure activity for workers, *beisbol* quickly caught fire, and local leagues have produced such major-league stars as Ruben Sierra and Roberto Clemente. A top-notch league of six teams—featuring many rising professionals honing their skills during the winter months—begins its season in October and plays in ballparks throughout the island. For a chance to see good baseball in a more intimate setting than is afforded in the major leagues, call **Professional Baseball of Puerto Rico** (tel. 809/765-6285) for information about minor-league games and, if available, a schedule.

BEACHES   With some 300 miles of Atlantic and Caribbean coastline, Puerto Rico obviously has plenty of beaches. The **Condado** and **Isla Verde** beaches are the most frequented. Good snorkeling is possible, and rental equipment is available for water sports. However, don't go walking along these beaches at night. Some, such as **Luquillo,** 30 miles east of San Juan, are overcrowded, especially on Saturday and Sunday. Others are practically deserted. If you find that secluded, hidden beach of your dreams, proceed with caution. On unguarded beaches you will have no way to protect yourself or your valuables should you be approached by a robber or mugger, which has been known to happen. For more information about the island's many beaches, call the **Department of Sports and Recreation** (tel. 809/722-1551).

Beaches in Puerto Rico are open to the public, although you will be charged for parking and for use of *balneario* facilities, such as lockers and showers. The public beaches on the north shore of San Juan at **Ocean Park** and **Park Barbosa** are good and can be reached by bus.

Public beaches are closed on Monday. If Monday is a holiday, the beaches are open but then close on Tuesday. In winter, beach hours are 9am to 5pm, to 6pm in summer.

Along the western coastal roads of Route 2, north of Mayagüez, lie what are reputed to be the best surfing beaches in the Caribbean. Surfers from as far away as New Zealand are attracted to these beaches. The most outstanding, comparable to the finest surfing spots in the world, according to competitors in the 1988 World Surfing Championship held there, is at **Punta Higuero,** on Route 413 near the town of Rincón. In the winter months especially, uninterrupted Atlantic swells with perfectly formed waves averaging 5 to 6 feet in height roll shoreward, and rideable swells sometimes reach 15 to 25 feet. The following balnearios start in the metropolitan area and continue clockwise around the island:

Punta Salinas (Rte. 868, Cataño)
Escambron (Puerta de Tierra, San Juan)

Isla Verde (Rte. 187, Isla Verde)
Luquillo (Hwy. 3, Luquillo)
Seven Seas (Rte. 987, Fajardo)
Sun Bay (Rte. 997, Vieques)
Punta Santiago (Hwy. 3, Humacao)
Punta Guilarte (Hwy. 3, Humacao)
Punta Guilarte (Hwy. 3, Arroyo)
Cana Gora (Rte. 333, Guánica)
Boquerón (Rte. 101, Boquerón)
Añasco (Rte. 410, Añasco)
Cerro Gordo (Rte. 690, Vega Baja)
Sardinera (Rte. 698, Dorado)

BOATING & SAILING   The waters off Puerto Rico provide excellent boating in all seasons. For sailors, winds average 10 to 15 knots virtually year-round. Marinas provide facilities and services on a par with any in the Caribbean, and many have powerboats or sailboats for rent, crewed or bareboat charter. Marinas include the San Juan Bay Marina; Isleta Marina, Puerto Chico, and Villa Marina in Fajardo; Marina del Mar and Palmas del Mar in Humacao; and Marina de Salinas in Salinas.

The Caribbean's largest and most modern marina, Puerto del Rey, is located on the island's east coast in Fajardo. Facilities for 70 boats are already completed, including docking and fueling for yachts up to 200 feet in length and haulout and repair for yachts up to 90 feet. The marina resort now includes accommodations for boat rentals, yacht charters, and water sports, in addition to several shops and a French restaurant.

Annual sailing regattas include the Copa Velasco Regatta for ocean racing, at Palmas del Mar Resort in Humacao.

CAMPING   The island abounds in sandy beaches and forested hillsides suitable (if permission is given by the landowner) for erecting a tent. More protected and much safer are sites throughout the island where simple cabins, sometimes with fireplaces, are maintained by the **Recreational Development Company of Puerto Rico.** Although accommodations are bare-boned minimalist, the costs are often less than those charged by hotels. For more information and an application to rent one of the units, call 809/722-1551 or 809/722-1771. Additional information about camping may be available from the **Parks and Recreation Association of Puerto Rico** (tel. 809/721-2800).

DEEP-SEA FISHING   It's top-notch! Allison tuna, white and blue marlin, sailfish, wahoo, dolphin, mackerel, and tarpon are some of the fish that can be caught in Puerto Rican waters, where 30 world records have been broken. Charter arrangements can be made through most major hotels and resorts.

It is said in deep-sea-fishing circles that **Capt. Mike Benitez,** who has chartered out of San Juan for more than 40 years, sets the standard by which to judge other captains. (In 1993, the Sport Fishing Tournament Guide listed him as one of the 15 most qualified sport-fishing captains in the world. Past clients have included, among others, ex-President Jimmy Carter, actor Timothy Bottoms, and most members of the singing group Huey Lewis and the News.) His Atlanta-born wife, Erin, handles the company's reservations and can be contacted directly at P.O. Box 5141, Puerta de Tierra, San Juan, PR 00906 (tel. 809/723-2292 daily until 9pm). The team offers two boats, one a 45-foot air-conditioned deluxe Hatteras, the *Sea Born;* the other, a 61-foot Davis (*Sea Born II*), a million-dollar almost-new yacht acquired after it was damaged during Hurricane Hugo in 1989. Depending on the boat, fishing tours, for up to six participants cost $390 to $625 for a half-day excursion and $690 to $1,200 for a full day, with all equipment included.

Some of the best year-round fishing in the Caribbean is found in the waters just off Palmas del Mar, the resort complex on the southeast coast. There, **Capt. Bill Burleson,** P.O. Box 8270, Humacao, PR 00792 (tel. 809/850-7442), operates charters on his fully customized 48-foot sport-fisherman, *Karolette,* which is electronically equipped for successful fishing. Burleson prefers to take fishing groups to Grappler Banks, 18 nautical miles away. The banks are two sea mounts, rising to about 240 feet below the surface and surrounded by deeps of 6,000 to 8,000 feet. They lie in the migratory paths of the wahoo, tuna, and marlin. The cost is $880 per day ($480 for a half day) for a maximum of six people. He also offers snorkeling expeditions to Vieques at $80 per person for a five-hour trip.

GOLF   Among the major tournaments held on Puerto Rico is the Hyatt Senior Tour Championship, in which the top 30 golfers of the Senior PGA Tour compete for a $1-million prize. The tournament is scheduled each December at the Hyatt Dorado Beach resort. Rums of Puerto Rico sponsors the annual Rums of Puerto Rico National Club Pro Am at the Hyatt Regency Cerromar Beach in November.

A golfer's dream, Puerto Rico has eight major courses, as well as many of lesser significance. Costs vary widely, depending on the course and the season, but usually range from $10 to $80 for 18 holes. The **Hyatt Resorts Puerto Rico** at Dorado (tel. 809/796-1234), with 72 holes, offers the greatest concentration of golf in the Caribbean. The 18-hole Robert Trent Jones courses at the Hyatt Regency Cerromar and the Hyatt Dorado Beach match the finest anywhere.

The **Club de Golf,** at Palmas del Mar, in Humacao (tel. 809/852-6000), is one of the best courses on Puerto Rico. On the southeast coast, it has a par-72, 6,690-yard layout designed by Gary Player. Crack golfers consider holes 11 through 15 the toughest five successive holes in the Caribbean.

The **Mayagüez Hilton,** at Mayagüez (tel. 809/831-7575), makes arrangements for guests to play at a 9-hole course at a nearby country club. The **Punta Borinquén Golf Club** (tel. 809/890-2987), at Aguadilla (the former Ramey Air Force Base), has an 18-hole public course, open daily from 7am to 7pm.

HORSE RACING   Great thoroughbreds and outstanding jockeys compete all year at **El Comandante,** avenida 65 de Infantería, Route 3, km 15.3, at Canovanas (tel. 809/724-6060), Puerto Rico's only race track. Post time is 2:15pm on Sunday and holidays, and at 3:45pm on Monday, Wednesday, and Friday. Clubhouse admission is $3; entrance to the grandstand is free. An air-conditioned terrace dining room opens at 12:30pm each race day. Telephone for luncheon reservations. Most credit and charge cards are accepted.

HORSEBACK RIDING   The equestrian center at **Palmas del Mar** (tel. 809/852-6000) has 42 horses, including English hunters for jumping, plus a variety of trail rides and instruction for all levels of ability. The land set aside for equestrian pursuits abuts the resort's airstrip and is bounded on one side by a stream. Trail rides skirt this creek, following paths through a coconut plantation and jungle and swinging along the beach. A trail ride lasts an hour and costs $20 per person.

MARATHON   The annual San Blas Half Marathon held in February attracts international as well as local competitors. It takes place in Coamo, in the south-central part of the island. Other races are scheduled year-round throughout the island.

SCUBA/SNORKELING   The continental shelf, which surrounds Puerto Rico on three sides, is responsible for an abundance of coral reefs, caves, sea walls, and trenches for scuba and snorkeling.

Open-water reefs off the central coast near Humacao are often visited by migrating whales and manatees. Many caves are located near Isabela on the west coast. The Great Trench, off the island's south coast, is ideal for experienced sport divers. Caves and the sea wall at La Parguera are also favorites. Vieques and Culebra, off the east coast, have coral formations. Mona Island, off the west coast, offers unspoiled reefs at depths averaging 80 feet; seals are one of the attractions. Uninhabited islands, such as Icacos, off the northeastern coast near Fajardo, are also popular with snorkelers and divers.

These sites are now within reach since many of Puerto Rico's dive operators and resorts offer packages that may include daily or twice-daily dives, scuba equipment, instruction, and excursions to the island's popular attractions. Four-dive packages, including equipment rental and air, are available for less than $200, and eight-dive programs can be purchased for less than $300. For instance, the **Caribbean School of Aquatics,** calle Taft 1, no. 10, San Juan, PR 00911 (tel. 809/723-4740), offers dive packages at La Concha Hotel, a resort in the Condado area of San Juan. There are day-long expeditions to several small offshore islands, including Mona Island and Icacos.

In San Juan, a highly recommended opportunity for underwater diving is through **Karen Vega's Carib Aquatic Adventures,** P.O. Box 2470, San Juan Station, San Juan, PR 00902 (tel. 809/729-2929, ext. 240). Its main office is in the lobby of the Radisson Normandie Hotel. The company offers diving certification from both PADI and NAUI following a 40-hour course priced at $330. A resort course for first-time divers costs $80. Also offered are Sunfish and laser rentals at $40 per hour, windsurfing (see below), and a choice of full-day diving expeditions to various reefs and wrecks surrounding the island.

Elsewhere on the island, several other companies offer scuba and snorkeling instruction.

Coral Head Divers & Water Sports Center, P.O. Box C.U.H.F., Humacao, PR 00792 (tel. 809/850-7208, or toll free 800/635-4529), is headquartered at the Palmas del Mar Resort (see Chapter 9). The dive center owns two fully equipped boats, measuring 26 and 44 feet. The center offers daily two-tank open-water dives for certified divers, plus snorkeling trips to Monkey Island and Vieques (see Chapter 11). The two-tank dive includes tanks, weights, and computer at $75. A snorkeling trip to Monkey Island includes use of equipment and beverages at $45 per person. A scuba resort lesson costs $40.

For reservations or more information about Puerto Rico diving packages, contact Kathy Rothschild at **Rothschild Travel Consultants** (tel. 212/662-4858 in New York City, or toll free 800/359-0747).

SPAS Puerto Rico has a number of spas and wellness centers:

The **Health Spa** at the El San Juan Hotel and Casino has a full range of facilities for men and women and an on-staff nutritionist available for guest consultations.

The **Plaza Spa** at the Condado Plaza Hotel & Casino features weight machines, steam room, sauna, whirlpool, facials, and massage.

The **Spa Caribe** at the Hyatt Regency Cerromar Beach offers health and exercise services, including "talking" Powercise machines, Swedish massage, European facials, and loofah polish. Spa packages also are available for guests of the Hyatt Dorado Beach Hotel.

The **Fitness Center** at Palmas del Mar Resort in Humacao offers a complete exercise program, including aerobics, stationary bicycles, hydraulic exercise, and other equipment. The center also has a juice bar and an aerobics and fitness clothing shop.

At **Parador Baños de Coamo** there are therapeutic thermal baths, a swimming pool, and a tennis court.

Each of these resorts will be discussed further in later chapters.

SURFING Puerto Rico's northwest beaches attract surfers from around the world. Called the Hawaii of the East, the island has hosted a number of international competitions. October through February are considered the best surfing months, but the sport is enjoyed in Puerto Rico from August through April. The most popular areas are from Isabela around Punta Borinquén to Rincón—with beaches such as Wilderness, Surfers, Crashboat, Los Turbos in Vega Jaja, Pine Grove in Isla Verde, and La Pared in Luquillo. Surfboards are available at many water-sports shops.

International competitions held in Puerto Rico have included the 1968 and 1988 World Amateur Surfing Championships, the annual Caribbean Cup Surfing Championship, and the 1989 and 1990 Budweiser Puerto Rico Surfing Challenge events, stops on the professional tour.

TENNIS There are approximately 100 tennis courts in Puerto Rico. Many are located at hotels and resorts, while others can be found in public parks throughout the island. Several paradores also have courts. A number of courts are lighted for nighttime play.

The twin resorts of **Dorado** and **Cerromar** (tel. 809/796-1234) maintain a total of 21 courts between them. Court fees are $15 an hour, rising to $18 from 6 to 8pm. Take your racquet and tennis outfit along (attire and equipment are often available in shops, but prices are high and the selection is minimal). Lessons are available for $50 per hour.

In San Juan, the **Caribe Hilton,** the **Condado Plaza,** the **Carib Inn,** and the **Condado Beach** and **La Concha** have tennis courts. Also in the area is a public court at the old navy base, Isla Grande, in Miramar. The entrance is from avenida Fernández Juncos at bus stop 11.

The **Tennis Center** at Palmas del Mar in Humacao (tel. 809/852-6000, ext. 51), the largest in Puerto Rico, features 20 courts. Court fees are $16 per hour for hotel guests during the day and $21 at night. Special tennis packages are available, including accommodations. Call for more information.

WINDSURFING   Windsurfing is another popular water sport on Puerto Rico, and the sheltered waters of the Condado Lagoon in San Juan are a favorite spot. Other sites include Ocean Park, Ensenada, Boquerón, Honda Beach, and Culebra. Throughout the island, many companies that offer snorkeling and scuba also provide windsurfing equipment and instruction, and dozens of hotels have facilities on their own premises. Puerto Rico hosted its first major windsurfing tournament, the Ray Ban Windsurfing World Cup, in June 1989.

One of the best places to arrange for windsurfing in San Juan is at **Karen Vega's Carib Aquatic Adventures,** P.O. Box 2470, San Juan Station, San Juan, PR 00902 (tel. 809/729-2929, ext. 240), whose main office is in the lobby of San Juan's Radisson Normandie Hotel. Rentals cost $25 per hour and lessons are $40.

Along the north shore, windsurfing is excellent at the carefully maintained beachfront of the Hyatt Dorado Beach Hotel. Here, the **Lisa Penfield Windsurfing School** (tel. 809/796-1234, ext. 3760, or 809/796-2188) offers 90-minute lessons for $55 each and two-hour board rentals for $45. Well supplied with a wide array of windsurfers, including some designed specifically for beginners and children, the school benefits from the almost uninterrupted flow of the north shore's strong, steady winds and an experienced crew of instructors.

9. FOOD & DRINK

Although Puerto Rican cooking is somewhat similar to both Spanish and Mexican cuisine, it has a unique style, using such indigenous seasonings and ingredients as coriander, papaya, cacao, nispero, apio, plantains, and yampee.

Cocina criola (Créole cooking) can be traced back to the Arawaks and Taínos, the original inhabitants of the island, who thrived on a diet of corn, tropical fruit, and seafood. When Ponce de León arrived with Columbus in 1493, the Spanish added beef, pork, rice, wheat, and olive oil to the island's foodstuffs. Soon after, the Spanish began planting sugarcane and importing slaves from Africa, who brought with them okra and taro (known in Puerto Rico as *yauita*). The mingling of flavors and ingredients passed from generation to generation among the different ethnic groups that settled on the island, resulting in the exotic blend of today's Puerto Rican cuisine.

APPETIZERS & SOUPS   Lunch and dinner generally begin with sizzling-hot **appetizers** such as *bacalitos,* crunchy cod fritters; *surullitos,* sweet plump cornmeal fingers; and *empanadillas,* crescent-shaped turnovers filled with lobster, crab, conch, or beef.

Soups are a popular beginning for meals on Puerto Rico. There is a debate about whether one of the best-known soups, *frijoles negros* (black-bean soup), is Cuban or Puerto Rican in origin. Nevertheless, it is still a savory, if filling, opening to a meal.

Another classic soup is *sopón de pollo con arroz*—chicken soup with rice—which manages to taste somewhat different in every restaurant. One traditional method of preparing this soup calls for large pieces of pumpkin and diced potatoes or yauitas (the starchy root of a large-leaved tropical plant whose flesh is usually yellow or creamy white).

The third classic soup is *sopón de pescado* (fish soup), prepared with the head and tail intact. Again, this soup varies from restaurant to restaurant and may depend on the catch of the day. Traditionally, it is made with garlic and spices plus onions and tomatoes, the flavor enhanced by a tiny dash of vinegar and a half cup of sherry. Galician broth (*caldo gallego*) is a dish imported from Spain's northwestern province of Galicia. It is prepared with salt pork, white beans, ham, and *berzas* (collard greens) or *grelos* (turnip greens), and the whole kettle is flavored with spicy chorizos (Spanish sausages).

Garbanzos (chickpeas), are often added to give flavor, body, and texture to Puerto Rican soups. One of the most authentic versions of this is *sopón de garbanzos con patas de cerdo* (chickpea soup with pig's feet). Into this kettle is added a variety of ingredients, including pumpkin, chorizos, salt pork, chile peppers, cabbage, potatoes, tomatoes, and fresh cilantro leaves.

Not really a soup, the most traditional Puerto Rican dish is **asopao,** a hearty gumbo made with either chicken or shellfish. One well-known version, consumed when the food budget runs low, is *asopao de gandules* (pigeon peas). Every Puerto Rican chef has his or her own recipe for asopao. *Asopao de pollo* (chicken asopao) takes a whole chicken, which is then flavored with spices such as oregano, garlic, and paprika, along with salt pork, cured ham, green peppers, chile peppers, onions, cilantro, olives, tomatoes, chorizos, and pimientos. For a final touch, green peas or asparagus might be added.

MAIN DISHES   The aroma that wafts from kitchens throughout Puerto Rico comes from *adobo* and *sofrito*—blends of herbs and spices that give many of the native foods their distinctive taste and color. Adobo, made by crushing together peppercorns, oregano, garlic, salt, olive oil, and lime juice or vinegar, is rubbed into meats before they are roasted. Sofrito, a potpourri of onions, garlic, and peppers browned in either olive oil or lard and colored with *achiote* (annatto seeds), imparts the bright-yellow color to the island's rice, soups, and stews.

Stews loom large in the Puerto Rican diet. They are usually cooked in a *caldero,* or heavy kettle. A popular one is *carne guisada puertorriqueña* (Puerto Rican beef stew). The ingredients that flavor the chunks of beef vary according to the cook's whims or whatever happens to be in the larder. These might include green peppers, sweet chile peppers, onions, garlic, cilantro, potatoes, olives stuffed with pimientos, or capers. Seeded raisins may be added on occasion. Meat pies (*pastelon de carne*) are the staple of many Puerto Rican dinners. Salt pork and ham are often used for the filling and are cooked in a caldero. This medley of meats and spices is covered with a pastry top and baked.

✪ Asopao, a hearty gumbo, is a classic of the Puerto Rican kitchen.

Other typical main dishes include fried beefsteak with onions (*carne frita con cebolla*), veal (*ternera*) à la parmesana, and roast leg of pork, fresh ham, lamb, or veal, à la criolla. These roasted meats are cooked in the Créole style, flavored with adobo.

Puerto Ricans also like such dishes as breaded calf's brains (*sesos empanados*), calf's kidney stew (*riñones guisados*), and stuffed beef tongue (*lengua rellena*).

A festive island dish is *lechón asado,* or **barbecued pig,** which is usually cooked for a party of 12 or 15. It is traditional for picnics and al fresco parties; one can sometimes catch the aroma of this dish wafting through the palm trees, a smell that must have been familiar to the Taíno peoples. The pig is basted with *jugo de naranja agria* (sour orange juice) and achiote coloring. Green plantains are peeled and roasted over hot stones, then served with the barbecued pig as a side dish. The traditional dressing served with the pig is *aji-li-mojili,* a sour garlic sauce. The sauce combines garlic, whole black peppercorns, and sweet seeded chile peppers, flavored further with vinegar, lime juice, salt, and olive oil.

Puerto Ricans adore **chicken,** which they flavor with various spices and seasonings. *Arroz con pollo* (chicken with rice) is the most popular chicken dish on the island, and it was brought long ago to the U.S. mainland. Other favorite preparations include chicken in sherry *(pollo al Jerez), pollo en agridulce* (sweet-and-sour chicken), and *pollitos asados à la parrilla* (broiled chickens).

Most visitors to the island seem to like the **fish and shellfish.** A popular dish is fried fish with Puerto Rican sauce *(mojo isleno).* The sauce is made with olives and olive oil, onions, pimientos, capers, tomato sauce, vinegar, and a flavoring of garlic and bay leaves. Fresh fish is often grilled, and perhaps flavored with garlic and an overlay of freshly squeezed lime juice—a very tasty dinner indeed. Caribbean lobster is usually the most expensive item on any menu, followed by shrimp. Puerto Ricans often cook shrimp in beer *(camarones en cerveza).* Another delectable shellfish dish is boiled crab *(jueyes hervidos).*

Many tasty **egg dishes** are served, especially *tortilla española* (Spanish omelet), cooked with finely chopped onions, cubed potatoes, and olive oil.

The rich and fertile fields of Puerto Rico produce a wide variety of **vegetables.** A favorite is the *chayote,* a pear-shaped vegetable called christophine throughout most of the English-speaking Caribbean. Its delicately flavored flesh is often compared to that of summer squash. Breadfruit, prepared in a number of ways, frequently accompanies main dishes. This large, round fruit from a tropical tree has a thick green rind covering its starchy, sweet flesh. The flavor is evocative of a sweet potato. *Tostones*—fried green breadfruit slices—accompany most meat, fish, or poultry dishes served on the island.

Tostones may also be made with **plantains.** In fact, the plantain seems to be the single most popular side dish served on the island. Plantains are a variety of banana that cannot be eaten raw. They are much coarser in texture than ordinary bananas and are harvested while green, then baked, fried, or boiled. When made into tostones, they are usually served as an appetizer with before-dinner drinks. Fried to a deep golden-yellow, plantains may accompany fish, meat, or poultry dishes.

DESSERTS Desserts usually include some form of flan (custard) or perhaps *nisperos de batata* (sweet-potato balls with coconut, cloves, and cinnamon). Equally traditional would be a portion of guava jelly with *queso blanco* (white cheese). Chefs take the bountiful harvest of Puerto Rican fruits and create any number of desserts, including orange layer cake, banana cupcakes, and guava cake. The most delicious dessert may be a freshly prepared fruit cocktail. The pumpkin, which grows in abundance on Puerto Rico, is used not only to flavor soups and as a side vegetable, but also to make the succulent base for a traditional Puerto Rican cake. Similarly, the sweet potato is used both as a side vegetable and in making a regional sweet-potato cake.

Coconut is probably the most common dessert ingredient. Many delectable desserts are made with its milk *(leche de coco),* including coconut flan, coconut cream desserts, crunchy coconut squares, coconut with meringue, and candied coconut rice. Another classic preparation is coconut bread pudding *(boudin de pasas con coco). Polvo de amor* ("love powder") is prepared with grated coconut meat after the milk has been extracted. The coconut is mixed with a lot of sugar and placed in a kettle to cook rapidly, then served crisp and golden brown.

Puerto Ricans make a number of preserves and jellies. Both sweet and sour guavas are used for various concoctions—not only guava jelly, but guava shells in syrup, guava paste, and guava pudding. Papayas are made into preserves or desserts with sugar, cinnamon, and vanilla extract. A mango dessert is made with virtually the same ingredients. Mangoes may be used for mamey preserve *(dolce de mamey)* or may be consumed raw.

DRINKS Finish your meal with strong, black, aromatic Puerto Rican **coffee,** which has been produced in the island's high-altitude interior for more than 300 years. Originally imported from the nearby Dominican Republic, coffee is still among the island's leading exports and is a suitable ending for any well-presented meal.

Because the island does not produce wine, it is entirely proper to order a cold **beer** before even looking at the menu. Beer, of course, is called *cerveza* throughout the Spanish-speaking world; the most popular brand on Puerto Rico is Medalla.

Rum is the national drink, and you can buy it in almost any shade. Puerto Rico is the world's leading rum producer; 80% of the rum consumed in the United States hails from the island.

Today's rum bears little resemblance to the raw and grainy beverage consumed by the renegades and pirates of the Spanish Main. Christopher Columbus brought sugarcane, from which rum is distilled, to the Caribbean on his second voyage to the New World, and in virtually no time it became *the* regional drink.

It is believed that Ponce de León introduced rum to Puerto Rico during his governorship, which began in 1508. In time, there emerged large sugarcane plantations. From Puerto Rico and other West Indian islands, rum was shipped to colonial America, where it lent itself to such popular and hair-raising 18th-century drinks as Kill-Divil and Whistle-Belly Vengeance. After America became a nation, rum was largely displaced as the drink of choice by whiskey, distilled from grain grown on the American plains.

It took almost a century before the rum industry regained its former vigor. This occurred during a severe whiskey shortage at the end of World War II. By the 1950s, sales of rum had fallen off again, as more and different kinds of liquor became available on the U.S. market. Rum had been a questionable drink because of inferior distillation methods and quality. Recognizing this problem, the Puerto Rican government drew up rigid standards for producing, blending, and aging rum. Rum factories were outfitted with the most

> ◐ **Strong, black, aromatic coffee has been produced in the island's interior for more than 300 years.**

modern and sanitary equipment, and sales figures (encouraged by aggressive marketing campaigns) began to climb.

The color of rum is usually gold, amber, or white. The lightest, driest rum is white. It can easily replace gin or vodka in dozens of mixed drinks that are eminently suited for consumption in the tropics. Many Puerto Ricans make Bloody Marys with rum instead of gin or vodka. The robust flavors of the gold or amber rums make them an effective substitute for whiskey. With white (clear) rum, orange juice and tonic water are the most popular mixers; amber rum is often served on the rocks. Puerto Ricans are fond of mixing it with various cola drinks. Gold rums, aged between four and six years (sometimes longer) in wooden casks are called *añejos*. They are considered the most flavorful and distinctive of the island rums. They are smooth; drink them straight or on the rocks.

Bacardi is the Puerto Rican rum most widely consumed in the United States. It is followed by other popular brands, including Ronrico, Castillo, and Don Q. The añejos rums carry such labels as Bacardi Gold Reserve, Ron del Barrilito, and Serralles' El Dorado.

Your best introduction to Puerto Rican rum making is to visit the Bacardi distillery in Catano, just a short ferryboat ride across the San Juan harbor.

Each bartender worthy of the profession in Puerto Rico likes to concoct his or her own favorite rum libation. Every resort offers the piña colada, which is made with cream of coconut, white Puerto Rican rum, and canned pineapple juice. The ingredients are thoroughly blended and served frappé-style in a tall cool glass, usually garnished with a maraschino cherry and a small paper parasol. But you may want to be more adventurous and sample some of the island's other cocktails, many of which are made with fresh fruit juices. Planter's punch, served over cracked ice, is the second most popular mixed rum drink for tourists. Often, it combines dark Puerto Rican rum, dark-brown Jamaican rum, citrus juice, and Angostura bitters. Of course, you can substitute rum in many mixed drinks such as rum collins, rum sour, rum screwdriver, and rum and tonic. The classic sangría, which is prepared in Spain with dry red wine, sugar, orange juice, and other ingredients, may be given a thoroughly Puerto Rican twist with a hefty dose of the island's rum.

10. RECOMMENDED BOOKS & RECORDINGS

BOOKS

GENERAL

Babin, Theresa Maria. *The Puerto Ricans' Spirit: Their History, Life, and Culture.* Collier Books, 1971. Provides good background information on the island's history and its people, along with a survey of its fine arts and literature.

Carrion, Arturo Morales. *Puerto Rico and the Non-Hispanic Caribbean: A Study in the Decline of Spanish Exclusivism.* University of Puerto Rico Press, 1984. Analysis of Puerto Rico's role within the English- and French-speaking Caribbean has been a neglected area of academic study. This book provides a Caribbean—rather than Spanish or North American—context to the Puerto Rican experience.

————. *Puerto Rico and the United States: The Quest for a New Encounter.* Editorial Academia, 1991. A tightly knit account of United States–Puerto Rico relationships during the 20th century. The book traces the development of these relationships from the early days of outright tutelage to the more recent era of improved understanding and close cooperation.

Garver, Susan, and Paula McGuire. *Coming to North America.* Dell, 1984. Explores the subject of the massive migration from Puerto Rico to America, where immigrants settled mainly in New York.

Gonzáles, José Luís. *Puerto Rico: The Four Storeyed Country.* Waterfront Press, 1990. A collection of essays examining Puerto Rican society, culture, and national identity; it assumes that you already know a lot about the island.

Gordon, Raoul. *Puerto Rican Culture: An Introduction.* Gordon Press, 1982. Provides an in-depth study of this subject for those interested in understanding the art and traditions of the island.

Hanberg, Clifford A. *Puerto Rico and the Puerto Ricans.* Hippocrene, 1975. Offers a look at the history and background of Puerto Rico.

Rodriquez, Clara E. *Puerto Ricans: Born in the U.S.A.* Westview Press, 1991. A highly politicized broad portrait of one of the largest segments of the Hispanic-American population. It looks at the unique position of Puerto Ricans on the mainland—Spanish-speaking U.S. citizens—and the impact of this on their lives and aspirations.

Santiago, Esmeralda. *When I Was Puerto Rican.* Addison-Wesley/Lawrence, 1993. The president of a film company describes her childhood as one of 11 Puerto Rican siblings, born into poverty. From the island countryside to the crime-ridden streets of Brooklyn, Santiago's memoir is rich in the ambience of Puerto Rican life.

Steiner, Stan. *The Islands.* Harper & Row, 1974. A journalistic portrayal of the island people, both within Puerto Rico itself and in North American *barrios*, such as those of the South Bronx.

HISTORY

Bonet, Walter A. Cardona. *Shipwrecks in Puerto Rico's History: 1502–1650.* Privately published in 1989. This carefully illustrated book is especially interesting to historians, marine scholars, or anyone interested in the many ships wrecked on the reefs and shoals off Puerto Rico, whose survivors contributed significantly to the island's racial and cultural mix and to its naval expertise. Available at bookstores in Old San Juan.

Carrion, Arturo Morales. *Puerto Rico: A Political and Cultural History.* W. W. Norton, 1983. One of the best major overviews of Puerto Rican history and culture. Most of the book focuses on the political history of the island, with extensive chapters devoted to 18th-century society, the plantation society, and the challenge to Spanish colonialism. Part Two traces the conflicts, hopes, and trauma that followed the U.S. takeover of the island in 1898. The final section provides a good cultural survey of Puerto Rico, covering folklore, literature, music, and art.

Dor-Ner, Zvi, and William G. Scheller. *Columbus and the Age of Discovery.* William Morrow, 1991. The companion book to the PBS series about the explorer. This is a good general survey of what is known about the voyages of Columbus.

Golding, Morton. *A Short History of Puerto Rico.* New American Library, 1973. For those who want their history readable and condensed.

Honychurch, Reginald. *The Caribbean People.* T. Nelson & Sons, 1981. In three volumes, this is a well-balanced account written by one of the so-called new historians of the Caribbean.

Scarano, Francisco A. *Sugar and Slavery in Puerto Rico: The Plantation Economy of Ponce, 1800–1850.* University of Wisconsin Press, 1984. A scholarly study of an agrarian region of Puerto Rico far removed from the Spanish-controlled capital of San Juan.

Tugwell, Rexford Guy. *The Story of Puerto Rico.* Greenwood Press, 1977. An expansive, scholarly history of Puerto Rico, from a highly politicized point of view.

Wagenheim, Kal, and Olga Jimenez, eds. *The Puerto Ricans: A Documentary History.* Waterford Press, 1973. An essential sourcebook providing a better understanding of Puerto Ricans. Its fast-paced rhythm makes it engrossing, if prejudicial, reading.

Williams, Eric. *From Columbus to Castro: The History of the Caribbean.* Vintage, 1970. The former prime minister of Trinidad and Tobago takes you on a grand tour of a region dominated by slavery, sugar, and often sheer greed.

POLITICS

Carr, Ramon. *Puerto Rico: A Colonial Experiment.* Random House, 1984. One of the most insightful views of island politics, which has been called the national religion of Puerto Rico. This book, funded by the Twentieth Century Fund (established in 1919 by philanthropist Edward A. Filene), discusses ways to loosen the economic bonds between a superpower and what is today a quasi-colonial possession.

Johnson, Roberta. *Puerto Rico: Commonwealth or Colony?* Praeger, 1980. This book attempts to answer the title's provocative question.

Melendez, Edgardo. *Puerto Rico's Statehood Movement.* Greenwood Press, 1980. Melendez reviews the statehood movement, presenting the pros and cons of a complicated issue.

Perl, Lila. *Puerto Rico, Island Between Two Worlds.* William Morrow, 1979. Describes the dilemma of an island caught between its Spanish heritage and its contemporary American ties.

Perusse, Roland I. *The United States and Puerto Rico: Breaking the Bonds of Economic Colonialism.* Robert E. Krieger, 1990. This book traces the history of trade relations in Puerto Rico, the second-largest Western trading partner of the United States, after Canada. A cultural and economic survey with a strongly politicized point of view.

Williams, Byron. *Puerto Rico: Commonwealth, State, or Nation?* Parents Magazine Press, 1972. A pointed discussion of the major Puerto Rican self-determination movements.

FICTION, LANGUAGE & LITERATURE

FICTION

Baldwin, James. *If Beale Street Could Talk.* Dial, 1974. An acclaimed work by the famed novelist. The setting of this story ranges from the streets of New York to Puerto Rico.

Coll y Toste, Cayetano. *Puerto Rican Tales, Legends of Spanish Colonial Times.* Translated and adapted by José Ramírez Rivera. Ediciones Libero, 1988. A highly readable collection of 12 Caribbean vignettes that provide an insight into the life of the Spanish conquistadores, the Taíno peoples, and the African slaves, in rich juxtaposition one to another. Dr. Ramírez Rivera, a medical academic, translated into English these original stories collected by Coll y Toste; originally published in the 1920s, they were quickly hailed as classics. There are tales of adventure, romance, religion and superstition, and history.

Michener, James A. *Caribbean.* Fawcett, 1989. Another good epic from the master. His sweep of the Caribbean, including Puerto Rico, begins with the 1310 conquest of the peaceful Arawaks by the cannibalistic Caribs and proceeds through seven centuries to Castro's Cuba. Perhaps it's a lot to cover in one book, but Michener has a way of recapturing the past that his many imitators don't.

Sapia, Yvonne V. *Valentino's Hair.* University of Colorado/Fiction Collective Two, 1991. The author of *The Fertile Crescent* presents a brooding and finely textured novel about an elderly Puerto Rican barber in New York City who once cut the hair of Rudolph Valentino. At Valentino's funeral he met a lovely woman and experienced a traumatic event that he vividly recalls upon his death bed 35 years later. The complex culture of Puerto Ricans transplanted to the South Bronx is explored.

LANGUAGE

Del Rosario, Ruben. *Vocabulario Puertorriqueño.* Troutman Press, 1965. The first major compilation of the "Puerto Rican vocabulary."

LITERATURE

Babin, Theresa Maria. *Borinquén: An Anthology of Puerto Rican Literature.* Vintage, 1974. A pioneering work and the best survey of several generations of island writing.

MISCELLANEOUS

Benedetti, Maria Dolores Hajosy. *Earth and Spirit: Healing Lore and More from Puerto Rico.* Waterfront Press, 1989. Written by a Puerto Rican-born allergist and dietitian living in New York today, this book discusses some of the occult and herbal lore of her island. The author describes her great-grandmother's role as a midwife in Mayagüez and a great-aunt's role as a spiritualist in the same town.

Bergman, Billy. *Hot Sauces: Latin and Caribbean Pop.* Quill, 1984. Has some good insights into the music of the West Indies, especially Puerto Rico.

Valldejuli, Carmen Aboy. *Puerto Rican Cookery.* Pelican, 1985. Traces the development of traditional Puerto Rican dishes in accurate and easy-to-follow details.

RECORDINGS

For the sounds produced by Puerto Rico's most famous stringed instrument, the cuatro, listen to the 19th-century compositions of native-born composer Don Felo, *100 Años con Don Felo,* performed by Edwin Colon Zayas (Estudio de Grabación/P.R.T. Recording Studios). In the same vein are the 19th-century folk pieces, adapted for piano and human voice by Narcisco Figueroa, that can be heard on *Canciones de Arte,* featuring soprano Elaine Arandes (Instituto de Cultura Puertorriqueña, Release no. ICP-C-20, vol. III).

Also important for an understanding of Puerto Rico's classical repertoire is a recording by a postwar musicologist, Ernesto Cordero, who returned from musical studies in Italy and Spain to arrange a collection of Puerto Rican folk melodies into formal orchestral scores. Some of the island's premier guitarists, sopranos, and tenors perform in this recording, *Musica de Ernesto Cordero* (Instituto de Cultura Puertorriqueña, Release no. ICP C-14).

The folk music of Puerto Rico's *jíbaros* (hillbillies) is considered one of the island's most enduringly popular musical forms. Among the best hillbilly singers are Andres Jimenez ("El Jíbaro"), Luís Miranda ("El Pico de Oro"), and a group of about 10 singers and guitarists collectively known as the Taller Campesino. The best-selling jíbaro album in many years, *Serenata Jíbara* (Nuevo Arte Recordings, NA 113 LP), features the talents of all three.

After World War II, there were hundreds of jazz and Big Band fans on Puerto Rico. Today's most original interpreter of jazz piano might be island-born Hilton Ruíz, whose recordings *Hilton Ruíz* (RCA, 3053-2-N) and *El Camino* (RCA/BMG, 3024-2-N) infuse the Big Band sound with a strong undercurrent of African rhythms and percussion.

Spanish has been called the language of love, and Puerto Rico has produced many interpreters of modern romantic ballads. The most popular of these are Danny Rivera and the immortal José Feliciano, whose *Canto a la Humanidad* (CBS, CD 80397) and *Contemporary Midline* (RCA/BMG, 2490-2-RL), respectively, are considered among the most representative and original recordings of this genre. Also important is Tony Croatta, a German-born former resident of Argentina, who has chosen to reside on Puerto Rico for many years. His recording *17 Obras Musicales de Puerto Rico* (Star Records, CDV 006) might induce any romantic to catch the next flight to San Juan.

More danceable is salsa, arguably the island's most memorable musical export. Although the movement has evolved and mingled with other musical traditions (mainly jazz) since the end of World War II, two of its long-reigning kings are Ismael Rivera ("El Sonero Mayor") and Rafael Cortijo. Their respective recordings, *De Todas Maneras Rosas* (Tico Records, TSLP 1415) and *Cortijo y su Combo* (Musical Productions, MP 3117 CD), are considered two of the early classics of the movement. More modern adherents of salsa make greater use of electronic amplification and African-derived percussion. Bobby Valentin's *Va a la Carcel* (Bronco Records, SLP 00102) made salsa and sociological history when it was recorded live during a much-publicized concert at Oso Blanco, the state penitentiary of Puerto Rico.

Modern experimental interpretations of salsa continue to proliferate. Jerry Gonzalez's *Rumba Para Monk* (Sunnyside Records, SSC 1036D) translates the Cuban and Puerto Rican salsa traditions back into jazz, much to the approval of anyone who loves to dance. Gonzalez's later album, *Obatala* (Enja, R2 79609), named in honor of a West African tribal god, infuses the traditional Hispanic dance music with more West African percussion and rhythms. On the cutting edge of Puerto Rico's avant garde is an album by island-born musician Angel "Cachete" Maldonado. Along with a group of African-Caribbean jazz artists, he produced *Batacumbele* (Montuno, MLP 525), whose powerful and quasi-experimental salsa encourages bodies and minds to zoom together into the sweet and sexy allure of the music.

CHAPTER 2

PLANNING A TRIP TO PUERTO RICO

This chapter and the next discuss the where, the when, and the how of your trip to Puerto Rico—everything required to plan your trip and get it on the road.

In this chapter I concentrate on what you need to do *before* you go. (See Chapter 3 for information on getting to and around Puerto Rico.) In addition to helping you decide when to take your vacation, I answer questions you might have about what to take, where to gather information, and what documents you need to obtain. I also include tips for special travelers and cover alternative and specialty travel options, such as educational and wilderness travel.

1. INFORMATION, ENTRY REQUIREMENTS, CUSTOMS & MONEY

SOURCES OF INFORMATION

For information before you leave home, contact one of the following, **Puerto Rico Tourism Company** offices: 575 Fifth Ave., New York, NY 10017 (tel. 212/599-6262, or toll free 800/223-6530); 200 SE 1st St., Suite 700, Miami, FL 33131 (tel. 305/381-8915); and 3575 W. Cahuenga Blvd., Suite 560, Los Angeles, CA 90068 (tel. 213/874-5991).

You may also want to contact the U.S. State Department for background bulletins. Write the Superintendent of Documents, **U.S. Government Printing Office,** Washington, DC 20402 (tel. 202/783-3238).

Other useful sources are, of course, **newspapers and magazines.** To find the latest articles about Puerto Rico, go to your library and ask for the *Readers' Guide to Periodical Literature* and look under "Puerto Rico" for listings.

A good travel agent can be a source of information. Make sure your agent is a member of the American Society of Travel Agents (ASTA). If you get poor service from an ASTA agent, you can then write to the **ASTA Consumer Affairs Department,** 1101 King St., Alexandria, VA 22314.

WHAT THINGS COST IN PUERTO RICO	U.S. $
Taxi from the airport to San Juan	10.00
Average taxi fare within San Juan	8.00
Typical bus fare	.25

	U.S. $
Local telephone call	.10
Double room at the Caribe Hilton (deluxe)	310.00
Double room at the Condado Lagoon (moderate)	95.00
Double room at the Casablanca (budget)	60.00
Lunch for one at Amadeus (moderate)	15.00
Lunch for one at La Bombonera (inexpensive)	10.00
Dinner for one at Ramiro's (deluxe)	44.95
Dinner for one at La Mallorquiña (moderate)	28.00
Dinner for one at Tony Roma's (inexpensive)	18.00
Glass of beer in a bar	1.50
Coca-Cola in a café	1.50
Glass of wine in a restaurant	2.25
Roll of ASA 100 color film, 36 exposures	7.25
Admission to Castillo San Felipe del Morro	Free
Movie ticket	4.50
Theater ticket	15.00

ENTRY REQUIREMENTS

American citizens do not need a passport or visa. **Canadians,** however, should carry some form of identification. Acceptable documents include an ongoing or return ticket, plus a current voter registration card or a birth certificate. In addition, you will need some photo ID, which could be a driver's license or an expired passport. Driver's licenses alone are not acceptable as ID.

PASSPORT   Visitors from the U.K., New Zealand, and most western European nations need only a passport for tourist travel so long as they plan to stay 90 days or less.

In the **United Kingdom,** citizens may apply at one of the regional offices in Liverpool, Newport, Glasgow, Peterborough, or Belfast, or in London if they live there. You can also apply in person at a main post office. The fee is £15, and the passport is good for 10 years. Documents required include a marriage certificate or birth certificate. Two photos must accompany the application.

In **New Zealand,** citizens may go to their nearest consulate or passport office to obtain an application and then file in person or via mail. Proof of citizenship is required, and the passport is good for 10 years. The fee is NZ$56.25, NZ$23.30 for children under 16.

In the **Republic of Ireland,** write in advance to the Passport Office, Setanta Centre, Molesworth Street, Dublin 2, Ireland (tel. 01/478-0822). The cost is IR$45. Applications will be sent by mail outlining requirements and procedures to follow. Irish citizens living in North America can contact the Irish Embassy, 2234 Massachusetts Ave. NW, Washington, DC 20008 (tel. 202/462-3939). The embassy can issue a new passport or direct you to one of the three North American consulates that have jurisdiction over a particular region. The cost of an Irish passport, if arranged by mail through Irish consulates, is $80 (U.S.). If a citizen arrives in person, there is a discount of $5.

VISA   Citizens of Australia and most other countries need both a passport and a visa to enter the United States, including Puerto Rico.

In **Australia,** citizens may apply at the nearest post office. Provincial capitals and all big cities, such as Sydney or Melbourne, have passport offices. The passport is valid for 10 years. Application fees are adjusted every three months. Call toll free 008/026-022 for the latest information. A departure stamp for A$20, sold at post offices and airports, is also required before leaving home. Children 11 and under are exempt.

DOCUMENT PROTECTION   Before leaving home, make two copies of your most valuable documents, including your passport, your driver's license, or any other identity document; your airline ticket; and any hotel vouchers. If you're on medication, you should also make copies of prescriptions.

CUSTOMS

All non–U.S. citizens are permitted to bring in items intended for their personal use, including tobacco, cameras, film, and a limited supply of liquor (usually 40 ounces). U.S. citizens can bring in whatever is legal if they are arriving by plane or ship from the mainland.

U.S. CUSTOMS   If you visit only Puerto Rico, you don't have to go through Customs at all because of its status as an American commonwealth. If you fly in from another Caribbean island, you will have to clear Customs, and this is true even if that island is one of the U.S. Virgin Islands. (Many visitors fly from Puerto Rico to St. Thomas on a shopping trip—see Chapter 12.) You can bring in $1,200 worth of merchandise every 30 days from the U.S. Virgin Islands. Those who go over the exemption are taxed at 5% rather than the usual 10%. If you're coming from another island—say, Jamaica or Martinique—you are allowed from $400 to $600 duty free, depending on the island.

Joint Customs declarations are possible for members of a family traveling together. For instance, a husband and wife with two children are allowed duty-free exemptions in the U.S. Virgins of up to $4,800 on their return to Puerto Rico or the United States. Unsolicited gifts can be sent to friends and relatives at the rate of $100 per day in the U.S. Virgins (or $50 a day on the other islands). From Puerto Rico the sky is the limit. So long as these gifts are under the limit, they don't have to be listed on your Customs declaration. U.S. citizens 21 years of age and over are allowed to bring in duty free 200 cigarettes, 100 cigars (but not Cuban), and one liter of liquor (or wine), if they are arriving from some non–U.S. destination.

Collect receipts for all purchases made abroad. Sometimes merchants suggest a false receipt, undervaluing your purchase. *Warning:* You could end up the target of a "sting" operation—the merchant might be an informer to U.S. Customs. You must also declare on your Customs form the nature and value of all gifts received during your stay abroad. It's prudent to carry proof that you purchased expensive cameras or jewelry on the U.S. mainland. If you purchased such an item during an earlier trip abroad, you should carry proof that you have previously paid Customs duty on the item.

If you use any medication containing controlled substances or requiring injection, carry an original prescription or note from your doctor.

For more specific guidance, write to the **U.S. Customs Service,** P.O. Box 7407, Washington, DC 20044, requesting the free pamphlet "Know Before You Go."

CANADIAN CUSTOMS   For information, write for the booklet "I Declare," issued by Revenue Canada Customs Department, Communications Branch, Mackenzie Avenue, Ottawa, ON K1A 0L5. Canada allows its citizens a $300 exemption; they can also bring back duty free 200 cigarettes, 2 pounds of tobacco, 40 ounces of liquor, and 50 cigars. Furthermore, Canadians may mail unsolicited gifts home from abroad at the rate of $40 (Canadian) a day (but *not* alcohol or tobacco). On the package, write "Unsolicited Gift, Under $40 Value." Declare all your valuables before departure from Canada on the Y-38 form, including serial numbers. *Note:* The $300 exemption can be used only once a year, and then only after an absence of seven days.

BRITISH CUSTOMS   On returning from Puerto Rico, if you arrive either directly in the U.K. or via a port in another EC country where you did not pass through Customs controls with all your baggage, you must go through U.K. Customs and declare any goods over and above the allowance, which is: 200 cigarettes or 100 cigarillos or 50 cigars or 250 grams of tobacco; 2 liters of table wine and 1 liter of spirits or strong liqueurs above 22% volume, or 2 liters of fortified or sparkling wine or other liqueurs, or 2 liters of additional table wine; 60ml of perfume; 250ml of toilet water; and £36 worth of other goods, including gifts and souvenirs. (No one under 17 years of age is entitled to a tobacco or drinks allowance.) Go through the Green "nothing to declare" passage only if you have no more than the Customs allowance and no prohibited or restricted goods. For further details on U.K. Customs, contact **HM Customs and Excise,** Excise and Inland Customs Advice Centre, Dorset House, Stamford Street, London SE1 9NG (tel. 071/202-4227).

AUSTRALIAN CUSTOMS   The duty-free allowance in Australia is A$400 or, for those under 18, A$200. Personal property mailed back from Puerto Rico should be labeled "Australian Goods Returned" to avoid payment of duty, providing the contents are correctly identified on the package. On returning to Australia, citizens can bring in 200 cigarettes or 250 grams of tobacco, and 1 liter of alcohol. If you're returning with valuable goods you owned before your trip, such as expensive foreign-made cameras, you should file form B263 before you leave Australia. A helpful brochure, "Customs Information for All Travellers," is available from Australian consulates or Customs offices.

NEW ZEALAND CUSTOMS   The duty-free allowance is NZ$500. Citizens over 16 years of age can bring in 200 cigarettes or 250 grams of tobacco or 50 cigars, and 4.5 liters of wine or beer or 1.125 liters of liquor. New Zealand currency does not carry restrictions regarding import or export. A Certificate of Export listing valuables taken out of the country (that is, items you already own) allows you to bring them back in without paying duty. Most questions are answered in a free pamphlet, "New Zealand Customs Guide for Travellers," available at New Zealand consulates and Customs offices.

IRISH CUSTOMS   Irish citizens may bring in 200 cigarettes, 100 cigarillos, 50 cigars, or 250 grams of tobacco; 1 liter of liquor with an alcohol content above 22% (such as whiskey, brandy, gin, rum, or vodka) or 2 liters of distilled beverages and spirits with a wine or alcoholic base of an alcoholic strength not above 22% by volume; 2 liters of other wine; and 50 grams of perfume. Other allowances include duty-free goods to a value of IR£34 per person (IR£17 for those under age 15).

MONEY

The U.S. dollar is the coin of the realm. All major U.S. banks are located in San Juan, and are open Monday through Friday from 8:30am to 2:30pm. Canadian currency is accepted by some big hotels in San Juan, although reluctantly. Foreigners, including visitors from the United Kingdom, should convert their currency into U.S. dollars.

TRAVELER'S CHECKS   Before leaving home, purchase traveler's checks denominated in U.S. dollars and arrange to carry some ready cash (usually about $250, depending on your habits and needs). In the event of theft, if the checks are properly documented, the value of your checks will be refunded. Most large banks sell traveler's checks, charging fees that average between 1% and 2% of the value of the checks you buy, although some out-of-the-way banks, in rare instances, have charged as much as 7%. If your bank wants more than a 2% commission, it may pay to call the traveler's check issuers directly for the address of outlets where this commission will be less.

THE POUND & THE U.S. DOLLAR

The U.S. dollar is commonly used throughout the Caribbean, except on the French islands of Martinique and Guadeloupe. It is widely accepted even on islands that print their own currency, and is the only currency accepted on Puerto Rico. Pounds sterling should be converted into dollars, even for use on islands that are British Crown Colonies. Since the exchange rate will fluctuate during the course of this edition, the following chart (based on £1 = $1.50 U.S.) should be used only as a guideline.

£	U.S.$	£	U.S.$
.05	.08	10	15.00
.10	.15	15	22.50
.25	.38	20	30.00
.50	.75	25	37.50
.75	1.13	30	45.00
1	1.50	35	52.50
2	3.00	40	60.00
3	4.50	45	67.50
4	6.00	50	75.00
5	7.50	75	112.50
6	9.00	100	150.00
7	10.50	125	187.50
8	12.00	150	225.00
9	13.50	200	300.00

American Express (tel. toll free 800/221-7282 in the U.S. and Canada) is one of the largest and most immediately recognized issuers of traveler's checks. No commission is charged to members of the American Automobile Association or to those who hold certain types of American Express cards. The company issues checks denominated in U.S. dollars, Canadian dollars, British pounds sterling, Swiss francs, French francs, German marks, and Japanese yen. For questions or problems that arise outside the United States and Canada, contact any of the company's many regional representatives.

Citicorp (tel. toll free 800/645-6556 in the U.S. and Canada, or 813/623-1709, collect, from anywhere else in the world), issues checks in U.S. dollars, British pounds, German marks, and Japanese yen.

Thomas Cook (tel. toll free 800/223-9920 in the U.S., or 609/987-7300, collect, from other parts of the world) issues MasterCard traveler's checks denominated in U.S. dollars, French francs, German marks, Dutch guilders, Spanish pesetas, Australian dollars, Japanese yen, and Hong Kong dollars. Depending on banking laws in various states, some of the above-mentioned currencies might not be available at every outlet.

Interpayment Services (tel. toll free 800/221-2426 in the U.S. and Canada, 800/453-4284 from most other parts of the world) sells VISA checks sponsored by Barclays Bank and/or Bank of America at selected branches in North America. Traveler's checks are denominated in U.S. or Canadian dollars, British pounds, Swiss or French francs, German marks, and Japanese yen.

CREDIT & CHARGE CARDS   Credit and charge cards are widely used in Puerto Rico. VISA and MasterCard are the major cards, although American Express and, to a lesser extent, Diners Club, are also popular.

2. WHEN TO GO — CLIMATE, HOLIDAYS & EVENTS

CLIMATE

Puerto Rico has one of the most unvarying climates in the world. Temperatures year-round range from 75°F to 85°F. The island is wettest and hottest in August, averaging 81°F and seven inches of rain. San Juan and the northern coast seem to be cooler and wetter than Ponce and the southern coast. The coldest weather is in the high altitudes of the Cordillera. Puerto Rico's lowest temperature (39°F) was recorded there.

THE "SEASON"

The "season" in Puerto Rico runs roughly from mid-December to mid-April. Hotels charge their highest prices during the peak winter period when visitors fleeing from cold north winds flock to the islands. Winter is generally the driest season but can be a wet period in mountainous areas.

If you plan to travel in the winter, make reservations two to three months in advance. At certain hotels it's almost impossible to secure accommodations at Christmas and in February. The mail is unreliable and takes a long time, so rather than writing to reserve a room, it's better to book through one of the many Stateside representatives used by major and many minor hotels or else to use a travel agent. You can also make arrangements with the hotel of your choice via telephone or fax.

THE "OFF-SEASON"

Increasingly, Puerto Rico is becoming a year-round destination. The island's "off-season" runs from late spring to late fall, and temperatures in the mid-80s prevail throughout most of the region. Trade winds assure comfortable days and nights, even in accommodations without air conditioning. Although the noonday sun may raise the temperature to around 90°F, cool breezes usually make the morning, late afternoon, and evening more comfortable than in many parts of the U.S. mainland.

Dollar for dollar, you'll spend less money by renting a summer house or fully equipped unit in Puerto Rico than you would on Cape Cod, Fire Island, Laguna Beach, or the coast of Maine.

20% TO 60% REDUCTIONS The off-season in Puerto Rico—roughly from mid-April to mid-December (rate schedules vary from hotel to hotel)—amounts to a summer sale. In most cases, hotel rates are slashed a startling 20% to 60%. It's a bonanza for cost-conscious travelers, especially families who like to go on vacations together. In the chapters ahead, I'll spell out in dollars the specific amounts hotels charge during the off-season.

OTHER OFF-SEASON ADVANTAGES Although Puerto Rico may appear inviting in the winter to those who live in northern climates, there are many reasons why your trip may be much more enjoyable if you go in the off-season.

- After the winter hordes have left, a less hurried way of life prevails. You'll have a better chance to appreciate the food, culture, and local customs.
- Swimming pools and beaches are less crowded—perhaps not crowded at all.
- Year-round resort facilities are offered, often at reduced rates, that may include snorkeling, boating, and scuba diving.
- To survive, resort boutiques often feature summer sales, hoping to clear the merchandise they didn't sell in February to accommodate stock they've ordered

for the coming winter. Duty-free items in free-port shopping are draws all year, too.

- You can often appear without a reservation at a top restaurant and get a table for dinner, a table that in winter would have required a reservation far in advance. Also, when waiters are less hurried, you'll get better service.
- The endless waiting game is over in the off-season: no waiting for a rented car (only to be told none is available), no long wait for a golf course tee-time, and quicker access to tennis courts and water sports.
- The atmosphere is more cosmopolitan in the off-season than it is in winter, mainly because of the influx of Europeans. You'll no longer feel as if you're at a Canadian or American outpost. Also, since the Antilleans themselves travel in the off-season, your holiday will become more of a multicultural experience.
- Some package-tour fares are as much as 20% lower, and individual excursion fares are also reduced between 5% and 10%.
- All accommodations, including airline seats and hotel rooms, are much easier to obtain.
- Summer is an excellent time for family travel, not usually possible during the winter season.
- Finally, the very best of Puerto Rican attractions remain undiminished in the off-season—sea, sand, and surf, usually with lots of sunshine.

THE HURRICANE SEASON   The curse of Puerto Rican weather, the hurricane season lasts—officially, at least—from June 1 to November 30. But there's no cause for panic. In general, satellite forecasts give adequate warnings so that precautions can be taken.

If you're heading for Puerto Rico during the hurricane season, you can call your local branch of the National Weather Service (listed in your phone directory under the U.S. Department of Commerce) for a weather forecast.

You can also obtain current weather information by calling WeatherTrak; for the telephone number for your chosen destination, dial 900/370-8725 (for a charge of 95¢ a minute, a taped message will give you the three-digit access code for the place you're interested in).

Average Temperatures on Puerto Rico

	Jan	Feb	Mar	Apr	May	June	July	Aug	Sept	Oct	Nov	Dec
Temp. (°F)	75	75	76	78	79	81	81	81	81	81	79	77

HOLIDAYS

Puerto Rico has many public holidays when stores, offices, and schools are closed: New Year's Day, January 6 (Three Kings' Day), Washington's Birthday, Good Friday, Memorial Day, July 4, Labor Day, Thanksgiving, Veterans' Day, and Christmas, plus such local holidays as Constitution Day (July 25) and Discovery Day (November 19).

PUERTO RICO
CALENDAR OF EVENTS

In addition to the individual events described below, Puerto Rico has three year-long series of special events:

The **LeLoLai VIP Program** gives visitors the opportunity to experience Puerto Rico's unique culture and its Spanish, Amerindian, and African heritage at substantial savings. Included are free performances of song and dance at various San Juan hotels, and discounted sightseeing tours of Old San Juan, Ponce, Rio Camuy Cave Park, El Yunque rain forest, and Luquillo Beach. Savings on folkloric shows and sightseeing tours add up to more than $250, not to mention discounts at shops, restaurants, and sporting activities throughout the island. For information and reservations, call 809/723-3135 or 809/722-1513.

Many of Puerto Rico's most popular events are the **Patron Saint Festivals** (*fiestas patronales*) in honor of the patron saint of each municipality. The festivities, held in each town's central plaza, include religious and costumed processions, games, local food, music, and dance.

At **Festival La Casita** prominent Puerto Rican musicians, dance troupes, and orchestras perform; puppet shows are staged; and painters and sculptors display their works. It's on every Saturday at Puerto Rico Tourism's "La Casita" Tourism Information Center, Plaza Darsenas, across from Pier 1, Old San Juan.

For more information about the events below, contact the **Puerto Rico Tourism Company,** 575 Fifth Ave., New York, NY 10017 (tel. 212/599-6262, or toll free 800/223-6530).

JANUARY

☐ **Three Kings Day,** islandwide. On this traditional gift-giving day in Puerto Rico there are festivals with lively music, dancing, parades, puppet shows, caroling troubadours, and traditional feasts. January 6.

☐ **De Hostos Day,** islandwide. Celebration honoring Eugenio María de Hostos (1839–1903), a Puerto Rican educator, writer, and patriot. January 11.

FEBRUARY

☐ **San Blas Marathon,** Coamo. International and local runners compete in a challenging 13.1-mile half marathon in the hilly town of Coamo. February 7.

☐ **Cristóbal L. Sanchez Carnival,** Arroyo. Costumes, floats, calypso, and popular music. High points include the naming of a Carnival queen, a parade, and the traditional "burial of the sardine." Daytime and evening activities. February 11–14.

☐ **Coffee Harvest Festival,** Maricao. This festival features folk music, a parade of floats, typical foods, crafts, and demonstrations of coffee preparation. It takes place in Maricao, a one-hour drive east of Mayagüez in the center of one of the island's coffee-growing districts. February 12–14.

☐ **Carnival Ponce.** The island's Carnival celebrations feature float parades, dancing, and street parties. One of the most vibrant festivities is held in Ponce, known for its masqueraders wearing brightly painted horned masks. Live music includes the folk rhythms of the *plena,* which originated in Africa. Festivities include the crowning of a Carnival queen and the closing "burial of the sardine." February 17–23.

☐ **Captain Correa Carnival,** Plaza Luís Muñoz Rivera, Arecibo. A parade of floats, costumes, music, and food. February 18–21.

☐ **Fish Festival,** on Route 308, Puerto Real, in Cabo Rojo. This annual festival features crafts, music, and a display of fish. February 19–21.

☐ **Coffee Harvest Festival,** Yauco. Music, crafts, foods, coffee, and demonstrations of coffee preparation. February 21–28.

MARCH

☐ **Feria Dulce Sueno,** Guayama. A two-day competition held in the southern city of Guayama features Puerto Rico's finest Paso Fino steeds, the island's own breed of smooth-gaited horses. March 5–7.

☐ **Regional Crafts Fair,** Ponce. One of the largest fairs on the island, dedicated to local authentic arts and crafts. March 19–22.

☐ **Emancipation Day,** islandwide. Commemoration of the emancipation of Puerto Rico's slaves in 1873, held at various venues. March 22.

☐ **Good Friday and Easter,** islandwide. Celebrated with colorful ceremonies and processions. Date varies.

APRIL

☐ **José de Diego Day,** islandwide. Commemoration of the birthday of José de Diego, a patriot, lawyer, writer, orator, and political leader who was the first president of the Puerto Rico House of Representatives under U.S. rule. April 19.

☐ **Mavi Festival,** at the town plaza in Juana Diaz. Costumes, floats, artistic shows, crafts, and mavi (local drink made from sassafras). April 22–25.

☐ **Puerto Rican Weaving Festival,** at Isabela, Route 2, km 115. Exhibitions of weaving, mundillo lace, and typical foods, drink, and music. April 30–May 2.

MAY

☐ **Virgin del Pozo Marathon,** Sabana Grande. The annual 13.1-mile half marathon starts in front of the sanctuary of the Virgin del Rosario. May 17.

☐ **Pineapple Festival,** Lajas. Celebration of the pineapple harvest, with musical presentations, shows, crafts, and typical foods. Dates vary.

JUNE

☐ **San Juan Bautista Day.** Puerto Rico's capital and other cities celebrate the island's patron saint with week-long festivities. At midnight, Sanjuaneros walk backward into the sea (or nearest body of water) three times to renew good luck for the coming year. June 23.

☐ **Aibonito Flower Festival,** at Road 722 next to the City Hall Coliseum, Aibonito. This annual flower competition festival features acres of lilies, anthuriums, carnations, roses, gardenias, and begonias. June 25–July 5.

☐ **Bomba y Plena Festival,** Ponce. The island's African-Caribbean heritage is celebrated with African-inspired music and dance. Dates vary.

JULY

☐ **Barranquitas Artisans Fair.** The island's oldest crafts fair marks its 31st year in 1994 with craft exhibitions by more than 130 artisans from around Puerto Rico; also features traditional music and food. July 15–18.

☐ **Muñoz Rivera's Birthday,** islandwide. A birthday celebration commemorating Luís Muñoz Rivera (1829–1916), statesman, journalist, poet, and resident commissioner in Washington, D.C. July 19.

☐ **Vieques Folk Festival.** There's a parade of floats and costumed celebrants, with music, food, and craft booths. July 22–25.

☐ **Loíza Carnival.** An annual folk and religious ceremony honoring St. James the Apostle. Colorful processions take place, with costumes, masks, and bomba dancers. A jubilant celebration reflecting the African and Spanish heritage of the northeastern town of Loíza. July 24–August 4.

SEPTEMBER

☐ **Mayagüez Light Tackle Tournament.** One of Puerto Rico's premier blue marlin tournaments. Dates vary.

OCTOBER

☐ **La Raza Day (Columbus Day),** islandwide. Commemoration of Columbus's landing in the New World. October 12.

☐ **National Plantain Festival,** Corozal. Annual festivity with crafts, paintings, agricultural products, exhibition, and sale of plantain dishes; *neuva trova* music and folk ballet are performed. Dates vary.

NOVEMBER

☐ **Discovery Day,** islandwide. Public holiday to celebrate Christopher Columbus's first sighting of Puerto Rico in 1493. November 19.

☐ **Jayuya Indian Festival.** Each year Puerto Rico celebrates its Taíno cultural heritage with craft shows, Amerindian ceremonies, folk dances, and visits to native tribal sites. November 19–22.

☐ **Arts and Crafts Fair,** in Mayagüez, Cabo Rojo, and other cities. Dates vary.

DECEMBER

☐ **Bacardi Arts Festival,** Cataño. More than 200 craftspeople exhibit and sell their works on the grounds of the world's largest rum-manufacturing plant. There are also music, troubadour singers, and food. December 5 and 12.

☐ **Senior PGA Tour Champions Golf Tournament,** at the Hyatt Dorado Beach Resort. The top 30 golfers of the Senior PGA Tour compete for $1 million in prize money. December 10–12.

☐ **Navidades,** islandwide. Christmas festivities featuring life-size nativity scenes on display in Old San Juan. Children's programs are presented at the Dominican Convent, La Fortaleza, and City Hall. The Puerto Rico Symphony performs special Christmas concerts. December 15–January 6.

☐ **Hatillo Festival of the Masks.** Colorful masks and costumes, folk music, and celebrations comprise the traditional festivity held annually in the northwestern town of Hatillo. December 25–28.

SAN JUAN
CALENDAR OF EVENTS

JANUARY

☐ **San Sebastián Street Festival,** calle San Sebastián in Old San Juan. Nightly celebrations with music, processions, crafts, and typical foods. January 17–20.

☐ **Equal Expo '95,** Ruben Rodríguez Stadium, Bayamón. Puerto Rico's equine celebration, featuring a world-class Paso Fino event, which showcases the island's breed of horse, a unique smooth-gaited variety. Dates vary.

APRIL

☐ **Puerto Rico Orchid Show,** Pedrin Zorrilla Coliseum, Hato Rey. Dates vary.

MAY

☐ **Semana de la Danza,** in the open-air court of the Dominican Convent, Old San Juan. A week-long celebration of the island's national dance form—*la danza*. Programs include a variety of dances, recitals, and choral concerts, as well as composer competitions. May 10–16.

JUNE

○ *CASALS FESTIVAL Sanjuaneros and visitors alike eagerly look forward to the annual Casals Festival, the Caribbean's most celebrated cultural event. The bill at San Juan's Performing Arts Center includes a glittering array of international guest conductors, orchestras, and soloists. They come to honor the memory of Pablo Casals, the renowned cellist who was born in Spain to a Puerto Rican mother. When Casals died in Puerto Rico in*

1973 at the age of 97, the Casals Festival was 16 years old and attracting the same class of performers who appeared at the Pablo Casals Festival he founded in France after World War II. When he moved to Puerto Rico in 1957 with his wife, Marta Casals Istomin (past artistic director of the John F. Kennedy Center for the Performing Arts), he founded not only this festival but also the Puerto Rico Symphony Orchestra to foster musical development on the island.

Where: Performing Arts Center in San Juan. When: Usually the second and third weeks in June (the dates vary). How: Ticket prices for the Casals Festival range from $20 to $40. A 50% discount is offered to students, senior citizens, and the disabled. Tickets are available through the Performing Arts Center in San Juan (tel. 809/725-7334). For full program information, contact the Festival Casals, P.O. Box 41227, Minillas Station, Santurce, PR 00940-1227 (tel. 809/721-7727). Information is also available from the Puerto Rico Tourism Company, 575 Fifth Ave., New York, NY 10017 (tel. 212/599-6262, or toll free 800/223-6530).

AUGUST

☐ **International Billfish Tournament,** at Club Nautico. This is one of the premier game-fishing tournaments and the longest consecutively held billfish tournament in the world. Fishermen from many countries angle for blue marlin that can weigh up to 900 pounds. August 28–September 3.

SEPTEMBER

☐ **Inter-American Festival of the Arts,** at the Performing Arts Center. A three-week series of musical art performances that includes classical, popular, and folk music; ballet and modern dance productions; and musical theater. September 20–October 10.

NOVEMBER

☐ **Start of Baseball Season,** in Hiram Bithorn Park in San Juan and throughout the island. Six Puerto Rican professional clubs compete. Professionals from North America also play here through February. Usually November 2.

☐ **Fiesta de la Música Puertorriqueña,** at the Dominican Convent in Old San Juan. This annual classical and folk music festival features a cuatro-playing contest. Free. Three successive weekends in November and December.

DECEMBER

☐ **Old San Juan's White Christmas Festival,** Old San Juan. Special musical and artistic presentations take place in stores, with window displays. December 1–January 12.

☐ **Lighting of the Town of Bethlehem,** between San Cristóbal Fort and Plaza San Juan Bautista in Old San Juan. During the Christmas season.

3. HEALTH, SAFETY & INSURANCE

HEALTH

Traveling to Puerto Rico should not adversely affect your health. Finding a good doctor in Puerto Rico presents no real problem, and most doctors speak English. See "Fast Facts: Puerto Rico" in Chapter 3 for the locations of hospitals.

HEALTH PROBLEMS If you have a chronic medical condition, speak to your doctor before leaving home. For conditions such as epilepsy, a heart condition, diabetes, or allergy, wear a **Medic Alert Identification Tag.** For a lifetime membership, the cost is $35 for a steel tag, $45 if silver plated, and $60 if gold plated. Contact the Medic Alert Foundation, P.O. Box 1009, Turlock, CA 95381-1009 (tel. toll free 800/432-5378). Medic Alert's 24-hour hotline enables a foreign doctor to obtain your medical records.

Although tap water is generally considered safe to drink, it's better to drink mineral water. Avoid iced drinks. Stick to beer, hot tea, or soft drinks.

Many visitors experience diarrhea, even if they follow the usual precautions. It usually passes quickly without medication if you eat simply prepared food and drink only mineral water until you recover. If symptoms persist, consult a doctor.

Sunburn The sun can be brutal, especially if you're coming from a winter climate and haven't been exposed to it in some time. Wear sunglasses to protect your eyes from the glare, a hat, and a coverup for your shoulders. Be sure to use a sunscreen. Experts also advise that you limit your time on the beach the first day. If you do overexpose yourself, stay out of the sun until you recover. If your exposure is followed by fever or chills, a headache, or a feeling of nausea or dizziness, see a doctor.

Insects and Pests Gnats (or "no-see-ums") are one of the biggest insect menaces in Puerto Rico. They appear mainly in the early evening, and even if you can't see these gnats, you sure can "feel-um," as any native Puerto Rican will agree. Screens can't keep these bugs out, so you'll need to use your favorite insect repellent.

Although mosquitoes are a nuisance, malaria-carrying mosquitoes in the Caribbean are confined largely to Haiti and the Dominican Republic.

Other Possible Dangers Dengue fever is widespread in Puerto Rico and other Caribbean islands, especially Barbados, Cuba, the Dominican Republic, and Haiti. To date, no satisfactory treatment for the ailment has been developed. Try to avoid mosquito bites, if that's possible.

Prickly heat, athletes foot, and other fungal infections are sometimes reported. For prickly heat, use talcum powder and wear loose clothing.

Intestinal worms, such as hookworm, are relatively common and can be contracted by just walking barefoot on an infected beach. Another disease, schistosomiasis (also called bilharzia), caused by a parasitic fluke, can be contracted by submerging your feet in rivers and lakes infested with a certain species of snail. This condition has been reported on St. Lucia, among other islands. You are less likely to be affected on Puerto Rico.

VACCINATIONS Vaccinations are not required for entry to Puerto Rico if you're coming from the United States or Canada.

Infectious hepatitis has been reported on such islands as Dominica, Haiti, and Montserrat, but less frequently on Puerto Rico. Consult your doctor about the advisability of getting a gamma-globulin shot before you leave home.

Other common immunizations include typhoid, poliomyelitis, and tetanus. Since these are not common diseases, inoculations are recommended mainly to visitors who plan to "rough it" in the wilds. If you're staying in a regular Puerto Rican hotel, such preventive measures are generally not needed, but your doctor can advise you, based on your destination and travel plans.

MEDICINES Take along an adequate supply of any prescription drugs that you need and a written prescription specifying the generic name of the drug—not the brand name. However, U.S. brand names are commonly available at most pharmacies. You may also want to take such over-the-counter items as first-aid cream, insect repellent, aspirin, and Band-Aids.

SAFETY

Will I be safe in Puerto Rico? This question is often asked by the first-time visitor, and it's one of the most difficult to answer. Can a guidebook writer safely recommend traveling to New York, Miami, Chicago, Los Angeles, or any major American city? Are you, in fact, free from harm in your own home?

In general, whenever you're traveling in an unfamiliar country, stay alert. Be aware of your immediate surroundings. Wear a moneybelt, carry your traveling funds in traveler's checks, and keep your check numbers in a separate place. Store valuables in the hotel safe and keep your hotel-room doors locked. Also, lock car doors and never leave your possessions within sight in an automobile. Don't leave valuables, such as cameras and cash-stuffed purses, lying unattended on the beach while you go for a swim. Puerto Rican tourist officials often warn visitors, "If you've got it, don't flaunt it." This will minimize the possibility of your becoming a victim of crime. Every society has its criminals. It's your responsibility to be aware and alert even in the most heavily touristed areas.

The Puerto Rican tourist board is increasingly sensitive to the treatment of visitors, because the economy is significantly dependent on tourism. Rudeness, room burglaries, anything that creates unfavorable publicity is damaging. As a result, Puerto Rican tourist officials are taking steps to make their own people more aware of the importance of tourism and of the desirability of treating guests as they themselves would want to be treated if they were travling abroad.

Of course, many of the problems have arisen from the tourists themselves. Tourists should take care to treat Puerto Ricans with respect and dignity. A smile usually wins a smile. In addition, many islanders, deeply religious, are offended by tourists who wear bikinis on shopping expeditions in town or appear nude on the beach.

Know that most Puerto Ricans are proud, respectable, and very proper; if you treat them as such, they will probably treat you the same way. Others—certainly the minority, but a visible minority—can be downright antagonistic and definitely "antigringo."

INSURANCE

Before purchasing insurance, check your current homeowner's, automobile, and medical insurance policies, as well as the membership contracts of automobile and travel clubs and credit/charge cards, for any coverage extended to you while you travel.

Many credit- and charge-card companies insure their users in case of a travel accident when the travel cost was paid with their card. Sometimes fraternal organizations have policies that protect members in case of sickness or accidents abroad.

Many homeowners' insurance policies cover theft of luggage during foreign travel and loss of such documents as your passport and your airline ticket. Coverage is usually limited to about $500. Remember that to submit a claim on your insurance, you'll need police reports or a statement from a local medical authority that you did suffer the loss or experience an illness. Some policies provide advances in cash or arrange for immediate transferals of funds.

If you feel you need additional insurance, check with the following companies:

Access America, 6600 W. Broad St., Richmond, VA 23230 (tel. 804/285-3300, or toll free 800/284-8300), offers a comprehensive travel insurance and assistance package, including medical expenses, on-the-spot hospital payments, medical transportation, baggage insurance, trip-cancellation/interruption insurance, and collision-damage insurance for a car rental. Their 24-hour hotline connects you to multilingual coordinators who can offer advice and help with medical, legal, and travel problems. Packages begin at $27.

Wallach and Co., 107 W. Federal St. (P.O. Box 480), Middleburg, VA 22117-0480 (tel. 703/687-3166, or toll free 800/237-6615), offers coverage for between 10 and 120 days at $3 per day; this policy includes accident and sickness coverage to the tune of $100,000. Medical evacuation is also included, along with $25,000 accidental death and dismemberment compensation. Provisions for trip cancellation and lost or stolen luggage can also be written into this policy at a nominal cost.

Mutual of Omaha, Mutual of Omaha Plaza, Omaha, NE 68175 (tel. toll free 800/228-9792), offers insurance packages priced from $113 for a three-week trip. Included in the packages are travel-assistance services, and financial protection against trip cancellation, trip interruption, flight and baggage delays, accident-related medical costs, accidental death and dismemberment, and medical evacuation coverage. Application for insurance can be taken over the phone for holders of major credit and charge cards.

At **Travelers Insurance Company,** Travel Insurance Division, One Tower Sq., 10 NB, Hartford, CT 06183-5040 (tel. toll free 800/243-3174), travel accident and illness coverage starts at $10 for 6 to 10 days; $500 worth of coverage for lost, damaged, or delayed baggage costs $20 for 6 to 10 days; and trip cancellation costs $5.50 for $100 worth of coverage. Written approval is necessary for cancellation coverage above $10,000.

4. WHAT TO PACK

Comfortable clothing with the "casual but chic" look is the rule for Puerto Rico. Cotton slacks or shorts are just fine for going around during the day. If you burn easily, wear a long-sleeved shirt and long pants.

Summer travelers don't need suits, but in winter men might want to wear a jacket with an open-neck shirt if they're dining in one of the more famous spots. Don't forget that evenings tend to be cooler, or you might go "up in the hills," so a light sweater or a jacket will come in handy. Sometimes restaurants and bars are overly air-conditioned. If you plan to visit nightclubs, casually chic dressy clothes are appropriate.

A wardrobe of lightweight cotton is preferable—avoid the synthetics and nylon that become hot and sticky in these climes. Khaki pants are acceptable for men in most places. Of course, anything that doesn't have to be ironed or dry-cleaned is always a good idea in the islands. Sometimes it's possible to get pressing done at hotels, but don't count on it. Be prepared to wash your lightweights, such as underwear, in your bathroom and hang them up to dry overnight. Take along at least two pairs of comfortable shoes.

If you want to bring along such items as an electric shaver or hairdryer, check to see if you need an electrical transformer or adapter plugs.

Remember that airlines are increasingly strict about both carry-on items and checked suitcases. Checked luggage should not measure more than a total of 62 inches (width plus length plus height), and carry-on pieces must fit under your seat or in the overhead bin.

5. TIPS FOR THE DISABLED, SENIORS, SINGLES, STUDENTS & FAMILIES

FOR THE DISABLED   Hotels rarely publicize what facilities, if any, they offer the disabled, so it's always better to contact the hotel directly, in advance. Tourist offices rarely have up-to-date information about such matters.

For more details, try **MossRehab,** 1200 W. Tabor Rd., Philadelphia, PA 19141 (tel. 215/456-9603)—this service is not a travel agent. MossRehab provides information to telephone callers only; call them for assistance with your travel-accessibility needs.

You can obtain a free copy of **"Air Transportation of Handicapped Persons,"** published by the U.S. Department of Transportation. Write for Free

Advisory Circular No. AC12032, Distribution Unit, U.S. Department of Transportation, Publications Division, M-4332, Washington, DC 20590.

Specialized Tours You may want to consider joining a tour specifically for disabled visitors. For names and addresses of such tour operators, contact the **Society for the Advancement of Travel for the Handicapped,** 347 Fifth Ave., Suite 610, New York, NY (tel. 212/447-7284). Yearly membership costs $45 for adults, $25 for senior citizens and students. Send along a self-addressed, stamped envelope.

FEDCAP Rehabilitation Services (formerly known as the Federation of the Handicapped), 211 W. 14th St., New York, NY 10011 (tel. 212/727-4268), operates summer tours to Europe and elsewhere for its members. Membership costs $6 yearly.

For the blind, the best source of travel information is the **American Foundation for the Blind,** 15 W. 16th St., New York, NY 10011 (tel. 212/620-2000, or toll free 800/232-5463). For those who are legally blind, it also issues identification cards for $6.

FOR SENIORS For information before you go, obtain a free copy of **"101 Tips for the Mature Traveler"** available from Grand Circle Travel, 347 Congress St., Suite 3A, Boston, MA 02210 (tel. 617/350-7500, or toll free 800/248-3737); this travel agency also offers escorted tours and cruises for seniors.

SAGA International Holidays, 22 Berkeley St., Boston, MA 02116 (tel. toll free 800/343-0273), is known for its all-inclusive tours and cruises for seniors, especially those 60 years of age or older. Insurance is included in the net price of any of their tours, except cruises.

The **AARP Travel Experience from American Express,** 400 Pinnacle Way, Suite 450, Norcross, GA 30071 (tel. toll free 800/927-0111 for land arrangements, 800/745-4567 for cruises, or 800/659-5678 for TTD), arranges travel for members of the American Association of Retired Persons, 601 E St. NW, Washington, DC 40049 (tel. 202/434-AARP). Travel Experience provides members with a wide variety of escorted, hosted, and go-any-day packages and cruises to most parts of the world.

Information is also available from the **National Council of Senior Citizens,** 1331 F St. NW, Washington, DC 20004-1171 (tel. 202/347-8800). A nonprofit organization, the council charges $12 per person/couple, for which you receive a regular magazine, part of which is devoted to travel tips. Discounts on hotel and auto rentals are provided.

FOR SINGLES Single travelers pay a penalty in an industry that's geared to "doubles." Jens Jurgen founded a company that makes heroic efforts to match single travelers with like-minded companions. New applicants desiring a travel companion fill out a form stating their preferences and needs; they then receive a minilisting of potential partners. Companions of the same or opposite sex can be requested. It is recommended that people meet and talk to each other before traveling together, which means that plenty of time should be allowed before embarking on a trip. Because his listings are extensive, it is quite likely that you will find a suitable traveling companion. He charges $36 to $66 for a six-month listing. A sample copy of his newsletter, filled with lots of travel tips for single travelers and 300 to 400 listings of others seeking traveling companions, is available postpaid for $4. For an application and more information, contact Jens Jurgen, **Travel Companion,** P.O. Box P-833, Amityville, NY 11701 (tel. 516/454-0880).

Singleworld, 401 Theodore Fremd Ave., Rye, NY 10580 (tel. 914/967-3334, or toll free 800/223-6490), operates tours for solo travelers. Two basic types are available: youth-oriented tours (for those in their 20s and 30s) and jaunts for any age. Annual dues are $25.

Grand Circle Travel, 347 Congress St., Boston, MA 02210 (tel. 617/350-7500, or toll free 800/248-3737), offers escorted tours and cruises for retired people, including singles. Once you book one of their trips, membership is included; you also get vouchers providing discounts for future trips.

FOR STUDENTS   Students can obtain a number of travel discounts. The most wide-ranging travel service for students is **Council Travel,** a subsidiary of the **Council on International Educational Exchange (CIEE),** 205 E. 42nd St., New York, NY 10017 (tel. 212/661-1450); it provides information about budget travel, study abroad, working permits, and insurance. It also issues a number of helpful publications and provides an International Student Identity Card (ISIC) for $16 to bonafide students. For a copy of its *Student Travels* magazine, which details all the Council Travel's services and CIEE's programs and publications, send $1 in postage.

FOR FAMILIES   Puerto Rico is a contender for top position on the world list of family vacation places. The smallest toddlers can spend blissful hours on sandy beaches and in the shallow sea water or pools specifically constructed for them. There's no end to the fascinating pursuits available for older children, ranging from boat rides to shell collecting to horseback riding, hiking, and even discoing. Perhaps your children are old enough to learn to snorkel and explore the wonderland of the underwater Puerto Rico. Skills such as swimming and windsurfing are taught, and there are a variety of activities unique to the islands.

There are important pointers to keep in mind when you're planning a family vacation anywhere on Puerto Rico. Most resort hotels will advise you of what there is in the way of fun for the young, and many have play directors and supervised activities for various age groups. However, to make the trip a success, parents need to attend to the following in advance:

Arrange ahead for such necessities as a crib, bottle warmer, and car seat (if you're driving anywhere) for the very young, as well as for cots in your room for older children. Find out if the place where you're staying stocks baby food, and, if not, take it with you.

Draw up rules for your family to follow during your holiday. These should be flexible, of course—after all, this trip is for fun. But guidelines on bedtime, eating, keeping tidy, being in the sun, and even shopping and spending money can help make everybody's vacation more enjoyable.

Take along protection from the sun. For tiny tots, this provision should include a sun umbrella, while the whole family will need sunscreen (one around "SPF 15" is a good idea) and sunglasses.

Take along anti-insect lotions and sprays. You'll probably need both repellents for such unwanted island denizens as mosquitoes and sand fleas, not to mention salves to ease the itching and other after effects of insect bites.

Babysitters can be arranged by most hotels, but you should insist that yours know at least rudimentary English. Talk with the sitter yourself and introduce her or him to your child(ren) before you leave the hotel room or nursery.

Family Travel Times, published 10 times a year by TWYCH (Travel With Your Children) includes a weekly call-in service for subscribers. Subscriptions cost $55 a year and can be ordered by writing to **TWYCH,** 45 W. 18th St., 7th Floor, New York, NY 10011 (tel. 212/206-0688). TWYCH also publishes two nitty-gritty information guides, *Skiing with Children* and *Cruising with Children,* which sell for $29 and $22, respectively, and are discounted for newsletter subscribers. An information packet describing TWYCH's publications, including a recent sample issue, is available by sending $2 to the above address.

6. ALTERNATIVE/ADVENTURE TRAVEL

EDUCATIONAL TRAVEL   The best information is available from the **Council on International Educational Exchange (CIEE),** 205 E. 42nd St., New York, NY 10017 (tel. 212/661-1450); see "For Students" in Section 5, above. Request a copy of the 318-page *Smart Vacations: The Traveler's Guide to Learning Adventures*

Abroad, which costs $14.95. If you'd like it mailed, add $1.50 for shipping. Hundreds of study tours, environmental trips, foreign-language courses, and arts programs are listed.

Elderhostel, 75 Federal St., Boston, MA 02110-1941 (tel. 617/426-7788), established in 1975, maintains an array of postretirement study programs, several of which are in the Caribbean. Most courses last for two or three weeks and represent good value considering that airfare, hotel accommodations in student dormitories or modest inns, all meals, and tuition are included. Courses involve no homework, are ungraded, and focus mostly on the liberal arts. Participants must be age 60 or older. However, if two members go as a couple, only one member needs to meet the age requirement. Write or call for their free newsletter and a list of upcoming courses and destinations.

A series of international programs combining travel and learning for people over 50 years of age is offered by **Interhostel,** developed by the University of New Hampshire. Each two-week program is escorted by a university faculty or staff member and arranged in conjunction with a host college, university, or cultural institution. Participants can stay beyond two weeks if they wish. For information, contact the University of New Hampshire, Division of Continuing Education, 6 Garrison Ave., Durham, NH 03824 (tel. 603/826-1147 between 1:30 and 4pm EST).

HOMESTAYS OR VISITS Servas ("to serve" in Esperanto), 11 John St., Suite 407, New York, NY 10038-4009 (tel. 212/267-0252), is a nonprofit, nongovernmental, international, interfaith network of travelers and hosts whose goal is to help build world peace, goodwill, and understanding by providing opportunities for personal contacts among people of diverse cultural and political backgrounds. Servas travelers are invited to stay without charge in private homes for visits lasting a minimum of two days. Visitors pay a $55 annual fee, fill out an application, and are interviewed for suitability; they then receive a Servas directory listing names and addresses of Servas hosts who will welcome visitors into their homes. This program embraces 110 countries, including many nations in the Caribbean.

Friendship Force, 575 South Tower, 1 CNN Center, Atlanta, GA 30303 (tel. 404/522-9490), is a nonprofit organization that fosters and encourages friendship among people worldwide. Dozens of branch offices throughout North America arrange en-masse visits, usually once a year. Because of group bookings, the airfare to the host country is usually less than the cost of individual APEX tickets. Each participant is required to spend two weeks in the host country. One full week is spent as a guest in the home of a family; most participants then spend the second week traveling in the host country.

TOURS FOR NATURALISTS Lectures on wildlife and the environment of Puerto Rico are offered by the Commonwealth of Puerto Rico Department of Natural Resources, especially for scientists and students. Also, private tours of the nature reserves and forests on the island can be arranged in advance. You need to specify the name of the reserve or forest you'd like to visit. Contact the **Department of Natural Resources,** Forest, Reserves and Refuge Area, P.O. Box 5887, San Juan, PR 00906 (tel. 809/721-5495 for the reserve and refuge, 809/723-1717 for the forest).

Tropix Wellness Tours (tel. 809/268-2173, or toll free 800/582-0613 in the U.S.) offers four tours to some of the island's varied natural treasures. Visitors can explore sea turtles' nesting sites on Culebra, the phosphorescent bay in Vieques, the Río Camuy Cave system in Camuy, and the dry, desertlike forest in Guánica.

The "Happy Turtle Tour" on Culebra includes a half-day kayaking/snorkeling expedition and a visit to the sea turtles' nesting sites during the spring/summer season. Culebra, ideally situated off the southeastern coast of Puerto Rico, is the home of the National Wildlife Refuge, which protects the habitats of the island's wildlife. The "Happy Turtle Tour," costing $315, includes four days'/three nights' accommodations and the airfare from Rivas Dominici Airport in Miramar to Culebra Airport. Rates are per person, based on double occupancy, and include continental breakfast and equipment for the escorted tours.

The "Phosphorescent Bay Tour" goes to Vieques, Puerto Rico's other offshore island; it also includes an expedition to Isla Nena, home of one of Puerto Rico's most spectacular reefs, bird sanctuaries, and deserted sandy beaches. The "Phosphorescent Bay Tour," which costs $325, includes four days'/three nights' accommodations at the Casa del Francés and the airfare from the Rivas Dominici Airport in Miramar to Vieques airport, as well as continental breakfast and equipment for the escorted expeditions.

The "Caveman Tour" in Camuy includes an expedition through one of the largest underground cave river systems in the world. Miles of natural waterways are surrounded by stalagmites, stalactites, sunless vegetation, and 20 different species of marsupials. The "Camuy Caveman Tour," which costs $275, includes four days'/three nights' accommodations at the Costa Dorado Hotel in Isabela, where the tour begins. Rates are per person, based on double occupancy, and include continental breakfast and equipment for the escorted tours.

The "Wet and Dry Tour" in Guánica includes two expeditions: the dry forest hike and mangrove kayaking at sunset. Southwestern Puerto Rico is the site of the world's largest remaining tract of tropical dry coast forest. This part of the island also features miles of mangrove channel systems. Visitors can explore these waterways by kayak as they are led to secluded Caribbean beaches. The "Wet and Dry Tour" costs $275 and includes four days'/three nights' accommodations at the Copamarina Hotel. Rates are per person, based on double occupancy, and include continental breakfast and equipment for the escorted expeditions.

HOME EXCHANGES House swapping keeps costs low—an advantage if you don't mind a stranger living in your mainland home or apartment. Sometimes the exchange includes use of the family car.

Many home-exchange directories are published. One problem is that there is no guarantee you'll find a house or apartment in the area you're seeking.

Intervac U.S., P.O. Box 590594, San Francisco, CA 94119 (tel. 415/435-3497, or toll free 800/756-HOME), is part of the largest worldwide home-exchange network. It publishes three catalogs a year, listing more than 8,800 homes in more than 36 countries. Members contact each other directly. The $62 charge (plus postage) includes the cost of all three catalogs (which will be mailed to you), plus your own listing in whichever catalog you choose. If you want to publish a photograph of your home, it costs $11 extra. Hospitality and youth exchanges are also available.

The Invented City, 41 Sutter St., Suite 1090, San Francisco, CA 94104 (tel. 415/673-0347, or toll free 800/788-CITY), publishes home listings in February, May, and November each year. For a $50 fee, they will list your home with your preferred time for an exchange, your occupation, and hobbies.

Vacation Exchange Club, P.O. Box 650, Key West, FL 33041 (tel. 305/294-3720, or toll free 800/638-3841), will send you four directories a year—including the one you're listed in—for $60.

HIKING The mountainous interior of Puerto Rico provides ample opportunities for hillclimbing and nature treks. These are especially appealing because of the panoramas that open at unexpected moments, often revealing spectacular views of the faraway sea.

The most popular and sought-after trekking spots include El Yunque National Park, the sprawling jungle maintained by the U.S. Forest Service, as well as the dozens of forest reserves scattered throughout the island. These range from coastal mangrove swamps teeming with bird life to densely forested palm groves in the high-altitude interior.

Equally suitable for hiking are the protected lands (especially the Río Camuy cave country) whose topography is characterized as karst (that is, limestone riddled with caves, underground rivers, and natural crevasses and fissures). Although these regions pose additional risks and technical problems for trekkers, some people prefer the opportunities they provide for exploring the territory both above and below its surface.

Information on hiking in the parks of Puerto Rico is available from several public and privately owned agencies: The **Department of Natural Resources Forest Service** (tel. 809/724-8774) administers some aspects of the park, although for the average hiker, more useful information may be available at the **El Yunque Catalina Field Office,** near the village of Palma, beside the main highway at the forest's northern edge (tel. 809/887-2875). They can provide material about hiking routes and, with 10 days' notice, help you plan overnight tours in the forest.

A *word of warning:* When you hike in the tropics, you can quickly become dehydrated and also sustain more serious insect bites and sunburn than you would while hiking in more temperate climes. Drink water frequently, wear a sun hat, and consider the advisability of long-sleeved shirts and sunscreen to protect yourself from heat exhaustion and sunstroke.

CHAPTER 3

ARRIVING IN PUERTO RICO

1. **GETTING THERE**
- **FROMMER'S SMART TRAVELER: AIRFARES**
2. **GETTING AROUND**
- **SUGGESTED ITINERARIES**
3. **WHERE TO STAY**
4. **WHERE TO DINE**
5. **WHAT TO BUY**
- **FAST FACTS: PUERTO RICO**

This chapter explores different possibilities for getting to Puerto Rico, including not only the most obvious ones but also some you may not have thought of. I also discuss various ways to travel around the island and suggest a number of itineraries to help you get the most out of your vacation time—whether it is one week or several weeks. You'll find tips on deciding where to stay, where to eat, and what to buy. Capping off the chapter is a quick-reference list of helpful information about Puerto Rico.

1. GETTING THERE

BY PLANE

Based on the number of flights from North America, Puerto Rico is by far the most accessible of all the Caribbean islands. It is, in fact, the airline capital of the West Indies. Even if you're not planning a holiday in Puerto Rico, chances are you'll pass through here if you do any extensive touring through the Caribbean Basin.

THE AIRLINES The most visible and dynamic airline in the entire region, **American Airlines** (tel. toll free 800/433-7300) has spent millions of dollars to make San Juan its most prominent Latin American hub. American offers nonstop daily flights to San Juan from New York (JFK), Newark, Boston, Miami, Dallas–Fort Worth, Washington (Dulles), Orlando, Tampa, Chicago, Baltimore, Hartford, Philadelphia, and Raleigh-Durham, as well as flights (with one intermediate stop in Chicago) to San Juan from both Montréal and Toronto. There are also two daily flights from Los Angeles to San Juan that touch down in either Dallas or Miami (depending on the schedule), offering the choice of daytime or nighttime travel. In all, the carrier now provides more than 27 daily nonstop flights to Puerto Rico, far more than any of its competitors.

American, through its wholly owned subsidiary, **American Eagle,** is also the undisputed leader among the short-haul commuter flights of the Caribbean. It specializes in these services, using propeller planes that carry 19 to 64 passengers. American Eagle links Puerto Rico with almost 100 daily incoming flights from nearly 40 destinations throughout the Caribbean.

Delta (tel. toll free 800/221-1212) flies daily to San Juan nonstop from Orlando, and also offers daily flights to San Juan from Los Angeles; some are nonstop, while others touch down briefly in Dallas and/or Atlanta. Delta's premier service to Puerto Rico, however, is from Atlanta, whose air routes Delta controls better and more efficiently than any other airline. From Atlanta, Delta makes seven daily flights to San Juan, six nonstop. Flights into Atlanta from around the world are staggeringly frequent, with excellent connections from points throughout Delta's network in the South and Southwest.

United Airlines (tel. toll free 800/538-2929), also a significant participant in international air travel, offers daily nonstop flights between Washington, D.C. (Dulles) and San Juan, and nonstop daily flights from Chicago to San Juan, with convenient connections through its widespread network.

Carnival Air Lines (tel. toll free 800/467-7415), a San Juan–based carrier wholly owned by the Carnival Group (of cruise-line fame), flies to both Ponce (Puerto Rico's second-largest city) and Aguadilla (on the northwestern coast) from Miami, Newark, and New York (JFK) three or four days a week, depending on schedules.

A handful of European carriers also flies to Puerto Rico, carrying winter-weary Europeans toward Caribbean sunshine. These include **British Airways** (tel. toll free 800/247-9297), which goes to San Juan twice a week (with an intermediate stop in Antigua) from London's Gatwick. **Lufthansa** (tel. toll free 800/645-3880) flies in from Frankfurt on Tuesday and Friday via Antigua, and on Wednesday and Saturday via St. Maarten. **Iberia** (tel. toll free 800/772-4642) flies to San Juan twice a week from Madrid.

FLYING TIMES The following lists the approximate nonstop flying time from various U.S. cities to San Juan:

Atlanta:	3 hrs. 15 min.	Miami:	2 hrs. 20 min.
Baltimore:	3 hrs. 45 min.	New Orleans:	3 hrs. 25 min.
Chicago:	4 hrs. 20 min.	New York:	3 hrs. 30 min.
Boston:	3 hrs. 45 min.	Philadelphia:	3 hrs. 25 min.
Los Angeles:	6 hrs. 25 min.	Washington:	3 hrs. 45 min.

REGULAR FARES Always shop around if you want to secure the lowest airfare. Keep calling the airlines. Sometimes you can purchase a lower-price ticket at the last minute, since airlines often discount tickets to try to achieve full passenger capacity.

In recent years, the traditional expectation that winter fares were higher than those in summer has changed. On their Caribbean routes, most airlines now divide their year into peak season and basic season, eliminating what used to be known as shoulder season. **Peak season** for fares between North America and Puerto Rico now generally means midwinter and midsummer, while the less expensive **basic season** covers spring and fall.

Also noteworthy is the fact that most airlines are eliminating business class on their routes from North America to Puerto Rico. Instead, they are offering first class (which is more expensive and has more lavish accessories) and economy class. (On most American Eagle flights, first class has been eliminated entirely in favor of single-service flights; since most intra-Caribbean American Eagle flights rarely exceed 90 minutes, no one seems to mind.)

Most airlines also offer periodic promotional fares, requiring advance purchase, minimum stays, and cancellation penalties; despite the restrictions, these flights tend to be heavily booked. The most common of these is **APEX** (Advance Purchase Excursion).

Land arrangements (that is, booking of hotel accommodations) are often tied in with promotional fares offered by airlines.

OTHER GOOD-VALUE CHOICES Proceed with caution through the next grab bag of suggestions. What constitutes good value keeps changing in the airline industry. It's hard to keep up, even if you're a travel agent. Fares, especially to Puerto Rico, change all the time—what was the lowest possible fare one day can change the very next day when a new promotional fare is offered.

Bucket Shops [Consolidators] The name originated in the 1960s in Britain, where the airlines gave that (then-pejorative) name to resalers of blocks of unsold tickets consigned to them by major carriers. "Bucket shop" has stuck as a label, but it might be more polite to call them "consolidators." They exist in a variety

FROMMER'S SMART TRAVELER: AIRFARES

1. Shop all the airlines that fly to your destination.
2. Always ask for the lowest fare—not just for a discount.
3. Keep calling the airlines—availability of cheap seats changes daily. Airlines would rather sell a seat than have it fly empty. As the departure date nears, additional low-cost seats become available.
4. Try to fly in spring or fall—fares are usually lower then.
5. Ask about the cost-conscious APEX (Advance Purchase Excursion) fare.
6. Sometimes it's cheaper to fly Monday through Thursday—check it out.
7. Read the section on "Other Good-Value Choices"—bucket shops, charter flights, rebators, promotional fares, and travel clubs.
8. Consider air-and-land packages, at considerably reduced rates.

of forms. In its purest sense, a bucket shop acts as a clearinghouse for blocks of tickets that airlines discount and consign during normally slow periods of air travel (for Puerto Rico, that usually means from mid-April to mid-December).

Charter operators (see below) and bucket shops used to perform separate functions, but their offerings have often become blurred in recent years. Many outfits perform both functions.

Tickets are sometimes—but not always—discounted as much as 20% to 35%. Terms of payment can vary, from perhaps 45 days prior to departure to the last minute. Discounted tickets can also be purchased through regular travel agents, who usually mark up the ticket 8% to 10%, maybe more, thereby greatly reducing your discount. A survey conducted of flyers who use consolidator tickets found only one major complaint: Such a ticket doesn't qualify you for an advance seat assignment, and so you are likely to be assigned a "poor seat" on the plane at the last minute.

Here's a possible hitch—many people who booked consolidator tickets reported no savings at all, since the airlines will sometimes match the price of the consolidator ticket by announcing a promotional fare. Because the situation is a bit tricky, you need to investigate carefully just how much you can expect to save.

Bucket shops abound from coast to coast. Look for their ads in your local newspaper's travel section; they're usually very small and a single column in width.

Although there are many air ticket discounters for transatlantic flights, there are few in the highly competitive Caribbean market. One of these is **TFI Tours International,** 34 W. 32nd St., 12th Floor, New York, NY 10001 (tel. 212/736-1140 in New York State, or toll free 800/745-8000 elsewhere in the U.S.) At press time, TFI offered tickets on TWA from New York to San Juan at prices a bit lower than what it would cost to buy them directly from TWA. The tickets are usually nonrefundable, or else carry penalties for any change in plans or itineraries.

Charter Flights These flights allow you to travel at rates lower than those of regularly scheduled flights. Many of the major carriers offer charter flights at rates that are sometimes 30% (or more) off the regular airfare.

There are some drawbacks to charter flights that you need to consider. Advance booking, for example, of up to 45 days or more may be required, and there are hefty cancellation penalties, although you can take out insurance against emergency cancellation. Also, you must depart and return on your scheduled dates or else you'll lose your money. If you don't have proper insurance, it will do you no good to call the airline and tell them you've had a ski accident in Aspen. If you're not on the plane, you can kiss your money good-bye.

Since charter flights are so complicated, it's best to go to a good travel agent and ask him or her to explain the problems and advantages. Sometimes charters require ground arrangements, such as prebooking hotel rooms.

One company that arranges charters is the **Council on International Educa-**

tional Exchange (Council Travel), 205 E. 42nd St., New York, NY 10017 (tel. 212/661-0311, or toll free 800/800-8222).

One of the biggest New York charter operators is **Travac,** 989 Sixth Ave., New York, NY 10018 (tel. 212/563-3303, or toll free 800/TRAV-800). Other Travac offices include 6151 W. Century Blvd., Los Angeles, CA 90045 (tel. 310/670-9692); 166 Geary St., San Francisco, CA 94108 (tel. 415/392-4610); and 2601 Jefferson St., Orlando, FL 32803 (tel. 407/896-0014).

Rebators To make matters even more confusing, in the past few years rebators have also begun to compete in the low-airfare market. Rebators are organizations that pass along to the passenger part of their commission, although many of them assess a fee for their services. And although rebators are not the same as travel agents, they sometimes offer roughly similar services. Sometimes a rebator will sell you a discounted travel ticket and also offer discounted land arrangements, including hotels and car rentals. Most rebators offer discounts averaging anywhere from 10% to 25% (but this varies from place to place), plus a $25 handling charge.

Rebators include **Travel Avenue,** 641 W. Lake St., Suite 201, Chicago, IL 60606-3691 (tel. 312/876-6866, or toll free 800/333-3335); and **The Smart Traveller,** 3111 SW 27th Ave. (P.O. Box 330106), Miami, FL 33133 (tel. 305/448-3338, or toll free 800/448-3338 in the U.S.). This agency also discounts hotel or condo packages and cruises

Promotional Fares From time to time, airlines announce promotional fares to Puerto Rico. You'll need a good travel agent or will have to do a lot of shopping or calling around yourself to learn what's currently available at the time of your intended trip

Travel Clubs Another possibility for low-cost air travel is the travel club, which supplies an unsold inventory of tickets with discounts in the range of 20% to 60%.

After you pay an annual fee, you are given a "hotline" number to call to find out what discounts are available. Many of these discounts become available several days before the departure, sometimes as long as a week and sometimes as much as a month beforehand—it all depends. Of course, you're limited to what's available, so you have to be fairly flexible.

Some of the best travel clubs include the following:

Discount Travel International, Ives Building, 114 Forrest Ave., Suite 203, Narberth, PA 19072 (tel. 215/668-7184), charges an annual membership of $45.

Moment's Notice, 425 Madison Ave., New York, NY 10017 (tel. 212/486-0500), has a members' 24-hour hotline (regular phone toll charges) and a yearly fee of $45 per family.

Sears Discount Travel Club, 3033 S. Parker Rd., Suite 1000, Aurora, CO 80014 (tel. toll free 800/255-1487), offers members, for $49, a catalog (issued four times a year), maps, discounts at select hotels, and a 5% cash bonus on purchases.

Encore Travel Club, 4501 Forbes Blvd., Lanham, MD 20706 (tel. toll free 800/638-8976), charges $49 a year for membership in a club that offers 50% discounts at well-recognized hotels around the country, sometimes during off-peak periods. It also offers substantial discounts on airfares, cruises, and car rentals through its volume purchase plans. Membership includes a travel package outlining the company's many services, and use of a toll-free phone number for advice and information

BY SHIP

CRUISE SHIPS If you'd like to sail the Caribbean in a hotel with an ocean view, a cruise ship might be for you. Cruises are slow and easy and are no longer enjoyed only by the idle rich who have months to spend away from home. Most cruises today appeal to the middle-income traveler who probably has no more than one or two weeks to spend cruising the Caribbean. Some 300 passenger ships sail the Caribbean, and in January and February that figure may increase another 100 or so. Puerto Rico is one of the major ports of call. Pick up a copy of *Frommer's Cruises* for more detailed information.

Most cruise-ship operators emphasize the concept of a total vacation. Some are mostly activity-centered, while others offer the chance to do nothing but relax. Cruise ships are self-contained resorts, offering a large variety of services and activities on board and sightseeing once you arrive in a port of call.

For those who don't want to spend all their time at sea, some lines offer a fly-and-cruise vacation. You spend a week cruising the Caribbean and another week staying at an interesting hotel at reduced prices. These total packages should cost less than the cruise and air portions purchased separately.

Another version of fly-and-cruise is to fly to and from the cruise. Most plans offer a package deal from the principal airport closest to your residence to the major airport nearest to the cruise-departure point. It's possible to purchase your air ticket on your own and book your cruise ticket separately, but you'll save money by combining the fares in a package deal.

Miami is the cruise capital of the world, but vessels also leave from San Juan, New York, Port Everglades (outside Fort Lauderdale), Los Angeles, and elsewhere.

Most cruise ships travel at night, arriving the next morning at the day's port of call. In port, passengers can go ashore for sightseeing, shopping, and a local meal. Cruise prices vary widely. Sometimes the same route with the same ports of call carries different fares, depending on the ship's luxury (as well as your accommodations on board). Consult a good travel agent for the latest offerings.

CHARTERS   There is perhaps no more dream-fulfilling way of enjoying a holiday in the Caribbean than from the deck of your own yacht. An impossible dream? Not really. No one said that you had to own that yacht. You can charter it or go on a prearranged cruise.

Experienced sailors and navigators can charter "bareboat," which means to rent a fully equipped boat without captain or crew. You're on your own and will have to prove your qualifications before you're allowed to rent such a craft. Even an experienced skipper may want to take along as a crew member someone familiar with local waters—they can be tricky in some places.

You can also charter a boat with a skipper and crew. Charter yachts, varying from 50 to more than 100 feet in length, can accommodate from four to a dozen people.

Most yachts are rented on a weekly basis and come with a fully stocked bar and equipment for fishing and water sports. However, more and more bareboat charterers are learning that they can save money and select menus more suited to their tastes by doing their own provisioning. The average charter carries four to six passengers and usually is reserved for one week. This doesn't mean that you can't go out for a shorter time, and you can certainly extend your sail. In summer, when business tends to be slow, you might be able to charter a boat for four or five days instead of a week or longer. For information about charters, call the following establishments:

The Moorings, Suite 402, 19345 U.S. 19N, Clearwater, FL 34624 (tel. 813/535-1446, or toll free 800/535-7289 in the U.S. and Canada), operates one of the biggest boat-charter operations in the Caribbean, with its main branch in the British Virgin Islands—cruise capital of the world. Charlie and Ginny Cary started the venture in 1969, and today preside over a mini-empire of seven Caribbean and Bahamian branches, each bristling with a regatta of yachts some of which are available for chartering. Depending on their size, yachts are rented to up to eight people at a time in comfort and style. Arrangements can be made either for bareboating (qualified sailors only) or for renting a yacht with a full crew and cook. Depending on circumstances, boats come equipped with barbecue, snorkeling gear, dinghy, and linens; the boats are serviced by an experienced staff of mechanics, electricians, riggers, and cleaners. If you're going out on your own, you'll get a thorough briefing about Caribbean waters, reefs, and anchorages.

Windjammer Barefoot Cruises Ltd., P.O. Box 120, Miami Beach, FL 33119 (tel. 305/534-7447, or toll free 800/327-2601), offers 6- and 13-day sailing adventures on classic tall ships through the Caribbean. Its *Flying Cloud* island-hops the British Virgins, its *Yankee Clipper* travels the Grenadines, its *Polynesia* and *Fantôme* sail through the West Indies, and its *Mandalay* cruises leisurely for 13 days through the

West Indies and the Grenadines. Its supply ship, the *Amazing Grace,* carries 96 passengers island-hopping from Freeport to Grenada. Rates start at $600. Air-sea package deals are offered. S/V (sailing vessel) *Fantôme,* S/V *Mandalay,* S/V *Polynesia,* S/V *Flying Cloud,* S/V *Yankee Clipper,* and M/V (motor vessel) *Amazing Grace* are registered in Honduras. All ships comply with international safety standards. Many people fly to Puerto Rico for a few days of rest and relaxation before taking a shuttle flight to the British Virgins for a week of sailing.

Nicholson Yacht Charters, 432 Columbia St., Suite 21A, Cambridge MA 02141-1043 (tel. 617/225-0555, or toll free 800/662-6066)—or P.O. Box 103, St. John's, Antigua, West Indies—one of the best in the business, handles charter yachts for use throughout the Caribbean basin, particularly the route between Dutch-held St. Maarten and Grenada and the routes around the U.S. and British Virgin Islands and Puerto Rico. Specializing in boats of all sizes, it can arrange rentals of motor or sailing yachts of up to 298 feet long. Especially popular are arrangements where two or more yachts, each sleeping eight guests in four equal double cabins, race each other from island to island during the day, anchoring near each other in secluded coves or at berths in Caribbean capitals at night. Nicholson offers a series of possibilities. The price for renting a yacht depends on the number in your party, the size of the vessel, and the time of the year. Rates range from $3,400 to $12,000 per week for a couple.

You can also cruise in the Caribbean on larger yachts that have scheduled sailing dates. On this type of craft, depending on its size, of course, there might be anywhere from 6 to 100 passengers.

Sunsail, 3347 NW 55th St., Fort Lauderdale, FL 33309 (tel. toll free 800/327-2276), specializes in yacht chartering from its bases in the British Virgin Islands, St. Lucia, the French West Indies, and The Bahamas. Bareboat and crewed yachts between 30 and 56 feet in length are available for cruising the waters around Puerto Rico and its neighbors. The company usually requires a deposit of 25% of the total rental fee, and arrangements must be made four to six months in advance. Clients with flexible schedules can reserve one month in advance.

PACKAGE TOURS

If you want everything done for you and want to save money as well, consider taking a package tour. Besides general tours, many have specific themes—tennis packages, golf packages, scuba and snorkeling packages, and honeymooners' specials. Puerto Rico is prominently featured in most of these offerings.

Economy and convenience are the chief advantages of a package tour—the costs of transportation (usually by plane), a hotel room, food (sometimes), and sightseeing (sometimes) are combined and neatly tied up with a single price tag. There are extras, of course, but in general you'll know in advance roughly what the cost of your vacation will be and you can budget accordingly. The disadvantage is that you may find yourself, for example, in a hotel you dislike but cannot leave because you've already paid for it.

Choosing the right package can be a bit of a problem. It's best to go to a travel agent, tell him or her what island (or islands) you'd like to visit, and see what's currently offered.

Packages are available because tour operators can mass-book hotels and make volume purchases. You generally have to pay the cost of the total package in advance. Transfers between your hotel and the airport are often included (this may be more of a break than it sounds at first since some airports are situated a $40-or-more taxi ride from a resort). Many packages carry several options, including the possibility of low-cost car rentals. Nearly all tour packages are based on double occupancy.

Some of the leading tour operators to the Caribbean include the following:

Caribbean Concepts, 575 Underhill Bend, Syosset, NY 11791 (tel. 516/496-9800, or toll free 800/423-4433), offers air and land packages to the islands, including apartments, hotels, or condo rentals. Car rentals and local sightseeing also can be arranged.

You might also want to consider one of the many tours offered by **American**

Airlines (tel. toll free 800/433-7300) or **American Express** (tel. 212/687-3700 in New York City, or toll free 800/YES-AMEX in the U.S. and Canada).

---

2. GETTING AROUND

BY PLANE American Eagle (tel. 809/749-1747) flies from Luís Muñoz International Airport to Mayagüez, which can be your gateway to western Puerto Rico. Most one-way fares are $45. For information about air connections to the offshore islands of Vieques and Culebra, see Chapter 11.

BY PUBLIC TRANSPORTATION *Públicos* are cars or minibuses that provide low-cost transportation and are designated with the letters "P" or "PD" following the numbers on their license plates. They serve all the main towns of Puerto Rico. Passengers are let off and picked up along the way. Rates are set by the Public Service Commission. Públicos usually operate during daylight hours, departing from the main plaza (central square) of a town. Information about the públicos is available at **Lineas Sultana,** calle Esteban González 898, Urbanización Santa Rita, Río Piedras (tel. 809/767-5205). The typical fare on a público from Río Piedras, for example, to San Juan is 50¢ (very cheap), but the route is slow and the vehicle stops frequently and is erratic. The typical fare from Río Piedras to faraway Mayagüez is $10, but it's quite inconvenient.

BY RENTAL CAR Rental cars are readily available, and some local agencies may tempt you with special reduced prices. But if you're planning to tour the island, you won't find any local branches to help you if you experience car trouble. And some of the agencies widely advertising low-cost deals won't take credit cards and want cash in advance. Also, watch out for "hidden" extra costs and the difficulties connected with regulating insurance claims, which sometimes proliferate among the smaller and not very well known firms.

If you're planning to do much touring on the island, it's best to stick with the old reliables: **Avis** (tel. 809/791-2500, or toll free 800/331-2112), **Budget** (tel. 809/791-3685, or toll free 800/527-0700), and **Hertz** (tel. 809/791-0840, or toll free 800/654-3001). At press time, Budget offered many reasonable rates from a fleet of well-maintained cars: A small but peppy Nissan Sentra with air conditioning and automatic transmission rented for $193 per week, with unlimited mileage. A more substantial mid-sized car, a Chevy Corsica (also with automatic transmission and air conditioning), rented for about $225 per week, also with unlimited mileage. These prices, as well as those offered by the competition, will undoubtedly change during the lifetime of this edition, although discounts are sometimes offered to members of organizations such as the AAA, depending on the policies of the rental companies.

Avis usually requires customers to be at least 21 years old; Budget and Avis prefer drivers to be 25 or older, although Budget will accept those who are 21 to 25 if they pay a small supplemental charge. In all cases, a valid credit or charge card must be presented at the time of rental; otherwise, a substantial cash deposit must be paid.

Each company offers an optional loss/damage waiver priced at around $12 a day. Purchasing the waiver eliminates most or all of the financial responsibility faced by the renter in case of an accident. (Without it, the renter would be liable for up to the full value of the car in case it was damaged.) Paying for the rental with certain credit or charge cards sometimes eliminates the need to buy this extra insurance, although prospective renters should check this matter with their card issuer.

Each of the big three companies offers minivan transport to their airport offices and car depots. Added security is achieved with an antitheft double-locking mechanism that has been installed in most rental cars available on Puerto Rico. Most rental cars are of Japanese make and perform well on narrow roads. Car theft is high on Puerto Rico, so use caution when choosing a parking spot.

Distances are often posted in kilometers rather than miles (1 kilometer equals 0.62 miles), but speed limits are reckoned in miles per hour.

Gasoline   There is usually an abundant supply of gasoline on Puerto Rico, especially on the outskirts of San Juan, where you'll see all the familiar signs, such as Mobil. Gasoline stations are also plentiful along the main arteries traversing the island. However, if you're going to remote areas of the island, especially on Sunday, it's advisable to start out with a full tank. *Caution:* On Puerto Rico, gasoline is sold by the liter, not by the gallon.

Driving Rules   Driving rules can be a source of some confusion. Speed limits are often not posted on the island, but when they are, they're given in miles per hour. For example, the limit on the San Juan–Ponce *autopista* (superhighway) is 70 m.p.h. Speed limits elsewhere, notably in heavily populated residential areas, are much lower. Since you're not likely to know what the actual speed limit is in some of these areas, it's better to confine your speed to no more than 30 m.p.h. The highway department places *lomas* (speed-bumps) at strategic points to deter speeders. Sometimes these are called "sleeping policemen." Puerto Ricans drive, as do U.S. motorists, on the right-hand side of the road. The older coastal highways provide the most scenic routes but are often congested. There are other blights that impede efficient motoring. Some of the roads of Puerto Rico, especially in the mountainous interior, are just too narrow for automobiles. Proceed with caution along these poorly paved and maintained roads, which most often follow circuitous routes. Cliffslides or landslides are not uncommon. Many readers have offered this advice: *Drive on Puerto Rico only if necessary.* Readers point out that local drivers are often dangerous, as evidenced by the number of fenders with bashed-in sides.

Highway Signs   Road signs using international symbols are commonplace in the San Juan metropolitan area and other urban centers. The following translations will also help motorists:

Spanish	English
Autopista	Expressway
Balneario	Public beach
Calle sin salida	Dead end
Carretera cerrada	Road closed to traffic
Carretera dividida	Divided highway
Carretera estrecha	Narrow road
Cruce	Crossroad
Cruce de peatones	Pedestrian crossing
Cuesta	Hill
Desprendimiento	Landslide
Desvío	Detour
Estación de peaje	Toll station
Manténgase a la derecha	Keep right
No entre	Do not enter
No estacione	Do not park
Parada de guaguas	Bus stop
Peligro	Danger
Puente estrecho	Narrow bridge
Velocidad máxima	Speed limit
Zona escolar	School zone

Road Maps   The best map both for touring the Puerto Rican countryside and for exploring some of its major cities is the *H. M. Gousha Roadmap of Puerto Rico* (about $2.50). Printed in an array of easy-to-decipher colors, it's available in bookstores throughout the island. In addition to showing the major and minor roads of the island, it contains blowups of Greater San Juan, Ponce, Arecibo, Aguadilla, Mayagüez, Carolina, and Caguas.

Breakdowns and Assistance   All the major towns and cities have garages that will come to your assistance and tow your vehicle in for repairs if necessary. There's no national emergency number to call in the event of a mechanical breakdown. If you have a rental car, call the rental company first. Usually, someone there will bring motor assistance to you. If your car requires extensive repairs because of a mechanical failure, a new one will be sent to replace it.

BY SIGHTSEEING TOUR **Castillo Watersports & Tours,** calle Don Tella 27, Punta La Marias, Santurce, PR 00913 (tel. 809/791-6195 or 809/726-5752), maintains offices at some of the capital's best-known hotels, including the San Juan Hilton, the El San Juan, and the Holiday Inn (Santurce). Using either its own vehicle (a 29-passenger van) or that of a subcontractor, it operates bus tours that pick up passengers at their hotel as an added convenience.

One of the most popular half-day tours departs most days of the week between 8:30 and 9am, lasts between four and five hours, and costs $25 per person. Departing from San Juan, it travels along the northeastern part of the island to El Yunque rain forest, later making a brief stop at Luquillo Beach.

The company also offers a city tour of San Juan which departs most mornings at 9am and, in some instances, at 1:30pm on Saturday, Sunday, and holidays. The four-hour trip costs $25 per person and includes a stopover at Bacardi's rum factory, where you're treated to a complimentary rum drink.

For a day sea excursion to the best islands, beaches, reefs, and snorkeling in the area, contact **Capt. Jack Becker,** Villa Marina Yachting (P.O. Box P), Fajardo, PR 00738 (tel. 809/860-0861). Captain Jack, a long-ago native of Washington, D.C., and a longtime resident of Puerto Rico, takes up to six passengers at a time on his Pearson-26 sloop. Participants appreciate the sun, the reefs, and the marine life that can be seen on this tour. Before departure, guests are directed to a nearby delicatessen, where they can buy drinks and a package lunch. The price for a five-hour swimfest is $40 per person. Reservations can be made any evening after 6pm.

BY FERRY There are no ferry services between Puerto Rico and the other islands of the Caribbean. There are, however, local ferries. The most frequented ferryboat run is between Old San Juan and Cataño every 30 minutes, seven days a week. Service begins at 6:15am, ending at 10pm.

The Fajardo Port Authority (tel. 809/863-0705) operates a ferryboat twice daily between Fajardo and the offshore island of Vieques. The trip takes 80 minutes. A ferryboat also operates between Fajardo and Culebra, making the one-hour trip either once or twice a day. Call for schedules and departure times, which may depend on weather and tides.

BY HITCHHIKING Although not illegal, hitchhiking is *not* recommended. You should neither hitch rides nor pick up hitchhikers. Countless cases of robbery, muggings, and even rapes have been reported on the roads of Puerto Rico. It's not worth taking a chance!

SUGGESTED ITINERARIES

IF YOU HAVE ONE WEEK

Day 1: Fly to San Juan and give yourself absolutely nothing to do the first day. Rest, relax, recuperate, have a rum punch, and listen to some salsa. Enjoy a typical Puerto Rican dinner, preferably at your hotel, to avoid the strain of having to find a local restaurant.

Day 2: After a long, leisurely morning and a late breakfast, take a taxi to Old San Juan for a day of lunching, shopping, and taking the walking tour detailed in Chapter 7. Try to schedule interior visits of El Morro Fortress and San Juan Cathedral.

Day 3: Head east for Luquillo, the most famous beach on Puerto Rico. If it's a weekend, both the highway to Luquillo and the beach itself are likely to be overcrowded. Try to schedule your visit for a weekday. Once a flourishing coconut plantation, the beach is protected by coral reefs that make its lagoon an ideal place to swim. Lockers, changing rooms, and showers are available, and it's possible to order local specialties at many open-air kiosks. Return to San Juan for the night.

Day 4: Head east again in the same direction of Luquillo, but this time spend the day exploring El Yunque rain forest—a lush, 28,000-acre site named after an Amerindian god. It's a world of ferns, vines, orchids, and a towering 3,532-foot peak (El Toro) on which 100 billion gallons of rainwater falls annually. There are 240 different species of trees here alone. Music is provided by millions of inch-long tree frogs (coquís).

Day 5: Back in the city, take a shopping tour of Old San Juan in the morning, looking specifically for Puerto Rican handcrafts. Have lunch at a Puerto Rican restaurant, such as El Patio de Sam or La Mallorquina. After lunch, head for the beaches of the Condado, one of the most glittering stretches of beachfront real estate in the Caribbean.

Day 6: Return to Old San Juan to see any of the sights you might not have had time for on Day 2's walking tour. Visit Fort San Cristóbal, La Fortaleza, Casa Blanca, and San José Church. If time remains, you might want to see the Pablo Casals Museum. Return to the beaches of the Condado in the afternoon, have a piña colada at sunset, and try to attend a Puerto Rican folk-culture show at night.

Day 7: Spend your final day touring "out on the island," taking in two of the major attractions of Puerto Rico. The first is Río Camuy Cave Park, one of the world's largest cave networks; guided tours allow you to see the world's second-largest underground river, along with caves and sinkholes. If time remains, try to visit Arecibo Observatory, the world's largest and most sensitive radar/radiotelescope, set in a 20-acre ancient sinkhole, about a two-hour drive west of San Juan, not far from the Río Camuy Cave Park. Return to San Juan in the evening for a night of casino and disco action.

IF YOU HAVE TWO WEEKS

Days 1–7: Spend the first week as outlined above.

Day 8: Leave San Juan in the morning for a day of exploring western Puerto Rico. Take Route 115 from Aguadilla to Rincón, one of the most scenic drives. At Rincón you'll find one of the world's greatest surfing beaches, attracting surfers from all over the world. If you can afford it, spend the night at Horned Dorset Primavera or at least enjoy a luncheon stopover there. There are also several budget-priced inns in the area where you can spend the night.

Day 9: Head south from Rincón to Mayagüez, the third-largest city on Puerto Rico. You can browse through its shops, many of which sell an intricate type of needlework that's a specialty of this part of the island. Also schedule a visit to the Mayagüez Zoo, a 45-acre tropical compound home to approximately 500 types of animals, ranging from Bengal tigers to tropical birds. Again, if you can afford it, schedule an overnight stop—or at least a buffet lunch—at the Mayagüez Hilton. If you have time in the afternoon, you can drive south of Mayagüez to Cabo Rojo, a former hangout of some of the Caribbean's most notorious pirates. Today it's a long stretch of white sandy beachfront, opening onto Canal de la Mona. At the end of Route 101, you reach Boquerón, one of the island's best beaches. You can either stay at one of the low-priced inns in the area or return to Mayagüez for the night.

Day 10: Spend a long, leisurely day exploring the southwestern corner of Puerto Rico. In the morning, head south along Route 2 to San Germán, a typical old town built during the 1600s in the Spanish style, with the oldest intact church under the U.S. flag. After walking through and exploring the town, drive south to Playa La Parguera for lunch at one of the simple seafood restaurants along the harbor. The fishing village lies south of San Germán at the termination of Route 304. Its main attraction is Phosphorescent Bay, but you'll need to stick around for a boat ride on a moonless night to see marine plankton light up the waters like a Christmas tree.

After some time on one of the nearby white sand beaches, you can continue eastward to spend the night in the city of Ponce.

Day 11: Spend the day seeing the attractions of Puerto Rico's second-largest city, including its red-and-black-striped firehouse and famed museum of art. Stroll through the historic town where major restoration continues on its turn-of-the-century buildings, constructed in a Ponce Créole and art deco style. In the afternoon, visit the beachfront strip south of Ponce and have a typical dinner at one of the seafood restaurants lining the shore. Return to Ponce for the night.

Day 12: Drive back leisurely along Route 52 to San Juan, where you can check into your hotel, perhaps along the Condado, and spend more time along this fabled beachfront strip of white sand, or you can return to Old San Juan for a shopping expedition, exploring Puerto Rican arts and crafts.

Day 13: Cram some sightseeing into this day, including a visit to the Bacardi Rum Plant, located beside the bay at San Juan. The tour takes about an hour, and the plant turns out 100,000 gallons of rum a day. You'll be offered a free sample. Later in the day, try to see the art collection at the University of Puerto Rico and explore its Botanical Gardens, which include more than 200 species of tropical and subtropical vegetation. If you still have enough stamina, return to Old San Juan to visit the Dominican Convent, now the Institute of Puerto Rican Culture. Try to have dinner in the old town at La Bombonera, a historic restaurant established in 1903 and known for its Puerto Rican coffee, savory stews, and Spanish pastries.

Day 14: For your final day in San Juan, make an important decision: You can either spend the entire day on the beach or see some of the attractions that you might have missed earlier, such as the Tapía Theater, Plaza de Colón, El Arsenal, the San Juan Gate, the City Hall, the House of the Buttresses, or the San Juan Museum of Art and History. In the evening, you might want to attend a Las Vegas–type show at one of the big resort hotels or do what the typical visitor to San Juan does—head for the casinos.

IF YOU HAVE THREE WEEKS

Days 1–14: Spend your first two weeks as outlined above.

Days 15 and 16: Head west from San Juan to Dorado, one of the best-developed resort areas in the Caribbean, famed for its Dorado Beach. Dorado is Puerto Rico's oldest resort town, known today for its deluxe Hyatt Dorado Beach Hotel and Hyatt Regency Cerromar Beach Hotel, with their glittering swimming pools, golf courses, and casinos. A shuttle bus runs between the resorts every 30 minutes. Two days pass quickly here, and there is much activity, both organized and spontaneous. In the unlikely event that you should tire of Dorado Beach, there are five other major beaches along the neighboring shorelines.

Days 17 and 18: For more Puerto Rican pleasure-seeking, continue east to Palmas del Mar, a residential resort community on the island's southeastern shore, 45 miles from San Juan, outside the town of Humacao. Again, two days will pass quickly here, with lots of swimming on the beaches as well as an active sports program that includes golf, tennis, scuba diving, sailing, deep-sea fishing, and horseback riding. You can even go hiking through a forest preserve with giant ferns, orchids, and hanging vines.

Day 19: Spend a day visiting the offshore island of Vieques, six miles east of the Puerto Rican "mainland." About twice the size of Manhattan, Vieques is ringed with scores of palm-lined white sand beaches. There's very little to do here, and that's why island aficionadoes seek it out.

Day 20: Head for Culebra, the other major offshore island—18 miles from Puerto Rico's eastern coast. It's about 7 miles long and 3 miles wide, with some 2,000 residents. If Vieques is sleepy, then Culebra is virtually drugged, it's that quiet and tranquil here. You'll have much of the island's beauty and beaches to yourself.

Day 21: Pulling yourself from the lethargy of Puerto Rico's offshore islands, return west to bustling San Juan. Try to grab a few final hours on the beaches of the Condado before packing for your homeward-bound trip the following morning.

Enjoy a typical San Juan night, devouring Puerto Rican specialties and listening to some of the best salsa in the world.

3. WHERE TO STAY

Few travel destinations in the West Indies offer the variety of accommodations that are available on Puerto Rico. San Juan itself has some of the finest resort hotels in the Caribbean, especially those in the Condado and Isla Verde areas.

The Hyatt hotel chain operates two major resorts at Dorado, and Palmas del Mar, in the east, is one of the largest and most luxurious resorts in the islands. Puerto Rico also offers a large number of moderately and budget-priced hotels. There are many small guesthouses in San Juan. Out on the island you'll find a scattering of *paradores* (country inns), plus small guesthouses and inns, all of which are modestly priced.

HOTELS & RESORTS There is no rigid classification of Puerto Rican hotels. The word "deluxe" is often used—or misused—when "first class" might have been a more appropriate term. First class itself often isn't. For that and other reasons, I've presented fairly detailed descriptions of the properties, so that you'll get an idea of what to expect once you're there. However, even in the deluxe and first-class properties, don't expect top-rate service and efficiency. "Things" don't seem to work as well in the tropics as they do in some of the fancy resorts of California or Europe. Life in the tropics has its disadvantages. When you go to turn on the shower, sometimes you get water and sometimes you don't. You may even experience island power failures.

Facilities often determine the choice of a hotel. For example, if golf is your passion, you may want to book into Palmas del Mar on the east coast. If scuba diving is your goal, then head for the offshore island of Culebra. Whatever your particular interest, there's probably a hotel that caters to it.

SPAS The Penthouse spa at the **El San Juan Hotel & Casino** has full amenities for men and women, including fitness evaluations, supervised weight-loss programs, aerobics classes, sauna, steam room, and massage. It's open seven days a week, year-round. A daily fee for individual services is assessed.

The Plaza Spa at the **Condado Plaza Hotel & Casino** features Universal weight-training machines, video exercycles, sauna, whirlpool, facials, and massages.

The fitness center at the **Palmas del Mar Resort** in Humacao features hydra-fitness exercise equipment, exercise programs, free-weight training, and computerized fitness evaluations. It's open seven days a week.

The Spa Caribe at the **Hyatt Regency Cerromar Beach** offers shape-up programs, including aerobics and "talking" Powercise machines, health evaluations, plus skin- and body-care treatments, such as massage facials.

At the **Parador Baños de Coamo** in Coamo there are therapeutic thermal springs—one hot, one cool. There are also two swimming pools (one for children) and a tennis court. It's open every day.

THE PUERTO RICAN GUESTHOUSE An entirely different type of accommodation is the guesthouse, where Puerto Ricans themselves usually stay when they travel. In Puerto Rico, the term "guesthouse" can mean anything. Sometimes they are like simple motels built around swimming pools. Others are small individual cottages with their own kitchenettes, constructed around a main building in which you'll often find a bar and a restaurant serving local food. Some are surprisingly comfortable, often with private baths and swimming pools. You may or may not have air conditioning. The rooms are sometimes cooled by ceiling fans or the trade winds, blowing through open windows at night.

For value the guesthouse can't be topped. Staying at a guesthouse, you can journey over to a big beach resort, using its seaside facilities for only a small charge, perhaps no more than $3. Although bereft of frills, the guesthouses I've recommended are clean

WHAT THE SYMBOLS MEAN

Travelers to Puerto Rico may at first be confused by classifications on hotel-room rate sheets. I've used these same classifications in this guide. One of the most common rates is **MAP,** meaning Modified American Plan. Simply put, that means room, breakfast, and dinner, unless the room rate is quoted separately in a listing, and then it means only breakfast and dinner. **CP** means Continental Plan—that is, room and a light breakfast. **EP** is European Plan—room only. **AP** (American Plan) is the most expensive rate because it includes your room and three meals a day.

and safe for families or single women. However, the cheapest ones are not places where you'd want to spend a lot of time because of their modest furnishings.

Puerto Rico's guesthouses, ranging in size from 7 to 25 rooms, offer a familial atmosphere. Many are on or near the beach, some have pools or sun decks, and a number serve meals. Rates are $40 to $90 for a double room. For further information, contact the **Puerto Rico Tourism Company,** 575 Fifth Ave., New York, NY 10017 (tel. 212/599-6262, or toll free 800/223-6530).

PARADORES Beyond San Juan's historic district, its hotels, casinos and nightlife, is the tranquil and natural beauty of Puerto Rico's countryside. In an effort to lure travelers "out on the island," the Puerto Rico Tourism Company offers the *paradores puertorriqueños*—Puerto Rico's charming country inns—which are comfortable bases for exploring the island's varied attractions. Vacationers seeking a peaceful idyll can also choose from several privately owned and operated guesthouses.

Using Spain's parador system as a model, the Puerto Rico Tourism Company established the paradores in 1973 to encourage tourism across the island. Each of the paradores is situated in a historic place or site of unusual scenic beauty and must meet high standards of service and cleanliness.

The paradores charge $53 to $83 a night, double occupancy; some are located in the mountains and others by the sea. Most have swimming pools, and all offer excellent Puerto Rican cuisine. Many are within easy driving distance of San Juan. To make a reservation at one of the paradores, call toll free 800/443-0266 in the U.S. (8am to noon and 1 to 4:30pm Atlantic time).

SELF-CATERING HOLIDAYS A housekeeping holiday can be one of the least expensive ways to vacation on Puerto Rico, particularly for a family or a group of friends. Self-catering accommodations are now available throughout Puerto Rico as well as on Culebra and Vieques. Some are individual cottages you can rent; others are housed in one building; some are private homes rented during the owners' absence. All have small kitchens or kitchenettes—you can do your own cooking and shop for groceries—nothing's better than freshly caught fish or Caribbean lobster bought at market. Most self-catering places include maid service in the rental fee, and you receive fresh linen as well. See "Rental Agencies," below, for specific agencies.

RENTAL VILLAS & VACATION HOMES Even Princess Margaret rents out her private villa on Mustique, in the Grenadines, to those who have the "proper references." Throughout the Caribbean, including Puerto Rico, you can often secure goods deals by renting privately owned villas and vacation homes.

Many villas have a staff, or at least a maid who comes in a few days a week, and they also provide the essentials of home life, including bed linen and cooking paraphernalia. Condos usually come with a reception desk and are often comparable to life in a suite at a big resort hotel. Nearly all condo complexes have swimming pools (some have more than one).

Private apartments are rented, either with or without maid service. This is more of a no-frills option than the villas and condos. The apartments may not be in buildings with swimming pools, and they may not have a front desk to help you. Cottages offer the most free-wheeling way to live among the major categories of vacation homes. Most cottages are fairly simple, many opening in an ideal fashion onto a beach, while others may be clustered around a communal swimming pool. Many contain no more than a simple bedroom together with a small kitchen and bath. For the peak winter season, reservations should be made at least five or six months in advance.

Dozens of agents throughout the United States and Canada offer these types of rentals (see "Rental Agencies," below, for some recommendations). You can also write to local tourist offices, which can advise you on vacation home rentals.

Travel experts agree that savings, especially for a family of three to six people, or two or three couples, can range from 50% to 60% of what a hotel would cost. If there are only two in your party, these savings don't apply.

RENTAL AGENCIES Agencies specializing in these rentals include the following:

Villas of Distinction, P.O. Box 55, Armonk, NY 10504 (tel. 914/273-3331, or toll free 800/289-0900), is one of the best offering "complete vacations," including airfare, rental car, and domestic help. Some private villas have two to five bedrooms, and almost every villa has a swimming pool.

Caribbean Connections Plus, P.O. Box 261, Trumbull, CT 06611 (tel. 203/261-8603), offers many apartments and villas in the Caribbean.

Hideaways International, 767 Islington St. (P.O. Box 4433), Portsmouth, NH 03802-4433 (tel. 603/430-4433), provides a 128-page guide with illustrations of its accommodations in the Caribbean so you'll get some idea of what you're renting. Most of its villas, which can accommodate up to three couples or a large family of about 10, come with maid service. You can also ask this travel club about discounts on plane fares and car rentals as well.

4. WHERE TO DINE

Much of Puerto Rico's food has to be imported, except the fish or Caribbean lobster that is caught locally and the excellent island-grown fruits and vegetables. A service charge is automatically added to most restaurant tabs, usually 10% to 15%. Even so, if the service has been good, it's customary to tip extra.

If you're booked into a hotel on the MAP (Modified American Plan, or half board), which is sometimes required during the peak winter season, you can sample local restaurants at lunch.

In summer, not many establishments require men to wear jackets, but some of the more sophisticated and posh havens do. Always check the policy of the restaurant or hotel dining room before going there. Check also to see if reservations are required. In winter you may find all the tables taken at some of the more famous places. Always wear a coverup when eating out; don't enter a restaurant attired in a bikini.

Whenever possible, stick to regional food. For main dishes, that usually means Caribbean lobster or fish. Don't eat too much meat; red meat is probably flown in and may have been in storage on the island for quite some time.

When you go out to dine, it's best to take a taxi. Roads in Puerto Rico are not marked very well; they are also badly lit and very narrow. In San Juan, of course, you'll have trouble finding a parking space. The restaurant or hotel where you're dining will call a cab for you, which should arrive within 30 minutes.

San Juan boasts some of the finest gourmet restaurants in the Caribbean, offering dishes from Spain, France, Italy, Germany, Mexico, Argentina, and Asia, as well as Puerto Rico. Traditional Puerto Rican cuisine is composed of an interesting mix of Spanish, Créole, and native Amerindian influences. Some of the island's best restaurants are the *mesones gastronómicos* (gastronomic inns), which feature local cuisine at reasonable prices. There are currently 45 *mesones gastronómicos* outside the San Juan urban area but close to major attractions. Membership in the program

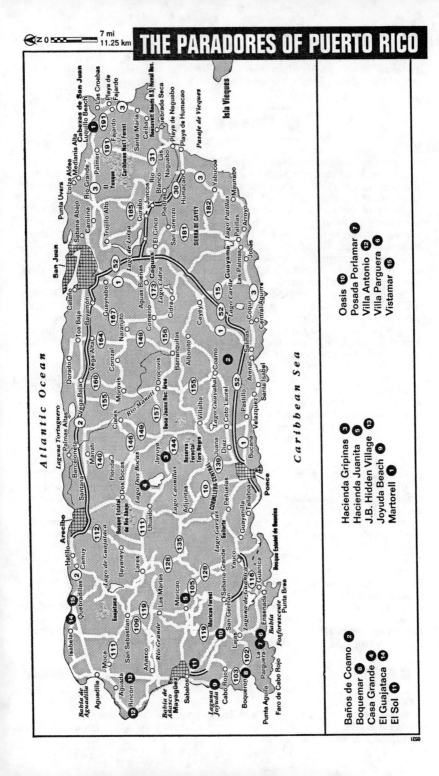

THE PARADORES OF PUERTO RICO

Baños de Coamo ②
Boquemar ⑧
Casa Grande ④
El Guajataca ⑭
El Sol ⑪

Hacienda Gripinas ③
Hacienda Juanita ⑤
J.B. Hidden Village ⑬
Joyuda Beach ⑨
Martorell ①

Oasis ⑩
Posada Porlamar ⑦
Villa Antonio ⑫
Villa Parguera ⑥
Vistamar ⑮

requires restaurants to have attractive surroundings and to comply with strict standards of service. Members must specialize in native foods and offer reasonably priced main dishes, some starting as low as $8.

5. WHAT TO BUY

Because the Commonwealth of Puerto Rico is part of the United States, no duty is charged on goods brought home by returning Americans. This boon, coupled with the international tastes of the island's people, results in one of the most desirable selections of merchandise in the Caribbean.

Many of the island's best shops advertise regularly in the glossy, photo-filled magazine *Qué Pasa?*, which is distributed free at airports, hotels, and tourist offices throughout Puerto Rico. A quick glance through its pages will give you an idea of what merchandise is available on the island.

Many visitors bypass the kiosks at the airport and their hotels, preferring instead to shop in the historic district of Old San Juan. For a combination of history and great shopping, Old San Juan simply cannot be beat in the Caribbean.

There is a more modern shopping center, akin to a sprawling California shopping mall but with a decided Hispanic flavor, in the Plaza Las Americas in the San Juan suburb of Hato Rey. More than 200 different shops comprise the largest and most densely packed shopping mall in the entire Caribbean. Somewhat less visited is the Plaza Carolina, in San Juan's Carolina district, where more than 150 shops are filled with stylish interpretations of European, U.S., and Puerto Rican fashion, home furnishings, and lifestyle accessories.

Despite the appeal of modern merchandise, most visitors prefer the kinds of traditional Puerto Rican crafts that have made the island famous. At the top of the list are ceramics, many of which are still decorated with geometric Taíno designs; musical instruments, which have made Puerto Rico one of the most musically entertaining islands anywhere (see "Performing Arts and Evening Entertainment" in Chapter 1); and the grotesque masks that are the trademark of dozens of different Puerto Rican festivals.

Other craft favorites include colorful hammocks (adapted from the Taíno *hamacas*); intricately woven baskets; and elaborately carved *santos,* representations of the dozens of Catholic saints. Paintings and sculptures can be bought at many different galleries throughout the island; they run the gamut from the most African to the most European of traditions, including even doses of Taíno inspiration.

Arts and crafts bargains are available in tin, tile, carved wood, papier-mâché, and textiles. Although some of these pieces might be viewed only as somewhat pretentious pieces of junk, artistic statements can indeed be found in many of them.

Regarding food and drink, don't overlook the many flavored, clear, or amber-colored rums that are considered a specialty of the island or the many spices and flavorings that help define Puerto Rican cuisine. Cans or vacuum-sealed plastic bags of ground Puerto Rican coffee make an excellent purchase, as does an array of spices, which are usually sold in jars or cans. Be aware that the U.S. Department of Agriculture forbids the importation to the U.S. mainland of many fresh tropical fruits, flowers, and vegetables, for fear of spreading agricultural diseases and pests to North American crops. Most processed or canned foods, however, are acceptable.

FAST FACTS   *PUERTO RICO*

American Express   See "Fast Facts: San Juan," in Chapter 4.

Area Code   The telephone area code for Puerto Rico is 809. For calls on the island, the area code is not used.

Babysitting This can be arranged through your hotel. You must specifically request a sitter who speaks English.

Banks All major U.S. banks are located on Puerto Rico; their hours are 8am to 2:30pm Monday through Friday and 9:45am to noon on Saturday.

Bookstores Most bookstores, especially those offering English-language editions, are located in San Juan. One of the best and largest selections of English-language titles can be found at The Book Store, calle San José 255 (tel. 724-1815). It's open daily from 9am to 7pm.

Business Hours Regular business hours are Monday through Friday from 8am to 5pm. Shopping hours vary considerably. Regular shopping hours are Monday through Thursday and Saturday from 9am to 6pm. On Friday, stores have a long day: 9am to 9pm. Many stores also open on Sunday from 11am to 5pm.

Camera and Film Nearly all well-known brands of film are sold on Puerto Rico. Rolls of film cost about what they do in your home town. It's relatively easy to get film processed on the island, especially in San Juan. It's important to protect your camera not only from theft but also from saltwater and sand; furthermore, the camera can become overheated and ruin any film it contains if left in the sun or locked in the trunk of a car. For the best commercial camera stores in Puerto Rico, see "Fast Facts: San Juan," in Chapter 4.

Car Rentals See "Getting Around," earlier in this chapter.

Climate See "When to Go," in Chapter 2.

Currency The U.S. dollar is the coin of the realm. Canadian currency is accepted by some big hotels in San Juan, although reluctantly.

Customs U.S. citizens do not need to clear Customs or immigration (but citizens of other countries do). On departure, your luggage must be inspected by the U.S. Agriculture Department, as laws prohibit bringing certain fruits and plants to the U.S. mainland.

Dentists and Doctors Dental emergencies can be taken care of at the San Juan Health Center, 200 De Diego Ave., Santurce (tel. 725-0202). This center also handles medical emergencies within the Greater San Juan area.

Documents American citizens do not need a passport or visa. Canadians, however, should carry some form of identification, such as a birth certificate. For further information, see "Information, Entry Requirements, Customs, and Money," in Chapter 2.

Driving Rules See "Getting Around," earlier in this chapter.

Drugs A branch of the Federal Narcotics Strike Force is permanently stationed on Puerto Rico, where drugs are a problem. Convictions for possession of marijuana can bring severe penalties, ranging from 2 to 10 years in prison. Possession of hard drugs, such as cocaine or heroin, can lead to 15 years in prison.

Drugstores Carry all prescription medications with you, enough for the duration of your stay. If you need any additional medications, you'll find many drugstores in San Juan and other leading cities. If you're going into the hinterlands, it's advisable to take along the medicines you'll need. One of the most centrally located pharmacies in Old San Juan is the Puerto Rican Drug Co., calle San Francisco 157 (tel. 725-2202); it's open Monday through Saturday from 8am to 9:30pm and on Sunday from 8:30am to 7pm.

Electricity The electricity is 110 volts A.C., as it is in the continental United States and Canada.

Embassies and Consulates Since Puerto Rico is part of the United States, there is no U.S. Embassy or Consulate. Instead, there are branches of all the principal U.S. federal agencies. Canada has no embassy or consulate either. In case of a problem, citizens of the United Kingdom can call 809/721-5193 to receive recorded directions on how to leave a message. They will be instructed to leave their name, address, telephone number, and a brief description of the problem; a staff member will eventually return the call.

Emergencies In an emergency, call the local police (tel. 343-2020), fire department (tel. 343-2330), ambulance (tel. 343-2550), or medical assistance (tel. 754-3535).

Etiquette   In social matters, Puerto Ricans tend to follow a more Spanish tradition than an American one. You should shake a woman's hand only if she extends it. Before you photograph anyone, on the streets of Old San Juan or in the countryside, you must always ask permission. Men are not usually required to wear jackets in the evening, except in the fanciest of restaurants (when in doubt, ask about the dress code when making your reservation).

Eyeglasses   See "Fast Facts: San Juan," in Chapter 4.

Hairdressers/Barbers   See "Fast Facts: San Juan," in Chapter 4.

Health Care   No special vaccinations are required to enter Puerto Rico. Medical-care facilities on the island are on par with those in the United States, with excellent hospitals and clinics. Hotels can arrange for a doctor in case of an emergency. Most major U.S. health insurance plans are recognized, but it's advisable to check with your carrier or insurance agent in advance of your trip, since medical attention is very expensive.

Hitchhiking   See "Getting Around," earlier in this chapter.

Holidays   See "When to Go—Climate, Holidays, and Events," in Chapter 2.

Hospitals   In a medical emergency, call 343-2550. The following facilities maintain 24-hour emergency rooms: Ashford Memorial Community Hospital, 1451 Ashford Ave. (tel. 721-2160), and the San Juan Health Center, avenida De Diego 200 (tel. 725-0202).

Information   See "Information, Entry Requirements, Customs, and Money," in Chapter 2.

Language   English is understood at the big resorts and in most of San Juan. Out in the island, Spanish is still *numero uno*.

Laundry   Your hotel can arrange to have your clothing laundered for you, but you'll pay a surcharge above what it would cost at a laundry. See "Fast Facts: San Juan," in Chapter 4, for specific recommendations.

Libraries   Puerto Rico does not have many public libraries. Most tend to specialize in law or engineering, and many are maintained by private foundations and universities. Exceptions include the Ateneo Puertorriqueño, which stocks mostly Spanish-language books, avenida Ponce de León 2, Puerto de Tierra (tel. 722-4839). The best university collection is probably the library at the University of Puerto Rico at Río Piedras (tel. 763-6199).

Liquor Laws   You must be 21 years of age to purchase liquor in stores or buy drinks in hotels, bars, and restaurants.

Lost and Found   There is no central clearinghouse for this. Your only hope is to go to the police, but in a poor commonwealth with a lot of unemployed people, it's unlikely that your property will be returned.

Maps   See "Getting Around," earlier in this chapter.

Newspapers/Magazines   *The San Juan Star,* a daily English-language newspaper, has been called the *"International Herald Tribune* of the Caribbean." It concentrates extensively on news from the United States. You can also pick up copies of *USA Today* at most news kiosks. If you read Spanish, you might enjoy *El Nuevo Dia,* the most popular local tabloid. Few significant magazines are published on Puerto Rico, although *Time* and *Newsweek* are available at most newsstands.

Passports   See "Information, Entry Requirements, Customs, and Money," in Chapter 2.

Pets   To bring your pet in, you must produce a health certificate from a mainland veterinarian and show proof of vaccination against rabies. Very few hotels allow animals, so check in advance. Many veterinarians are listed in the yellow pages of the local telephone book.

Police   Call 343-2020.

Postal Services   Since the U.S. Postal Service is responsible for handling mail on the island, the regulations and tariffs are the same as on the mainland. Stamps may be purchased at any post office, each of which is open Monday through Friday from 8am to 5pm. Saturday hours are 8am to noon (closed Sunday). As on the mainland, one can purchase stamps at vending machines in airports, stores, and hotels.

Radio and Television   An all-English station, Radio WOSO (1030 AM), broadcasts news and music throughout the day. Soft rock music is played on Radio Fidelity (95.7 FM). The major TV stations, broadcasting in Spanish, include WKAQ (Channel 2), WAPA (Channel 4), and TELE ONCE (Channel 11). English-language television is available only on cable TV, which is provided by most of the major hotels on the island. With cable TV, you can receive most of the major channels from the U.S. mainland, including CNN.

Restrooms   There are no public toilets on Puerto Rico. Visitors often use the facilities of a bar or restaurant; to do so, it's polite to order something, even if just mineral water, since theoretically these facilities are restricted to patrons. Toilets can be found at public beaches and at various rail and bus terminals.

Safety   Crime exists here as it does everywhere. Use common sense and take precautions. Muggings have been reported on the Condado and Isla Verde beaches, so you might want to confine your moonlit beach nights to the fenced-in and guarded areas around some of the major hotels. The countryside of Puerto Rico is safer than San Juan, but caution is always the rule. Avoid small and narrow little country roads and isolated beaches, either night or day.

Shoe Repairs   See "Fast Facts: San Juan," in Chapter 4.

Taxes   In addition to the government tax of 7% in regular hotels or 10% in hotels with casinos, some hotels add a 10% service charge to your bill. If they don't, you're expected to tip for services rendered. There is no airport departure tax.

Telephone, Telex, and Fax   Coin-operated phones are found throughout the island. After depositing your coin, you can dial a seven-digit number at the sound of the dial tone. If you're calling long distance, in either Puerto Rico or the U.S. Virgin Islands, simply dial "1" before the numbers. For long-distance calls elsewhere, dial "1," the area code, then the number. An operator will tell you how much money to deposit. For operator-assisted calls, dial "0" (zero). Most phone booths contain printed directions for dialing. Most hotels will send a telex or a fax for you. In San Juan, you can also go to Fax & Telex Service, Pereira Diversified Communications, 1020 Ashford Ave., Santurce (tel. 723-8233). Many hotels impose extremely high surcharges for long-distance calls made from your hotel room. If you wish to place an international call and want to circumvent these surcharges, go to the many public telephones available at World Service Telephone (AT&T), Pier 1, Old San Juan (tel. 721-2520).

Time   Puerto Rico is on Atlantic Standard Time year-round, which is one hour later than Eastern Standard Time. However, when the eastern United States goes on Daylight Saving Time, Puerto Rico does not, and so the time is the same.

Tipping   Tip as you would in the United States. That usually means 15% in restaurants, except for fast-food places; 10% in bars; and 10% to 15% for taxi drivers, hairdressers, and other services, depending on the quality of the service rendered. Tip a porter, either at the airport or at your hotel, between 75¢ and $1 per bag.

Tourist Offices   Before you leave home, refer to "Information, Entry Requirements, Customs, and Money," in Chapter 2. For local information, contact the Puerto Rico Tourism Company, paseo de la Princesa, Old San Juan, PR 00901 (tel. 809/721-2400).

Transit Information   For flight information, call either your airline or Luís Muñoz Marín International Airport (tel. 791-4670 or 791-5823). For bus information in the Greater San Juan area, call the Metropolitan Bus Authority (tel. 767-7979). For taxis in the San Juan area, call 723-2460.

Visas   U.S. and Canadian citizens do not need a visa to enter Puerto Rico. Visa requirements for nationals of other countries are the same as for entering the United States. Foreigners should check with their local embassies or consulates to learn the specific requirements; also, see "Information, Entry Requirements, Customs, and Money," in Chapter 2.

Water   There is ample water for showers and bathing in Puerto Rico, but it's always wise to conserve. Most visitors drink the local tap water with no harmful after effects. Others, more prudent or with more delicate stomachs, might want to stick to bottled water. In any event, because your body may be unaccustomed to the heat of Puerto Rico, you should probably increase your intake of fluids.

Weights and Measures   Most weights and measures on the island are metric, due to the Spanish tradition. Road distances are given in kilometers, although speed limits appear in miles per hour. Gasoline is sold by the liter, and meats and poultry are measured by the kilogram; however, reflecting the cultural confusion of the island, liquids, such as beer, are sold by the ounce.

Yellow Pages   All Puerto Rican phone directories contain yellow pages, but they won't be of much help unless you read Spanish. The blue pages of these directories list U.S. and local government offices. As an aid to English-speaking visitors, the phone company publishes the *Tourist Quick Guide,* a compilation of the local yellow pages, with addresses and services, plus phone numbers, printed in English.

CHAPTER 4

GETTING TO KNOW SAN JUAN

San Juan, the capital of Puerto Rico, is today an urban sprawl, one municipality flowing into another to form a great metropolitan area. San Juan will introduce you to Puerto Rico; the look of this old city ranges from decaying ruins reminiscent of the Spanish Empire to modern beachfront hotels that resemble Miami Beach.

The historic district of Old San Juan is a seven-square-block area that was once completely enclosed by a wall. The most powerful fortress in the Caribbean—erected by the Spanish with slave labor—was able to hold off would-be attackers. By the 19th century, however, this former military stronghold had become one of the most charming residential and commercial areas of the Caribbean. Today it's a setting for restaurants and shops; most of the major resort hotels (see Chapter 5) are located along the Condado beachfront and at Isla Verde.

San Juan is the second-oldest city in the Americas, surpassed only by Santo Domingo (once called Ciudad Trujillo). It presents two completely different faces to the world: One is the historic district, and the other is the urban sprawl that has grown around Old San Juan, with towering concrete buildings and expressways.

About one-third of all Puerto Ricans live in metropolitan San Juan; concentrated within 300 square miles, San Juan is not only the capital city but also the political base, economic powerhouse, and social center for most of the island's big events.

1. ORIENTATION

ARRIVING

BY PLANE   Arrivals are at **Luís Muñoz Marín International Airport** (tel. 809/791-4670, or toll free 800/791-5823), the major transportation hub of the Caribbean. Both American Airlines and its subsidiary, American Eagle, use it as their Caribbean hub. The international and domestic flights of other airlines also land here. The airport is situated on the easternmost side of the city, rather inconvenient to nearly all hotels unless you're staying at one of the resorts or small inns at Isla Verde.

The airport offers an array of services—not only the usual toilets and fast-food restaurants but also barbershops and hairdressers, coin lockers to store luggage (particularly useful if you're visiting one of the smaller islands on a shuttle plane),

WHAT'S SPECIAL ABOUT SAN JUAN

Beaches
☐ Condado, once filled with the private villas of the rich, now the most frequented beachfront strip of the Caribbean, with long bands of white sand.

Historic Buildings
☐ El Morro Fortress, in Old San Juan, Puerto Rico's grand architectural legacy of the Spanish Empire.
☐ Casa Blanca, a gem of Old San Juan—a 16th-century nobleman's house built for Ponce de León.
☐ La Fortaleza, one of the oldest executive mansions in the western hemisphere—some 300 years older than the White House.

Ace Attractions
☐ The entire historic walled town of Old San Juan, a restored masterpiece of Spanish colonial architecture.

Religious Shrines
☐ The Dominican Convent, built in 1523 on land donated by Ponce de León and closed as a convent in 1838, now the Institute of Puerto Rican Culture.
☐ Church of San José, the oldest church still in use in the Americas.
☐ Cathedral of San Juan, not completed until 1852, but whose interior dates to 1521.

Parks and Gardens
☐ Botanical Garden, Río Piedras, with more than 200 species of tropical and subtropical vegetation from around the island.

Special Events
☐ Casals Festival, honoring the famed Spanish–Puerto Rican cellist, the premier cultural event of the Caribbean; staged annually in June.

---

bookstores, banks, money-exchange kiosks, and even a bar (open daily from noon to 4pm) offering a sampling of the best Puerto Rican rums in all their many hues and flavors. The tourist information center at the airport is open daily from 9am to 5:30pm.

Those with little luggage can take the T1 bus, which runs to the center of the city.

Most visitors head for the Condado area by taxi or limousine. Although taxis are metered, make sure when you get in that the meter is turned off and that it registers zero. You don't want to end up paying the previous passenger's fares as well as your own.

Fares can vary widely, depending on traffic conditions. However, it will probably cost $8 to $12 to reach one of the Condado hotels or about $15 to $18 if you want to be delivered to the far end of the city—Old San Juan. Dozens of taxis line up outside the airport to meet arriving flights, so you rarely have to wait.

Although technically cab drivers should turn on their meters, more often than not they'll quote a flat rate before starting out, which is usually within the price ranges quoted above.

BY CRUISE SHIP The Port of San Juan is the busiest ocean terminal in the West Indies. It's estimated that half the trade in the Caribbean passes through here. The harbor where both commercial cargo and cruise ships arrive lies outside San Juan Bay, a body of water that's about 3 miles long and 1 mile wide—and almost completely landlocked. The long bay protects vessels from any roughness in the Atlantic Ocean.

The major cruise ships of the Caribbean, such as the *Sovereign of the Seas,* anchor alongside the various piers. There are about 710 cruise-ship arrivals every year, bringing nearly 851,000 passengers.

From the docks, a spacious walkway connects the piers to the cobblestone streets of Old San Juan. Most cruise-ship passengers head for this district to shop. One can also take a waiting taxi and head for the beaches of Condado. For advice and maps, contact the Tourist Information Center at La Casita, near Pier 1 in Old San Juan (tel. 722-1709). The dock area, now restored, is an attractive place for strolling, with its plazas, fountains, promenades, and beaches.

BY CAR   If you enter San Juan by car, follow one of the signs to a garage, park your car, then stroll about on foot or take a trolley around the city.

If you're driving in from the airport, head west along Route 26, which becomes Route 25 as it enters Old San Juan. If you stay on Route 25 (also called avenida Muñoz Rivera), you'll have the best view of the ocean and the monumental city walls.

Just before reaching the Capitol building, turn left between the Natural Resources Department and the modern House of Representatives office building. Go two blocks until you reach the intersection of paseo de Covadonga, then take a right past the Treasury Building and park your car in the Covadonga Parking Garage on the left. This garage is open 24 hours a day. A free shuttle bus service loops the old town from here on two different routes.

BY BUS   You can also arrive in Old San Juan by air-conditioned bus. The fare is only 25¢. You can take one of these buses from the Condado or Isla Verde hotels to Old San Juan. You'll be deposited at the main bus terminal across the street from the Cataño ferry pier and the Plaza de Colón. This section of San Juan is the starting point for many metropolitan bus routes.

For example, bus 2 goes from the Plaza de Colón along the Condado, eventually reaching the commercial section of San Juan, Hato Rey. Bus A7 also passes from Old San Juan to the Condado and goes on to avenida Isla Verde, and T1 heads for avenida De Diego in the Condado district, then makes a long run to Isla Verde and the airport.

For more information about bus travel in San Juan, call 767-7979.

TOURIST INFORMATION

Tourist information is available at the **Luís Muñoz Marín Airport** (tel. 809/791-1014). Another office is at **La Casita,** Pier 1, Old San Juan (tel. 809/722-1709). Out on the island other offices are at the **Casa Armstrong Poventud,** Plaza Las Delicias, Ponce (tel. 809/840-5695); and **Rafael Hernández Airport,** Aguadilla (tel. 809/890-3315).

CITY LAYOUT

Metropolitan San Juan includes the old walled city on San Juan Island; the city center on San Juan Island, containing the Capitol building; Santurce, on a larger peninsula, which is reached by causeway bridges from San Juan Island (the lagoonfront section here is called Miramar); Condado, the narrow peninsula that stretches from San Juan Island to Santurce; Hato Rey, the business center; Río Piedras, site of the University of Puerto Rico; and Bayamón, an industrial and residential quarter.

The Condado strip of beachfront hotels, restaurants, casinos, and nightclubs is separated from Miramar by a lagoon. Isla Verde, another resort area, is near the airport, which is separated from the rest of San Juan by an isthmus.

FINDING AN ADDRESS   Finding an address in San Juan isn't always easy. You'll have to contend not only with missing street signs and numbers but also with street addresses that appear sometimes in English and at other times in Spanish. The most common Spanish terms for thoroughfares are *calle* (street) and *avenida* (avenue). When they are used, the street number will follow them; for example, the Gran Hotel El Convento is located at calle del Cristo 100, in Old San Juan. Locating a building in Old San Juan is relatively easy, with the odd numbers on one side of the street and the even numbers on the other. The area is only seven square blocks, so by walking around it's possible to locate most addresses.

San Juan ★
PUERTO RICO

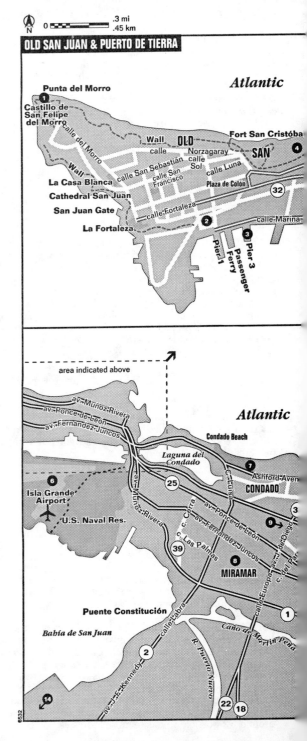

OLD SAN JUAN & PUERTO DE TIERRA

0   .3 mi
      .45 km
N

Atlantic

Punta del Morro **1**
Castillo de San Felipe del Morro
Wall
calle
Norzagaray
OLD
Fort San Cristóbal **4**
SAN
calle del Morro
Wall
calle San Sebastián
calle San Francisco
calle Sol
calle Luna
La Casa Blanca
Cathedral San Juan
San Juan Gate
Plaza de Colón
32
calle Fortaleza
La Fortaleza
2
calle Marina
Pier 1
Pier 3
Passenger Ferry
3

area indicated above

av. Muñoz Rivera
av. Ponce de León
av. Fernández Juncos

Atlantic

Condado Beach
Laguna del Condado
7
Ashford Aven
CONDADO
6
Isla Grande Airport
25
c. Cruise
av. Ponce de León
3
av. Muñoz Rivera
c. Cerra
av. Fernández Juncos
9
c. Diego
U.S. Naval Res.
39
Las Palmas
8
MIRAMAR
calle Europa
1
Puente Constitución
calle Labra
Bahía de San Juan
Caño de Martín Peña
2
av. J.F. Kennedy
R. Puerto Nuevo
14
22
18

6532

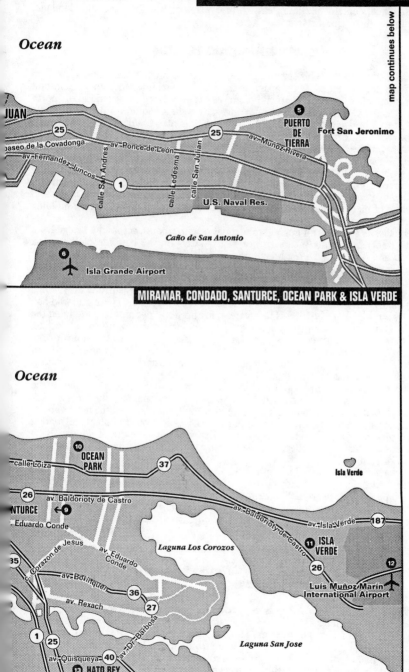

SAN JUAN ORIENTATION

Ocean

JUAN

paseo de la Covadonga

av. Fernandez Juncos

av. Ponce de León

calle San Andres

calle Ledesma

calle San Julian

25

25

1

av. Muñoz Rivera

5

PUERTO DE TIERRA

Fort San Jeronimo

U.S. Naval Res.

Caño de San Antonio

6

Isla Grande Airport

map continues below

MIRAMAR, CONDADO, SANTURCE, OCEAN PARK & ISLA VERDE

Ocean

calle Loiza

10

OCEAN PARK

37

Isla Verde

26

av. Baldorioty de Castro

NTURCE

9

Eduardo Conde

35

Corazon de Jesus

av. Borinquen

av. Rexach

av. Eduardo Conde

Laguna Los Corozos

av. Baldorioty de Castro

av. Isla Verde

187

11

ISLA VERDE

26

12

Luis Muñoz Marín International Airport

36

27

av. Dr. Barbosa

1

25

av. Quisqueya

40

13 HATO REY

Laguna San Jose

Airport

STREET MAPS *Qué Pasa?*, the monthly tourist magazine distributed free by the tourist office, contains accurate, easy-to-read maps of San Juan and the Condado, pinpointing the major attractions.

NEIGHBORHOODS IN BRIEF

Old San Juan This seven-square-block area is probably the most historic in the West Indies. Filled with Spanish colonial architecture and under constant restoration, it lies on the western end of an islet. It's encircled by water: On the north is the Atlantic Ocean and on the south and west is the tranquil San Juan Bay. Ponte San Antonio bridge connects the old town with "mainland" Puerto Rico. Ramparts and old Spanish fortresses form its outer walls.

Puerto de Tierra Translated as "gateway to the land" or "gateway to the island," Puerto de Tierra lies just east of the old city walls of San Juan. This section of metropolitan San Juan is split by avenida Ponce de León and interconnects the historic peninsula of Old San Juan with the Puerto Rican "mainland." The settlement, founded by freed black slaves, today functions as the island's administrative center and is the site of many military and government buildings, including the Capitol building and various U.S. naval reserves.

Miramar This is an upscale residential neighborhood, across the bridge from Puerto de Tierra. Many yachts anchor in its waters on the bay side of Ponte Isla Grande, and some of the finest homes on Puerto Rico are found here. It's also the site of Isla Grande Airport, where you can board flights to the offshore islands of Vieques and Culebra.

Condado/Santurce The Condado is the glittering beachfront strip of San Juan—site of most of the major hotels. It's linked to Puerto de Tierra and Old San Juan by a bridge built in 1910. The greater neighborhood of Santurce, adjoining the Condado, was once the most exclusive in San Juan. However, now it's in sad decline.

Hato Rey Santurce's loss was Hato Rey's gain. Situated to the south of the Martín Peña canal, this area today is the Wall Street of the West Indies, filled with many high-rises, a large federal complex, and many business and banking offices. Actually, it was once a marsh until landfill and concrete changed it forever.

Río Piedras South of both Hato Rey and Santurce, this is the site of the University of Puerto Rico and its student population. It's dominated by the landmark Roosevelt Bell Tower, named for Theodore Roosevelt, who donated the money for its construction. The main thoroughfare is paseo de Diego, site of a popular local market where produce is sold. The Agricultural Experimental Station of Puerto Rico maintains a Botanical Garden; there are many tropical plants here, including 125 species of palms.

Bayamón The San Juan sprawl has reached this once-distant southwestern suburb, which had been farmland before industry moved in and took over. Some 200,000 people and nearly 200 factories are now located in this geographically large district. Bus no. 46 from the center of San Juan runs out here. At Route 2, km 6.4, in Guayanobo are the ruins of Caparra, the first colonial settlement on the island.

2. GETTING AROUND

BY FERRY The *Agua Express* connects Old San Juan with the industrial and residential communities of Hato Rey and Cataño, across the bay. Ferries depart daily every 30 minutes from 6am to 9pm. The one-way fare to Hato Rey is 75¢, and the one-way fare to Cataño is 50¢. Departures are from the San Juan Terminal at the pier in Old San Juan. However, it's best to avoid rush hours since hundreds of locals who work in town use this ferry. Each ride lasts about 20 minutes. For more information, call 751-7055.

BY TAXI Taxis—operated by the Public Service Commission (PSC)—are metered in San Juan, or are supposed to be. The initial charge is $1, plus 10¢ for each one-tenth of a mile and 50¢ for every suitcase. The minimum fare is $3. Various taxi companies are listed in the yellow pages of the phone book under "Taxis," or you can call the PSC at 791-3725 to request information or report any irregularities.

BY BUS The Metropolitan Bus Authority operates buses in the greater San Juan area. Bus stops are marked by upright metal signs or yellow posts reading PARADA. The bus terminal in San Juan is in the dock area and at the Plaza de Colón. A typical fare is only 25¢. For more information about routes and schedules, call 767-7979.

BY MINIVAN OR LIMOUSINE Be aware that a wide variety of vehicles at the San Juan airport call themselves *limosinas* (their Spanish name). One outfit whose sign-up desk is in the arrivals hall of the international airport, near American Airlines, is the **Airport Limousine Service** (tel. 791-4745). They offer minivan service from the airport to various San Juan neighborhoods for prices that are lower than what a taxi would charge. If eight passengers can be rounded up to share a minivan, the fare per person for transportation, with luggage, to any hotel in Isla Verde is $2.50; to the Condado district, $3; and to Old San Juan, $3.50.

For conventional limousine service, **Bracero Limousine** (tel. 740-0444) offers plushly upholstered cars with drivers to meet you and your entourage at the arrivals terminal of the airport for luxurious and strictly private transportation to your hotel. The charge within San Juan ranges from $85 to $120, depending on your destination; arrangements should be made before your arrival.

BY TROLLEY When you tire of walking around Old San Juan, you can board one of the free trolleys that run through the historic area. Departure points are the Marina and La Puntilla, but you can get on anyplace along the route. Relax and enjoy the sights as the trolleys rumble through the old and narrow streets.

ON FOOT This is the only way to explore Old San Juan. All the major attractions can easily be covered in a day. However, if you're going from Old San Juan to Isla Verde, you'll need to rely on public transportation.

Walking can, of course, be risky. Muggings are sometimes reported during the daylight hours, although nighttime is certainly more dangerous. Take extreme caution if walking in Old San Juan at night. Never walk along the Condado beaches at night; the muggers there are just waiting for you.

 SAN JUAN

American Express The agency is represented in San Juan by **Travel Network,** 1035 Ashford Ave., Condado (tel. 725-0950). After hours, call American Express directly (tel. toll free 800/327-1267).

Area Code See "Fast Facts: Puerto Rico," in Chapter 3.

Babysitting There's no central service in San Juan that arranges sitting. Most assignments are made through hotels, and you need to specify an English-speaking sitter.

Banks See "Fast Facts: Puerto Rico," in Chapter 3.

Bookstores The Book Store, at calle San José 255 (tel. 724-1815), in Old San Juan, has one of Puerto Rico's best selections of English-language titles.

Business Hours See "Fast Facts: Puerto Rico," in Chapter 3.

Camera and Film Both Cinefoto (tel. 753-7238) and Rabola (tel. 753-8778), located in the Plaza Las Americas Shopping Mall in Hato Rey, offer a wide variety of photographic supplies.

Car Rentals See "Getting Around," in Chapter 3. It's best to reserve a car before you leave home. However, it's also possible to reserve a car once you arrive at the San Juan airport, where all the major car-rental companies have kiosks. In Puerto Rico call 791-5212 to reserve a car at Avis, 791-3685 to reserve a car at Budget, and 725-5537 to reserve a car at Hertz.

Currency   See "Fast Facts: Puerto Rico," in Chapter 3.

Currency Exchange   Most banks will provide this service. You can also exchange money at the Luís Muñoz Marín Airport. Otherwise, in Old San Juan, go to Caribbean Foreign Exchange, calle Tetuan 201B (tel. 722-8222).

Drugstores   One of the most centrally located pharmacies is the Puerto Rican Drug Co., calle San Francisco 157 (tel. 725-2202), in Old San Juan. It's open Monday through Saturday from 8am to 9:30pm and on Sunday from 8:30am to 7pm. Walgreen's, 1130 Ashford Ave., Condado (tel. 725-1510), is open 24 hours a day.

Emergencies   In an emergency, call the local police (tel. 343-2020), fire department (tel. 343-2330), ambulance (tel. 343-2550), or medical assistance (tel. 754-3535). Dental emergencies are handled at the San Juan Health Center at avenida De Diego 200 in Santurce (tel. 725-0202).

Eyeglasses   Go to Pearle Vision Express, Plaza Las Americas Shopping Mall (tel. 753-1033).

Hairdresser/Barber   One of the best is unisex Los Muchachos, calle Tetuan 301, Old San Juan (tel. 723-4883).

Hospitals   Ashford Memorial Community Hospital, 1451 Ashford Ave. (tel. 721-2160), and the San Juan Health Center, avenida De Diego 200 (tel. 725-0202), both maintain 24-hour emergency rooms.

Information   See "Information, Entry Requirements, Customs, and Money," in Chapter 2.

Laundry/Dry Cleaning   Any hotel receptionist can probably give you the location of a nearby coin-operated laundry, but if you're stuck, try the Soft-Dry Cleaning and Laundromat, 4-SS Fidalgo Diaz, Villa Fontana, Carolina (tel. 769-0875). A reliable dry cleaner, usually with same-day service, is Albano One Hour Martinizing, calle Loíza 1702, Santurce (tel. 728-7643).

Libraries   Two public libraries in the Greater San Juan area are the Ateneo Puertorriqueño, avenida Ponce de León 2, Puerto de Tierra (tel. 722-4839), and the Volunteer Library League, avenida Ponce de León 250, Santurce (tel. 725-7672).

Luggage Storage   Facilities are available at the Luís Muñoz Marín International Airport (tel. 791-4670).

Maps   See "Getting Around," in Chapter 3.

Postal Service   See "Fast Facts: Puerto Rico," in Chapter 3, for more information. In San Juan, the General Post Office is at 585 Roosevelt Ave., San Juan, PR 00936 (tel. 767-3604). If you don't know your address in San Juan, you can ask that your mail be sent here "c/o General Delivery." This main branch is open Monday through Friday from 8am to 4:30pm and on Saturday from 8am to noon. A letter from Puerto Rico to the U.S. mainland will arrive in about four days.

Radio and Television   See "Fast Facts: Puerto Rico," in Chapter 3.

Religious Services   Protestants can attend services at the Freedom Chapel, Assemblies of God, avenida Ponce de León 654, Santurce (tel. 721-4187); Catholics, at the San Juan Cathedral, calle Cristo 153, Old San Juan (tel. 722-0861); and Jews at the Jewish Community Center of Puerto Rico, avenida Ponce de León 9032 (tel. 724-4157).

Restrooms   See "Fast Facts: Puerto Rico," in Chapter 3.

Safety   Stay away from the back streets of San Juan and don't venture onto the unguarded public stretches of the Condado and Isla Verde beaches at night.

Shoe Repairs   You can go to Zapateria Condado, corner of Barranquitas and Ashford Avenues at the Condado (tel. 725-8462), which is convenient to most of the big resort hotels.

Telephone, Telex, and Fax   Many public telephones are available at World Service Telephone (AT&T), Pier 1, Old San Juan (tel. 721-2520). To send a fax or telex, go to Fax & Telex Service, Pereira Diversified Communications, 1020 Ashford Ave., Santurce (tel. 723-8233). See also "Fast Facts: Puerto Rico," Chapter 3.

Tourist Offices See "Fast Facts: Puerto Rico," in Chapter 3.
Transit Information See "Fast Facts: Puerto Rico," in Chapter 3.
Yellow Pages See "Fast Facts: Puerto Rico," in Chapter 3.

3. NETWORKS & RESOURCES

FOR STUDENTS Although there are no organizations offering special services to visiting students, the **University of Puerto Rico** in Río Piedras is a good place to meet fellow students, nearly all of whom speak English. You can wander around the campus and shop at the large sprawling market near the bus terminal. Students often play guitars outdoors on the campus, which has a mellow atmosphere. You can visit the José M. Lazaro Library, largest on the island.

You can also wander through the **Río Piedras Market,** on avenida De Diego, where students go to shop, especially for fresh fruits such as papaya and pineapples. Many eat this fresh fruit for lunch. There are also fast-food places, popular with students, with such names as Taco Market and Energy (a health-food store and restaurant).

FOR GAY MEN & LESBIANS Before going to Puerto Rico, you can order the *Damron Address Book* ($13.95) for gay men or *Ferrari's Places for Women* ($12) from Giovanni's Room, 1145 Pine St., Philadelphia, PA 19107 (tel. 215/923-2960; fax 215/923-0813). *Spartacus,* the international gay guide, is available for $29.95, but I don't think it's the best guide for someone going to Puerto Rico.

FOR WOMEN The **American Association of University Women** presents evening discussions of "women's issues," often at the Second Union Church on avenida Alto Apolo. Call 789-4205 for more information. The **San Juan Christian Women's Club** sponsors brunch meetings, with guest speakers, music, and other features. Call 726-4273 for more information.

CHAPTER 5

WHERE TO STAY IN SAN JUAN

Whatever your preferences in accommodations—a beachfront resort or a place in the midst of historic Old San Juan, sumptuous luxury or an austere, inexpensive base from which to reconnoiter the sights—you can find a perfect fit in San Juan.

In addition to checking the recommendations listed here, you may want to confer with a travel agent; there are package deals galore that can save you money and match you with an establishment that meets your requirements.

In general, hotels charging more than $210 a night for a double room are considered "Very Expensive," those asking $150 to $210 for a double are "Expensive," and those costing $95 to $150 are "Moderate." Anything under $95 is regarded as "Inexpensive" or "Budget." Every hotel listed here in the first three groups has a bath in every room, unless otherwise noted.

Tax and Service Charges All hotel rooms in Puerto Rico are subject to a 7% tax, which is *not* included in the rates given here. Most hotels also add a 10% service charge. When booking a room, it's always best to inquire about these added charges.

Reservations You may make your reservations by telephone, mail, or fax. If you're booking into a chain hotel, such as a Hilton, you can call toll free in North America and easily make your reservations by phone. Whenever this service is available, the toll-free numbers are indicated.

You can usually cancel a room reservation one week ahead of time and get a full refund. A few hotelkeepers will return your money on cancellations up to three days before the reservation date; others won't return deposit money, even if you cancel far in advance. It's best to clarify this issue in advance. It's a good idea to include a stamped, self-addressed envelope with your payment.

If you arrive without a reservation, begin your search for a room as early in the day as possible. If you arrive late at night and without a reservation, you may have to take what you can get, often in a price range much higher than you'd like to pay.

1. OLD SAN JUAN

CASA SAN JOSÉ, calle San José 159, San Juan, PR 00901. Tel. 809/723-1212, or toll free 800/443-0266 in the U.S. and Canada. Fax 809/723-7620. 4 rms (all with bath), 6 suites. TEL **Bus:** A7, T1, or 2.

$ Rates (including continental breakfast): Winter, $190 single; $210–$230 double; $315 suite. Off-season, $150 single; $170 double; $200 suite. AE, DC, MC, V. **Parking:** Free.

This restored 17th-century mansion—now converted into a small hotel—was the first new hotel to open in Old San Juan in about three decades. Situated near the City Hall and Plaza de Armas, it's an old house with marble floors and one of the few elevators to be found in colonial-era Old San Juan. Accommodations are furnished comfortably with elegant antiques.

Balconies surround the interior patio, a quiet green place where you can hear the bubbling of water in the fountain. Particularly noteworthy is the second-floor Salon Grande, spanning the entire width of the house—a lovely place to enjoy afternoon tea, gather for cocktails, or sit and enjoy a book. Furnished as a room in an old country house with light pretty colors, spacious sofas, books, and a grand piano, the salon can come to feel like a home away from home. Breakfast is served in the adjoining dining room. Children under 12 are not accommodated.

GALERÍA SAN JUAN, calle Norzagaray 204-206, San Juan, PR 00901. Tel. 809/722-1808. Fax 809/724-7360. 5 rms (4 with bath), 3 suites. **Bus:** A7, T1, or 21

$ Rates (including continental breakfast): Year-round, $85 single or double without bath; $95 single or double with bath; $150–$175 suite. AE, MC, V. **Parking:** Three free spaces (other parking available on street).

Set on a hilltop in Old San Juan, across the street from a sweeping view of the sea, this unusual and charming hotel encloses its guests in a maze of verdant courtyards and interconnected art studios. During the 1700s, the premises were built to serve as headquarters for an aristocratic Spanish family. Today, the Galeria is one of the most whimsically bohemian hotels in the Caribbean, with trompe l'oeil paintings and a labyrinthine layout which has been compared to a large and intriguing piece of sculpture. All but two of the accommodations have air conditioning; none has a TV or phone, but guests seldom mind because of the charming and dynamic presence of the Connecticut-born owner, Jan D'Esopo. A noted painter, sculptor, and silk-screen artist, she maintains an art studio and metalworking foundry on the premises, contributing to a kind of creative chaos which many guests find enormously appealing. She is assisted by her husband, Manuco Gandía, who offers horseback tours and trail rides for around $20 for a 75-minute session. There's a simple courtyard-style café on the premises, but many visitors prefer to dine at one of the old city's innumerable restaurants instead.

2. PUERTO DE TIERRA

CARIBE HILTON, calle Los Rosales, San Juan, PR 00903. Tel. 809/721-0303, or toll free 800/HILTONS in the U.S., 800/268-9275 in Canada. Fax 809/725-8849. 616 rms, 52 suites. A/C MINIBAR TV TEL **Bus:** A7.

$ Rates: Winter, $285–$395 single; $310–$430 double; from $495 suite. Off-season, $195–$285 single; $220–$320 double; from $350 suite. Children stay free in parents' room. Continental breakfast from $10.50 extra. AE, DC, MC, V. **Parking:** $5.

The Hilton stands near the old Fort San Jerónimo, which has been incorporated into its complex. With Old San Juan at its doorstep and San Juan Bay as its backyard, it can be called the gateway to walled city. Built in 1949 in a 17-acre tropical park, the hotel underwent a major $40-million renovation in the early 1990s. The bedrooms have been given a fresh, modern styling and pastel-colored shades, with color-coordinated carpets, fabrics, and draperies. Some of the rooms are located in the 20-story tower (added in 1972), and the Garden Wing units have a tropical decor. You can walk to the 16th-century fort or spend the day on a tour of Old San Juan, then come back and enjoy the beach and swimming cove.

Dining/Entertainment: The Caribe Terrace restaurant complex features cuisines from all over the world, with a different menu each night. The hotel's restaurants and entertainment facilities include El Batey del Pescador, a fish restaurant; Rôtisserie, focusing on continental cuisine; the Peacock Paradise Chinese restaurant; and the Carib Bar, with deep and comfortable chairs and huge windows.

Services: Room service (6:30am to 11pm), laundry/valet, babysitting.

Facilities: Two freshwater swimming pools, health club, lighted tennis courts.

RADISSON NORMANDIE, avenida Muñoz Rivera (at the corner of Los Rosales), San Juan, PR 00902. Tel. 809/729-2929, or toll free 800/333-3333. Fax 809/729-2930. 174 rms, 6 suites. A/C MINIBAR TV TEL **Bus:** A7.

$ Rates: Winter, $200–$230 single; $210–$240 double; $500 suite. Off-season, $145–$190 single; $165–$210 double; $430 suite. Continental breakfast $8 extra. AE, DC, MC, V. **Parking:** $5.

Geared to the upscale business traveler but also a haven for vacationers, the Normandie first opened in 1939, then reopened in 1989 after a $20-million renovation and reconstruction. Designed in the shape of the famous French ocean liner, the *Normandie*, the hotel is a monument to art deco. Adorned with columns, cornices, and countless decorations, it was built originally for a Parisian cancan dancer (she'd married a construction tycoon). Next door to the Caribe Hilton, the hotel is located just a five-minute walk from Old San Juan, and its beachside setting adjoins the Sixto Escobar Stadium.

The elegant and elaborate rooms are well furnished, each with a private bath and all the amenities. The more expensive units are executive rooms.

Dining/Entertainment: There are two good restaurants, and the Atrium Lounge is set in a swirl of greenery. A French menu is offered in the formal Normandie Restaurant.

Services: Room service (to 11pm), laundry.

Facilities: Freshwater swimming pool, bar.

3. CONDADO

Once this area was filled with the residences of the very wealthy, but all that changed with the construction of the Puerto Rico Convention Center. Private villas gave way to high-rise hotel blocks, restaurants, and nightclubs. The Condado shopping area, along Ashford and Magdalena Avenues, attracted an extraordinary number of boutiques. There are good bus connections into Old San Juan, or you can take a taxi.

VERY EXPENSIVE

CONDADO PLAZA HOTEL & CASINO, 999 Ashford Ave., San Juan, PR 00902. Tel. 809/721-1000, or toll free 800/624-0420. Fax 809/253-0178. 544 rms, 22 suites. A/C MINIBAR TV TEL **Bus:** A7.

$ Rates: Winter, $255–$365 single; $275–$385 double; from $575 suite. Off-season, $185–$315 single; $205–$335 double; from $400 suite. Continental breakfast $12 extra. AE, DC, MC, V. **Parking:** $5.

In this two-in-one hotel complex, the original oceanfront structure is linked by an elevated passageway across Ashford Avenue to its Laguna section. In the Laguna wing, which has its own lobby with direct access from the street, every room has a private terrace and a king-size or double bed. The deluxe part of the hotel, the Plaza Club, has 75 units with five bilevel suites. This section has a VIP lounge reserved for the use of its guests, and accommodations have cable TVs and private check-in/check-out service. The least expensive rooms offered by the hotel are labeled "Ashford," while the higher-priced units are called either "Laguna View" or "Oceanfront."

The hotel is linked to El San Juan Hotel (the facilities of one can be charged to a room at the other), and a frequent shuttle service runs between the two hotels.

Dining/Entertainment: The Lotus Flower is one of the island's premier Chinese restaurants (see Chapter 6). Sweeney, one of the best seafood houses, offers a choice of both Caribbean and Maine lobster along with Florida stone crab. The Capriccio has seafood prepared northern Italian style as well as a variety of other classic Italian dishes. There are also Las Palmas and Tony Roma's. La Posada, open 24 hours, is known for its prime beef and seafood. For nighttime entertainment, La Fiesta offers live Latin music, or you can dance to the disco beat at Isadora's. The glittering modern casino at the Condado Plaza is perhaps the most frequented in the entire Caribbean.

Services: Room service, laundry, chaise longues, and towels provided free at beach and pool.

Facilities: Five swimming pools, water sports, fitness center in the Laguna wing, two lit Laykold tennis courts, business center.

RADISSON AMBASSADOR PLAZA HOTEL & CASINO, 1369 Ashford Ave., San Juan, PR 00907. Tel. 809/721-7300, or toll free 800/468-8512. Fax 809/723-6151. 146 rms, 87 suites. A/C TV TEL **Bus:** A7.
$ Rates: Winter, $200–$330 single; $210–$340 double; from $410 suite. Off-season, $175–$265 single; $185–$275 double; from $335 suite. Breakfast $10 extra. AE, DC, MC, V. **Parking:** $5.

Although it had always enjoyed an enviable reputation on the Condado, the Radisson Ambassador Plaza emerged as a star-studded hotel after New York entrepreneur Eugene Romano poured more than $40 million into its restoration in 1990. The hotel offers rich doses of glamour as well as big-time pizzazz, with its Czech and Murano chandeliers; hand-blown wall sconces; acres of Turkish, Greek, and Italian marble; and yards of exotic hardwoods.

The accommodations are located in a pair of high-rise towers, one of which is devoted exclusively to suites. Each suite is decorated in a style inspired by 18th-century Versailles, 19th-century London, Imperial China, or art deco California and Paris. Each has cable color TV with remote control and a choice of about half a dozen pay-per-view movies, plus a breeze-filled balcony with outdoor furniture.

Dining/Entertainment: The restorers took care not to diminish the stature of perhaps the most famous Howard Johnson restaurant in the chain—the only one catering to late-night gamblers. More intriguing is Giuseppe's, for its northern Italian cuisine. The Jade Beach Chinese restaurant offers Mandarin decor and Szechuan and Cantonese cuisine. The casino has an impressive battery of ringing bells, flashing lights, more slot machines than any casino on the Condado, and a resident singer/pianist who performs in a quiet corner bar.

Services: 24-hour concierge, VIP floors with extra amenities and enhanced services, a social director who offers a changing array of daily activities, room service (daily 6:30 to midnight), babysitting, laundry.

Facilities: Penthouse-level fitness and health club, beauty salon, four different bar/lounges, rooftop swimming pool, business center (staffed with typists, translators, guides, and stenographers).

EXPENSIVE

THE CONDADO BEACH TRIO, 1061 Ashford Ave., Condado, San Juan, PR 00907. Tel. 809/721-6090, or toll free 800/468-2775 in the U.S. Fax 809/468-2775. 241 rms, 4 suites (Condado Beach Hotel); 219 rms, 17 suites (La Concha Hotel). A/C TV TEL **Bus:** T1.
$ Rates: Condado Beach Hotel, winter, $180–$205 single; $190–$215 double; from $255 suite. Off-season, $135–$150 single; $145–$165 double; from $220 suite. La Concha Hotel, winter, $150–$185 single; $160–$190 double; from $275 suite. Off-season, $125–$145 single; $135–$155 double; from $180 suite. Breakfast $8–$12 extra. AE, DC, MC, V. **Parking:** $5.

In 1991, Carnival Cruise Lines and other investors bought a sprawling trio of Condado properties and (after renovation) incorporated them into a coherent whole. The original hostelries were El Centro (built in the 1970s as the largest convention center in the Caribbean), La Concha, and the Condado Beach Hotel.

San Juan ✪
PUERTO RICO

Caribe Hilton **4**
Casa San Jose **1**
Casablanca **12**
Condado Beach Trio **8**
Condado Lagoon **9**
Condado Plaza **5**
El Canario by the Lagoon **10**
El Canario Inn **11**
El San Juan Hotel & Casino **16**
Empress Oceanfront **17**
Excelsior **6**
Galeria San Juan **2**
Holiday Inn Crowne Plaza **18**
La Condesa Inn **14**
Radisson Ambassador Plaza **13**
Radisson Normandie **3**
Ramada Hotel Condado **8**
Regency Hotel **7**
Sands Hotel & Casino **15**

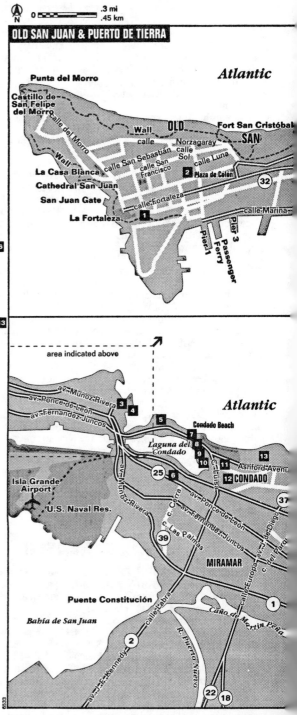

.3 mi
0 ━━━━━
.45 km
N

OLD SAN JUAN & PUERTO DE TIERRA

Punta del Morro

Castillo de San Felipe del Morro

Atlantic

Wall

OLD

Fort San Cristóbal

calle Norzagaray

SAN

calle del Morro

calle San Sebastián
calle San Francisco
calle Sol
calle Luna

Wall

La Casa Blanca

Cathedral San Juan

San Juan Gate

2 Plaza de Colón

32

calle Fortaleza

calle Marina

La Fortaleza **1**

Pier 3

Pier 1

Passenger Ferry

area indicated above

av. Muñoz Rivera
av. Ponce de León
av. Fernández Juncos

3 **4**

5

Atlantic

Condado Beach

7

Laguna del Condado

8

9

10

11 Ashford Avenue

13

Isla Grande Airport

25 **6**

12 CONDADO

37

U.S. Naval Res.

av. Muñoz Rivera

c. Cerra

av. Ponce de León
av. Fernández Juncos

c. de Diego

39

c. Las Palmas

MIRAMAR

calle Europa
av. del Parque

Puente Constitución

c. del Parque

1

Bahía de San Juan

calle Labra

Caño de Martín Peña

2

av. J.F. Kennedy

R. Puerto Nuevo

22 **18**

0533

SAN JUAN ACCOMMODATIONS

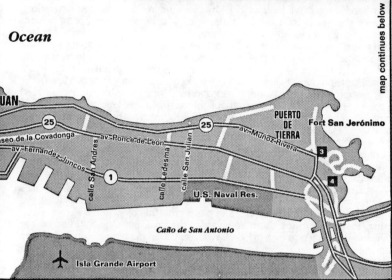

Ocean

JUAN

(25) paseo de la Covadonga

av. Fernandez Juncos

(25) av. Ponce de León

calle San Andres

(1)

calle Ledesma

calle San Julian

(25) av. Muñoz Rivera

PUERTO DE TIERRA

Fort San Jerónimo

3

4

U.S. Naval Res.

Caño de San Antonio

✈ Isla Grande Airport

map continues below

Airport

MIRAMAR, CONDADO, SANTURCE, OCEAN PARK & ISLA VERDE

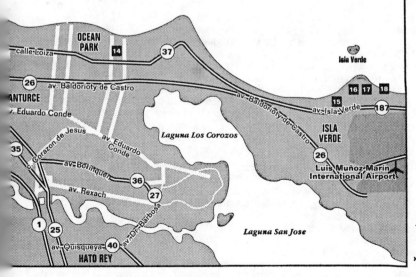

Ocean

calle Loiza

OCEAN PARK

14

(37)

(26) av. Baldorioty de Castro

SANTURCE

av. Eduardo Conde

Corazon de Jesus

av. Eduardo Conde

(35)

av. Botinquen

(36)

av. Rexach

(27)

(1) (25)

av. Quisqueya

(40)

HATO REY

Laguna Los Corozos

Laguna San Jose

Isla Verde

av. Baldorioty de Castro

16 **17** **18**

15

av. Isla Verde

(187)

ISLA VERDE

(26)

Luis Muñoz Marin
International Airport ✈

Airport ✈

Each part of the new trio has a distinct identity that can still be recognized: The Condado Beach Hotel was built in 1919 by the Vanderbilts as the first hotel along what is now the heavily congested Condado. Although its once-elaborate gardens were long ago swallowed up by the surrounding neighborhood, it still has its dignified colonial facade, which some visitors feel resembles an archbishop's palace in Spain. An unglitzy hotel favored for the weddings and catered celebrations of local families, it retains some of its dignified grandeur as well as a legendary double staircase in the lobby—a favorite place for Puerto Rican newlyweds to be photographed. Most of the hotel's accommodations are in a rambling modern wing (invisible from the street) whose red-tile roof mimics the detailing of the original core. Guests have included Randolph Churchill, Henry Morgenthau, Jr., Ted Kennedy, Jack Benny, Bob Hope, Tyrone Power, Plácido Domingo, Julio Iglesias, Michael Bolton, and the Spanish actress Isabel Pantoja.

La Concha Hotel, which is separated from its more glamorous neighbor by the convention center, was originally built in 1959; it comprises one of the longest spans of reinforced concrete in Puerto Rico. Most of its spacious bedrooms are located in a slightly outdated concrete-sided wing, where each enjoys an ocean view. La Concha's rooms, usually priced 15% to 20% less than those at the Condado Beach Hotel, are functionally comfortable and decorated in pastel tropical colors.

Dining/Entertainment: Both hotels share the small but elegant casino on the lobby level of the Condado Beach Hotel. Restaurants on the premises include Vivas (recommended separately in Chapter 6) and the Café del Arte (in the Condado Beach Hotel), and an Italian restaurant (Adagio) in La Concha. Cabaret shows—some of the best on the island—are often presented at El Teatro, in the Convention Center. Also recommended separately is Sirena's (in La Concha), the most architecturally interesting nightclub on the island.

Services: Room service (7am to 11pm), same-day laundry, babysitting, a sports and activities desk, easy access to tour companies and rental-car agencies.

Facilities: Guests at both hotels have free use of all facilities in the trio. Both hotels have their own freshwater pools (with bars and well-accessorized sun decks), two beaches (the one at La Concha is sandier and wider), an array of water-sports options, and two tennis courts. An open-air seaside promenade interconnects the two hotels, away from the traffic congestion of Ashford Avenue.

RAMADA HOTEL CONDADO, 1045 Ashford Ave., San Juan, PR 00907. **Tel. 809/723-8000,** or toll free 800/468-2040. Fax 809/721-8230. 96 rms, 2 suites. A/C MINIBAR TV TEL **Bus:** A7 or 10.
$ Rates: Winter, $150–$170 single or double; from $300 suite. Off-season, $120–$140 single or double; from $200 suite. Continental breakfast $8 extra. AE, MC, V. **Parking:** $5.

Catering to both vacationers and business travelers, this first-class hotel is right on the beach in the heart of the Condado section. You can bask in the sun by the pool or on the sandy beach, have lunch or drinks on the sun deck, and dance the night away in the Polo Lounge to live music that alternates between Latin rhythms and soft romantic melodies. The intimate Ocean View Restaurant serves local specialties and continental fare from 6 to 11pm—but in winter only. Shopping, sights, and island nightlife are within walking distance or just a short ride away. The rooms are classified as standard, superior, or deluxe. Laundry service is available.

REGENCY HOTEL, 1005 Ashford Ave., San Juan, PR 00907. **Tel. 809/721-0505,** or toll free 800/468-2823 in the U.S. Fax 809/722-2909. 109 rms, 18 suites. A/C TV TEL **Bus:** A7.
$ Rates (including continental breakfast): Winter, $135–$175 single or double; $220 suite. Off-season, $135 single or double; $190 suite. Third occupant in any room $20 per day extra. AE, DC, MC, V. **Parking:** $5.

Clean, comfortable, and recently remodeled, this pink-and-white-sided hotel is close to more expensive competitors in a desirable and prominent neighborhood of the Condado. You'll register in a small and deliberately simple lobby before taking an elevator to one of the uncomplicated, pastel-colored bedrooms. Most of the accommodations offer a balcony with ocean or city views. On the premises there's a bar as well as the St. Moritz restaurant, an elegant dining enclave with conservatively classic food. Although the hotel has its own small-scale freshwater swimming pool, some guests prefer to use the pool, the casino, and the dining and drinking facilities of the Condado Plaza next door.

MODERATE

CONDADO LAGOON HOTEL, calle Clemenceau 6 (P.O. Box 13145), San Juan, PR 00908. Tel. 809/721-0170. Fax 809/724-4356. 46 rms, 2 suites. A/C MINIBAR TV TEL **Bus:** A7.

$ **Rates** (including continental breakfast): Winter, $85 single; $95 double; $150 suite. Off-season, $70 single; $80 double; $130 suite. AE, MC, V. **Parking:** Free.

 In Condado at the corner of Joffre Street, this hotel is small and personal. If you're booking from the States, allow plenty of lead time (two or three weeks will do) since rooms go fast both in- and off-season. All the rooms, suitably furnished, have refrigerators, and guests can enjoy the hotel's swimming pool. Meals are available at the Ajili Mojili restaurant if you learn to pronounce it—it's named after a garlic-and-onion sauce created at the hotel. Although the establishment isn't on the beach, the sands are only a short walk away; it's a block from the main street of Condado. Babysitting is available, and room service is offered from 7am to 10pm.

EL CANARIO BY THE LAGOON HOTEL, calle Clemenceau 4, San Juan, PR 00907. Tel. 809/722-5058, or toll free 800/533-2649. Fax 809/723-8590. 40 rms. A/C TV TEL **Bus:** A7 or 2.

$ **Rates** (including continental breakfast and morning newspaper): Winter, $85–$95

Ⓕ FROMMER'S SMART TRAVELER: HOTELS

VALUE-CONSCIOUS TRAVELERS SHOULD TAKE ADVANTAGE OF THE FOLLOWING:

1. Off-season reductions. All hotels grant them (from 20% to 60%) from mid-April to mid-December.
2. Greatly reduced rates for children who stay in a parent's room. Sometimes children under 12 stay free.
3. Reductions in rates if you pay cash.
4. Accommodation at a Puerto Rican guesthouse in a room with a shared bath.
5. Air-and-land packages, which in the long run usually work out cheaper for you.
6. The Modified American Plan (MAP), which is usually cheaper than ordering meals à la carte.
7. Any special packages offered for honeymooners, divers, tennis players, golfers, and so on.

QUESTIONS TO ASK IF YOU'RE ON A BUDGET

1. Is there a surcharge for local or long-distance calls? Usually there is. In some hotels it can be an astonishing 40%.
2. Is service included in the rates quoted, or will 10% to 15% be added to your final bill? It makes a big difference.
3. Is breakfast included? If not, it can easily add as much as $80 per week to your final bill.
4. Is the 7% government tax included in the quoted rate? It can make a big difference in your final bill after a few days.

single; $95–$105 double. Off-season, $65–$75 single; $75–$85 double. AE, DC, MC, V. **Parking:** Free.

A European-style bed-and-breakfast hotel operated by Keith and Jude Olson, El Canario is situated in a quiet residential neighborhood just a short block from Condado Beach. The attractive rooms all have their own balconies and cable TVs, and the hotel has a guest laundry and an in-house tour desk. A relaxing, informal atmosphere prevails.

INEXPENSIVE

CASABLANCA, calle Caribe 57, San Juan, PR 00907. Tel. 809/722-7139. Fax 809/722-7139. 7 rms (all with bath). **Bus:** A7, T1, or 2.

$ Rates: Winter (including continental breakfast), $50–$65 single; $60–$75 double. Off-season, $35–$50 single; $45–$60 double. AE, MC, V.

This informal guesthouse occupies a valuable plot of land just a few paces from the Condado. Originally built as a guesthouse in the 1940s, it was expanded by a former resident of Massachusetts, Alex Leighton. You'll find it behind a wraparound veranda, a wall, and a garden across Ashford Avenue. Inside, the small and simple guest rooms have ceiling fans or air conditioners and copies of movie posters from the golden age of Hollywood. An honor bar is open throughout the day, turning the front porch into a social center for guests. You shouldn't expect the Ritz if you select this place, but you'll probably benefit from the advice that the management has accumulated since they've been on the Condado. Only street parking is available.

EL CANARIO INN, 1317 Ashford Ave., San Juan, PR 00907. Tel. 809/722-3861, or toll free 800/443-0266. Fax 809/722-0391. 25 rms (all with bath). A/C TV TEL **Bus:** M3 or M7.

$ Rates (including continental breakfast and morning newspaper): Winter, $75 single; $85 double. Off-season, $60 single; $70 double. Two-night minimum stay required in winter. AE, DC, MC, V.

This inn offers one of the best bed-and-breakfast values in San Juan. You'll recognize the building by its arched veranda and porte-cochère (an extended porchlike roof), which covers a side yard filled with plants, a fountain, and a gazebo. Keith and Jude Olson are the accommodating owners. The hotel, completely remodeled in 1988, consists of a main house and two nearby sets of servants' quarters, all linked by a terrace. On the premises are an outdoor breakfast bar and lots of quiet corners for conversation. Each room is furnished with two double beds, twin beds, or a double bed. There is a communal kitchen, useful if you feel like cooking, although many restaurants are close by. The beach is a short block away, and a tour desk is available in the lobby.

4. MIRAMAR

Miramar, a residential sector, is very much a part of metropolitan San Juan, and a long brisk walk will take you where the action is. The beach, regrettably, is at least half a mile away.

HOTEL EXCELSIOR, avenida Ponce de León 801, San Juan PR 00907. Tel. 809/721-7400, or toll free 800/223-9815. Fax 809/723-0068. 130 rms, 10 suites. A/C TV TEL **Bus:** T1 or 2.

$ Rates: Winter, $121–$149 single; $137–$165 double; $179 suite. Off-season, $93–$121 single; $107–$134 double; $145 suite. Children under 10 stay free in parents' room; cribs free. Continental breakfast $3.95 extra. AE, MC, V. **Parking:** Free.

Handsome accommodations and good service are offered at this hotel. The bedrooms have been completely refurbished; many have fully equipped kitchenettes, and all have hairdryers, two phones (one in the bathroom), and marble vanities. Included in the rates are use of the swimming pool, daily coffee, a newspaper, shoeshines, and transportation to the nearby beach, as well as parking in the underground garage or the adjacent parking lot. This hotel is known for its excellent maintenance and meticulous housekeeping.

The award-winning Augusto's Restaurant is open for lunch Tuesday through Friday and for dinner Monday through Saturday; El Gazebo serves breakfast daily at poolside. A cocktail lounge, an exercise room, and a beauty shop complete the hotel's facilities. Services include laundry and babysitting.

5. OCEAN PARK

LA CONDESA INN, calle Cacique 2071, San Juan, PR 00911. Tel. 809/727-3698. 16 rms (all with bath). A/C TV **Directions:** Take a taxi.
$ Rates: Winter, $73 single; $73–$85 double. Off-season, $48–$61 single; $61–$73 double. Breakfast $6 extra; lunch or light dinner from $12. AE, MC, V.
The former private residence of the Spanish consul is now La Condesa Inn, located directly east of the airport in the residential Ocean Park–Condado area, just 60 yards from San Juan's most spacious beach and about a five-minute drive from most of the casinos, restaurants, and entertainment centers. Because this guesthouse is small, reserve and plan accordingly. All the comfortably furnished bedrooms have air conditioning and private bath, cable color TV, and clock radio. There's a swimming pool and Jacuzzi. The bar is open until midnight daily. Street parking is available.

6. ISLA VERDE

Beach-bordering Isla Verde is closer to the airport than the other sections of San Juan. The hotels here are farther from Old San Juan than those in Miramar, Condado, and Ocean Park. However, a few of these establishments are among the deluxe showcases of the Caribbean. If you don't mind the isolation and want to be near fairly good beaches, then you might consider one of the following hotels:

VERY EXPENSIVE

EL SAN JUAN HOTEL AND CASINO, Isla Verde Ave. (Rte. 37; P.O. Box 2872), San Juan, PR 00902. Tel. 809/793-1000, or toll free 800/468-2818. Fax 809/253-0178. 372 rms, 20 suites. A/C MINIBAR TV TEL **Bus:** A7, M7, or T1.
$ Rates: Winter, $285–$405 single; $305–$425 double; from $520 suite. Off-season, $215–$335 single; $235–$355 double; from $410 suite. Breakfast buffet $5 extra. AE, DC, MC, V. **Parking:** $5.
★ For dozens of reasons involving more than its spectacular building and lavishly decorated interior, this is considered the best hotel in Puerto Rico and possibly the entire Caribbean basin. Built in the 1950s, it was restored with the infusion of $45 million. The hotel is surrounded by 350 palms, century-old banyans, and gardens. The sandy beach with its almond trees is probably the finest in the San Juan area. At the hotel's river pool, currents and cascades evoke a freshwater jungle stream with lagoons.

The hotel's lobby may be the most opulent and memorable in the Caribbean. Totally sheathed in russet-colored marble and hand-carved mahogany paneling, the public rooms stretch on almost endlessly.

The accommodations have intriguing touches of high-tech. Each makes maximum use of irregular spaces to include such amenities as dressing rooms, three phones,

---

(F) FROMMER'S COOL FOR KIDS: HOTELS

El San Juan Hotel and Casino *(see p. 103)* This hotel, although expensive, offers more programs for children than any other hotel on Puerto Rico. Its supervised Kids Klub provides daily activities—ranging from face painting to swimming lessons—for children 5 to 12 years of age.

Empress Oceanfront Hotel *(see p. 105)* Although this moderately priced hotel doesn't provide specific activities for children, all its units have two double beds. Thus, two children under 12 can stay here free.

Caribe Hilton *(see p. 95)* Children under 16 stay free in their parents' room at this deluxe hotel, which has two swimming pools and is situated in a 17-acre tropical park.

---

video-linked TVs, and ceiling fans. A few feature Jacuzzis. Each benefits from a harmonious color scheme of restful but stimulating Caribbean colors. About 150 of the accommodations are in the outer reaches of the garden. Each is designed as a rustic but comfortable bungalow. Known as casitas, they include the accessories that most honeymooners fantasize about, including Roman tubs, atrium showers, and access to the fern-lined paths of a tropical jungle a few steps away.

Dining/Entertainment: La Veranda Restaurant, near the sands, is open 24 hours. Dar Tiffany, a steak-and-seafood restaurant, is open nightly; or you might prefer Don Juan, an upscale restaurant offering nouvelle Caribbean cuisine. Good Italian food is served for lunch and dinner at La Piccola Fontane. Or you can promenade down a re-creation of a Hong Kong waterfront street to a Chinese restaurant called Back Street Hong Kong. The in-house casino is open daily from noon to 4am.

Services: 24-hour room service, dry cleaning, babysitting, massage.

Facilities: Rooftop health club, water sports, steam room, sauna.

SANDS HOTEL & CASINO, 187 Isla Verde Ave., Isla Verde, PR 00913. Tel. 809/791-6100, or toll free 800/443-2009. Fax 809/791-8525. 397 rms, 17 suites. A/C TV TEL **Bus:** A7, M7, or T1.

$ Rates: Winter, $265–$325 single; $285–$345 double; from $390 suite. Off-season, $200–$250 single; $220–$270 double; from $340 suite. Breakfast $11.50 extra. AE, DC, MC, V. **Parking:** $5.

Originally built about 40 years ago as the Americana, this hotel received a new lease on life in 1987, when it was overhauled and became a Caribbean version of the Sands Hotel in Atlantic City. Today, amid verdant plantings, pink marble floors, and a somewhat stripped-down version of its 1987 renovation, it enjoys a high occupancy rate and the attention of many tour operators throughout the Americas. The bedrooms are comfortable but simple, often with sea views and (unstocked) refrigerators. The most desirable guest rooms are in the Plaza Club, a mini-hotel within the hotel. It offers a private entrance, concierge service, complimentary food and beverage buffets, and private spa and beach facilities.

Dining/Entertainment: The hotel's most upscale restaurant is Valentino's, which serves northern Italian cuisine. Equally appealing is Ruth Chris Steak House, and Tucano's is a 24-hour tropical theme restaurant serving seafood and Caribbean cuisine. Simple beachfront dining is offered at the Boardwalk Grill. The in-house nightclub offers revue-style spoofs of Hollywood legends and glittery Vegas-inspired revues, depending on bookings. The in-house casino is also popular.

Services: 24-hour room service, babysitting, laundry, limousine, massage.

Facilities: The resort boasts what is said to be the Caribbean's largest free-form swimming pool, complete with waterfalls, rockscapes, and a swim-up bar. There are also a business center and scuba-diving facilities.

EXPENSIVE

HOLIDAY INN CROWNE PLAZA HOTEL & CASINO, Rte. 187 km 1.5, San Juan, PR 00979. Tel. 809/253-2929, or toll free 800/HOLIDAY in the U.S. and Canada. Fax 809/253-0079. 22 rms. 32 suites. A/C TV TEL **Bus:** T1.
$ Rates: Winter, $175.50–$215.50 single; $175.50–$225.50 double; from $250.50 suite. Off-season, $155.50–$195.50 single; $165.50–$205.50 double; from $230.50 suite. Breakfast $12.25 extra. AE, DC, MC, V. **Parking:** $10 (valet), $6 (self).

This is one of the newest and most easterly of the grand modern hotels of San Juan, and it's the leading Caribbean showcase of the Holiday Inn chain. Set on a landscaped plot of seafront close to the airport, the hotel incorporates tropical themes and colors into its decor. Rising 12 soundproofed stories above a beach, the resort has attracted a loyal clientele from North America and the Caribbean since it opened in 1991.

You register in a large but simple lobby sheathed with beige marble. Each bedroom offers an ocean view and is decorated in pastel shades of peach or mint green. Bathrooms, constructed in both marble and tile, are equipped with hairdryers and a phone. Each accommodation is double insulated against noise from the nearby airport.

Dining/Entertainment: The premier dining spot is Windows on the Sea, an oceanfront emporium serving international and Puerto Rican food. The Crowne Room is a 55-seat steak-and-seafood restaurant. The Tropics Lounge offers drinking and dancing for an adult crowd every evening beginning at 5pm. The hotel also has a large casino, El Tropical, whose unusual decor includes illuminated replicas of puffy overhead clouds, carpeting whose colors reflect the hues of the rain forest, and hints of jungle vegetation amid hundreds of slot machines.

Services: Laundry, room service (6:30am to 11pm daily), babysitting. On those floors offering enhanced facilities and services, a concierge staff provides free continental breakfast and complimentary early-evening hors d'oeuvres.

Facilities: A large, free-form swimming pool with swim-up bar, a sandy beachfront studded with palm trees and sea grapes, car-rental facilities, a tour desk, children's game room, children's pool, fitness center, an in-house gift shop, and both a sports club and a beach club offering land and water sports.

MODERATE

EMPRESS OCEANFRONT HOTEL, calle Amapola 2, Isla Verde, PR 00913. Tel. 809/791-3083, or toll free 800/678-0757. Fax 809/791-1423. 30 rms. A/C TV TEL **Bus:** T1.
$ Rates: Winter, $128 single; $148–$168 double. Off-season, $68 single; $88–$128 double. Breakfast from $5.25 extra. AE, DC, MC, V. **Parking:** Free for hotel guests.

Set on 2½ acres of rocky headlands jutting out from the coastline of a quiet neighborhood in Isla Verde, this four-story pink-sided hotel, built on the site of a former private home, is efficiently run by a local Anglo-Latino family who immigrated to Puerto Rico from Brooklyn. From its enclosed swimming pool terrace, you'll enjoy one of the most sweeping views anywhere of the high-rise hotels and valuable real estate nearby.

On the premises is a popular evening bar, the Blue Dolphin, and a likeable restaurant, Sonny's Oceanfront Place for Ribs (see Chapter 6). There's a Jacuzzi near the pool; the pleasantly airy decor is inspired by the tropics.

WHERE TO DINE IN SAN JUAN

San Juan has the widest array of restaurants in the Caribbean. In addition to local fare, you can enjoy continental, American, and even Chinese, Mexican, and Japanese cuisines. In recent years, many restaurants have shown a greater appreciation for traditional Puerto Rican cooking; local specialties now appear on the menus of leading restaurants, as well as wide-ranging cuisines. Whenever possible, chefs make use of local ingredients, which enhances all their dishes.

Before searching for a local restaurant, you might want to review "Food and Drink," in Chapter 1.

Many of San Juan's best restaurants are in the resort hotels along the Condado and at Isla Verde. Some require reservations, but others don't. The listings indicate policy on reservations.

Most restaurants serve lunch from noon to 2:30pm and dinner from 8 to 10pm, although the hours vary from establishment to establishment. There has been a restaurant explosion in San Juan in the past few years. Many of the newer ones are off the beaten tourist path. However, some of these newer places have not achieved the fine quality found at many of the older and more traditional restaurants.

In Puerto Rico, a "Very Expensive" restaurant is one charging more than $50 per person for a meal, excluding drinks and service. In restaurants classified as "Expensive" or "Moderate," meals range from $25 to $50, and from $15 to $25, respectively. Any meal under $15 is definitely "Inexpensive."

1. OLD SAN JUAN

EXPENSIVE

AMADEUS, calle San Sebastián 106. Tel. 722-8635.
 Cuisine: CARIBBEAN. **Reservations:** Recommended. **Bus:** M2, M3, or T1.
$ Prices: Appetizers $3–$9; main courses $7–$16. AE, MC, V.
 Open: Tues–Sun noon–2am (kitchen closes at 12:30am).
Housed in a brick-and-stone building that was constructed in the 18th century by a wealthy merchant, Amadeus offers Caribbean food with a nouvelle twist. You might enjoy an appetizer of fried green plantains with caviar and fish mousse, fried dumplings in guava sauce, a cassoulet of shrimp with black beans and sausages, or rabbit with prunes and red-wine sauce. The establishment lies in the heart of the old city, across from the side of the Church of San José.

LA CHAUMIÈRE, calle Tetuan 367. Tel. 722-3330.

Cuisine: FRENCH. **Reservations:** Recommended. **Bus:** A7, T1, or 2.
$ Prices: Appetizers $5.50–$12.50; main courses $21.50–$36.50. AE, DC, MC, V.
Open: Dinner only, Mon–Sat 6pm–midnight. **Closed:** July–Aug.

✪ Behind the Tapía Theater, La Chaumière is decorated like an inn in provincial France, with heavy ceiling beams, black-and-white checkerboard floors, large rows of wine racks, and half-timbered walls. Menu items include fresh goose liver in port-wine sauce; rack of baby lamb provençal; chateaubriand for one; pâté maison made with pork, chicken, and duck liver; and daily specials, such as fish soup. Veal Oscar and oysters Rockefeller also appear on the menu.

YUKIYU, calle Recinto Sur 311. Tel. 721-0653.
Cuisine: JAPANESE. **Reservations:** Recommended. **Bus:** A7, T1, or 2.
$ Prices: Appetizers $4–$6.95; main courses $13.95–$17.95; fixed-price dinners $19.95–$35.75; sushi $2.50 apiece. AE, MC, V.
Open: Lunch Mon–Sat noon–2:20pm; dinner Mon–Fri 5–11pm, Sat 7–11pm.

Traditional Japanese and Oriental cooking techniques are combined in this restaurant in the old town. Its sushi bar is acclaimed as the best in the Caribbean, although the tabs mount quickly. Sushi is available at both lunch and dinner, although the teppanyaki grill at the front, where your own personal chef will attend to you, is open only for dinner. The dining room itself is postmodern, all gray, and monochromatic.

Against this backdrop, the various chefs tempt you with hibachi chicken or chicken with scallops and sesame seeds. You might begin with miso soup or steamed pork dumplings, then go on to a shrimp-and-vegetable tempura, perhaps filet of sole with capers. Fresh yellowfin tuna with teriyaki is a favorite, as is the chicken teriyaki. The sushi bar features everything from squid and octopus to sea urchins and raw clams, although the most popular items are the raw butterfly shrimp and raw salmon.

MODERATE

AL DENTE, calle Recinto Sur 309. Tel. 723-7303.
Cuisine: SICILIAN. **Reservations:** Recommended. **Bus:** A7, T1, or 2.
$ Prices: Appetizers $4.50–$8; main courses $10–$15. AE, MC, V.
Open: Mon–Sat noon–10pm.

Located in the heart of Old San Juan, this restaurant has a decor that might remind you of the trattoria you enjoyed in Palermo, and the food is faithful to the recipes that placed Sicily on the gastronomic map of Europe. Both the dress code and the ambience are relaxing and casual. You might begin with a selection of seafood antipasti, followed by gnocchi with pesto, fettuccine maestro, ravioli, well-seasoned calamari, a savory version of roast goat, or one of the traditional veal or chicken dishes. Brochettes of fresh tuna laced with pepper and Mediterranean herbs is an excellent choice.

EL PATIO DE SAM, calle san Sebastián 102. Tel. 723-1149.
Cuisine: AMERICAN/PUERTO RICAN. **Reservations:** Not required. **Bus:** A7, T1, or 2.
$ Prices: Appetizers $2.50–$7; main courses $9–$28. AE, DC, MC, V.
Open: Sun–Thurs 11am–midnight, Fri–Sat 11am–1:30am.

Located across from the Church of San José, the oldest building on the island, this restaurant faces the statue of Ponce de León, the island's first governor. A popular gathering spot for American expatriates, newspeople, and shopkeepers in the old town, it's known for having the best hamburgers in San Juan. Even though the dining room is not outdoors, it has been transformed into a patio. The illusion is so credible you'll swear you're dining al fresco: Every table is strategically placed near a cluster of potted outdoor plants, and canvas panels and awnings cover the skylight. For a cooling and satisfying lunch, ideal after you've strolled through the streets of Old San

San Juan ★
PUERTO RICO

Al Dente **6**
Amadeus **2**
Augusto's **11**
Back Street Hong Kong **24**
Bombonera, La **3**
Butterfly People Café **8**
Caribe Hilton Hotel **10**
Casona, La **20**
Chart House **17**
Chaumière, La **9**
Che's **23**
Compostela **16**
Dar Tiffany **24**
El Patio
  (Gran Hotel El Convento) **1**
El Patio de Sam **2**
Faisanes, Los **15**
Giuseppe's **18**
Hard Rock Café **5**
Howard Johnson's **18**
L. K. Sweeney & Son, Ltd. **12**
Lotus Flower **12**
Mallorquina, La **4**
Martino's **19**
Mona's Mexican Restaurant **21**
NoNo's **3**
Oasis **13**
Piccola Fontana **24**
Ramiro's **15**
Repostería Kassalta **22**
Scotch & Sirloin **14**
Sonny's Oceanfront Place
  for Ribs **25**
Tasca del Callejon, La **8**
Tony Roma's **12**
Vivas **14**
Yukiyu **7**

OLD SAN JUAN & PUERTO DE TIERRA

.3 mi
0 _____ .45 km

Atlantic

Punta del Morro
Castillo de San Felipe del Morro
Wall
OLD
calle del Morro
calle San Sebastián
Norzagaray
calle Sol
Fort San Cristóbal
SAN
Wall
calle San Francisco
calle Luna
La Casa Blanca
Plaza de Colón
Cathedral San Juan
San Juan Gate
calle Fortaleza
calle Marina
La Fortaleza
Pier 1
Pier 3
Passenger Ferry

32

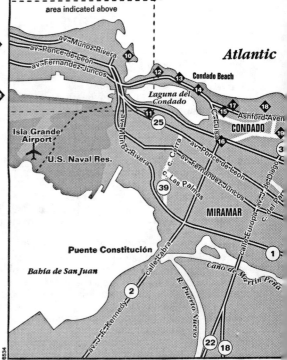

area indicated above

Atlantic

av. Muñoz Rivera
av. Ponce de León
av. Fernández Juncos
Condado Beach
Laguna del Condado
Ashford Aven
CONDADO
Isla Grande Airport
U.S. Naval Res.
c. c. Sierra
av. Muñoz Rivera
c. Luisa
av. Ponce de León
av. Fernández Juncos
c. Las Palmas
MIRAMAR
Puente Constitución
Bahía de San Juan
calle Labra
av. J. F. Kennedy
R. Puerto Nuevo
Caño de Martín Peña
calle Europa

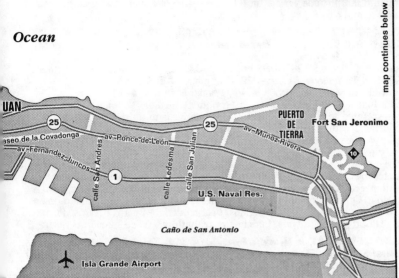

Ocean

UAN

25

aseo de la Covadonga

av.-Ponce-de-León

av.-Fernández-Juncos

calle San Andrés

calle Ledesma

calle San Julián

1

25

av.-Muñoz-Rivera

PUERTO DE TIERRA

Fort San Jeronimo

10

U.S. Naval Res.

Caño de San Antonio

Isla Grande Airport

map continues below

MIRAMAR, CONDADO, SANTURCE, OCEAN PARK & ISLA VERDE

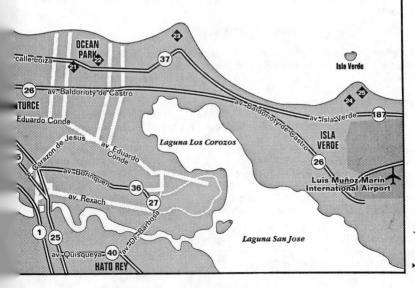

Ocean

OCEAN PARK

calle-Loiza

21

22

23

37

Isla Verde

26

av.-Baldorioty-de-Castro

TURCE

Eduardo Conde

c.-Corazon-de-Jesus

av.-Eduardo Conde

Laguna Los Corozos

av.-Baldorioty-de-Castro

24

25

av.-Isla-Verde

187

ISLA VERDE

av.-Borinquen

36

av. Rexach

27

26

Luis Muñoz Marin International Airport

1

25

av.-Quisqueya

40

c.-Dr.-Barbosa

HATO REY

Laguna San Jose

Airport ✈

Juan, try the black-bean soup, followed by the burger platter and then a key lime tart. Other main dishes include various steaks, barbecued ribs, filet of sole stuffed with crab, and fish and chips.

LA MALLORQUINA, calle San Justo 207. Tel. 722-3261.
   Cuisine: PUERTO RICAN. **Reservations:** Not accepted at lunch, recommended at dinner. **Bus:** A7, T1, or 2.
$ Prices: Appetizers $3.25–$8.95 at lunch, $3.25–$8.95 at dinner; main courses $8.95–$26.95 at lunch, $13.95–$29.95 at dinner. AE, DC, MC, V.
   Open: Lunch Mon–Sat 11:30am–4pm; dinner Mon–Sat 4–10pm.

⑤ San Juan's oldest restaurant was founded in 1848. A bit of Old Spain transplanted to the New World, the restaurant is in a three-story, glassed-in courtyard with arches and antique wall clocks. Even if you've already eaten, you might want to visit just to perch at the old-fashioned wooden bar running the length of the left wall as you enter. The chef specializes in the most typical Puerto Rican rice dish—asopao. You can have it with chicken, shrimp, or lobster and shrimp (if you're feeling extravagant). Arroz con pollo is almost as popular. I suggest that you get your dinner rolling by ordering garlic soup. If that frightens you, relax, gazpacho is also available. Other recommended main dishes are red snapper in a tomato-onion sauce and lobster rice with fried plantains, beef tenderloin Puerto Rican style, and assorted seafood stewed in wine. Lunch is busy, but dinners are sometimes quiet.

LA TASCA DEL CALLEJÓN, calle Fortaleza 317. Tel. 721-1689.
   Cuisine: SPANISH. **Reservations:** Recommended. **Bus:** A7, T1, or 2.
$ Prices: Tapas $3.50–$14.95; main courses $12–$25. AE, DC, MC, V.
   Open: Mon–Thurs noon–11pm, Fri–Sat noon–2am, Sun 5–11pm.

This is the only combination cabaret and taverna in Puerto Rico, and the entertainment is as important as the cuisine. In a large brick-sided room reminiscent of those in Old Iberia, an attractive staff will interrupt their service to sing, dance, or play the guitar for an enthusiastically applauding crowd.

The specialty here is tapas, an array of hot or cold appetizers that, when ordered in different combinations, make for both a satisfying and a fun meal. Specific dishes include cannelloni stuffed with pâté, octopus in vinaigrette, fabada asturiana (the bean dish of northern Spain), a hearty potato-and-kale soup called caldo gallego, grilled New York sirloin, and paella. No one will mind if you order only a single dish of tapas and drink the night away. Shows usually begin around 7:30pm and continue for several hours.

INEXPENSIVE

BUTTERFLY PEOPLE CAFE, calle Fortaleza 152. Tel. 723-2432.
   Cuisine: CONTINENTAL/AMERICAN. **Reservations:** Not required. **Bus:** A7, T1, or 2.
$ Prices: Appetizers $3.25–$4.50; main courses $8.50–$10. AE, DC, MC, V.
   Open: Lunch only, Mon–Sat 10am–6pm.

On the second floor of a restored mansion in Old San Juan, next to the world's largest gallery devoted to butterflies (see "Savvy Shopping," in Chapter 7), you can dine in this café, which opens onto a patio, with 15 tables serving lunch and drinks. The café specializes in tropical and light European fare prepared with fresh ingredients.

You might begin with gazpacho or vichyssoise, follow with quiche or one of the daily specials, and top it all off with chocolate mousse or the tantalizing raspberry-chiffon pie with fresh raspberry sauce. A full bar offers tropical specialties featuring piña coladas; fresh-squeezed Puerto Rican orange juice; and Fantasias—a frappé of seven fresh fruits. Wherever you look, framed butterflies will delight you.

HARD ROCK CAFE, calle Recinto Sur 253. Tel. 724-7625.
   Cuisine: AMERICAN. **Reservations:** Not required. **Bus:** A7, T1, or 2.
$ Prices: Appetizers $3.25–$8.95; main courses $8.95–$15.95. AE, MC, V.
   Open: Daily 11am–midnight. (Bar, daily 11am–2am.)

Filled with rock 'n' roll memorabilia, this café lies in a historic section of Old San

Juan. Serving a "classic" American cuisine against a backdrop of loud rock music, it is firmly entrenched. Between drinks and burgers, diners look at the café's collection of artifacts from the rock 'n' roll hall of fame, ranging from a wig worn by Elton John to a jacket worn by John Lennon. There's also Pink Floyd's guitar and Phil Collins's drumsticks. Throughout the day, well-stuffed sandwiches and juicy burgers are served, although many prefer to come here for dinner, filling up on fajitas, barbecued chicken, pork ribs, or even the catch of the day. The chili will set you ablaze. There's even a selection of salads. This is probably the most frequented dining spot in the old town, and there's even a gift shop selling such merchandise as Hard Rock Café T-shirts.

LA BOMBONERA, calle San Francisco 259. Tel. 722-0658.
   Cuisine: PUERTO RICAN. **Reservations:** Recommended. **Bus:** M2, M3, or T1.
$ Prices: Main courses $5–$11. AE, MC, V.
   Open: Daily 7:30am–8:30pm.

 This long-enduring favorite was established in 1902, and ever since it has been offering homemade pastries and endless cups of coffee (said to be the best served in Old San Juan) in a traditional colonial decor. For decades it was a rendezvous for the island's literati and for old San Juan families, but now it has been discovered by foreign visitors. The food is authentic and inexpensive. La Bombonera serves sandwiches, but most patrons prefer one of the main regional dishes, perhaps rice with squid, roast leg of pork, or seafood asopao. For dessert, you might choose an apple, pineapple, or prune pie or one of many types of flan. Service is polite, if a bit rushed, and the place fills up quickly at lunch.

2. CONDADO

VERY EXPENSIVE

GIUSEPPE'S, in the Radisson Ambassador Plaza Hotel, 1369 Ashford Ave. Tel. 721-7300.

Ⓕ FROMMER'S SMART TRAVELER:
RESTAURANTS

VALUE-CONSCIOUS DINERS SHOULD
CONSIDER THE FOLLOWING:

1. Daily specials, which are often cheaper than the regular fare on the à la carte menu.
2. The cost of alcohol. Your tab will mount rapidly with liquor and especially wine. Have your cocktails before happy hour ends (usually 7pm at most places).
3. A meal at a restaurant serving Puerto Rican dishes, such as La Mallorquina and La Bombonera. These restaurants are invariably cheaper than the French/continental establishments.
4. Having a light lunch of sandwiches or hamburgers at one of the many beach bars and cafés during the day and saving your big meal for the evening.
5. Fixed-price menus, which are often more economical than ordering à la carte.
6. Whether service is included. Most restaurants add 10% to 15% to the bill, and there's no need to tip unless service has been exceptionally good.

Cuisine: ITALIAN. **Reservations:** Recommended. **Bus:** A7.
$ Prices: Appetizers $8.50–$10.50; main courses $17–$40. AE, DC, MC, V.
Open: Lunch Mon–Fri noon–3pm; dinner Mon–Sat 6pm–midnight, Sun noon–10pm.

This is one of the more sophisticated Italian restaurants in San Juan, catering to a clientele who appreciate the nuances of fine cuisine and service. The decor of neutral colors, stucco arches, and unobtrusive trompe l'oeil murals seems designed to enhance the attractiveness of patrons.

Menu items include just about everything in the major repertoire of northern Italian cuisine. You'll find a specialty version of Caesar salad; fresh mushrooms in garlic sauce; a succulent half-melted version of fresh mozzarella *in carozza;* a variety of seafood, veal, chicken, and beef dishes; and virtually any pasta dish ever created, which, if not on the menu, will be specially concocted by the kitchen staff.

LOS FAISANES, avenida Magdalena 1108, Condado. Tel. 725-2801.
Cuisine: INTERNATIONAL. **Reservations:** Recommended. **Bus:** A7, T1, or 2.
$ Prices: Appetizers $6–$12; main courses $17–$35. AE, DC, MC, V.
Open: Sun–Fri noon–11:30pm, Sat 6–11:30pm.

Located in a masonry-sided Iberia-inspired house on a relatively quiet corner of the Condado, this is considered one of the finest and most discreetly elegant restaurants in San Juan. The restrained decor is reminiscent of what you might find in a comfortably sedate private home. There's a sophisticated array of wines and a selection of dishes inspired by the cuisines of France, Italy, and the Hispanic world. Several pheasant preparations are usually available (including one with sherry and mango sauce), as well as a changing variety of chicken, beef, veal, and seafood dishes, several of which will be prepared at your table. One specialty is Hemingway-style fresh filet of tuna, cooked with onions, chardonnay, lemon juice, and olive oil.

RAMIRO'S, avenida Magdalena 1106. Tel. 721-9049.
Cuisine: SPANISH/INTERNATIONAL. **Reservations:** Recommended. **Bus:** A7, T1, or 2.
$ Prices: Appetizers $6.95–$29.95; main courses $21.95–$32.95; fixed-price five-course meal $44.95. AE, DC, MC, V.
Open: Lunch Mon–Fri noon–3pm, Sun noon–3:30pm; dinner Mon–Thurs 6:30–10:30pm, Fri–Sat 6:30–11pm, Sun 6–10pm.

Here you'll find a refined cuisine and a touch of Old Spain. One of the most distinguished dining places on Puerto Rico, this elegantly decorated restaurant prepares what it terms a *cocina imaginativa,* sometimes called "New Créole" cooking—a style pioneered by its owner and chef, Jesús Ramiro. You might begin with breadfruit mille feuille with local crabmeat and avocado. For your main course, you can request any fresh fish or meat charcoal-grilled. Rack of lamb is one of the house specialties; you can also enjoy fresh filet of grouper with two different sauces (tamarind sauce and caper sauce). Among the many homemade desserts are caramelized mango on puff pastry with strawberry-and-guava sauce, and "four seasons" chocolate.

EXPENSIVE

CHART HOUSE, 1214 Ashford Ave. Tel. 728-0110.
Cuisine: STEAK/SEAFOOD. **Reservations:** Required on weekends, recommended otherwise. **Bus:** A7, T1, or 2.
$ Prices: Appetizers $4.95–$8.95; main courses $16.50–$24.95. AE, DC, MC, V.
Open: Dinner only, Sun–Thurs 6–11pm, Fri–Sat 6pm–midnight.

This restaurant, one of the best on the island, attracts literally hundreds of locals on any night. It's in a lattice-trimmed villa built in 1910, once the home of the German consul. Today the heavy ceiling beams have been exposed, track lighting has been installed, and paintings have been hung to create a warm ambience. The food is well prepared, with prime rib a specialty. You also can order New England clam chowder, top sirloin, shrimp teriyaki, Australian lobster, Hawaiian chicken, and a copious salad. The special dessert is "mud pie." The Chart House belongs to a chain of restaurants that's based in California.

LOTUS FLOWER, in the Laguna wing of the Condado Plaza Hotel and Casino, 999 Ashford Ave. Tel. 722-0940.
   Cuisine: CHINESE. **Reservations:** Required. **Bus:** A7, T1, or 2.
$ **Prices:** Appetizers $2.50–$14; main courses $15.50–$35. AE, DC, MC, V.
   Open: Lunch Mon–Fri noon–3pm; dinner Mon–Sat 6–11:30pm, Sun 1–11:30pm.

One of the finest Chinese restaurants in the Caribbean overlooks the Condado Lagoon. The chef here is equally at home turning out Hunan, Szechuan, or Cantonese cookery. Specialties include lemon chicken, beef with scallops and shrimp in a hot sauce, and Szechuan Phoenix, made with prime beef and chicken in a hot sauce. Begin your meal with the noodles in sesame sauce, a delectable dish.

MARTINO'S, in the Dutch Inn Hotel & Casino, 55 Condado Ave. Tel. 722-5256.
   Cuisine: ITALIAN. **Reservations:** Recommended. **Bus:** A7.
$ **Prices:** Appetizers $5–$11; main courses $14.95–$34. AE, DC, MC, V.
   Open: Dinner only, daily 6pm–midnight.
Under a steel-and-glass canopy on the 13th (top) floor of this well-known hotel and casino, Martino's offers not only some of the finest service on the Condado, but also a classic Italian cuisine. A critically acclaimed restaurant, it is the domain of its chef and owner, Martin Acosta. His picture windows offer stunning views of the Atlantic and the night lights of the Condado. Even if diners come primarily for the view, they're likely to be pleased with the northern Italian cuisine. Appetizers include hot seafood antipasti or Caesar or spinach salads. You can order one of the homemade pasta dishes for a main course, or seafood suprême, vitello Martino (with shrimp), gnocchi with cream sauce and parmesan, or filet mignon Monnalisa (flambéed at your table). In fact, you can request tableside flambé for almost any dish. Good and reasonably priced wines enhance your dining pleasure.

RESTAURANT COMPOSTELA, avenida Condado 106. Tel. 724-6088.
   Cuisine: SPANISH/PUERTO RICAN. **Reservations:** Recommended. **Bus:** 2.
$ **Prices:** Appetizers $7–$14; main courses $15–$29. AE, DC, MC, V.
   Open: Lunch Mon–Fri noon–3pm; dinner Mon–Sat 6:30–10:30pm.

With a comfortably unpretentious pine-trimmed decor, this restaurant achieves formality through its battalion of formally dressed waiters whose manners evoke Old Spain. Established by a Galician-born family, who named it after the most famous religious shrine (Santiago de Compostela) in northern Spain, the restaurant has achieved a reputation as one of the best in the capital.

Specialties include roasted peppers stuffed with salmon mousse, brochettes of filet studded with truffles, grilled shellfish with brandy sauce, rack of lamb, duck with kiwi sauce, lobster au gratin, breast of partridge with a foie-gras stuffing, a seasonal version of roast pheasant prepared in the chef's style, and two different versions of paella. The wine list is appropriately international.

SCOTCH & SIRLOIN, in La Rada Hotel, 1020 Ashford Ave. Tel. 722-3640.
   Cuisine: STEAKS/SEAFOOD. **Reservations:** Recommended. **Bus:** A7, T1, or 2.
$ **Prices:** Appetizers $3–$9; main courses $18.95–$39; dinner special (5:30–7:30pm) $16.95. AE, DC, MC, V.
   Open: Daily 5:30pm–midnight.
It's probably the most famous independent restaurant on the Condado, long affiliated

with names from show biz and the nearby casinos. (Jackie Gleason, a frequent and loyal client, used to come here with his entourage and order staggering amounts of food and drink.) Set on the lower level of a hotel/condominium complex, the restaurant offers seating on a covered, open-air terrace near a swimming pool overlooking the lagoon. Despite the view outside, I prefer a table inside, where sophisticated and evocative paintings complement the soothing lighting and colors. Everywhere, you'll find a reassuring and warmly masculine allure reflected in the establishment's name.

Menu specialties include ale-battered shrimp, prime aged beef, broiled fresh salmon steak, barbecued pork ribs, chicken or sirloin teriyaki, and a selection of "reef dishes" that are usually brought in fresh each morning. All main courses include the complimentary well-stocked salad bar, which also offers a superb banana bread and a soup of the day; the salad bar selections could constitute a meal in itself.

VIVAS, in the Condado Beach Trio, Ashford Ave. Tel. 721-6090.
   Cuisine: LATIN. **Reservations:** Recommended. **Bus:** T1.
$ **Prices:** Appetizers $6–$11.50; main courses $19.75–$28; Sun brunch $26.75. AE, DC, MC, V.
   Open: Lunch Mon–Fri noon–3pm; dinner daily 6:30–10:30pm; brunch Sun noon–4pm.

Opened in 1992, this restaurant deserves to be better known, even though it's in the most important landmark hotel on the Condado. You can begin your evening listening to music in the Vivas Lounge, and sampling fine champagnes and sparking wines from around the world, among other drinks. The chef calls his cuisine "New World" because it combines the classic traditional dishes of Latin America, ranging from Mexico to Argentina (and even Puerto Rico), together with his own innovative dishes. Appetizers from Brazil might include white-bean quenelles with Malagueta pepper, Dende oil, and a cilantro sauce, or a roasted corn, conch, and red-pepper tamale. Soups are likely to include Dorado shrimp chowder (with corn and potato) or ginger chicken with shiitake mushrooms. Among the more inventive main dishes are grilled Florida swordfish in a ginger/soy/cream sauce and a classic Puerto Rican dish of stuffed pork loin with sausage, olives, peppers, and ham. The lavish Sunday brunch is one of the well-attended events along the Condado.

INEXPENSIVE

OASIS, 1043 Ashford Ave. Tel. 724-2005.
   Cuisine: CUBAN/INTERNATIONAL. **Reservations:** Not required. **Bus:** A7, T1, or 2.
$ **Prices:** Appetizers $2.50–$3.95; main courses $5.50–$22.50. AE, DC, MC, V.
   Open: Lunch daily noon–3pm; dinner daily 6–11pm.

This budget eatery manages to hold its own along the Condado beachfront where prices are sometimes astronomical in the better-known establishments. It's really a family-style dining room with a large variety of "Cuban Créole" dishes, as well as international and Puerto Rican regional specialties. The tables in back, with views of the ocean, are usually taken first.

Although the menu is in English, Spanish may be the only language you'll hear. Caldo gallego, that rich flavored soup of beans and greens, with meat and sausage, is a hearty opener, followed by any number of main courses, such as stuffed Cornish hen, oxtails in a Créole sauce, breaded red snapper filet, or lobster asopao. Paella is another specialty, although at least two diners must order this dish. Good value, good food (and plenty of it), and an informal, relaxed atmosphere keep this place going year after year while other restaurants along the Condado come and go with the seasons.

TONY ROMA'S, in the Condado Plaza Hotel, 999 Ashford Ave. Tel. 721-1000, ext. 2123.
   Cuisine: BARBECUE. **Reservations:** Not accepted. **Bus:** A7.
$ **Prices:** Appetizers $2.75–$5.95; main courses $8.95–$15.95. AE, DC, MC, V.
   Open: Daily noon–midnight.

Efficient and unpretentious, this is Puerto Rico's busiest branch of a chain of eateries that now maintains outlets throughout North America. It's probably one of the least expensive restaurants in the Condado, and as such, is well appreciated for its spicy barbecued food. Menu selections include a wide range of barbecued dishes, such as chicken and several varieties of ribs, as well as hamburgers and large loaves of onion rings.

3. SANTURCE

EXPENSIVE

LA CASONA, calle San Jorge 609, at the corner of avenida Fernández Juncos. Tel. 727-2717.
   Cuisine: SPANISH/INTERNATIONAL. **Reservations:** Required. **Bus:** 1.
$ Prices: Appetizers $6–$12; main courses $17–$35. AE, DC, MC, V.
   Open: Mon–Fri noon–11pm, Sat 6–11pm.

⭐ One of the finest dining rooms on Puerto Rico offers the kind of experience usually found in Madrid, complete with a strolling guitarist. Since 1972 the chefs here have dispensed their special blend of Spanish and international dishes in a turn-of-the-century mansion surrounded by gardens. Guests pass by sweet-scented plants and trailing bougainvillea to enter a much-renovated but still charming and sophisticated dining room. The place draws some of the most fashionable diners in Puerto Rico. Paella marinara, prepared for two or more diners, is a specialty, as is a zarzuela de mariscos, or seafood medley. Another tasty dish is filet of grouper in Basque sauce.

4. MIRAMAR

EXPENSIVE

AUGUSTO'S, in the Hotel Excelsior, avenida Ponce de León 801. Tel. 725-7700.

FROMMER'S COOL FOR KIDS: RESTAURANTS

Caribe Hilton *(see p. 118)* The Sunday brunch here—which is half price for children—is an all-you-can-eat buffet. There's even a clown on hand to delight the children.

NoNo's *(see p. 118)* While touring Old San Juan, you might want to drop in here if your child is yearning for familiar U.S. food. Try the NoNo burger; the prices are low, too.

Butterfly People Café *(see p. 110)* Children take delight in eating lunch in this fantasy world of mounted butterflies. A favorite drink is Fantasia—a frappé made from seven fresh fruits.

Cuisine: INTERNATIONAL. **Reservations:** Required. **Bus:** A7, T1, or 2.
$ **Prices:** Appetizers $5.50–$21; main courses $22–$25; fixed-price lunches $23–$35. AE, MC, V.
Open: Lunch Tues–Fri noon–3pm; dinner Tues–Sat 7–9:30pm. **Closed:** July 7–Aug 1.

An interesting choice is this enclave of European aesthetics and cuisine in the middle of San Juan, although tropical ingredients are used to a significant degree. Augusto's is run by one of Puerto Rico's most successful chefs, Austrian-born August Schreiner, who first came to prominence on the island during his long stay at the Caribe Hilton, where he won many awards for outstanding international cuisine. The restaurant has a sophisticated decor with light-gray walls and masses of fresh flowers. The menu changes frequently, but you might begin with iced zucchini bisque or a Caesar salad with croutons, followed by fresh elk medallions in a juniperberry sauce or roast rack of lamb in a mustard-and-herb crust. For dessert, try the chocolate soufflé if it's available. Other desserts are made from fresh fruits.

5. ISLA VERDE

VERY EXPENSIVE

DAR TIFFANY, in the Hotel El San Juan, Isla Verde Ave. Tel. 791-7272.
Cuisine: SEAFOOD/AMERICAN. **Reservations:** Required. **Bus:** M4 or T1.
$ **Prices:** Appetizers $11.95–$13.95; main courses $18.95–$31.95. AE, DC, MC, V.
Open: Dinner only, daily 6:30–11:30pm.

One of the best choices in San Juan for a taste of the good life, Dar Tiffany is usually jammed, especially on weekends, with the island's resident literati and glitterati, including everybody from Joan Rivers to Eddie Murphy and Raul Julia. On the ground floor of Puerto Rico's most glamorous hotel, it provides considerate service and an elegant etched-glass decor in a multilevel room, with lots of plants and tropical furniture. The wine list is actually more extensive than the food menu, which offers such carefully aged or seasonal specialties as prime rib, filet mignon, veal chops, sea scallops, and filet of fresh Norwegian salmon. Prime dry-aged steaks are a specialty, as are live Maine lobsters and the fresh fish of the day. Salads are superb, especially the Caesar and spinach varieties.

EXPENSIVE

BACK STREET HONG KONG, in the Hotel El San Juan, Isla Verde Ave. Tel. 791-1224.
Cuisine: CHINESE. **Reservations:** Recommended. **Bus:** M4 or T1.
$ **Prices:** Appetizers $2–$10.50; main courses $15.50–$31.50. AE, MC, V.
Open: Mon–Sat 6pm–midnight, Sun noon–midnight.

To reach this restaurant, you head down a re-creation of a waterfront street in Hong Kong. Disassembled from its original home at the 1964–65 New York World's Fair, it was rebuilt with the exposed electrical meters and lopsided facades of its original design intact. A few steps later you enter one of the best Chinese restaurants in the Caribbean, serving Mandarin, Szechuan, and Hunan dishes. Beneath a soaring redwood ceiling, surrounded by teakwood lattices and iron filigree, and served by formally dressed employees, you can enjoy pineapple fried rice served in a real pineapple, a superb version of scallops with orange sauce, Szechuan beef with chicken, or a Dragon and Phoenix (lobster mixed with shrimp).

LA PICCOLA FONTANA, in El San Juan Hotel and Casino, Isla Verde Ave. Tel. 791-1000, ext. 1271.
Cuisine: ITALIAN. **Reservations:** Required. **Bus:** T1.
$ **Prices:** Appetizers $5.50–$11.25; main courses $19–$36. AE, DC, MC, V.

Open: Lunch Mon–Fri noon–3pm; dinner daily 6pm–midnight.

⭐ Right off the luxurious Palm Court in this previously recommended hotel (see Chapter 5), this restaurant serves perhaps the finest classic northern Italian cuisine on Puerto Rico. From its white linen to its classically formal service, La Piccola Fontana enjoys a worldwide reputation. Small and intimate, it's like a jewel box, an octagonal Neo-Palladian room with lattices and crystal chandeliers. Look for the daily specials, such as fish of the day (depending on the catch), or else try one of the eight classic veal dishes. From the sea come such main courses as hot seafood suprême and calamari marinara. However, many diners prefer one of the pasta dishes as their main course, perhaps the homemade manicotti or baked ziti. To begin, there are such temptations as hot seafood antipasti and a Caesar salad. The chocolate cheesecake, a chef's specialty, is a smooth finish.

6. OCEAN PARK

INEXPENSIVE

MONA'S MEXICAN RESTAURANT, calle María Moczó 57. Tel. 728-0140.
  Cuisine: MEXICAN. **Reservations:** Not accepted. **Bus:** T1.
$ **Prices:** Appetizers $3.25–$9.75; main courses $2.25–$10. AE, MC, V.
  Open: Daily 11:30am–midnight. (Bar, open till 2am.)
Occupying pleasant premises in the residential neighborhood of Ocean Park not far from the big resorts of Isla Verde, this restaurant re-creates the allures and textures of Old Mexico in a tropical setting. Consider enjoying a tart margarita at the ample bar area before heading to your table. Specialties include a full array of Tex-Mex specialties—chimichangas, carnitas, enchiladas, tacos, burritos, and nachos.

REPOSTERIA KASSALTA, calle McLeary 1966. Tel. 727-7340.
  Cuisine: SPANISH/PUERTO RICAN. **Reservations:** Not accepted. **Bus:** T1.
$ **Prices:** Full American breakfast $5; soups $4; sandwiches $1.50–$5; pastries from 75¢ each. MC, V.
  Open: Daily 6am–10pm.
This is probably the most famous of the cafeteria/bakery/delicatessens of San Juan because of its reasonable prices and eat-in and take-out foods. It's in Ocean Park, a commercial neighborhood four miles east of Old San Juan. When you get there, you'll enter a cavernous room flanked with modern sun-flooded windows and endless ranks of glass-fronted display cases. Depending on the season, these will be filled with meats, sausages, and pastries appropriate to Christmas, Easter, Thanksgiving, or whatever the forthcoming holiday.

At one end of the room, patrons line up to place their order at a cash register, then carry their selections, cafeteria style, to one of the establishment's many tables. (A knowledge of Spanish is helpful, but not essential.) Among the selections offered are steaming bowls of the best caldo gallego in Puerto Rico. (Served in thick earthenware bowls; laden with collard greens, potatoes, and sausage slices; and accompanied with hunks of bread, this soup makes a meal in itself.) Also popular are Cuban sandwiches (made with sliced pork, cheese, and fried bread), steak sandwiches, octopus salad, and an assortment of omelets.

7. PUNTA LAS MARÍAS

MODERATE

CHE'S, calle Caoba 35. Tel. 726-7202.

Cuisine: ARGENTINE/ITALIAN. **Reservations:** Recommended for lunch, required for dinner. **Bus:** T1.
$ Prices: Appetizers $2.75–$9; main courses $9.50–$30. AE, DC, MC, V.
Open: Sun–Thurs noon–midnight, Fri–Sat noon–1:30am.
Named after the most colorful Latino revolutionary (Che Guevara), this place re-creates some of the color and drama of the Argentine pampas. It's about two miles east of the Condado's resorts. Many of the specialties are grilled in the style preferred by cowherding gauchos. If you're not in the mood for highly seasoned flank steak or any of the grilled meats, you can choose a variety of pastas and veal dishes.

8. SPECIALTY DINING

HOTEL DINING

L. K. SWEENEY & SON LTD., in the Condado Plaza Hotel, 999 Ashford Ave. Tel. 723-5551.
Cuisine: SEAFOOD/INTERNATIONAL. **Reservations:** Recommended. **Bus:** A7.
$ Prices: Appetizers $4.50–$11.90; main courses $16.95–$25.95. AE, MC, V.
Open: Dinner only, daily 6–11pm.
⭐ Imbued with an architectural elegance that resembles a Nantucket version of a London gentleman's club, this stylish eatery is one of the most desirable in a district filled with unusual restaurants. Many diners choose an apéritif (perhaps with a platter of clams, oysters, or shrimp) amid the burnished mahogany, stained glass, and polished marble of Sweeney's Oyster Bar, where a pianist plays every night between 6pm and midnight.
Dining room specialties include clams casino, grilled king salmon, individual rack of lamb, fresh fish imported daily from the markets of Boston and New York (sautéed, poached, or blackened), crab cakes, an herb-laced version of Caribbean seafood stew, and a wide variety of thick and juicy steaks. Jackets for men are recommended.

SUNDAY BRUNCH

CARIBE HILTON, calle Los Rosales. Tel. 721-0303.
Cuisine: INTERNATIONAL. **Reservations:** Recommended. **Bus:** A7.
$ Prices: All-you-can-eat buffet brunch $35.95 for adults, $18.50 for children under 10. AE, DC, MC, V.
Open: Sun only, 12:30–3:30pm.
Every Sunday this brunch—served in the first hotel along the Condado beachfront strip—captivates the imagination of island residents with its combination of food, glamour, and entertainment. There's a clown for the amusement of children, as well as live music on the bandstand for anyone who cares to dance. Champagne is included in the price. Food is arranged at several different stations: Puerto Rican food, seafood, paella, ribs, cold cuts, steaks, pastas, and salads. Afterward, you might like to stroll amid the boutiques and seafront facilities of this famous hotel.

FAST FOOD

NONO'S, calle San Sebastián 100. Tel. 725-7819.
Cuisine: AMERICAN/FAST FOOD. **Bus:** A7, T1, or 2.
$ Prices: Appetizers $2.75–$6; hamburgers and main courses $3.50–$10.95; drinks from $3.50. AE, MC, V.
Open: Daily 11am–9pm. (Bar, daily 11am–4am.)
At the corner of calle Cristo in the heart of Old San Juan, NoNo's brings Stateside food to those eager for a taste of the salads, mozzarella sticks, three-decker sandwiches, chicken-fried steaks, hamburgers (here called NoNo burgers), and onion rings they've been missing. You'll sit beneath a beamed ceiling in one of the oldest

buildings in San Juan, near a large and accommodating bar whose clientele seems only peripherally interested in the establishment's food service. Drinks are colorfully (sometimes embarrassingly) named, including such specialties as the B-52 (made with Kahlúa, Grand Marnier, and bay leaves), the Sex on the River, and the Sex on the Beach. (These are made with varying amounts of vodka, schnapps, and orange and cranberry juices.)

DINING WITH A VIEW

SONNY'S OCEANFRONT PLACE FOR RIBS, in the Empress Oceanfront Hotel, calle Amapola 2, Isla Verde. Tel. 791-3083.
 Cuisine: AMERICAN. **Reservations:** Not required. **Bus:** T1.
 $ Prices: Appetizers $3.75–$5.95; sandwiches $2.95–$5.95; main courses $7.95–$16.50. AE, DC, MC, V.
 Open: Daily 8am–11pm.
Located at street level in an Isla Verde hotel (see Chapter 5), this restaurant offers an all-white, well-scrubbed, and solidly built decor overlooking the sea and the hotel's terraced swimming pool. From its terrace you can get a good view of the nightlife of the Condado. The cuisine is unpretentious and guaranteed to satisfy your hunger for U.S. mainland food. The menu includes hamburgers, several different types of barbecued ribs, pastas, at least four different preparations of chicken, four kinds of omelets, and steaks.

BREAKFAST

EL PATIO, in the Gran Hotel El Convento, calle Cristo 100 Tel. 722-7419.
 Cuisine: AMERICAN/PUERTO RICAN. **Reservations:** Not required. **Bus:** A7, T1, or 2.
 $ Prices: Full breakfast $5–$10.
 Open: Breakfast daily 7–10:30am.
By anyone's standards, the building accommodating this sunlit restaurant is the oldest hotel in Puerto Rico. Adjacent to the San Juan Cathedral in Old San Juan, it was built as a Carmelite convent during the 1600s and exudes a rich sense of history to anyone who passes beneath its towering portals. Its sheltered courtyard, protected from the rain with a greenhouselike canopy, is best appreciated in the early morning, when many people stop by for breakfast. Uniformed waiters serve bottomless cups of coffee and breakfasts that include the traditional ham, bacon, and eggs, as well as a selection of Puerto Rican breakfasts (for example, fried eggs served on a bed of stewed rice with green pigeon peas or fried plantains and eggs on a hamburger patty with diablo sauce and cornmeal tortillas).

AMERICAN

HOWARD JOHNSON'S, in the Radisson Ambassador Plaza Hotel & Casino, 1369 Ashford Ave. Tel. 721-7300.
 Cuisine: AMERICAN. **Reservations:** Not required.
 $ Prices: Appetizers $3.50–$6; main courses $8.50–$12; full American breakfasts $6–$12. AE, DC, MC, V.
 Open: Mon–Thurs 6:30am–12:30am, Fri–Sun 6:30am–2:30am.
On the lobby level of one of the best-recommended hotels of the Condado, this comfortable and cozy eatery reigns supreme as the most famous Howard Johnson's in the Caribbean and as one of the most consistently popular restaurants anywhere on the Condado. Despite its downhome image, it attracts some of the most prestigious politicians and financiers on Puerto Rico to its booths and tables. (Many of these luminaries live nearby and consider it their neighborhood diner, frequenting it particularly for breakfast.) In addition, it's the only Howard Johnson's in the world that caters, during the wee hours, almost exclusively to a clientele of gamblers, who presumably come to its cozy premises for comfort and stability after the wild ups and downs of the nearby casino.

Depending on the time of day, you can order pancakes, omelets, muffins, hash-brown potatoes, and sausages; or you can order lunch and dinner foods such as fish fries, teriyaki steaks, the famous Hojo clam platters, and an array of sandwiches and burgers. Don't overlook the many varieties of ice cream, which still retain a potent hold on any dessert-lover's imagination.

PICNIC FARE & WHERE TO EAT IT

Puerto Rico is usually ideal for picnicking year-round. The best place to fill a picnic basket is **Reposteria Kassalta** (see "Ocean Park," earlier in this chapter)—a cafeteria/bakery/deli with lots of goodies. Puerto Rican families often come here to order delicacies for their Sunday outings. The best places for a picnic are **Muñoz Marín Park,** along Las Américas Expressway, west of avenida Piñero, and the Botanical Gardens operated by the University of Puerto Rico in the Río Piedras section. For more information about these gardens, see "Parks and Gardens" under "Attractions," in Chapter 7.

WHAT TO SEE & DO IN SAN JUAN

Around 1521 the Spanish began to settle in the area now known as Old San Juan. At the outset, the city was called Puerto Rico ("rich port"), and the whole island was known as San Juan.

The streets are narrow and teeming with traffic, but a walk through Old San Juan—in Spanish, *El Viejo San Juan*—is like a stroll through five centuries of history. You can do it in less than a day. In the historic seven-square-block area of the western side of the city, you can see many of Puerto Rico's chief sightseeing attractions and do some shopping along the way. Many of the museums in Old San Juan close for lunch between 11:45am and 2pm.

SUGGESTED ITINERARIES

IF YOU HAVE ONE DAY To make the most of a short stay, head immediately for Old San Juan for an afternoon of sightseeing and shopping. You should definitely schedule a visit inside El Morro Fortress. Try to spend two hours at Condado beach. Enjoy a Puerto Rican dinner at a local restaurant, and listen to some salsa music while enjoying a rum punch before retiring for the night.

IF YOU HAVE TWO DAYS The first day, spend the morning shopping and sightseeing in Old San Juan. Schedule interior visits to El Morro Fortress and San Juan Cathedral, then relax on Condado beach for the rest of the day. Enjoy a Puerto Rican dinner and some local music before retiring.

On your second day, spend the morning exploring El Yunque rain forest, a lush 28,000-acre site east of San Juan. Schedule two or three hours at nearby Luquillo Beach, the finest on Puerto Rico. Buy lunch from one of the open-air kiosks. Return to San Juan for the evening, attending either a folk-culture show (if available) or a Las Vegas–type revue. Visit the casinos for some action before retiring.

IF YOU HAVE THREE DAYS Follow my suggestions above for your first two days.

On your third day, return to Old San Juan to see some of the sights you missed on your first visit: Fort San Cristóbal, La Fortaleza, the Casa Blanca, and the Iglesia de San José. If time remains, you might want to visit the Pablo Casals Museum. Return to the beaches of the Condado to enjoy what's left of the afternoon, then have a piña colada at sunset and promise yourself a return trip to Puerto Rico.

? DID YOU KNOW . . . ?

- Juan Ponce de León, seeker of the "Fountain of Youth," was the first governor of Puerto Rico.
- The typical tourist who patronizes San Juan's casinos spends 17 hours at the tables or slots during a four-day visit.
- The annual per capita income on Puerto Rico is the highest in Latin America.
- When the Caribe Hilton opened in 1950, an ocean-view room cost $14 a night.
- San Juan is the oldest city—and capital—in the territorial United States.
- The Church of San José is the oldest church still in use in the Americas.
- La Fortaleza is the oldest executive mansion in the western hemisphere.
- The former naval station of El Arsenal, dating from 1800, was the last place on Puerto Rico to be held by the Spanish, who turned it over to the United States in 1898.

IF YOU HAVE FIVE DAYS For the first three days, follow my suggestions above.

Spend the fourth day touring "out on the island," visiting two of the major attractions: Río Camuy Cave Park, one of the world's largest cave networks (guided tours are offered); and Arecibo Observatory, with the world's largest and most sensitive radar/radiotelescope set in a 20-acre ancient sinkhole. Return to San Juan in the evening for a night of casino and disco action.

On your fifth day, head to the southern coast to visit Ponce, Puerto Rico's second-largest city. Stroll through the historic inner city, where major restoration continues on its turn-of-the-century buildings. If time remains, either visit San Germán, a historic Spanish colonial city in the west, or relax on Playa Ponce, the local white sand beach strip to the south. Return to San Juan before dark and enjoy a Puerto Rican dinner, perhaps in the old town.

1. ATTRACTIONS

Although I have outlined a walking tour of Old San Juan later in this chapter, here is an introduction to some of the sights mentioned there, as well as others you may wish to seek out yourself.

FORTS

CASTILLO SAN FELIPE DEL MORRO, at the end of calle Norzagaray. Tel. 729-6960.

Called "El Morro," this fort stands on a rocky promontory dominating the entrance to San Juan Bay. Ordered built in 1540, the original fort was a round tower which can still be seen deep inside the lower levels of the castle. Additional walls and cannon-firing positions were constructed, and by 1787 the fortification had attained the complex design we see today. This fortress was attacked repeatedly by both the English and the Dutch. The U.S. National Park Service oversees the fortifications of Old San Juan, which have been declared a World Heritage Site by the United Nations. Offering some of the most dramatic views in the Caribbean, El Morro is an intriguing labyrinth of dungeons, barracks, vaults, lookouts, and ramps. A video is presented in English and Spanish. Free tours, in English and Spanish, are given daily from 10am to 4pm. The closest parking to the historic fort is the underground facility beneath the Quincentennial Plaza at the Ballajá Barracks on calle Norzagaray.
   Admission: Free.
   Open: Daily 9am–5pm. **Bus:** T1.

FORT SAN CRISTÓBAL, calle Norzagaray, uphill from Plaza de Colón. Tel. 729-6960.

This fort in the northeast corner of Old San Juan, begun in 1634 and redesigned 200 years ago, is one of the largest defenses ever built in the Americas. Its walls rise more than 100 feet above the sea, a marvel of military engineering. Protecting San

Juan against attackers coming by land, San Cristóbal is connected to El Morro by half a mile of massive walls filled with cannon-firing positions. Tunnels and dry moats connect the center of San Cristóbal to its "outworks" (trenches, traps, bunkers, and bastions arranged defensively, layer upon layer, over a 27-acre site). You'll get the idea of the defenses if you look at a scale model on display. Like El Morro, this fort is administered by the National Park Service. Museum exhibits depict what a soldier's life was like in the late 18th century, and a video is shown in English and Spanish. Free tours, in English or Spanish, are given daily from 10am to 4pm. Because of the steep hillside and enormous 18th-century walls, there are only a small number of parking spaces available.

Admission: Free.
Open: Daily 9am–5pm. **Bus:** T1.

FORT SAN JERÓNIMO, east of the Caribe Hilton, at the entrance to Condado Bay. Tel. 724-5949.
Completed in 1788, this fort was badly damaged during the English assault of 1797. Reconstructed in the closing year of the 18th century, it has now been taken over by the Institute of Puerto Rican Culture. A museum has been established here, with life-size mannequins wearing military uniforms. Ship models and charts are also on display.

Admission: Free.
Open: Wed–Sun 9am–noon and 1–4:30pm. **Bus:** T1.

CHURCHES

CAPILLA DE CRISTO, calle del Cristo.
The Cristo Chapel was built to commemorate a legendary miracle. Horse racing down calle del Cristo was the highlight of the fiestas on St. John's Day, which honored the patron saint of the city. In 1753 a young rider lost control of his horse and plunged over the precipice. Moved by the accident, a spectator, the secretary of the city, Don Mateo Pratts, invoked Christ and the youth was saved. To express his thanks, the young man had the chapel built later that same year. Today, the chapel is a landmark in the old city and one of the best-known historical monuments. The chapel's Campeche paintings and gold-and-silver altar can be seen through its glass doors.

Since the chapel is open only one day a week, most visitors have to settle for a view of its exterior. The chapel lies directly west of paseo de la Princesa.

IN THEIR FOOTSTEPS

Pablo Casals (1876–1973) Famed for his interpretations of works for the cello and a composer of works for the violin, piano, full orchestra, and chorus, he is also one of the best-known musicians of the 20th century.

• **Birthplace:** Born in Spain to a Puerto Rican mother, he made his debut as a soloist in 1898. He was especially noted for his brilliant interpretations of Bach.

• **Accomplishments:** In 1957 he moved to Puerto Rico with his wife, Marta Casals Istomin, past artistic director of the John F. Kennedy Center for the Performing Arts. Casals gained worldwide renown as a cellist, touring frequently from 1901.

• **Favorite Haunts:** Old San Juan, where he founded the Casals Festival, which celebrates its 38th year in 1994—the most prestigious cultural event in the Caribbean.

• **Resting Place:** His beloved Puerto Rico, where he died in 1973 at the age of 97.

Admission: Free.
Open: Tues 10am–4pm. **Bus:** T1.

CATEDRAL DE SAN JUAN, calle del Cristo 151. Tel. 722-0861.

The San Juan Cathedral, standing at the corner of calle del Cristo and caleta San Juan in Old San Juan, was begun in 1540 and has been subjected to some rough treatment through the years. It hardly resembles the thatch-roofed building that stood here until 1529, when it was wiped out by a hurricane. Hampered by lack of funds, church officials slowly added a circular staircase and two adjoining vaulted Gothic chambers to the cathedral. But along came the Earl of Cumberland in 1598 to loot it and a hurricane in 1615 to blow off its roof. In 1908 the body of Juan Ponce de León was brought here. After he died in 1521 from a poisoned-arrow wound in Florida, his body was first taken to the Iglesia de San José. Extensively renovated in recent years, the cathedral faces the Plaza de las Monjas (Nuns' Square), a tree-shaded old-town spot where you can rest and cool off.
Admission: Free.
Open: Daily 8:30am–4pm. **Bus:** T1.

CONVENTO DE LOS DOMINICOS, Plaza de San José, calle Norzagaray 98. Tel. 724-5949.

The Dominican Convent was established by Dominican friars in 1523, shortly after the city itself was founded. It was the first convent in Puerto Rico, and women and children often hid here during Carib attacks. The friars lived here until 1838, when the Crown closed down the monasteries and turned this building into an army barracks. The American army used it as its headquarters until 1966. Gregorian chants help re-create the long-ago atmosphere. On the ground floor is a small Chapel Museum displaying religious artifacts, including a medieval altarpiece; in another section the Arts Museum displays some of the city's fine arts collection.
Admission: Free.
Open: Chapel Museum, Wed–Sun 9am–noon and 1–4:30pm; Arts Museum, Mon–Sat 9:15am–4:15pm. **Bus:** T1.

IN THEIR FOOTSTEPS

José Ferrer (1912–92) This Broadway actor and director, best known for his portrayals of Cyrano de Bergerac and Toulouse-Lautrec, was the most versatile actor ever to come out of Puerto Rico. He maintained homes in Coconut Grove (Florida) and New York City. His portrayal of Cyrano won him Broadway's first best actor Tony award in 1947; this was followed by his Oscar-winning film version of the same play in 1950.

• **Birthplace:** Ferrer was born on January 8, 1912, in Santurce, Puerto Rico, and he went on to receive a bachelor's degree at Princeton before making a one-line Broadway debut in 1935.

• **Accomplishments:** Some of Ferrer's best-known roles included his portrayal of Toulouse-Lautrec in *Moulin Rouge* (1953), followed by *The Caine Mutiny* with Humphrey Bogart (1954) and *Lawrence of Arabia* (1962) with Peter O'Toole. The versatile star also appeared in and directed a number of films, including *The Shrike* (1955) and *I Accuse!* (1958). Some of his greatest stage roles included *Charley's Aunt* (1940) and *Stalag 17* (1952).

• **Favorite Haunts:** The Coconut Grove Playhouse, where, as artistic director, he drew a salary of $1 a year and brought in first-rate stars such as Kim Hunter and major revivals of plays such as Tennessee Williams's *The Glass Menagerie*.

• **Resting Place:** Coral Gables, Florida. He was survived by his wife, Stella Daphne Magee, as well as six children and eight grandchildren

IGLESIA DE SAN JOSÉ, calle del Cristo. Tel. 725-7501.
The Church of San José is centered in Plaza de San José, right next to the Dominican monastery. Initial plans for the church were drawn in 1523 and construction, supervised by Dominican friars, began in 1532. Before going into the church, look for the statue of Ponce de León on the adjoining plaza. It was made from British cannons captured during Sir Ralph Abercromby's unsuccessful 1797 attack on San Juan.

Both the church and its monastery were closed by decree in 1838, the property confiscated by the royal treasury. Later, the Crown turned the convent into a military barracks. The Jesuits restored the badly damaged church. The church had been the place of worship for Ponce de León's descendants, who are buried here under the family's coat-of-arms. The conquistador was interred here until his body was removed to the cathedral in 1908.

Although looted several times over the years, the church still has some treasures, including *Christ of the Ponces,* a carved crucifix presented to Ponce de León. Packed in a crate, the image survived a terrible shipwreck outside San Juan Harbor. The church has four oil paintings by José Campeche and two large works by Francisco Oller. Many miracles have been attributed to a painting in the Chapel of Belém, a 15th-century Flemish work called *The Virgin of Bethlehem.*
Admission: Free.
Open: Church, Mon–Sat 8:30am–3:30pm; Chapel of Belém, Mon–Fri 10am–4pm, Sun 11:30am–4pm. **Bus:** T1.

MUSEUMS

MUSEO DE ARTE Y HISTORIA DE SAN JUAN, calle Norzagaray. Tel. 724-7171.
Located at the corner of calle MacArthur, this is a contemporary cultural center today, but in the mid-19th century it was a marketplace. Local art is displayed in the east and west galleries, and audiovisual materials reveal the history of the often-beleaguered city. Sometimes major cultural events are staged in the museum's large courtyard. English-language audiovisual shows are presented Monday through Friday at 11am and 1:15pm.
Admission: Donations requested, $1 adults, 50¢ children.
Open: Mon–Fri 9am–noon and 1–4pm, Sat–Sun 10am–noon and 1–4pm. **Bus:** T1.

MUSEO DE PABLO CASALS, calle San Sebastián 101. Tel. 723-9185.
Adjacent to the Iglesia de San José, at the corner of Plaza de San José, this museum houses the memorabilia left by the famed musician to the people of Puerto Rico. The maestro's cello is here, along with a library of videotapes (played on request) of some of his festival concerts. This small 18th-century house also contains Casals's manuscripts and photographs. Born in 1876, he achieved fame as a cellist as well as a conductor and composer. His Casals Festival draws worldwide interest and attracts some of the greatest performing artists. The festival is held the first two weeks of June every year.
Admission: Free.
Open: Tues–Sat 9:30am–5:30pm, Sun 1–5pm. **Bus:** T1.

MUSEUM OF THE UNIVERSITY OF PUERTO RICO, avenida Ponce de León, Río Piedras. Tel. 764-0000, ext. 2452.
Here you'll find good collections of paintings by Puerto Rican artists, including Francisco Oller (late 19th and early 20th century) and José Campeche (18th century). There is also a large collection of pre-Columbian Puerto Rican Amerindian artifacts from the Ingeri, sub-Taíno, and Taíno civilizations. In the museum's temporary exhibition hall, you can see the work of contemporary Puerto Rican artists, retrospectives of important aspects of Puerto Rican art, and exhibits of the work of other U.S. artists.

Admission: Free.
Open: Mon–Tues and Wed–Fri 9am–4:30pm, Thurs 9am–9pm, Sat 9am–3pm.
Bus: Take the bus marked RÍO PIEDRAS from Plaza de Colón in Old San Juan.

HISTORIC SIGHTS

San Juan Gate, calles San Francisco and Recinto Oeste, built in 1639 just north of La Fortaleza, was the main gate and entry point into San Juan—that is, if you arrived by ship in the 18th century. The gate is the only one remaining of the several entries to the old walled city. Bus: T1.

Plazuela de la Rogativa, caleta de las Monjas, basks in legend. In 1797 the British across San Juan Bay at Santurce held the old town under siege. However, that same year they mysteriously sailed away. Later, the commander claimed he feared that the enemy was well prepared behind those walls—he apparently saw many lights and believed them to be reinforcements. Some people believe that those lights were torches carried by women in a *rogativa*, or religious procession, as they followed their bishop. A handsome statue of a bishop, trailed by a trio of torch-bearing women, was donated to the city on its 450th anniversary. Bus: T1.

The **City Walls,** calle Norzagaray, around San Juan were built in 1630 to protect the town against both European invaders and Caribbean pirates. The thickness of the walls averages 20 feet at the base and 12 feet at the top, with an average height of 40 feet. Between Fort San Cristóbal and El Morro, bastions were erected at frequent intervals. You can start to see the walls as you approach from Fort San Cristóbal on your way to El Morro. Bus: T1.

The **San Juan Cemetery,** calle Norzagaray, officially opened in 1814 and has since been the final resting place for many prominent Puerto Rican families. The circular chapel, dedicated to Saint Magdalene of Pazzis, was built in the 1860s. Aficionados of old graveyards can wander among marble monuments, mausoleums, and statues, marvelous examples of Victorian funereal statuary. However, since there are no trees or any form of shade here, it would be best not to go exploring in the noonday sun. In any case, be careful here—the cemetery is often a venue for illegal drug deals and can be dangerous. Bus: T1.

CASA BLANCA, calle San Sebastián 1. Tel. 724-4102.
Juan Ponce de León never lived here, although construction of the house (in 1521)

FROMMER'S FAVORITE
SAN JUAN EXPERIENCES

A Day at Condado Beach This is a spectacular loop of white sand, with calm waters on one side and an array of glittering resort hotels on the other.

Shopping in Old San Juan Nowhere in the Caribbean can you shop in such a historic district—filled with Spanish colonial architecture and store after store brimming with bargains, especially in jewelry and clothing.

Listening to Salsa Bands They're all over the place—at hotels, clubs, sometimes restaurants, and even in public parks. Aficionados rate Puerto Rican salsa the best in the Caribbean—hot rhythms, hot music, and hot nights.

Touring the Forts San Juan has the most impressive military fortresses in the West Indies, a legacy of the island's Spanish colonial days. Touring from El Morro to Fort San Cristóbal is like walking through the pages of history.

is sometimes attributed to him. The house was erected two years after the explorer's death, as ordered by his son-in-law, Juan García Troche. The parcel of land was given to Ponce de León as a reward for services rendered to the Crown. Ponce de León's descendants lived here for about 2½ centuries until the Spanish government took it over in 1779 to use as a residence for military commanders. The U.S. government later used it as a home for army commanders.

This historic residence now houses two museums. On the first floor, the Juan Ponce de León Museum is furnished with antiques, paintings, and artifacts from the 16th through the 18th centuries, illustrating the various uses of the house. On the second floor, the Taíno Indian Ethno-Historic exhibit opens with a series of 16th-century European maps of the known world, reproductions of famous paintings of Columbus, and charts of his voyage. Taíno life is depicted through artifacts, ceremonial objects, everyday articles, and a model of an Amerindian village.

Admission: $2 adults, $1 children.

Open: Wed–Sun 9am–noon and 1–4:30pm. **Bus:** T1.

CASA DE LOS CONTRAFUERTES [House of the Buttresses], calle San Sebastián 101. Tel. 724-5949.

Adjacent to the Museo de Pablo Casals, this building, which has thick buttresses, is believed to be the oldest residence remaining in Old San Juan. The complex also contains a Pharmacy Museum, which in the 19th century was a working business located in the town of Cayey. If you go upstairs, you'll find a Graphic Arts Museum, displaying an exhibit of prints and paintings by local artists.

Admission: Free.

Open: Wed–Sun 9am–4:30pm. **Bus:** T1.

EL ARSENAL, La Puntilla. Tel. 724-5949.

The Spaniards used a shallow craft to patrol lagoons and mangroves in and around San Juan. Needing a base for these vessels, they constructed El Arsenal around 1800. It was at this base that they staged their last stand on Puerto Rico, flying the Spanish colors until the final Spaniard was removed in 1898, at the end of the Spanish-American War. There are exhibits in the building's three galleries.

Admission: Free.

Open: Wed–Sun 9am–4:30pm. **Bus:** T1.

LA CASA DEL LIBRO, calle del Cristo 255. Tel. 723-0354.

This restored 19th-century building houses a library devoted to the arts of printing and bookmaking, with examples of fine printing dating back eight centuries, as well as some medieval illuminated manuscripts.

Admission: Free.

Open: Tues–Sat 11am–4:30pm. **Bus:** T1.

LA FORTALEZA AND MANSION EJECUTIVA, calle Fortaleza, overlooking San Juan Harbor. Tel. 721-7000, ext. 2211.

The office and residence of the governor of Puerto Rico is the oldest executive mansion in continuous use in the western hemisphere, and it has served as the island's seat of government for more than three centuries. It dates back even further, to 1553, when construction began on a fortress to protect San Juan's Spanish settlers during raids by Carib tribesmen and pirates. The original medieval towers remain, but as the edifice was subsequently enlarged into a palace, other modes of architecture and ornamentation were incorporated, including baroque, Gothic, neoclassical, and Arabian. La Fortaleza has been designated a national historic site by the U.S. government. Informal but proper attire is required. Tours of the gardens, conducted in both Spanish and English, are given every hour, and there are guided tours of the second floor of the mansion at 9:30, 10, 10:30, and 10:50am.

Admission: Free.

Open: Mon–Fri 9am–4pm. **Bus:** T1.

ALCALDÍA [San Juan City Hall], calle San Francisco. Tel. 724-1227.
The City Hall, with its double arcade flanked by two towers resembling Madrid's City Hall, was constructed in stages from 1604 to 1789. Still in use, this building is more than a historical site—it's a unique place full of monuments and legends.
Admission: Free.
Open: Tours by appointment, Mon–Sat (except holidays) 8am–3pm. **Bus:** T1.

PARKS & GARDENS

BOTANICAL GARDEN, Barrio Venezuela. Tel. 766-0740.
Administered by the University of Puerto Rico, this is a lush tropical garden with some 200 species of vegetation, located in Río Piedras. You can pack a picnic lunch and bring it here if you choose. The orchid garden is exceptional, and the palm garden is said to contain some 125 species. Footpaths blaze a trail through heavy forests opening onto a lotus lagoon. The garden is at the intersection of Routes 1 and 847.
Admission: Free.
Open: Tues–Sun 9am–4:30pm (if Mon is a holiday the park is open, but closed the following Tues). **Bus:** 19.

MUÑOZ RIVERA PARK, avenida Ponce de León. Tel. 763-0787.
Some 50 years ago, this rectangular park was built along the waterfront to honor Luís Muñoz Rivera, the Puerto Rican statesman, poet, and journalist. It's filled with picnic areas, wide walks, shady trees, landscaped grounds, and recreational areas. Sometimes cultural and handcraft exhibits are held here at the Peace Pavilion. Cable cars link the parking lot with the main park.
Admission: Free.
Open: Tues–Fri 9am–6pm, Sat–Sun 8:30am–6pm. **Directions:** Take the Los Américas Expressway to avenida Piñero, then head west until you reach the entrance. Parking costs $1 per car.

SAN JUAN CENTRAL PARK, calle Cerra. Tel. 722-1646.
Built in 1979 for the Pan-American Games, this mangrove-bordered park lies southwest of Miramar. One of the best places in San Juan for jogging, it's also a good venue for playing tennis.
Admission: Free.
Open: Mon 2–10pm, Tues–Sat 8am–10pm, Sun 10am–6pm.

2. NEARBY ATTRACTIONS

SAN JUAN ENVIRONS The outskirts of metropolitan San Juan have some interesting attractions; all you'll need to see them is a car and about half a day's time for touring.
From the Santurce area, take Route 2 southwest to km 6.4. To the right you'll see a small park containing the ruins of the house erected in 1509 by Ponce de León in Caparra—this was the first Spanish settlement in Puerto Rico.
Continue west on Route 2 until you reach **Bayamón.** Facing the town plaza is an old church built in 1877, an excellent example of period architecture.
From here, turn right onto Route 167 north, heading toward Cataño, and take a left at km 5.2. Within a short distance you'll find yourself in the **Barrilito Rum Distillery.** To the left is a 200-year-old mansion with grand outdoor staircases leading to the second-floor galleries. This is the original mansion of the former 2,400-acre Santa Ana plantation and is still occupied by members of the family, the owners of the distillery. There's an office on the right, near a tower that was originally a windmill from which the entire valley and bay could be seen. Along the bay is the **Bacardi Rum Plant,** where 100,000 gallons of rum are distilled each day. Guided tours are available.

intended as an adjunct to El Morro fortress. Today, like its twin, it is maintained by the National Park Service and can be visited throughout the day.

4. SAVVY SHOPPING

Puerto Rico has the same tariff barriers as the U.S. mainland. That's why you don't pay duty on purchases brought back to the United States, and that means you don't walk away with great bargains either. Nevertheless, there are many boutiques and specialized stores—especially in the old town—that may tempt you to do some shopping.

Native handcrafts can be good buys. Look for *santos,* hand-carved wooden religious figures, needlework (women are no longer paid 3¢ an hour for it!), straw work, ceramics, hammocks, guayabera shirts for men, papier-mâché fruit and vegetables, and paintings and sculptures by Puerto Rican artists.

Many stores are open from 9am until 6pm, and certain shops also open on Sunday, especially when large cruise ships are in port. The streets of the old town, such as calle San Francisco and calle del Cristo, are the major venues for shopping.

The biggest and most up-to-date shopping plaza in the Caribbean Basin is **Plaza Las Américas,** which is situated in the financial district of Hato Rey, right off Las Américas Expressway. The complex, with its fountains and modern architecture, has more than 200 shops, most of them upscale. The plaza is open Monday through Thursday and on Saturday from 9:30am to 6pm, and on Friday from 9:30am to 9:30pm.

ANTIQUES

JOSÉ E. ALEGRIA & ASSOCIATES, calle del Cristo 152-154. Tel. 721-8091.

Opposite El Convento Hotel, this shop is housed in an impressive, old Spanish building dating from 1523 with rooms opening onto patios and courtyards. It displays antique furniture and paintings, and the collection is considered the finest in San Juan. The specialty here is 18th-century furniture and paintings, and there is also a collection of French furnishings and Spanish exhibits from the 16th to the 19th century. Intermingled are the paintings of contemporary artists from Puerto Rico and elsewhere. Prices are not low, but the quality is very high. There is also a wine boutique in the old cellars.

ART

GALERÍA BOTELLO, calle del Cristo 208. Tel. 723-2879.

A contemporary Latin American art gallery, Galería Botello is a living tribute to the success story of the late Angel Botello, one of Puerto Rico's outstanding artists,

---

Ⓕ FROMMER'S SMART TRAVELER: SHOPPING

1. Know prices in your hometown so you can identify bargains in San Juan.
2. Take advantage of the greatly reduced prices on jewelry, clothing, and handcrafts.
3. Island-made handcrafts are especially good buys—jewelry, straw products, locally made clothing, leather sandals, santos, and the like.
4. If you're making a big purchase, do some old-fashioned bargaining with the shopkeeper. Sometimes it doesn't work, but often it does.

who died in 1986. Born in a small village in Galicia, Spain, he fled after the Spanish Civil War to the Caribbean and spent 12 years in the art-conscious country of Haiti. His paintings and bronze sculptures, evocative of his colorful background, are done in a style uniquely his own. This *galería* is his former home, a colonial mansion that he restored himself. Today a setting to display his paintings and sculptures, it also offers a large collection of Puerto Rican antique santos—small, carved wooden figures of saints.

BOOKS

THE BOOK STORE, calle San José 255. Tel. 724-1815.
This is the leading bookstore in the old town, with the largest selection of titles. It sells a number of books on Puerto Rican culture and also good touring maps of the island. It will ship purchases back to the States.

BUTTERFLIES [MOUNTED]

BUTTERFLY PEOPLE, calle Fortaleza 152. Tel. 723-2432.
Butterfly People is a gallery and café (see Chapter 6) in a handsomely restored building in Old San Juan. Butterflies, sold here in artfully arranged boxes, cost from $20 for a single butterfly to as much as $70,000 for a swarm. The butterfly wings are preserved by a secret formula so that the color lasts forever. The dimensional artwork is sold in limited editions, and the gallery ships boxes worldwide. This is the largest privately owned collection of mounted butterflies in the world, second only to the collection at the Smithsonian Institution. The store doesn't use endangered species, although its butterflies come from virtually every tropical region of the world—the most beautiful are from the densest jungles of Borneo and Malaysia.

CLOTHING

HATHAWAY FACTORY OUTLET, calle del Cristo 203. Tel. 723-8946.
The selection of dress shirts, known for the "Red H," varies widely in this factory outlet, but if you happen to be here just after a new shipment has been received, you can stock up at bargain prices on shirts that could easily cost twice as much back home. Most items are top-quality dress and knit shirts from the Hathaway factories in Waterville, Maine, but also include articles by Chaps, Ralph Lauren, Christian Dior, and Jack Nicklaus, reduced by 35% to 50%.

GONZÁLEZ PADIN, Plaza de Armas. Tel. 721-5700.
This is the flagship for a 10-member chain of clothing stores scattered throughout the island. It has three floors of clothing for men, women, and children. Especially well-stocked is the collection of guayabera shirts, which Puerto Rican men often substitute for jacket and tie.

JOLIE BOUTIQUE, 1015 Ashford Ave. Tel. 723-5575.
One of the best-known specialty shops on the island, it offers a large, exclusive selection of imported bathing suits, maillots, bikinis, and pareos, as well as high-fashion loungewear and beachwear. It's near the Condado Plaza Hotel and the Regency Hotel complex, and there is free parking.

LEVEL I, 1004 Ashford Ave. Tel. 725-0223.
Both formal and casual clothes for women by the best local and international designers are sold at this restored old mansion located on a bustling commercial district between the Condado Plaza Hotel and the Condado Beach Trio.

LONDON FOG, calle del Cristo 156. Tel. 722-4334.
London Fog often has sales on men's wear, including a wide selection of raincoats

(which today are often made in Korea) and casual-wear winter jackets. Women's clothing is on the ground floor.

NONO MALDONADO, 1051 Ashford Ave. Tel. 721-0456.

Named after its owner, a Puerto Rico–born designer who worked for many years as the New York–based fashion editor of *Esquire* magazine, this is one of the most fashionable and upscale haberdashers in the Caribbean. Selling both men's and women's clothing, the shop has everything from socks to dinner jackets, as well as ready-to-wear versions of Maldonado's twice-a-year collections. Both ready-to-wear and couture are available here. Although this is the main store for the designer (midway between the Condado Plaza and the Condado Beach Trio), the establishment also maintains a boutique in El San Juan Hotel in Isla Verde.

POLO RALPH LAUREN FACTORY STORE, calle del Cristo 201. Tel. 722-2136.

This is one of the best shops in the old town if you're looking for men's, women's, or children's sportswear. At certain times of the year, discounts of 40% to 50% are offered.

W. H. SMITH, on the lobby level of the Condado Plaza Hotel, 999 Ashford Ave. Tel. 723-1125.

This outlet sells mostly women's clothing—everything from bathing suits and beach attire to jogging suits and a collection of semiformal evening wear. For men, there are shorts, bathing suits, and jogging suits. There's also a good selection of books.

GIFTS & HANDCRAFTS

BARED & SONS, calle Fortaleza 206, at the corner of calle San Justo. Tel. 724-3215.

This store sells Lladró figurines and hand-embroidered tablecloths at something like 25% to 30% off Stateside prices. It also offers a nice selection of jewelry and watches.

IN THEIR FOOTSTEPS

Jimmy Smits (b. 1955) "L. A. Law"'s hot Puerto Rican star went from playing stock Hispanic characters to the upper echelons of cinema. He still remembers fondly his work in the New York Shakespeare Festival, where he appeared in *Hamlet,* directed by Joseph Papp.

• **Birthplace:** Born in New York of a Dutch father and a Puerto Rican mother, Smits graduated from Brooklyn College (where he studied drama) and later obtained a Master of Fine Arts degree at Cornell University.

• **Accomplishments:** Smits is equally at home in theater, television, and cinema, although he became best known as the idealistic Hispanic lawyer Victor Sifuentes in TV's "L. A. Law." He received Emmy Award nominations for best supporting actor in a drama series in his first three seasons with the show, eventually garnering the award in 1991. One film critic wrote that Smits "seems to be doing for the Latin image what Bill Cosby has done for black America through his TV role as Doctor Huxtable."

• **Favorite Haunts:** Often charity events, such as the René Enriquez Celebrity Tennis Tournament at San Juan's Caribe Hilton, with funds going to Proyecto Amor, an AIDS hospice in Loíza Aldea.

OLÉ, calle Fortaleza 105. Tel. 724-2445.

Even if you don't buy anything, you can still learn a lot about the crafts shown here, where practically everything that wasn't made in Puerto Rico comes from South America. Every object is artistically displayed in a high-ceilinged room decorated clear to the top. If you want a straw hat from Ecuador, hand-beaten Chilean silver, Christmas ornaments, or Puerto Rican santos, this is the place to buy them.

PUERTO RICAN ARTS & CRAFTS, calle Fortaleza 204. Tel. 725-5596.

In a colonial building, this unique store is probably the premier outlet on the island for authentic Puerto Rican artifacts. From modern contemporary ceramics to traditional crafts such as hand-carved santos, you will experience Puerto Rico in a special way. Of particular interest are the papier-mâché carnival masks from the south-coast town of Ponce, whose grotesque and colorful features were originally made to chase away evil spirits.

ROVERDALES, calle del Cristo 99. Tel. 722-5424.

Roverdales, big on brass, also carries a wide selection of gift items, including a collection of inexpensive but authentic Puerto Rican santos, local handcrafts, and small easy-to-pack art objects from around the world. A Panama-style hand-woven palm hat is a hot item.

JEWELRY

BARRACHINA'S, calle Fortaleza 104, between calle del Cristo and calle San José. Tel. 725-7912.

Revered as the acknowledged birthplace, in 1963, of the piña colada, the store consists of a series of departments sprawling over a single floor. A favorite of visiting cruise-ship passengers, it offers one of the largest selections of jewelry, perfume, and gifts in San Juan. There's a patio—a calm oasis amid the commercial hubbub—where you can order a piña colada. You will also find a Bacardi rum outlet, a costume-jewelry department, a gift shop, and a section for authentic jewelry. Watches by Raymond Weil, Movado, Bulova, and Rado are available.

LETRAN, calle Fortaleza 201. Tel. 721-5825.

This store, which focuses on jewelry and watches, is one of the best-established and most reputable jewelers in Old San Juan.

RIVIERA, calle Cruz 205. Tel. 725-4000.

This jewelry shop specializes in first-class gemstones and excellent watches by Rolex and Patek Philippe. The third-generation owner, Julio Abislaiman, and his staff will respond to your needs. They don't sell costume jewelry.

200 FORTALEZA, calle Fortaleza 200, at the corner of calle Cruz. Tel. 723-1989.

Known as a leading place to buy fine jewelry in Old San Juan, this shop has famous-name watches; you also can purchase 14-karat Italian gold chains and bracelets, which are measured, fitted, and sold by weight and priced according to the gold market. You can buy your diamond initials pendant set in 14-karat white and yellow gold. 200 Fortaleza Jewelry Center has always carried the most recent designs in Italian jewelry.

YAS MAR, calle Fortaleza 205. Tel. 724-1377.

This shop sells convincingly glittering fake diamonds for those afraid or unwilling to wear the real thing. It also stocks real diamond chips, emeralds, sapphires, and rubies.

LEATHER

LEATHER & PEARLS, calle del Cristo 202. Tel. 724-8185.

Majorca pearls and fine leather garments, bags, and accessories (by Gucci, Fendi, and Paloma Picasso, among others) are sold here. The shop is located one block from the cathedral.

SHOES

DEXTER SHOE OUTLET, calle San José 252. Tel. 721-6079.
This is the factory outlet for a Maine-based shoe manufacturer. Shoes sometimes sell at 50% of their retail price in the United States. Women's shoes are available up to size 12 and men's shoes up to size 15.

5. EVENING ENTERTAINMENT

San Juan nightlife comes in all varieties: From the vibrant performing-arts scene to street-level salsa or the casinos, discos, and bars, there's plenty of entertainment available almost any evening. Here's a listing of some of the favorites:

THE LELOLAI VIP PROGRAM

S For $10, the cost of membership in Puerto Rico's LeLoLai VIP (Value in Puerto Rico), visitors to the island can enjoy the equivalent of up to $250 in travel benefits. Admission to folkloric shows and discounts on guided tours of historic sites and natural attractions, as well as on lodgings, meals, shopping, sports activities, and more, add up to significant savings.

By presenting the LeLoLai VIP membership card, visitors receive 10% discounts on car rentals from Avis, Budget, and Thrifty (Hertz offers $5 off on daily rentals or $25 off on weekly rentals). The *paradores puertorriqueños,* the island's modestly priced network of country inns, offer 20% off their room rates Monday through Thursday. Discounts of 10% to 15% are available at many restaurants, from San Juan's toniest hotels to several *mesones gastronómicos* (government-sponsored restaurants out on the island that serve Puerto Rican fare). There are shopping discounts at many stores and boutiques and, best yet, 10% to 50% discounts at many island attractions.

The folkloric shows alone are worth the card's membership price. Showcasing Puerto Rico's musical traditions are three different evening shows at leading San Juan hotels and an afternoon performance at the Casa Blanca, the island's "White House."

Fantasia . . . Puerto Rico, on Sunday evening at 8:30pm at the Convention Center, features the Taller de Voces Ballet with musical selections from traditional 19th-century Puerto Rican classics to modern compositions.

My Island Sings for You, Monday at 9pm at the Condado Plaza Hotel & Casino, features music of contemporary Puerto Rican composers performed by the popular Perla del Sur dance company.

Caribbean rhythms are highlighted on Tuesday afternoon at 4pm in *Colorful Puerto Rico,* performed at the historic Casa Blanca in Old San Juan. Built for Puerto Rico's first governor, Juan Ponce de León, the Casa Blanca was restored at a cost of $275,000 and now houses two museums juxtaposing the indigenous Amerindian culture with that of the Spanish explorers.

Traditional jíbaro (hillbilly) music and dancing from the mountains of Puerto Rico enliven Wednesday evening beginning at 8:30pm at the Caribe Hilton International's Caribe Terrace.

Discounted guided tours under the LeLoLai VIP program include:

• Half-day tours on Monday of Fort San Cristóbal and El Morro Castle, the fortifications of Old San Juan.

- Full-day walking tours of historic sites in Old San Juan on Tuesday.
- Full-day tours of the Río Camuy Cave Park on Wednesday.
- Full-day tours of Ponce, on the southern coast, Puerto Rico's second city including the Ponce Museum of Art, Serralles Castle, and the famed 19th-century Parque de Bombas red-and-black firehouse, Tibes Indian Ceremonial Park, and more than 500 restored 19th-century buildings.
- Full-day tours to El Yunque rain forest and the east coast, including the historic El Faro lighthouse and Cabezas de San Juan Nature Reserve.

Membership in the LeLoLai VIP program, valid for one week, can be obtained at the airport on arrival, at the tourism information center next to the American Airlines baggage claim area, and at La Casita Information Center near the cruise-ship piers in Old San Juan. It's also available at participating San Juan hotels, including the Condado Plaza, Condado Caribe Hilton, Regency, and the Condado Beach Trio; as well as at such authorized travel agencies as Travel Network, Turismo Internacional, Condado Travel, and Prime Market Travel.

THE PERFORMING ARTS

Qué Pasa, the official visitors' guide to Puerto Rico, lists cultural events, including music, dance, theater, film, and art exhibits. It's distributed free by the tourist office.

The **Condado Plaza Hotel & Casino,** 999 Ashford Ave. (tel. 721-1000), stages a folkloric show, the LeLoLai Festival, every Monday night at 9pm. Events include singing, dancing, and presentations of Puerto Rico mountain music. The $15 admission cost includes one free drink, and the show lasts about 75 minutes.

Sometimes, usually on Friday or Saturday, the **Institute of Puerto Rican Culture** presents folkloric shows to celebrate the island's cultural diversity at various theaters, churches, or auditoriums around town. It changes venue according to the availability of the artists and the anticipated demand for tickets. The admission charge is around $10, although some events are presented free. Be aware that the shows are usually presented in a theaterlike setting, not a nightclub, and so drinks are not served. For information, check a local newspaper or call 724-1000.

CENTRO DE BELLAS ARTES, avenida Ponce de León 22. Tel. 724-4747.

Built in 1981, in the heart of Santurce, the Performing Arts Center is a six-minute taxi jaunt from most of the hotels on Condado Beach. Costing $18 million (relatively modest for such a complex), the center has 1,883 seats in the Festival Hall, 760 in the Drama Hall, and 210 in the Experimental Theater. Some of the events here will be of interest only to those who speak Spanish, while others attract an international audience. **Bus:** 1.

Admission: Tickets, $12–$30 (prices are determined by the producers of the various shows).

EL TEATRO, in El Centro, the Condado Beach Trio, Ashford Ave. Tel. 721-6090.

In San Juan's convention center, part of the previously recommended Condado Beach Trio complex of hotels and restaurants, this room is known for the most spectacular show revues in San Juan. Usually these are in the *Olé Latino* style, with colorful costumes, Latin music, and dancing. A "taste of the tropics" is promised and ultimately delivered. However, since this room is also used for special events, call to find out what's scheduled at the time of your visit. Shows usually begin at 10pm (but confirm by phone). **Bus:** A7.

Admission: $28 (but the price varies, depending on the show or special event).

TEATRO TAPÍA, avenida Ponce de León. Tel. 722-0407.

The Tapía Theater was paid for by taxes on bread and imported liquor. Standing across from the Plaza de Colón, it's one of the oldest theaters in the western hemisphere, built about 1832. In 1976 a restoration returned the theater to its original appearance. Much of Puerto Rican theater history is connected with the Tapía, named after the island's first prominent playwright, Alejandro Tapía y Rivera (1826–82). Adelina Patti (1843–1919), the most popular and highly paid singer of her day, made her operatic debut here when she was barely 14.

Various productions—some musical—are staged here throughout the year, a repertoire of drama, dance, and cultural events. You'll have to call the box office (open Monday through Friday from 9am to 5pm). **Bus:** T1.

Admission: Tickets, $10–$30 (prices are determined by the producers of the various shows).

THE CLUB & MUSIC SCENE

AMADEUS DISCO, in El San Juan Hotel, avenida Isla Verde, Isla Verde. Tel. 791-1000.

Its conservative art deco interior welcomes a widely divergent collection of the rich and beautiful, the merely rich, and a gaggle of onlookers pretending to be both. The Amadeus Disco is in the most exciting hotel in San Juan (see Chapter 5) and a visit here offers a chance to explore the adjacent casino and the best-decorated lobby in Puerto Rico. The duplex area has one of the best sound systems in the Caribbean. The disco is open Tuesday through Sunday from 10pm to 3:30am. **Bus:** A7, T1, or 2.

Admission (including two drinks): $10–$15.

COPA, in the Sands Hotel & Casino, avenida Isla Verde, Isla Verde. Tel. 791-6100.

This is one of the major showrooms for revues along the San Juan beachfront strip. Although I can't predict what show may be featured at the time of your visit, previous revues have included *Hollywood Legends,* with impersonators appearing as Liza, Cher, or Tina Turner. There might also be a major Las Vegas–type headliner from the mainland. Shows are Wednesday through Sunday at 10:30pm. **Bus:** A7, T1, or 2.

Admission (including two drinks): $28, but the price can vary.

EL CHICO BAR, in El San Juan Hotel, avenida Isla Verde, Isla Verde. Tel. 791-1000.

Located just off the expansive and richly paneled lobby of the most glamorous hotel in San Juan, this bar provides live music that permeates most of the hotel's bustling lobby. Decorated in shades of scarlet, with risqué paintings evocative of a brothel in turn-of-the-century San Francisco, it is avidly appreciated by local residents, who court, flirt, converse, celebrate anniversaries, and dance on the sometimes-crowded dance floor. It's open Monday through Saturday from 9pm to 1:30am. Drinks begin at $3.50. **Bus:** A7, T1, or 2.

Admission: Free.

EL TROPICORO, in El San Juan Hotel, avenida Isla Verde, Isla Verde. Tel. 791-1000.

The format and nature of the shows presented here change frequently, although visitors can usually be assured of lots of glittering lights and plenty of theatricality. Currently, most of the shows include a bit of flamenco, as well as a bit of fashionably revealing décolletage from a bevy of feathered-and-beaded beauties. The hotel usually presents two shows a night, each of which lasts an hour and usually begins at 9pm or at 11pm. Call ahead to find out about the show and to make reservations. **Bus:** A7, T1, or 2.

Admission (including two drinks): $28.

LA LAGUNA NIGHT CLUB, calle Barranquitas 53, Condado. Tel. 725-4249.

This is one of the best-known gay nightlife centers in San Juan, which is unofficially considered the gay capital of the Caribbean. The club is known for its male "revues" at 1am on Tuesday, Thursday, Friday, and Saturday. Happy hour is nightly from 9 to 10pm, when drink prices are reduced. The club is open seven nights a week from 9pm "until whenever." There's dancing every night.

Admission (including first drink): Free Mon, $5 Tues–Sun.

PEGGY SUE, 1 Roberto H. Todd Ave. Tel. 722-4750.

This is one of the busiest nightclubs for young, upwardly mobile singles. There's a dance floor well worn by years of boogeying feet, although many visitors come only for drinks at the long and very accommodating bar. The decor was inspired by 1950s retro-chic, the music embraces most of the major musical movements since the 1960s, and people can usually meet and mingle easily.

There's live music every Friday and Saturday night. Jeans are not allowed. Its transformation from a bar into a crowded disco usually occurs around 9pm. It's open daily from 5pm to 3am. **Bus:** T1.

Admission (including one or two drinks): $5–$10, depending on the night of the week and the time you arrive.

SIRENA'S, in the Condado Beach Trio, Ashford Ave. Tel. 721-6090.

Animated and fun, and accustomed to packing in as many as 400 dancers on a Saturday night, this disco is situated in one of the most unusual concrete structures on Puerto Rico. Designed like the upper half of a clam shell and surrounded by raised patios that offer a view of the sea, La Concha (seashell) was the name of the original hotel before it became part of the Condado Beach Trio. Once you're past the doorman, you can sit at one of the many tables, dance beneath the shell, or make conversation at the elongated bar area. It's open Wednesday through Sunday from 7pm to 3am. **Bus:** A7.

Admission: $5–$15.

THE BAR SCENE

THE BLUE DOLPHIN BAR, calle Amapola 2, Isla Verde. Tel. 791-3083.

Set on a wooden terrace jutting out above the surf from a point near the Empress Oceanfront Hotel, this pleasant and often-animated bar offers one of the most exciting views of the dozens of oceanfront skyscrapers of Isla Verde. The house specialty drink, a Blue Dolphin, is made from Blue Curaçao liqueur and several kinds of rum. The place can be fun and the view is splendid. Admission is free, and drinks start at $4. The bar is open daily from noon to 4am; the disco hops Wednesday through Saturday from 9pm to 4am. **Bus:** A7, T1, or 2.

DON PABLO BAR-GALERÍA, calle del Cristo 103. Tel. 724-1008.

In long, narrow, and high-ceilinged street-level premises on a sloping street about a

---

IN THEIR FOOTSTEPS

Raul Julia (b. 1940) Known for his dramatic power and skill at portraying offbeat and isolated protagonists, this actor was perfectly cast as Gomez Addams in *The Addams Family* and in *Addams Family Values*. In these films, he heated up the screen with Morticia (Anjelica Huston) while portraying a character based on the original Charles Addams cartoons and the popular television series.

- **Birthplace:** San Juan, Puerto Rico.
- **Accomplishments:** Raul Julia's performances have ranged from the suave defense lawyer in *Presumed Innocent* with Harrison Ford to the political prisoner Valentin in the 1985 *Kiss of the Spider Woman*, with William Hurt. He's been called a "combination of Rudolph Valentino and John Barrymore."
- **Favorite Haunts:** Any meeting of the Hunger Project, the group he and others founded to end world hunger by the year 2000.

block from the Catedral de San Juan, this bar is of visual interest because of its collection of modern paintings; an arts-oriented crowd gathers here every evening. You can order one of the potent rum-based drinks that are the specialty of the establishment's friendly barman and owner. Live music is usually performed every Saturday night. Beer and rum drinks begin at $1.50. The house special is a 30-ounce Papajac, made with tequila, rum, and passionfruit, at $5. Open Wednesday through Saturday from 9pm to 3am. **Bus:** T1.

FIESTA BAR, in the Condado Plaza Hotel & Casino, 999 Ashford Ave. Tel. 721-1000.

This bar succeeds at attracting a nice mixture of local residents who mingle happily with hotel guests. The margaritas are appropriately salty, the rhythms are hot and typically Latin, and the free admission may help you forget any losses you may have suffered at the nearby casinos. Drinks are priced from $6. It's open Sunday through Thursday from 5pm to 1am and on Friday and Saturday from 5pm to 3am. **Bus:** T1.

MARÍA'S, calle del Cristo 204.

Perched on a stool here, you'll be served some of the coolest and most refreshingly original drinks in the capital—a banana, pineapple, or chocolate frost; an orange, papaya, or lime freeze; or a mixed-fruit frappé. The students, TV personalities, writers, and models who gather here also enjoy the Mexican dishes, such as chili with cheese, tacos, or enchiladas. If that sounds too heavy on a hot day, then I suggest the fruit salad. Tacos cost $3.50, enchiladas are about $4, and most frothy drinks go for $3.50 and up. Open daily from 11am to 2am. **Bus:** T1.

PALM COURT, in El San Juan Hotel, avenida Isla Verde, Isla Verde. Tel. 791-1000.

Many of its aficionados consider this to be the most beautiful bar on the island—perhaps in the entire Caribbean. Set amid the russet-colored marble and burnished mahogany of the hotel, and designed as an oval that wraps around a sunken bar area, the Palm Court is graced with one of the world's largest chandeliers and an undeniable sense of style. After 9pm Monday through Saturday, live music emanates from an adjoining room (El Chico Bar). Otherwise, patrons can relax while watching one of the most animated lobbies on the island. It's open daily from 11am to 2:30pm. Drinks cost $5 to $6.

SHANNON'S IRISH PUB, calle Loíza 1503, Santurce. Tel. 728-6103.

Ireland and its ales become "tropicalized" at this pub with a Latin accent and seven TV monitors. It's the regular watering hole for many of the island's university students, a constant supplier of high-energy rock 'n' roll, and the after-hours hangout of the staff from many of the city's restaurants. Happy hours occur twice daily, from noon to 2pm and 4 to 9pm, when drinks are half price. There are pool tables if you feel like playing, and a simple café serves inexpensive lunches daily from noon to 2pm. Beer costs $2.50, except during happy hour, when it's $1.25. Light lunches begin at $10 each. It's open Sunday through Thursday from 11:30am to 3:30am and on Friday and Saturday from noon to 4:30am. **Bus:** 1.

TIFFANY'S SALON, calle del Cristo 213. Tel. 722-3651.

Many young guests have wandered into this popular spot expecting a quick piña colada or daiquiri, only to stay all evening. Tropical drinks and frappés are also popular. The establishment is on one of the main streets of Old San Juan. Hard drinks start at $3. Open daily from 11am to 3am. **Bus:** T1.

VIOLETA'S, calle Fortaleza 56. Tel. 723-6804.

Stylish, comfortable, and sophisticated, Violeta's occupies the ground floor of a 200-year-old beamed house two blocks from the landmark Gran Hotel El Convento. A pianist at the oversize grand piano provides live music every Friday and Saturday night from 8pm to 1am, working with a singer who sings in five different languages. An open courtyard in back provides additional seating. Margaritas, at $4, are probably the most popular drink. Open daily from 1pm to 3am. **Bus:** T1.

CASINOS

Casinos are one of the island's biggest draws. Many visitors come here on package deals and stay at one of the posh hotels at Condado or Isla Verde with just one intention—to gamble at games ranging from blackjack to baccarat.

You can try your luck at the **Caribe Hilton** (one of the better ones), the **Condado Beach Trio, El San Juan Hotel and Casino** at Isla Verde, and the **Condado Plaza Hotel & Casino.** There are no passports to flash, admissions to pay, or whatever, as is often the case in European gambling casinos. The **Radisson Ambassador Plaza Hotel and Casino** is another deluxe hotel noted for its casino action. There's yet another casino at the **Dutch Inn Hotel & Casino,** 55 Condado Ave. One of the latest casinos to open on the island is at the **Holiday Inn Crowne Plaza Hotel and Casino,** on Route 187.

The largest casino on the island is the **Sands Casino** at the Sands Hotel & Casino at Isla Verde, on Isla Verde Road. Open from noon to 4am daily, this 10,000-square-foot gaming facility is an elegant rendezvous. One of its Murano crystal chandeliers is longer than a bowling alley. The casino offers 197 slot machines, 22 blackjack tables, five dice tables, six roulette wheels, two regular baccarat tables, and one minibaccarat table. Puerto Rican law provides that a percentage of gaming revenues be set aside for education funding.

The best casinos "out on the island" are those at the **Hyatt Regency Cerromar Beach** and **Hyatt Dorado Beach.** In fact, you can drive to either of these from San Juan to enjoy their nighttime diversions. There's also a casino at **Palmas del Mar** and yet another at the **Mayagüez Hilton** in western Puerto Rico. Puerto Rico's "second city," Ponce, now has a major casino—the **Ponce Hilton and Casino.**

Most casinos are open daily from 1 to 4pm and again from 8pm to 4am. Jackets for men are sometimes requested, since the commonwealth wants to maintain a "dignified, refined atmosphere."

MOVIES

Movie theaters in San Juan showing films in English include the **UA Paramount,** avenida Ponce de León 1313, Santurce (tel. 725-1101); **Metro 1, 2, 3,** avenida Ponce de León 1255, Santurce (tel. 722-0465); and **Fine Arts Cinema,** avenida Ponce de León 654, Santurce (tel. 721-4288).

CHAPTER 8

ISLAND DRIVES

**1. RAIN FORESTS &
BEACHES OF THE
EAST**

**2. KARST COUNTRY/
WEST & SOUTH
COASTS**

Although San Juan has traditionally been the focus of tourism in Puerto Rico, the rest of the island now has an appeal of its own. A rental car (for information, see Chapter 3) will allow visitors to add new dimensions to their experience, such as seeing some of the 79 towns and cities on the island, each of which has a unique charm and flavor. Puerto Rico also has a panoramic countryside, centuries-old coffee plantations and sugar estates, an almost lunar subterranean landscape of caves, and enormous boulders with mysterious petroglyphs carved by the Taíno peoples—the vanished indigenous culture of the island.

Puerto Rico is a relatively small island, barely 100 miles long and about 35 miles wide, but there is a wide variety of natural scenery. From your car, you can see terrain ranging from the rain forests and lush mountains of El Yunque to the lime deposits of the north and the arid stretches along the south shore, where irrigation is necessary and cacti grow wild. Seasonal changes also transform the landscape: In November the sugarcane fields are in bloom, and in January and February the flowering trees along the roads are covered with red and orange blossoms. Springtime brings delicate pink flowers to the Puerto Rican oak and deep-red blossoms to the African tulip tree, while summer is a flamboyant time when the roadsides seem to be on fire with blooming flowers.

Puerto Rico has colorful but often narrow and steep roads. While driving on mountain roads, blow your horn before every turn; this will help you avoid an accident. Commercial road signs are forbidden, so make sure you take along a map and this guide to keep you abreast of restaurants, hotels, and possible points of interest. There are white roadside markers noting distances in kilometers (1 kilometer is equivalent to 0.62 miles) in black lettering. Remember that speed limits are given in miles per hour.

Two programs that have helped the Puerto Rico Tourism Company successfully promote Puerto Rico as "The Complete Island" are the *paradores puertorriqueños* and the *mesones gastronómicos.*

The paradores puertorriqueños are a chain of privately owned and operated country inns under the auspices and supervision of the Commonwealth Development Company. These hostelries are easily identified by the Taíno grass hut that appears in the signs and logos of each one. The Puerto Rico Tourism Company started the program in 1973, modeling it after Spain's parador system. Each parador is situated in a historic or particularly beautiful spot. They vary in size, but all share the virtues of affordability, hospitable staffs, and high standards of cleanliness.

The paradores are also known for their food—each serves Puerto Rican cuisine of excellent quality, with meals starting at $15. There are now paradores at locations throughout the island, many within an easy drive of San Juan. For reservations or further information, contact the **Paradores Puertorriqueños Reservation Office,** Old San Juan Station, San Juan, PR 00905 (tel. 809/721-2884, or toll free 800/443-0266 in the U.S.).

As you tour the island, you'll find few well-known restaurants, except for those in major hotels. However, there are plenty of roadside places and simple taverns.

Visitors to Puerto Rico who long for authentic island cuisine can rely on mesones gastronómicos ("gastronomic inns"). This established dining "network," sanctioned by the Puerto Rico Tourism Company, highlights restaurants recognized for excellence in preparing and serving Puerto Rican specialties at modest prices.

Mesón gastronómico status is limited to restaurants outside the San Juan area that are close to major island attractions. Membership in the program requires that restaurants have attractive surroundings and comply with strict standards of good service. Members must specialize in native foods, but if you ask for any fresh fish dish, the chances are you'll be pleased.

What follows are two driving tours of the Puerto Rican countryside. The first will take you to the lush tropical forests and sandy beaches of eastern Puerto Rico, the second to the subterranean sights of Karst Country and on to the west and south coasts. They are both extended tours—the first takes approximately two days to complete and the second approximately six days—but Puerto Rico's small size and many roads will give you many places to pick up or leave the tour. In fact, there are several points in the tours where I give you the opportunity to cut your tour short and head back to San Juan.

DRIVING TOUR 1 —— RAIN FORESTS & BEACHES OF THE EAST

Start: San Juan.
Finish: San Juan.
Time: Allow approximately 2 days, although you may wish to stay longer at places along the way.
Best Times: Any sunny day Monday through Friday.
Worst Times: Saturday and Sunday when the roads are often impossibly crowded.

This tour will take you through some of Puerto Rico's most spectacular natural scenery, including El Yunque forest and Luquillo Beach. You will travel through the small towns of Trujillo Alto, Gurabo, Fajardo, Naguabo, Humacao, Yabucoa, San Lorenzo, and Caguas before returning to San Juan.

From downtown San Juan, go to Río Piedras and take Route 3 (avenida 65 de Infantera, named after the Puerto Rican regiment that fought in World War II and the Korean War). Turn south onto Route 181 toward Trujillo Alto, then take Route 851 up to Route 941. At the end of the valley you can spot the:

1. **Lake of Loíza.** Houses can be seen nestled on the surrounding hills. You may even see local farmers (jíbaros) riding horses laden with produce going to or from the marketplace. The lake is surrounded by mountains. Your next stop is the town of:
2. **Gurabo.** This is tobacco country, and you'll know that you're nearing the town from the sweet aroma enveloping it (tobacco smells sweet before it's harvested). Part of the town of Gurabo is set on the side of a mountain and the streets consist of steps.
   Leave the town by heading east on Route 30. Near Juncos, turn left onto Route 185 north, follow it up through Lomas, and then get on Route 186 south. This road offers views of the ocean beyond the mountains and valleys. At this point you'll be driving on the lower section of the Caribbean National Forest; the vegetation is dense, and you'll be surrounded by giant ferns. The brooks descending from the mountains become small waterfalls on both sides of the road. At about 25 miles east of San Juan is:
3. **El Yunque.** Consisting of about 28,000 acres, it's the only tropical forest in the U.S. National Forest system. It is said to contain some 240 different tree species native to the area (only half a dozen of these are found on the mainland United

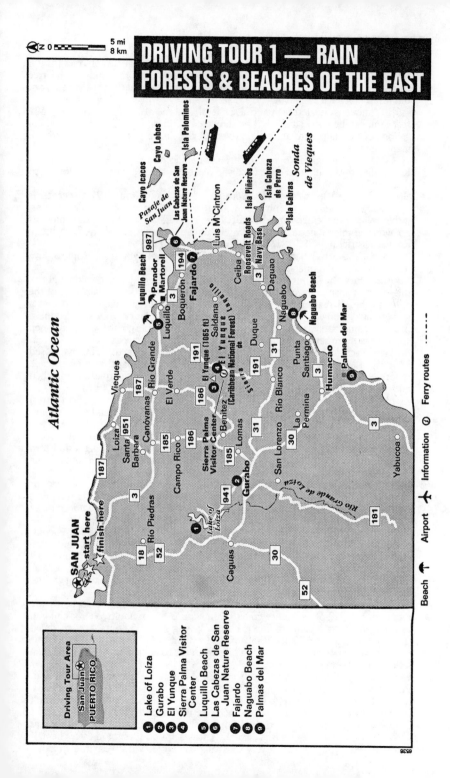

DRIVING TOUR 1 — RAIN FORESTS & BEACHES OF THE EAST

Atlantic Ocean

N 0 | 5 mi / 8 km

Driving Tour Area
San Juan ★
PUERTO RICO

1 Lake of Loíza
2 Gurabo
3 El Yunque
4 Sierra Palma Visitor Center
5 Luquillo Beach
6 Las Cabezas de San Juan Nature Reserve
7 Fajardo
8 Naguabo Beach
9 Palmas del Mar

Beach | Airport | Information | Ferry routes

SAN JUAN
start here
finish here

Cayo Icacos
Cayo Lobos
Isla Palominos
Las Cabezas de San Juan Nature Reserve
Pasaje de San Juan
Luis M. Cintron
Roosevelt Roads
Isla Piñeros
Isla Cabeza de Perro
Navy Base
Isla Cabras
Sonda de Vieques

Luquillo Beach
Parador Martorell
Luquillo
Boquerón
Fajardo
Ceiba
Daguao
Naguabo
Naguabo Beach
Palmas del Mar

Vieques
Río Grande
El Verde
Loíza
Santa Bárbara
Canóvanas
Campo Rico
Sierra Palma Visitor Center
Benítez
Lomas
El Yunque (1065 ft)
El Yunque (Caribbean National Forest)
Saldaña
Duque
Punta Santiago
Humacao

Río Piedras
Gurabo
San Lorenzo
Río Blanco
La Permina
Yabucoa

Lake of Loíza
Caguas

Rio Grande de Loíza

987
194
3
191
186
185
941
951
187
185
18
52
31
30
52
181
3
30
31
191
3

6538

States). In this world of cedars and satinwood (draped in tangles of vines), you'll hear chirping birds, see wild orchids, and perhaps hear the song of the tree frog—the *coquí*. The entire forest is a bird sanctuary and may be the last retreat of the rare Puerto Rican parrot.

El Yunque is situated high above sea level, and the peak of El Toro is at 3,532 feet. You can be fairly sure you'll be showered upon, since more than 100 billion gallons of rain falls here annually. However, the showers are brief and there are many shelters.

Continue driving on Route 186 through Benitez and El Verde until you reach Route 986. Turn south and drive until you reach Route 191, which will take you to the:

4. **Sierra Palma Visitor Center.** Located at km 11.6 on Route 191, the center is open daily from 9:30am to 5pm. Guides here give lectures and show slides; groups, if they make arrangements in advance, can go on guided hikes. Since the center has no working telephone, call the Administrative Headquarters of the El Yunque Ranger District (tel. 887-2875) for information about the area.

To make your way back, backtrack on Route 191 until you reach Route 3. Five miles east from the intersection is:

5. **Luquillo Beach.** About 30 miles east of San Juan, edged by a vast coconut grove, this crescent-shaped beach is not only the best on Puerto Rico but also one of the finest in the Caribbean. You pay $1 to enter with your car, and you can rent a locker, take a shower, and use the changing rooms to put on your suit. Luquillo Beach becomes rather crowded on weekends, so if possible go on a weekday when you'll have more sand to yourself. Picnic tables are available as well.

The beach is open Tuesday through Sunday from 9am to 5pm; it's closed Monday (if Monday is a holiday, the beach will shut on Tuesday that week instead). Before entering the beach, you may want to stop at one of the roadside thatched huts that sell Puerto Rican snacks and pick up the makings for a picnic.

Not far from the beach is the Parador Martorell, where you can spend a restful night at the seaside (see "Where to Stay Along the Way," at the end of this tour).

From Luquillo, return to Route 3 east until the first exit to Fajardo, where you make a left onto Route 194. At the traffic light at the corner of the Monte Brisas Shopping Center, turn left; stay on this road until the next traffic light and turn right. Continue on this road until it intersects with Route 987. Turn left onto Route 987 and continue until you reach the entrance to:

6. **Las Cabezas de San Juan Nature Reserve,** better known as *El Faro,* or "The Lighthouse." In the northeast corner of Puerto Rico, north of Fajardo, this is one of the most beautiful and important areas of the island—unique because of the number of different ecological communities that flourish here.

Surrounded on three sides by the Atlantic Ocean, the 316-acre site encompasses forest land, mangroves, lagoons, beaches, cliffs, offshore cays, and coral reefs. El Faro serves as a research center for the scientific community. Home to a vast array of flora and fauna (such as sea turtles and other endangered species), including abundant and varied underwater life, it is an important spawning ground for fish and crustaceans, and for shore and migratory birds.

The nature reserve is open Friday through Sunday; since reservations are required, call 722-5882 before going. Admission is $4 for adults, $1 for children under 12 (parking included). Guided tours, lasting 2 to 2½ hours, are scheduled three times daily: at 9:30am, 10:30am, and 1:30pm.

After visiting the reserve, you can take the same road back to Route 3 and then follow the highway signs into:

7. **Fajardo.** This fishing port was hotly contested during the Spanish-American War. Puerto Ricans are fond of giving nicknames to people and places—for many years, the residents of Fajardo have been called *cariduros* ("the hard-faced ones"). Don't let the label mislead you; the people here are very friendly.

Sailors and fishers are attracted to the shores of Fajardo and nearby Las Croabos, which has a lot of fish restaurants. Rosas Seafood is a good eatery here. If you have time, you can take a very satisfying trip by ferry from Fajardo to either

Vieques or Culebra, small islands off the Puerto Rican coast that make urban troubles seem far, far away (see Chapter 11).

Continue south on Route 3, following the Caribbean coastline. At Cayo Lobos, just off the Fajardo port, the Atlantic meets the Caribbean. Here, the vivid colors of the Caribbean seem subdued compared to those of the ocean.

Go through the town of Ceiba, near the Roosevelt Navy Base, until you reach:

8. Naguabo Beach. Here you can have coffee and *pastelillos de chapín,* pastry turnovers that were actually used as tax payments during Spanish colonial days. At km 70.9 of Route 3, take a brief detour to the town of Naguabo and enjoy the town plaza's scented, shady laurel trees, imported from India.

Continue south along Route 3, going through Humacao and its sugarcane fields. When the cane blooms during November and December, the tops of the fields change colors according to the time of day. Humacao itself isn't of much interest, but it has a balneario-equipped beach with changing facilities, lockers, and showers. From here you can detour to the sprawling resort of:

9. Palmas del Mar. A full discussion of the offerings of this sun-and-sports paradise would be impossible here; see Chapter 9 for details.

After this stopover, you can continue along Route 3 through Yabucoa, nestled amid some hills. The view along the road opens up at Cerro La Pandura, a mountain from which there's a spectacular outlook over giant boulders onto the Caribbean.

At the town of Maunabo, leave Route 3 for Route 181, which passes through the mountains to San Lorenzo. There, Route 183 will lead you to Caguas, where you may choose between the scenic tour (Route 1) or the speedy highway (Route 52) back into San Juan.

WHERE TO STAY ALONG THE WAY

IN LUQUILLO

PARADOR MARTORELL, 6A Ocean Dr., Luquillo, PR 00773. Tel. 809/880-2710. Fax 809/889-4520. 10 rms (4 with bath). TV **Directions:** At km 36.2 along Route 3, turn toward the shore, then turn left and drive four short blocks.

$ Rates (including continental breakfast): $55 single without bath; $70 double with bath. MC, V. **Parking:** Free.

Ⓢ Back in 1800 the Martorell family came to Puerto Rico from Spain and fell in love with the island. Today their descendants own and operate this Luquillo parador near the island's most impressive beach. When you arrive at the parador, you'll enter an open courtyard by a tropical garden. Meals in the patio of the guesthouse are enhanced by the fragrant flowers, the hummingbirds that inhabit the garden, and the occasional music of the coquí, the tiny Puerto Rican tree frog that few people are privileged to see. Breakfast always features plenty of freshly picked fruit and baskets full of homemade breads and compotes. The main reason for staying at the Martorell remains Luquillo Beach, which has shady palm groves, crescent beaches, coral reefs for snorkeling and scuba diving, and a surfing area.

A PLACE TO DINE IN FAJARDO

ROSAS SEAFOOD, Playa Puerto Real, Fajardo. Tel. 863-0213.
Cuisine: PUERTO RICAN/SEAFOOD. **Reservations:** Not required. **Directions:** Take Route 195 from Fajardo all the way to the end.
$ Prices: Appetizers $1–$8; main courses $8.95–$25. MC, V.
Open: Thurs–Tues 11am–11pm.

Ⓢ This is a charming but simple *mesón gastrónomico,* in business for more than 25 years with a devoted local clientele. Situated at the edge of the river, near the sea, it offers a beach-inspired ambience, dining rooms on two different floors, and windows overlooking the river. A family favorite, it's most popular on Sunday. Specialties include lobster or conch à la Rosa, and smashed plantains stuffed with seafood.

DRIVING TOUR 2 — KARST COUNTRY/WEST & SOUTH COASTS

Start: San Juan.

Finish: San Juan.

Time: Between 2 and 6 days, depending on how much of the itinerary you want to complete. The tour could run longer if you spend extra time out at some of the stops along the way.

Best Times: Monday through Friday, any sunny day.

Worst Times: Saturday and Sunday, when the roads are overcrowded with drivers from San Juan.

This tour begins with a foray into the famous Karst district of Puerto Rico. Along the way, you'll see the Taíno Indian Ceremonial Ball Park, Pagan Pagan's Cave, Río Camuy Cave Park, and Arecibo Observatory. You will then emerge from the island's interior to begin a roundabout tour of the west and south coasts, taking in Guajataca Beach, Mayagüez, San Germán, Phosphorescent Bay, Ponce, Coamo, and numerous other towns and attractions.

Starting out from San Juan, take Route 2 west through the town of Manati, after which you will pass the pineapple region. At km 57.9 turn left at Cruce Dávila and follow Route 140 south to the village of Florida. At km 25.5 you'll find a coffee cooperative where, during harvest time, the beans are processed, ground, and packed. At km 30.7, turn right toward the:

1. **Hacienda Rosas.** A coffee plantation, interesting at all times, is especially so from September to December or January, when groups of pickers walk under the bushes and gather the crimson beans while other workers process the yield.

   Shortly thereafter, you may leave Route 140 for Route 141, which will take you on an interesting detour to:

2. **Jayuya.** This village in the middle of the Cordillera Central is home to the Parador Hacienda Gripinas, a former coffee plantation where you can avail yourself of a very authentic and unique glimpse of the old days (see "Where to Stay and Dine Along the Way," at the end of the tour).

   If you decide to make this restful side trip, pick up the trail again by returning on Route 141 to Route 140, then travel west on Route 140 until you pass Lake Caonillas. There, turn onto Route 111 west, and you'll soon reach the town of:

3. **Utuado.** A small mountain town, Utuado boasts the Parador La Casa Grande, with accommodations, a restaurant, a swimming pool, and a good place to stop at after a day's touring in the area (see "Where to Stay and Dine Along the Way," at the end of the tour).

   From Utuado, continue west on Route 111 to km 12.3, where you'll find the:

4. **Taíno Indian Ceremonial Ball Park.** Archeologists have dated this site to approximately two centuries before Europe's discovery of the New World. It is believed that the Taíno chief Guarionex gathered his subjects on this site to celebrate rituals and practice sports. Set on a 13-acre field surrounded by trees are some 14 vertical monoliths with colorful petroglyphs, all arranged around a central sacrificial stone monument. The ball complex also includes a museum, open daily from 9am to 5pm; admission is free. There is also a gallery, Herencia Indigena, where visitors can purchase Taíno relics at very reasonable prices, including the sought-after Cemis (Taíno idols) and figures of the famous little frog, the coquí.

   Continue next on Route 111 to the town of Lares, then turn onto Route 129 north. Drive about 3½ miles, then turn right onto Route 4456, and you'll soon reach the:

5. **Río Camuy Cave Park.** Río Camuy, the third-largest underground river in the world, runs through a network of caves, canyons, and sinkholes that have been

DRIVING TOUR 2—KARST COUNTRY/ WEST & SOUTH COASTS

N

Atlantic Ocean

Caribbean Sea

SAN JUAN
start here

finish here

Driving Tour Area

PUERTO RICO

San Juan

1 Hacienda Rosas
2 Jayuya
3 Utuado
4 Taino Indian Ceremonial Ball Park
5 Rio Camuy Cave Park
6 La Cueva de Pagan Pagan
7 Arecibo Observatory
8 Quebradillas
9 Mayagüez
10 San Germán
11 Porta Coeli
12 Boquerón Beach
13 La Parguera
14 Phosphorescent Bay
15 Ponce
16 Coamo
17 Guayama

Airport ✈   Beach ⚓

0   14 mi
    22.5 km

6537

cut through the island's limestone base over the course of millions of years. The caves, known to both the pre-Columbian Taíno peoples and local Puerto Rican farmers, came to the attention of speleologists in the 1950s. Developed by the Puerto Rico Land Administration, they were opened to the public in 1987.

Gardens in the focal point of the park surround buildings where tickets can be purchased. Visitors first see a short film about the caves, then descend to where open-air trolleys carry them on the downward journey to the actual caves. The trip takes you through a 200-foot-deep sinkhole, a chasm where tropical trees, ferns, and flowers flourish, supporting many birds and butterflies. The trolley then goes to the entrance of Empalme Cave, one of the 16 in the Camuy Caves network, where visitors begin a 45-minute cave walk, viewing the majestic series of rooms rich in stalagmites, stalactites, and huge sculptures carved out and built up through the centuries. In 1989, the park opened Tres Pueblos Sinkhole, measuring 650 feet in diameter with a depth of 400 feet—room enough to accommodate all of San Juan's El Morro Fortress. Tres Pueblos lies on the boundaries of the Camuy, Hatillo, and Lares municipalities. In Tres Pueblos, visitors can walk along two platforms: one on the Lares side facing the town of Camuy and the other on the Hatillo side overlooking Tres Pueblos Cave and the Río Camuy.

The caves are open Wednesday through Sunday from 8am to 5pm, with the last tour starting at 4pm. Tickets are $6 for adults ($3 for seniors), $4 for children 2 to 12, free for children under 2. For more information, phone the park at 756-5555.

For more spelunking, drive to km 13.6 of Route 129. There, take Route 489 south to La Cueva de la Luz ("Cave of Light"). From there, continue on Route 489 to the Barrio Aibonito, Pagan sector. If you're not sure of your whereabouts, ask anyone to help you find:

6. La Cueva de Pagan Pagan ("Pagan Pagan's Cave"). A narrow road will lead you to a general store where you can receive directions to Pagan. Only the agile and those who like to explore should venture inside the cave. The cave is lit by daylight, but the floor is rough and irregular. (It's advisable to wear slacks and good walking shoes here.) There are no bats in the cave. Inside, a stone vessel contains fresh water that some believe has rejuvenating qualities. Other caves in this area have not been explored fully, but relics from the native peoples have been found in some of them.

A short drive from Pagan Pagan's Cave is the:

7. Arecibo Observatory. To get there, backtrack on Route 489 to Route 635; then turn right and travel east for a short distance until you reach Route 625. Turn right and take this road to the observatory.

Arecibo Observatory, also called the National Astronomy and Ionosphere Center of Cornell University, has the world's largest and most sensitive radar/radiotelescope. The telescope features a 20-acre dish or radio mirror set in an ancient sinkhole. It's 1,000 feet in diameter and 167 feet deep, allowing scientists to examine the ionosphere, planets, and moon with powerful radar signals and to monitor natural radio emissions from distant galaxies, pulsars, and quasars. It has been used by scientists as part of the Search for Extraterrestrial Intelligence (SETI), a research effort based on the proposition that possible advanced civilizations elsewhere in the universe might communicate via radio waves; thus Arecibo Observatory is called an "ear to the heavens."

Unusually lush vegetation flourishes under the giant dish, benefiting from the filtered sunlight and rain. There are ferns, grasses, and other plants such as wild orchids and begonias. Creatures such as mongooses, lizards, frogs, dragonflies, and an occasional bird have taken refuge under the dish. Suspended in outlandish fashion above the dish is a 600-ton platform similar in design to a bridge. Hanging as it does in midair, it resembles a space station.

The observatory (tel. 878-2612) is open for self-guided tours Tuesday through Friday from 2 to 3pm and on Sunday from 1 to 4pm. There's a souvenir shop on the grounds.

When you're ready to leave the observatory, follow Routes 625 and 635 back out to Route 129 and consider the time of day and your own inclinations when deciding whether to head south to one of the paradores in Utuado or Jayuya; head north to Arecibo and Route 2, the main north coast highway, where you can turn toward attractions and accommodations to the west; or return to San Juan.

Going west on Route 2 from Arecibo, the next stop on the tour is:

8. Quebradillas. Beautiful Guajataca Beach and two paradores are only a 15-mile trip from Arecibo along Route 2 in the vicinity of this small town near the sea. Guajataca is fine for sunning and collecting shells, but a *playa peligrosa* (dangerous for swimming unless you're a strong swimmer). Parador El Guajataca and Parador Vistamar are located fairly close to each other (see "Where to Stay and Dine Along the Way," at the end of the tour, for full descriptions).

From Quebradillas, take Route 113 south to Route 119, which will bring you to the artificial Guajataca Lake. Follow the lake's shoreline for about 2½ miles and turn left at km 19 to Route 455; you will soon cross a bridge spanning the Guajataca River, which runs through the lush mountains.

Return to Route 119, which you follow west to San Sebastián. There, take Route 109 across coffee plantations through the town of Anasco and on to Route 2, where you turn south and head for:

9. Mayagüez. For a complete discussion of where to stay and eat and what to see in the environs of this western port city, see Chapter 10. When you're ready to leave Mayagüez, continue southeast along Route 2 until you reach:

10. San Germán. This town, a little museum piece, was founded in 1512 and destroyed by the French in 1528. Rebuilt in 1570, it was named after Germain de Foix, the second wife of King Ferdinand of Spain. Once it rivaled San Juan in importance, although it has settled into a slumber, albeit one that has preserved the feel of the Spanish colonial era. Gracious old-world–style buildings line the streets, and flowers brighten the patios as they do in Seville. Also as in a small Spanish town, many of the inhabitants stroll in the plaza in the early evening. San Germán is the site of the Parador Oasis, not a satisfactory stopover.

On a knoll at one end of the town stands the chapel of:

11. Porta Coeli (Gate of Heaven). Dating from 1606, this is the oldest church in the New World. Restored by the Institute of Puerto Rican Culture, it contains a museum of religious art with a collection of ancient santos, the carved figures of saints that have long been a major branch of Puerto Rican folk art. Admission is free; the hours are Tuesday through Sunday from 9am to noon and 2 to 4:30pm. Guided tours are offered Wednesday through Saturday (tel. 892-5845).

Easily accessible from either Mayagüez or San Germán via Route 102 to Route 100 south is:

12. Boquerón Beach. This is one of Puerto Rico's best bathing beaches, and there's a comfortable parador with a good restaurant only two blocks away. For more information about Parador Boquemar, see "Where to Stay and Dine Along the Way," at the end of this tour.

From San Germán, take Route 320 to Route 101 into Lajas, where Route 116 will lead to Route 304, which will take you to:

13. La Parguera. There are two paradores in this small fishing village, the Parador Villa Parguera and the Parador Posada Porlamar (see "Where to Stay and Dine Along the Way," at the end of the tour). If you have the good fortune to find yourself in La Parguera on a moonless night, I recommend going to:

14. Phosphorescent Bay. A boat leaves Villa Parguera pier nightly from 7:30pm to 12:30am, depending on the demand, and heads for this small bay to the east of La Parguera. There, a pitch-black night will facilitate a marvelous show, since you can see fish leave a luminous streak on the water's surface and watch the boat's wake glimmer in the dark. This phenomenon is produced by a large colony of dinoflagellates, a microscopic form of marine life that produces sparks of chemical light when their nesting is disturbed.

To travel on, take Route 304 up to Route 116 and drive west through Ensenada. At Guánica, you may turn south and follow Route 333 out to Caña

154 · ISLAND DRIVES

Gorda Beach for lunch or a swim. While there, look for the cacti that flourish in this unusually dry region. Back on Route 116, drive north to Palomas, where you can take Route 2 into:

15. Ponce. A complete discussion of the many interesting eateries, inns, and sights in this old colonial city can be found in Chapter 10.

When you're ready to leave Ponce, take Route 1 east in the direction of Guayama. At the town of Santa Isabel, you may want to take an interesting detour north along Route 153 to:

16. Coamo. Along the way to this town, you'll see signs pointing to the Baños de Coamo. Legend has it that these hot springs were the Fountain of Youth sought by Ponce de León. It is believed that the Taíno peoples, during pre-Columbian times, held rituals and pilgrimages here as they sought health and well-being. For more than 100 years (1847–1958), the site was a center for rest and relaxation for Puerto Ricans as well as others, some on their honeymoon, others in search of the curative powers of the geothermal springs, which lie about a five-minute walk from Parador Baños de Coamo (see "Where to Stay and Dine Along the Way," at the end of the tour).

Return to Route 1, driving east onto Route 3 and on into:

17. Guayama. The small town of Guayama is green and beautiful, with steepled churches and one of the finest museums around, the Museo Cautino. The old mansion is a showplace of fine turn-of-the-century furnishings and pictures of the prize horses for which the Guayama area is famous. Just minutes from town is Arroyo Beach, a tranquil place to spend an afternoon.

To begin the final leg back to San Juan, take Route 15 north. If you take this road in either spring or summer, you'll be surrounded by the brilliant colors of flowering trees.

At km 17.1, in Jajome, you can see the governor's former summer palace, an ancient building now restored and enlarged as a roadside inn. Continue on Route 15, then take Route 1, which goes directly back to the capital.

WHERE TO STAY & DINE ALONG THE WAY

AT JAYUYA

PARADOR HACIENDA GRIPINAS, Rte. 527 km 2.5 (P.O. Box 387), Jayuya, PR 00664. Tel. 809/828-1717. Fax 809/828-1719. 19 rms (all with bath). **Directions:** From Jayuya, head east via Route 144; at the junction with Route 527, go south for 1½ miles.

$ Rates: Year-round, $50 single; $60 double. Breakfast $5 extra. AE. **Parking:** Free.

A former coffee plantation about 2½ hours from San Juan, in the very heart of the Cordillera Central (Central Mountain Range), this is reached by a long, narrow, and curvy road. This home-turned-inn is a delightful blend of the hacienda of days gone by and the conveniences of today. The plantation's ambience is found everywhere—ceiling fans, splendid gardens, hammocks on a porch gallery, and more than 20 acres of coffee-bearing bushes. You'll taste the home-grown product when you order the inn's aromatic brew.

The restaurant features a Puerto Rican and international cuisine. Most of the modest rooms come with ceiling fans. You can swim in the pool (away from the main building), soak up the sun, or enjoy the nearby sights, such as the Taíno Indian Ceremonial Ball Park at Utuado. Boating and plenty of fishing are just 30 minutes away at Lake Caonillas. The parador is also near the Río Camuy Cave Park.

AT UTUADO

PARADOR LA CASA GRANDE, P.O. Box 616, Caonillas, Utuado, PR 00761. Tel. 809/894-3939. Fax 809/894-3939. 20 rms (all with bath).

Directions: From Utuado, head south via Route 111 until you reach Route 140; then head west until you come to the intersection with Route 612 and follow 612 south for about half a mile.

$ Rates: Year-round, $58.85 single or double. Breakfast $5 extra. AE, MC, V. **Parking:** Free.

Parador La Casa Grande lies in the district of Caonillas Barrios, in the mountainous heartland of the island, about 2½ hours from San Juan. Situated on 107 acres of a former coffee plantation, it has a cocktail lounge, a restaurant with both Puerto Rican and international specialties, and a swimming pool. All the comfortably furnished bedrooms have ceiling fans.

AT QUEBRADILLAS

PARADOR EL GUAJATACA, Rte. 2 km 103.8 (P.O. Box 1558), Quebradillas, PR 00742. Tel. 809/895-3070. Fax 809/895-3589. 38 rms (all with bath). A/C TV TEL **Directions:** From Quebradillas, continue northwest on Route 2 for one mile (the parador is signposted).

$ Rates: Year-round, $77.04 single; $80.25–$88.80 double. Breakfast from $4 extra. AE, DC, MC, V. **Parking:** Free.

You'll find this place along the north coast 70 miles west of San Juan. Service, hospitality, and the natural beauty surrounding El Guajataca—plus modern conveniences and a family atmosphere—add up to a good visit. The parador is set on a rolling hillside that reaches down to the surf-beaten beach. Each room is like a private villa with its own entrance and private balcony opening onto the turbulent Atlantic.

Room service is available, but meals are more enjoyable in the glassed-in dining room where all the windows face the sea. Dinner is an experience, with a cuisine that blends Créole and international specialties. A local musical group plays for dining and dancing on weekend evenings. The bar is open daily from 11am to 10pm (until 1am on Friday and Saturday).

There are two swimming pools (one for adults, another for children), two tennis courts (free for guests), plus a playground for children.

PARADOR VISTAMAR, 6205 Rte. 113N (P.O. Box T-38), Quebradillas, PR 00678. Tel. 809/895-2065. Fax 809/895-2294. 55 rms (all with bath). A/C TV TEL **Directions:** At Quebradillas, head northwest on Route 2, then go left at the junction with Route 113 for half a mile.

$ Rates: Year-round, $69.55–$90.95 single or double. Up to two children under 13 stay free in parents' room. Breakfast $6 extra. AE, DC, MC, V. **Parking:** Free.

High atop a mountain, overlooking greenery and a seascape in the Guajataca area, this parador, one of the largest on Puerto Rico, sits like a sentinel surveying the scene. There are gardens and intricate paths carved into the side of the mountain where you can stroll while you enjoy the fragrance of the tropical flowers that grow in the area. Or you may choose to search for the calcified fossils that abound on the carved mountainside. For a unique experience, visitors can try their hand at freshwater fishing in the only river on Puerto Rico with green waters, just down the hill from the hotel. Flocks of rare tropical birds are frequently seen in the nearby mangroves.

A short drive from the hotel will bring you to the Punta Borinquén Golf Course. Tennis courts are just down the hill from the inn itself. Sightseeing trips to the nearby Arecibo Observatory—the largest radar/radiotelescope in the world—and to Monte Calvario (a replica of Mount Calvary) are available. Another popular visit is to the plaza in the town of Quebradillas, where you can tour the town in a horse-driven coach. Back at the hotel, prepare yourself for a typical Puerto Rican dinner, or choose from the international menu, in the dining room with its view of the ocean.

AT BOQUERÓN BEACH

PARADOR BOQUEMAR, 101 Rte. 307, Boquerón, Cabo Rojo, PR 00622. Tel. 809/851-2158. Fax 809/851-7600. 64 rms (all with bath). A/C

TV **Directions:** From either Mayagüez or San Germán, take Route 102 into Cabo Rojo and then get Route 100 south; turn right onto Route 101 and the hotel will be two blocks from the beach.
$ Rates: Year-round, $65 single; $65–$75 double. Breakfast $5 extra. AE, DC, MC, V. **Parking:** Free.

Parador Boquemar, built in the late 1980s, lies near Boquerón Beach (considered one of the best bathing beaches on the island) in the southwest corner of the island, between Mayagüez and Ponce. The hotel is not right on the beach, but it's just a short block away. There is also a swimming pool, popular with Puerto Rican families, in back of the hotel. The Boquemar rents comfortable bedrooms with modern furnishings and has one of the best restaurants in the area, Las Cascadas; reservations aren't necessary. Meals, starting at about $15, include such specialties as mofongo filled with lobster and lobster asopao.

AT LA PARGUERA

PARADOR POSADA PORLAMAR, Rte. 304 (P.O. Box 405), La Parguera, Lajas, PR 00667. Tel. 809/899-4015. 18 rms (all with bath). A/C **Directions:** Drive west along Route 2 until you reach the junction of Route 116; then head south along Route 116 and Route 304.
$ Rates: Year-round, $64.20 single; $69.55 double. AE, MC, V. **Parking:** Free.

S Life in a simple fishing village plus all the modern conveniences you want in a vacation are what you'll find at this "Guesthouse by the Sea" in the La Parguera section of Lajas, in the southwestern part of the island. The area is famous for its Phosphorescent Bay and good fishing, especially for snapper. The guesthouse, built in 1960, is near several fishing villages and other points of interest. If you like to collect seashells, you can beachcomb. Other collectors' items found here are fossilized crustacea and marine plants. If you want to fish, you can rent a boat at the nearby villages, and you can even cook your catch in a communal kitchen. Otherwise, meals are not served—not even breakfast.

PARADOR VILLA PARGUERA, 304 Main St. (P.O. Box 273), La Parguera, Lajas, PR 00667. Tel. 809/899-7777. Fax 809/899-6040. 62 rms (all with bath). A/C TV TEL **Directions:** Drive west along Route 2 until you reach the junction with Route 116; then head south along Route 116 and Route 304.
$ Rates: Sun–Thurs, $80.25 single or double; Fri–Sat (including half board), $299 double-occupancy packages (for two days). Two children under 10 stay free in parents' room. AE, DC, MC, V. **Parking:** Free.

Although the water in the nearby bay is too polluted for swimming, guests can still enjoy a view of the water and the swimming pool. Situated on the southwestern shore of Puerto Rico, this parador is known for its seafood dinners (the fish is not caught in the bay), its comfortable rooms, and its location next to the phosphorescent waters of one of the coast's best-known bays. The dining room offers daily specials, as well as such chef's favorites as filet of fish stuffed with lobster and shrimp. Meals are served daily from noon to 5pm and 6 to 9:30pm. The rooms are furnished in a simple modern style. Because the inn is popular with the residents of San Juan on weekends, there's a special weekend package for a two-night minimum stay; $299 covers the price of the double room, welcome drinks, breakfasts, dinners, flowers, and dancing with a free show.

AT COAMO

PARADOR BAÑOS DE COAMO, P.O. Box 540, Coamo, PR 00769. Tel. 809/825-2186. Fax 809/825-4739. 48 rms (all with bath). A/C TV TEL **Directions:** From Route 1, turn onto Route 153 at Santa Isabel; then turn left onto Route 546 and drive west for one mile.
$ Rates: Year-round, $50 single; $60 double. Breakfast $7 extra. AE, DC, MC, V. **Parking:** Free.

S The spa at Baños de Coamo features a parador offering hospitality in the traditional Puerto Rican style, although this place has a somewhat Mexican atmosphere. The buildings range from a lattice-adorned, two-story motel unit with wooden verandas to a Spanish colonial pink stucco building housing the restaurant. The cuisine here is both Créole and international, and the coffee Baños style is a special treat. The bedrooms draw a mixed reaction from visitors, so ask to see your prospective room before deciding to stay here.

Coamo is inland on the south coast, about a two-hour drive from San Juan; swimming is limited to an angular pool, but you can easily drive to a nearby public beach. The Baños has welcomed many notable visitors over the years, including Franklin D. Roosevelt, Frank Lloyd Wright, Alexander Graham Bell, and Thomas Edison.

CHAPTER 9

DORADO & THE EAST COAST

Three of the Caribbean's premier resorts— Palmas del Mar and El Conquistador on Puerto Rico's east coast, and the Hyatt Cerromar Beach and the Hyatt Dorado Beach to the west of San Juan—are the subject of this chapter.

Often people who book into one of the resorts at Palmas del Mar, Las Croabas, or Dorado see San Juan only on their way to or from the airport since the facilities at these places are so all-encompassing.

If you're going to Puerto Rico for the first time, you may want to spend a day or so sightseeing and shopping in San Juan before heading to your chosen resort since it's quite likely that once you're there you won't want to leave the grounds. The hotels are self-contained, with beach, swimming, golf, tennis, dining, and nightlife activities. For those who don't want to pay for accommodations at these luxury hotels, a fairly short trip will get you there for lunch and an afternoon on the splendid beaches.

1. DORADO

18 miles W of San Juan

GETTING THERE   By Limousine   Daily service leaving from the airport from 11:30am to 9:30pm is provided by Dorado Transport Co-op (tel. 796-1214). The fare is $14 per person (minimum of four).

By Car   From San Juan, take Highway 2 west to Route 693 north to Dorado (trip time: 40 min.)

ESSENTIALS   Tourist information and rental cars must be acquired in San Juan; for information, see Chapter 4, and for car rentals, see Chapter 3.

Once you're in Dorado, you can get around via the shuttle bus that travels between the two hotels every 30 minutes during the day.

The name itself evokes a kind of magic. Along the north shore of Puerto Rico, not far from the capital, a world of luxury resorts and villas unfolds. The big properties of the elegant Hyatt Dorado Beach Hotel and the newer, larger Hyatt Regency Cerromar Beach Hotel sit on the choice white-sand beaches here.

The site was originally purchased in 1905 by Dr. Alfred T. Livingston, a Jamestown, N.Y., physician, who had it developed as a 1,000-acre grapefruit and coconut plantation. Dr. Livingston's daughter, Clara, widely known in aviation circles and a friend of Amelia Earhart, owned and operated the plantation after her father's death. It was she who built the airstrip here. The building that houses Su Casa Restaurant (see "Where to Dine," below) was for many years the plantation home of the Livingstons.

WHAT'S SPECIAL ABOUT DORADO & THE EAST COAST

Beaches

☐ Playa Dorado, at Dorado, actually a term for a total of six white sandy beaches along the northern coast, reached by a series of winding roads.

☐ Palmas del Mar beaches—called "the New American Riviera"—three miles of white sandy beaches on the eastern coast of the island.

☐ Palomino Island, owned by El Conquistador, a private island paradise with sandy beaches and recreational facilities.

Great Towns and Villages

☐ Palmas del Mar, largest resort on the island, lying to the south of Humacao on 2,800 acres of a former coconut plantation—now devoted to luxury living and the sporting life.

☐ Dorado, the island's oldest resort town, center of golf courses, casinos, and two major Hyatt resorts.

☐ Las Croabas, a fishing village on the northernmost tip of Puerto Rico's east coast, site of the island's major resort, El Conquistador.

Sports and Recreation

☐ Hyatt Resorts Puerto Rico at Dorado, with 72 holes of golf, the greatest concentration in the Caribbean—all designed by Robert Trent Jones.

☐ The Club de Golf, Palmas del Mar, one of the leading golf courses of the Caribbean, lying on the southeast coast, with a par-72, 6,690-yard layout designed by Gary Player.

☐ Equestrian Center, Palmas del Mar, the finest riding center on the island, with trails cut through an old plantation and jungle along the beach.

☐ The "water playground" at the Hyatt Regency Cerromar Beach Hotel, Dorado, with a 1,776-foot-long "fantasy pool"—the world's longest freshwater swimming pool.

For the Kids

☐ The Palmas del Mar supervises summer activities program for children 5 to 14.

☐ Camp Coquí, at El Conquistador, which offers everything from building sandcastles to learning arts and crafts.

☐ Camp Hyatt, where children 3 to 15, supervised by bilingual, CPR-certified counselors, take part in daily activities from swimming and kite flying to arts and crafts and Spanish lessons.

WHERE TO STAY

HYATT DORADO BEACH HOTEL, Dorado, PR 00646. Tel. 809/796-1234, or toll free 800/233-1234. Fax 809/796-2022. 281 rms, 17 casitas. A/C MINIBAR TV TEL

$ Rates: Winter, $325–$435 single or double; from $605 casita. Off-season, $150–$200 single or double; from $245 casita. MAP $58 per person extra. AE, DC, MC, V. **Parking:** Free.

The two Hyatt hotels in Dorado sprawl across the former Livingston estate, which now bristles with palms, pine trees, and purple bougainvillea and has a two-mile stretch of sandy ocean beach. Two side-by-side 18-hole championship golf courses, designed by Robert Trent Jones, are their big draw (see "Sports and Recreation," in Chapter 1). The Dorado Beach, an elegantly outfitted low-rise building, is the more tranquil of the two Hyatts. Opened in 1958, it was originally designed by Laurance Rockefeller, and many repeat guests, including celebrities, have been coming back ever since.

The Hyatt Hotels Corporation, the present owner, has spent millions of dollars on improvements. The renovated bedrooms have marble baths and terra-cotta flooring throughout. Rooms are available on the beach or in villas tucked into nooks in the lushly planted grounds. The casitas are private beach or poolside houses.

Dining/Entertainment: Breakfast can be taken on your private balcony and lunch on an outdoor Ocean Terrace. Dinner is served in a three-tiered main dining room where you can watch the surf. Hyatt Dorado chefs have won many awards, and the food at the hotel restaurants, and at Su Casa Restaurant (not included in the MAP), is considered among the finest in the Caribbean. And don't forget the casino.

Services: 24-hour room service, laundry/dry cleaning, babysitting.

Facilities: Two 18-hole golf courses, seven all-weather tennis courts, two swimming pools, a children's camp, a private airfield. Also on the grounds is one of the best windsurfing schools in Puerto Rico—the Lisa Penfield Windsurfing School (see "Sports and Recreation," in Chapter 1).

HYATT REGENCY CERROMAR BEACH HOTEL, Dorado, PR 00646. Tel. 809/796-1234, or toll free 800/233-1234. Fax 809/796-4647. 461 rms, 43 suites. A/C MINIBAR TV TEL

$ Rates: Winter, $280–$395 single or double; from $605 suite. Off-season, $150–$225 single or double; from $300 suite. MAP $58 per person extra. AE, DC, MC, V. **Parking:** Free.

The high-rise Cerromar Beach's name is a combination of two words—*cerro* ("mountain") and *mar* ("sea")—and it is indeed surrounded by mountains and ocean and stands on its own crescent beach. The Cerromar Beach shares the Robert Trent Jones golf courses and other facilities with the Dorado Beach Hotel next door; a shuttle bus runs back and forth between the two resorts every half hour.

All rooms have first-class appointments and are well maintained; the majority have private balconies. The floors throughout are tile, and furnishings are casual and tropical, in soft colors and pastels. All rooms have honor bars and in-room safes.

Dining/Entertainment: The outdoor Swan Café has three levels, connected by a dramatic staircase; some tables overlook a lake populated by swans and flamingos. Other dining choices include Sushi Wong's and Chi Chi Steakhouse, both winter offerings, and the hotel's pride and joy, Medici's. The Flamingo bar offers a wide, open-air expanse overlooking the sea and the water playground.

Services: 24-hour room service, laundry/dry cleaning, babysitting.

Facilities: The water playground encompasses the world's longest freshwater swimming pool—a 1,776-foot-long fantasy pool, opened in 1986, that actually has a riverlike current, created as water flows through five connected free-form pools set at descending heights. It takes 15 minutes to float from one end of the pool to the other. There are also 14 waterfalls, a subterranean Jacuzzi, water slides, walks, bridges, and a children's pool—all amid tropical landscaping. A full-service spa and health club provides both body and skin care (including Swedish massages) and a "Powercise" machine that "talks" to you, coaching you during exercises. In addition there are 14 tennis courts.

WHERE TO DINE

EL MALECÓN, Rte. 693 km 8.2, Dorado. Tel. 796-1645.
   Cuisine: PUERTO RICAN. **Reservations:** Not required.
$ Prices: Appetizers $3–$6.75; main courses $9–$31. AE, MC, V.
   Open: Sun–Thurs 11am–10pm, Fri–Sat 11am–11pm.

If you'd like to discover an unpretentious local place with good Puerto Rican cuisine, then head for El Malecón, a simple concrete structure located in a small shopping center 2 miles east of the Hyatt Dorado Beach Hotel. Established around 1985, it has a cozy family ambience and is especially popular on

ⓕFROMMER'S COOL FOR KIDS: HOTELS

Hyatt's Resorts (*see p. 159*) These hostelries offer "family getaway" packages at Camp Hyatt, featuring professionally supervised day and evening programs for children ages 3 to 15. Children also receive a 50% discount on meals.

Palmas del Mar Resorts (*see p. 165*) This resort complex features a supervised activities program for children ages 5 to 14 in June and July; offerings include swimming, volleyball, aerobics, handcrafts, bowling, table games, sack races, table tennis, bingo, aquatic polo, basketball, and ring toss. Kids also delight in the 3 miles of beaches.

El Conquistador (*see p. 163*) There are a special activities area and game room just for kids. Camp Coquí (daily from 9am to 3pm) for children ages 3 to 12 costs $38 per day. Activities may include arts and crafts, fishing, sailing, and cooking lessons. Children under 12 stay free in their parents' room, and babysitting services are available.

weekends. Some staff members speak English, and the chef's specialty is fresh seafood, which most diners seem to order. If the ingredients are available, the chef can also prepare a variety of dishes not listed on the menu.

MEDICI'S, in the Hyatt Regency Cerromar Beach Hotel. Tel. 796-1234, ext. 3047.
  Cuisine: INTERNATIONAL. **Reservations:** Required.
$ **Prices:** Appetizers $5.50–$12; main courses $20–$28. AE, DC, MC, V.
  Open: Dinner only, daily 6:30–9:30pm.
Medici's is an elegant 340-seat dining room. On the way to your table, your attention will be torn between a view of the sprawling gardens and a look at the lavish antipasto table. The tables are situated on tiers at several levels, each of which has been angled for views of one of the gardens. The staff sets the mood of relaxed formality, the music is "upbeat classical," and the wine cellar is broad based and diversified. Guests can take their pick—from steak to "spa cuisine," from osso buco to Caribbean flavors. The kitchen also turns out a light Italian cuisine, and most dishes, including pastas, are available as appetizers, main courses, or side dishes. Try the grilled salmon on spinach with a dill sauce. Herb granita (Italian ice) is served between courses.

SU CASA, in the Hyatt Dorado Beach Hotel. Tel. 796-1234.
  Cuisine: SPANISH/CONTINENTAL. **Reservations:** Required.
$ **Prices:** Appetizers $6.50–$19; main courses $25–$45. AE, DC, MC, V.
  Open: Dinner only, daily 6:30–9pm. **Closed:** June–Oct.
⭐ Su Casa is the 19th-century Livingston family plantation home on the resort property. The Spanish colonial building with tile courtyards has been a favorite dining place for the rich and famous ever since the Rockefellers entertained guests at their posh Dorado Beach hideaway. Diners sit at candlelight tables and, while partaking of Spanish and classical European dishes, are serenaded by strolling entertainers. The chef produces an innovative cuisine, using Puerto Rican fruits and vegetables whenever possible, including plantain, spinach, and eggplant. Specialties include pastel de langosta (lobster fried in a corn tortilla with tomato-and-cilantro sauce), filete de res "Carlos V" (filet mignon with a Spanish brandy sauce on eggplant), rack of lamb, paella mixta (a very special blend of fresh seafood and spices, and Bien me sabe (a house special dessert), made with Caribbean coconut and biscuit. Don't plan to rush through a meal at Su Casa—allow enough time to enjoy the quality of your dinner in this relaxed tropical setting.

SUSHI WONG'S, in the Hyatt Regency Cerromar Beach Hotel, Dorado. Tel. 796-1234.
Cuisine: CHINESE/JAPANESE. **Reservations:** Required.
$ Prices: Appetizers $5.50–$9.75; main courses $12.50–$29.50. AE, DC, MC, V.
Open: Dinner only, daily 6:30–9:30pm. **Closed:** Spring–fall.

In this Oriental restaurant, a combined Chinese and Japanese cuisine is featured, along with what is acclaimed by some food critics as one of the best sushi bars on Puerto Rico. At least 200 diners can be seated. The tasteful Oriental decorations, soft lighting, and Asian music give the three-level restaurant an exotic, elegant, yet casual atmosphere.

The menu is traditional; all the dishes are familiar, even to those who frequent only neighborhood Chinese eateries. You might begin, for example, with wonton soup or shrimp tempura, then follow with salmon in black-bean sauce, sweet-and-sour pork or chicken, or Peking duck—oven roasted, glazed, and crisp. Many diners prefer to come here for the sushi bar combinations, including a sampling of almost everything on the Sushi platter deluxe: tuna, octopus, yellowtail, shrimp, eel, crab, salmon, tuna, and smelt roe. Children's portions are available at half price.

EVENING ENTERTAINMENT

When you tire of the casinos, try Puerto Rico's liveliest sports bar, **El Coquí,** in the Hyatt Regency Cerromar Beach Hotel (tel. 796-1234). An electronic temple for the sports-minded, it contains arrays of basketball simulators, board games, large-screen video TVs, and a high-amplification sound system left over from the establishment's former status as a disco. Drinks begin at $4, and the bar is open daily from 7pm to 2am.

2. LAS CROABAS

31 miles E of San Juan

GETTING THERE By Car From San Juan, head east on Route 3 toward Fajardo. At the intersection, cut northeast on Route 195 and continue to the intersection with Route 987, at which point turn north.

ESSENTIALS El Conquistador greets all guests personally at the San Juan airport and transports them to the resort (alert the hotel to the time of your arrival): On arrival, you will be escorted to El Conquistador's airport Welcome Center. Then you will ride in one of El Conquistador's motor coaches. During the 31-mile (45-minute) trip to the resort, you will be preregistered by a concierge, served refreshments, shown a video of the resort's features, and presented with sightseeing commentary.

For nearly two decades, from the '60s through the late '70s, the acknowledged leader in luxury resorts in the Caribbean was El Conquistador. Its site atop a 300-foot cliff at the northeastern tip of Puerto Rico overlooks both the Caribbean Sea and the Atlantic Ocean. It closed in 1980. But the name El Conquistador still evokes pleasurable memories among its numerous former guests. A new $250-million El Conquistador—reborn, redesigned, and distinctive—opened on the same site on October 1, 1993. George Bush was among the first guests.

The developers of the original El Conquistador were Hugh McPherson and Raymond J. Burmeister, who met on Puerto Rico in 1958. McPherson purchased 120 acres of land that had served as a U.S. Navy observation post during World War II and built his home nearby.

The developers hired architect Robert Alderdice, a Carnegie Tech graduate who was working in Puerto Rico, to design an 84-room hotel at a cost of $1.2 million, and they applied for a loan from the Government Development Bank of Puerto Rico. The planned name for the hotel was Trade Winds. But when a bank official hinted that if the developers wanted government funding the hotel should have a Spanish name, Burmeister stayed up all night going through a Spanish-English dictionary until he was inspired by the word "conquistador." After the hotel opened on July 14, 1962, it soon became the "in" place to stay.

But El Conquistador was too small ever to be profitable. Planning began immediately for a massive expansion from 84 rooms to 388. Construction began at the conclusion of the 1966 high season, and the hotel was closed for only six months. It remained open during the rest of the construction, which lasted two years.

The initial budget for the hotel's expansion was $15 million. By the time the new "El Conquistador Hotel and Club" was completed and furnished in September 1968, the cost had doubled. A circular casino, in black and stainless steel, appeared in the last scene of the James Bond movie *Goldfinger*. A nightclub named Anything Goes at Sugar's had 250 lavender seats, each of which was different (they included a 1932-style bathtub, a rowboat, an electric chair, and a Volkswagen). An 18-hole championship golf course, designed by Robert von Hagge, featured swans—imported from Switzerland—on its lakes.

The grand inaugural took place the weekend of November 1, 1968. From New York this Friday, Trans-Caribbean Airways flew its new DC8, *El Magnifico,* which seated 222 passengers. The plane, chartered by the hotel, was at full capacity with press, stage, screen, and literary luminaries. Among the celebrities were Elaine May, Jack Gilford, Celeste Holm, (with her husband and two poodles), Elaine Stritch (and her dog), Amy Vanderbilt, Jack Palance, Burt Bachrach and Angie Dickinson, Omar Shariff, Marc Connelly, Maureen O'Sullivan, and Xavier Cugat.

In its glory days, El Conquistador epitomized the luxurious Caribbean resort. Crippled by the Middle East oil embargo during the mid-1970s and the recession that followed, Puerto Rico's tourist business declined and the hotel was financially devastated.

Less than seven years after its inaugural, El Conquistador was in serious trouble. In May 1977 the hotel reduced its staff 50%, and one month later it closed. Reopened in 1978 with an infusion of new investor money, it declared bankruptcy a year later. By May 1980 it was all over—the once-glamorous resort was shuttered.

In 1982, a religious organization, Maharishi International Caribbean, Inc., paid $2.5 million for the property to use as a meditation center and university, but these plans never materialized. The buildings began to decay and fall apart.

In 1988 the Commonwealth of Puerto Rico expropriated the property because $12 million was owed in back taxes. Then a dedicated search began to find a developer who would finance and re-create a new world-class resort. Finally, Mitsubishi and the Williams Hospitality Group of San Juan infused more than $250 million into the project and opened the new hotel.

WHERE TO STAY

EL CONQUISTADOR RESORT & COUNTRY CLUB, Las Croabas (P.O. Box 70001, Fajardo), PR 00738. Tel. 809/863-1000, or toll free 800/468-5228 in the U.S. Fax 809/860-3280. 802 rms, 122 suites. A/C MINIBAR TV TEL
$ Rates: Winter, $265–$415 single or double; from $950 suite. Off-season, $165–$320 single or double; from $950 suite. Extra person $40. Children under 12 stay free in parents' room. Breakfast $12 extra. AE, DC, MC, V. **Parking:** $7.

One of the most spectacular and impressive properties anywhere in the tropics, El Conquistador is *the* destination for many people. Rebuilt in 1993 by Mitsubishi and the Williams Hospitality Group at a cost of $250 million, it incoporates $1 million worth of art, a charming staff, and five different hotels on 500 acres of forested hills whose edge slopes down to the sea. The architecture was inspired by Mediterranean models, including the interconnected town houses of the Spanish colonial empire, the Moorish gardens of medieval Seville, and the grandiose neoclassical elegance of northern Italy. Each of the far-flung elements of the resort is interconnected by carefully landscaped serpentine walkways, and with a railroad-style funicular which makes frequent trips up and down the verdant hillside. Throughout, gardens are interspersed with trompe l'oeil murals, world-class paintings and sculptures, and some of the most sophisticated decorative elements in the Caribbean. The accommodations are designed to please, with comfortable and stylish furniture, soft tropical colors, and about half a dozen unexpected amenities (such as bathrobes and ironing boards) which make a stay very pleasant. One of its special aspects is the resort's staff, each of whom seems pleased to welcome guests to "their" hotel.

Dining/Entertainment: Altogether there are 16 different restaurants, one of which is a 24-hour tropical deli. Several others are highlighted in "Where to Dine," below. A casino incorporates dignified glamour with live music from a nearby piano bar. Among the bars and nightlife is the formal Drake's Library, outfitted with books, mahogany, leather, a vaulted ceiling, and a billiards table; and Amigos Bar and Lounge, where live merengue and salsa artists maintain a convivial ambience until the wee morning hours.

Services: Room service, babysitting, men's and women's beauty salon, laundry/ dry cleaning, massage.

Facilities: The hotel is the sole owner of a forested "fantasy island" (Palomino Island) about half a mile offshore, with caverns, nature trails, and a wide choice of water sports (such as scuba diving, windsurfing, and snorkeling). Private ferries run between the island and the main hotel at frequent intervals. There's also a 55-slip marina (several boats are available for rent), six swimming pools, numerous Jacuzzi tubs, and some of the largest and most up-to-date conference facilities in the world. There are lighted tennis courts and an 18-hole championship golf course designed by Arthur Hills with "unbelievable views." An arcade of shops includes branches of W. H. Smith bookstore and New York–based Reinhold Jewelers, a family-run shop which is the exclusive outlet for Tiffany's on Puerto Rico.

WHERE TO DINE

BLOSSOMS, in El Conquistador Resort. Tel. 863-1000.
  Cuisine: CHINESE/JAPANESE. **Reservations:** Recommended.
$ Prices: Appetizers $3–$4.25; main courses $21–$45. AE, DC, MC, V.
  Open: Dinner only, daily 6pm–midnight.
This restaurant opened at Christmas 1993 on the Mirador level and became an instant success. It features three culinary styles, including a sushi bar, and boasts some of the freshest seafood in eastern Puerto Rico. Sizzling delights are prepared on teppanyaki tables, and there's a zesty selection of Hunan and Szechuan specialties. On the teppanyaki menu, you can choose dishes ranging from chicken to shrimp, from filet mignon to lobster. Sushi-bar selections range from eel to squid, from salmon roe to giant clams.

ISABELA'S, in El Conquistador Resort. Tel. 863-1000.
  Cuisine: INTERNATIONAL. **Reservations:** Recommended.
$ Prices: Appetizers $5.50–$12; main courses $23–$42; Sun buffet lunch $35 per person. AE, DC, MC, V.
  Open: Dinner daily 6pm–midnight; buffet lunch, Sun only, noon–3pm.
Of the resort's 16 restaurants, Isabela's is considered the premier. Its echoing and dignified room was inspired by an aristocratic monastery in Spain, and it's flanked by one of the most beautiful pieces of ironwork (a gate similar to those in Spanish cathedrals) on Puerto Rico. There's additional seating on an open-sided terrace for diners who want to be exposed to the sea and the trade winds. The service is impeccable and the food is among the finest on the island. The menu might include roast lamb with Dijon sauce, grilled filet of beef with red wine sauce and exotic

mushrooms, roast chicken with natural juices (or fresh ginger sauce), and baked Caribbean lobster tail with drawn butter. Black-bean soup is one of the favorite appetizers.

LOS GAUCHOS, in El Conquistador Resort. Tel. 863-1000.
Cuisine: ARGENTINEAN. **Reservations:** Not required.
$ Prices: Appetizers $4.50–$12; main courses $19–$32. AE, DC, MC, V.
Open: Dinner only, daily 6:30pm–midnight.

Gauchos are the Argentinean prairie riders whose lifestyles resemble those of American cowboys. Meats are grilled here in the authentic Argentinean tradition. Located at Las Olvas Village, the restaurant offers many specialties of the house, including an Argentine tableside grill with various traditional meats as well as the popular Argentine "skirt steak." Seafood is also offered, including mahi-mahi broiled with olive oil, garlic, and parsley. Another favorite dish is beef-and-shrimp brochette. You might begin with barbecued Argentine sausages or a plate of turnovers filled with either seasoned meat or cheese and onion.

OTELLO'S, in El Conquistador Resort. Tel. 863-1000.
Cuisine: NORTHERN ITALIAN. **Reservations:** Required.
$ Prices: Appetizers $5.50–$12.50; main courses $19–$36.50. AE, DC, MC, V.
Open: Dinner only, daily 6pm–midnight.

You can dine by candlelight in the old-world tradition at Otello's, with a choice of either indoor or outdoor seating. Located across from Drake's Library on the Mirador level of the hotel, Otello's cuisine is authentic northern Italian. You might begin with one of the soups, perhaps pasta fagioli or minestrone, or else select one of the zesty Italian appetizers, such as hot seafood antipasto or clams areganata. Pastas, which can be ordered as either a half-portion appetizer or a main dish, include the likes of homemade manicotti or spaghetti carbonara. The chef is known for his many veal dishes, ranging from veal marsala to veal chop valdostana. Poultry and vegetarian dishes are offered nightly, along with several shrimp and clam dishes. The chef's special is a seafood suprême served in a seasoned marinara sauce over linguine.

3. PALMAS DEL MAR
46 miles SE of San Juan

GETTING THERE By Plane Humacao Regional Airport, three miles north of Palmas del Mar, has a 2,300-foot strip for private planes. No airline currently schedules regular flights to this airport.

By Bus The resort (tel. 809/852-6000) will arrange minivan or bus transport from Luís Muñoz Marín International Airport in San Juan to Humacao. The fare is $16 each way.

By Car From downtown San Juan, take Highway 52 south to Caguas, then take Highway 30 east to Humacao (trip time: 1 hour).

ESSENTIALS Beach fees: $1 for parking, 25¢ for use of changing room and a locker. Before going, see "Tourist Information" in "Orientation," Chapter 4.

Billing itself as the "Caribbean side of Puerto Rico," this residential resort community lies on the island's southeastern shore. Once there, you'll find plenty to do: One of the most action-packed sports programs in the Caribbean offers golf, tennis, scuba diving, sailing, deep-sea fishing, and horseback riding. Hiking on the resort's grounds is another favorite activity. There is a forest preserve with giant ferns, orchids, and hanging vines. There's even a casino.

Palmas del Mar's land is an attraction in its own right. There are more than 6 miles of Caribbean ocean frontage here, 3½ miles of which is sandy beach; the balance is rocky cliffs and promontories. Large tracts of the 2,700-acre property have harbored sugar and coconut plantations over the years, and a wet, tropical forest covering about 70 acres flourishes near the resort's geographic center.

One of Palmas del Mar's greatest assets is its location on the southeastern shore of Puerto Rico. Thus the property is exposed to the Caribbean trade winds that steadily blow across this section of the island all year; the winds have a pleasing effect and help to stabilize the weather. The temperatures are balmy year-round. Together, the wind and weather patterns make Palmas del Mar ideal for a great many outdoor sports. The wet season extends from May into September; rainfall amounts to about 9 inches a month during this period. The dryer season, from December to April, averages 3 to 5 inches of rain a month.

Guests can be accommodated in either hotel rooms or villas, depending on their space needs. The two hotels are the luxurious Palmas Inn and the Candelero Hotel. The villas are surrounded by a marina, the beach, a tennis complex, and a championship golf course. There are also some privately owned condominiums that are available for guests when the owners are away.

Most guests book into Palmas del Mar on a package plan, perhaps choosing one of the sports options, such as the golf package. Most packages are for seven days/six nights in winter, four days/three nights in summer. For more information, call toll free 800/468-3331 in the U.S.

WHERE TO STAY

CANDELERO HOTEL, at Palmas del Mar, P.O. Box 2020, Humacao, PR 00661. Tel. 809/852-6000, or toll free 800/468-3331 in the U.S. Fax 809/850-4445. 101 rms (all with bath) A/C TV TEL

$ Rates: Winter, $240 single or double. Off-season, $130 single or double. MAP $68 extra per person in winter, $55 off-season. AE, DC, MC, V. **Parking:** Free.

The rooms here come in a variety of sizes, some with king-size beds. High cathedral ceilings accentuate the space, which is extended even farther by patios on the ground floor. Some of the superior and deluxe accommodations have private balconies. The main dining establishment, Las Garzas, is discussed in "Where to Dine," below. The beach and golf course are close by.

PALMAS INN, at Palmas del Mar, P.O. Box 2020, Humacao, PR 00661. Tel. 809/852-6000, or toll free 800/468-3331. Fax 809/850-4445. 23 junior suites. A/C TV TEL

$ Rates (including breakfast): Winter, $320 suite for two. Off-season, $180 suite for two. MAP $65 per person extra in winter, $55 off-season. AE, DC, MC, V. **Parking:** Free.

This gem has only deluxe junior suites, each with a panoramic vista of sea and mountains. The general decor here evokes the feeling of a Mediterranean villa, with a spacious airiness; the rooms themselves have a Spanish antique style. The inn also houses the Palm Terrace Restaurant, discussed in "Where to Dine," below.

VILLA SUITES, at Palmas del Mar, P.O. Box 2020, Humacao, PR 00661. Tel. 809/852-6000, or toll free 800/468-3331 in the U.S. Fax 809/852-2230. 10 studios, 135 villas. A/C TV TEL

$ Rates: Winter, $195 studio; $320–$430 one-bedroom villa; $432–$565 two-bedroom villa; $564–$710 three-bedroom villa. Off-season, $140 studio; $193–$265 one-bedroom villa; $262–$340 two-bedroom villa; $340–$420 three-bedroom villa. MAP $68 per person extra in winter, $55 off-season. Three-day minimum stay in winter. AE, DC, MC, V. **Parking:** Free.

Adjacent to the Candelero Hotel, this complex of red-roofed, white-walled, Iberian-inspired villas would be a suitable vacation headquarters for a family. Each of the villas, furnished and decorated according to the taste of its absentee owners, contains a full working kitchen and enough privacy to allow a feeling of relaxed well-being. Prices in each category of villa depend on the building's proximity to either the beachfront or the golf course; several additional villas have been built against a steep hillside overlooking the tennis courts.

WHERE TO DINE

Palmas del Mar has a wide variety of restaurants. The Palm Terrace Restaurant is arguably the best, serving northern Italian food, but if management continues its policy of a dine-around plan, MAP guests need not become bored. Currently, MAP guests can choose among six specialty restaurants on the grounds, as well as five restaurants off the property. They can also enjoy five theme dining nights, including a western night and a Mexican night.

The following is only a partial listing of dining possibilities. Undoubtedly, you will discover several more on your own. All the restaurants are open during the winter season; in summer, only three or four may be fully functioning.

CHEZ DANIEL/LE GRILL, Marina de Palmas del Mar. Tel. 850-3838.
  Cuisine: FRENCH. **Reservations:** Required.
$ **Prices:** Appetizers $4.50–$8; main courses $19.50–$26.50. AE, MC, V.
  Open: Lunch Wed–Mon noon–3pm; dinner Wed–Mon 6:30–10pm. **Closed:** June 15–July 10.

It's French, it's nautical, it's fun, and it's the preferred dining spot for those whose yachts are moored at the adjacent pier. Daniel Vasse, the executive chef, presents a menu that might begin with fish soup or stuffed mussels, followed by such main courses as bouillinade (a traditional Catalán-style bouillabaisse) or lobster and chicken sautéed with butter in tarragon-and-lemon sauce. Filet mignon in a Roquefort sauce is another delectable choice. For dessert, you might enjoy a soufflé Grand-Marnier.

LAS GARZAS, in the Candelero Hotel. Tel. 852-6000, ext. 50.
  Cuisine: PUERTO RICAN. **Reservations:** Not required.
$ **Prices:** Appetizers $3.75–$7.50; main courses $15.50–$26.50. AE, DC, MC, V.
  Open: Breakfast daily 7–11am; lunch daily noon–3pm; dinner daily 6–10:30pm.

Cooled by trade winds, this outstanding restaurant overlooking a courtyard and swimming pool is an ideal choice for breakfast, lunch, or dinner. Lunch always includes sandwiches and burgers galore, and if you want heartier fare, ask for the Puerto Rican specialty of the day, perhaps red snapper in garlic butter, preceded by black-bean soup. Dinner is more elaborate. You might begin with a chilled papaya bisque served in half a coconut, followed by Caribbean lobster, New York sirloin, paella, or the catch of the day. On Wednesday an island buffet features Puerto Rican specialties, and on Friday a lavish seafood buffet is presented. A barbecue is held on the terrace every Saturday night.

PALM TERRACE RESTAURANT, in the Palmas Inn. Tel. 852-6000, ext. 52.
  Cuisine: CARIBBEAN/CONTINENTAL. **Reservations:** Recommended.
$ **Prices:** Appetizers $4.95–$8.50; main courses $15.95–$26.95. AE, MC, V.
  Open: Dinner only, daily 6–11pm.

In the Palmas Inn, near the casino, this restaurant offers a hilltop vantage point for views of Candelero Beach and the Caribbean Sea. This restaurant provides what many consider the finest dining in and around this sprawling resort. The chefs feel equally at home in both Caribbean and continental cuisine. A zarzuela (mixed medley) of shellfish might tempt you, as would the Caribbean lobster or perhaps baked island wahoo. Meat fanciers might enjoy such dishes as medallions of beef tenderloin. For appetizers, you can sample the likes of fried conch, squid flavored with garlic, or black-bean soup. The restaurant has an Iberian colonial decor, with wide expanses of glass to enhance the view.

EVENING ENTERTAINMENT

The **casino** (tel. 852-6000, ext. 13513) in the Palmas del Mar complex, near the Palmas Inn, is in the Culebra Room on the second floor. It features nine blackjack tables, two roulette wheels, a craps table, and dozens of slot machines. The casino is open from 6pm to 3am daily (in summer, closed Monday and Tuesday). Guests are requested to dress with "casual elegance." Under Puerto Rican law, drinks cannot be served in a casino, but you can enjoy one in the Palm Terrace Lounge.

CHAPTER 10

PONCE, MAYAGÜEZ & RINCÓN

1. PONCE
- **WHAT'S SPECIAL ABOUT PONCE, MAYAGÜEZ & RINCÓN**
- **WALKING TOUR: PONCE**
2. MAYAGÜEZ
3. RINCÓN

For those who want to see a less urban side of Puerto Rico, Ponce on the southern coast and Mayagüez and Rincón on the western coast offer a variety of places to stay, and each also makes a good center for sightseeing. Founded in 1692, Ponce, the second-largest city of Puerto Rico, has received much attention because of its inner-city restoration, and it is home to the preeminent art gallery on Puerto Rico.

Puerto Rico's third-largest city, Mayagüez is a port located about halfway down the west coast. Mayagüez may not be as architecturally remarkable as Ponce, but it is a base for exploring some sights and good beaches within the area. Rincón, to the north of Mayagüez, is even smaller, but it boasts the finest country hotel in Puerto Rico—the Horned Dorset Primavera—and has some world-class surfing beaches.

Not too far from all three towns is Boquerón Beach, a mile-long west-coast white-sand beach, one of the finest on the island. The Cabo Rojo Lighthouse, at the southwesternmost corner, is another interesting place to visit.

---

1. PONCE

75 miles SW of San Juan

GETTING THERE   By Plane   American Eagle (tel. toll free 800/433-7300) flies three times a day between San Juan and Ponce (flying time: 30 min.). The fare is $60 to $70 round-trip, depending on the ticket.

By Car   Take Route 1 south to Highway 52, then continue south and west to Ponce.

ESSENTIALS   Maps and information can be found at the tourist office, on the second floor of the Citibank Building, on Plaza de Las Delicias (tel. 841-8160).

Ponce—"the Pearl of the South"—was named after Loíza Ponce de León, great-grandson of Juan Ponce de León. Founded in 1692, it is today Puerto Rico's

WHAT'S SPECIAL ABOUT PONCE, MAYAGÜEZ & RINCÓN

Beaches

- ☐ Boquerón Beach, a mile-long west-coast white sandy beach, south of Mayagüez, where San Juan citizens flock for fun on the weekend.
- ☐ Playa de Ponce, on the southern coast west of Ponce—beaches of white sand opening onto the tranquil Caribbean, with rows of seafood restaurants.
- ☐ Playa Punta Higuero, Route 413 near Rincón, one of the finest windsurfing beaches in the world.

Great Towns and Villages

- ☐ Ponce, Puerto Rico's "second city," with possibly the best weather on the island.
- ☐ Mayagüez, its "third city," on the west coast, with some of the island's best swimming and surfing.

Architectural Highlights

- ☐ The central district of Ponce, a blend of Ponce Créole and art deco architectural styles dating from the 1890s to the 1930s.

Museums

- ☐ Museo de Arte de Ponce, leading art museum of Puerto Rico, with major American and European schools of the past five centuries represented.
- ☐ Museo Castillo Serrallés, Ponce, a Spanish Revival mansion built by a wealthy rum distillery owner.

Churches

- ☐ Cathedral of Our Lady of Guadalupe, founded in 1660, the best-known church in southern Puerto Rico.

Ancient Monuments

- ☐ Tibes Indian Ceremonial Center, outside Ponce, the oldest cemetery in the Antilles.

Ace Attractions

- ☐ Mona Island, off the west coast of Puerto Rico, often called the "Galapagos of the Caribbean," because of its rich marine life.

principal shipping port on the Caribbean. The city is well kept and attractive, as reflected by its many plazas, parks, and public buildings. A suggestion of a provincial Mediterranean town lingers in its air. Look for the *rejas,* or framed balconies, on the handsome colonial mansions.

Timed to coincide with 1992's 500th anniversary celebration of Christopher Columbus's voyage to the New World, the $440-million renovation of Ponce has brought new life to a once-decaying city. The streets are lit with gaslamps and lined with neoclassical buildings, just as they were a century ago. Horse-drawn carriages clop by, and strollers walk along sidewalks edged with pink marble. The restoration recalls the turn of the century, when Ponce rivaled San Juan as a wealthy business and cultural center.

Most of Ponce's distinctive architecture—a blend of Ponce Créole and art deco—dates from the 1890s to the 1930s, when it flourished as the hub of the island's sugarcane, rum, and shipping industries. At that time, Ponce was also home to many of the island's artists, poets, and politicians.

WHAT TO SEE & DO

In addition to the attractions listed below, the **marketplace** at calles Atocha and Castillo is colorful, **La Perla Theater** historic, and the **Serrallés rum distillery** is worth a visit. Perhaps you'll want to simply sit in the plaza, watching the Poncenos at one of their favorite pastimes—strolling about town.

If you feel a yen for shopping, head for the Fox-Delicias Mall at the intersection of calle Reina Isabel and the Plaza de Las Delicias. It is Ponce's most innovative shopping center. Among the many interesting shops in the mall is **Regalitos y Algo Mas,** located on the upper level. It specializes in unusual gift items from around Puerto Rico. Look especially for the unusual Christmas-tree ornaments, crafted from wood, metal, colored porcelain, or bread dough, and for the exotic dolls chosen and displayed by the owners. Purchases can be shipped anywhere in the world.

CATHEDRAL OF OUR LADY OF GUADALUPE, calle Concordia/calle Union. Tel. 842-0134.

In 1660 a rustic chapel was built on this spot on the western edge of the Plaza de Las Delicias, and since then fires and earthquakes have razed the church repeatedly. In 1919 a team of priests collected funds from local parishioners to construct the Doric- and Gothic-inspired building that stands here today. Designed by architects Francisco Porrato Doría and Francisco Trublard in 1931, featuring a pipe organ installed in 1934, it remains an important place for prayer for many of Ponce's citizens. The cathedral, named after a famous holy shrine in Mexico, is probably the best-known church in southern Puerto Rico.

Admission: Free.
Open: Daily 8am–noon and 3–6pm.

MUSEO DE ARTE DE PONCE, avenida de Las Américas 25. Tel. 848-0505.

If you follow calle Concordia from Plaza de Las Delicias 1½ miles south to avenida de Las Américas, you'll reach this excellent museum, donated to the people of Puerto Rico by Luís A. Ferré, a former governor. The museum building was designed by Edward Durell Stone (who also designed the John F. Kennedy Center for the Performing Arts) and has been called the "Parthenon of the Caribbean." Its collection represents the principal schools of American and European art of the past five centuries.

Admission: $3 adults, $2 children under 12, $1 students with ID.
Open: Mon and Wed–Fri 10am–noon and 1–4pm, Sat 10am–4pm, Sun and holidays 10am–5pm.

MUSEO CASTILLO SERRALLÉS, El Vigía 17. Tel. 259-1774.

Two miles north of the center of town is the largest and most imposing building in Ponce, built during the 1930s high on El Vigía Hill (see below) by the Serrallés family, owners of a local rum distillery. Considered one of the architectural gems of Puerto Rico, it is likely the best evidence of the wealth produced by the turn-of-the-century sugar boom. Guides will escort you through the Spanish Revival house, where Moorish and Andalusian details include panoramic courtyards, a baronial dining room, a small café and souvenir shop, and a series of photographs showing the tons of earth that were brought in for the construction of the terraced gardens. The roads leading to the museum are a confusing labyrinth of run-down unnamed residential streets; it's best to take a taxi; the cost is about $3 each way.

Admission: $3 adults, $2 seniors, $1.50 children under 12.
Open: Tues–Sun 10am–5pm.

MUSEUM OF THE HISTORY OF PONCE (CASA SALAZAR), calle Reina Isabel 53, at calle Mayor. Tel. 844-7071.

Located in the Casa Salazar and opened on December 12, 1992, this museum traces the history of the city from the time of the Taíno peoples to the present. Interactive displays help visitors orient themselves and locate other attractions. The museum includes a conservation laboratory, library, souvenir and gift shop, cafeteria, and conference facilities.

Casa Salazar ranks close to the top of Ponce's architectural treasures. Built in 1911, it combines neoclassic with Moorish styles and displays much decorative detail typical of Ponce: stained-glass windows, mosaics, pressed-tin ceilings, fixed jalousies, wood or iron columns, porch balconies, interior patios, and the use of doors as windows.

One of Ponce's main residential streets, calle Reina Isabel itself offers textbook examples of seven Ponceño architectural styles: European-neoclassic, Spanish colonial, Ponce-Créole, town Créole, neoclassic, and superior neoclassic.

Admission: $3 adults, $2 seniors, $1 children.

Open: Mon, Wed, and Fri 10am–5pm; Sat 10am–9pm; Sun 11am–7pm.

MUSEO DE LA MÚSICA PUERTORRIQUEÑA, calle Cristina 70. Tel. 844-9722.

The Museum of Puerto Rican Music was established in 1990 in a pink-and-white neoclassical inner-city villa located half a block east of Plaza de Las Delicias and built during the 19th century by a wealthy merchant. The museum's gracefully restored interior contains a complete retrospective of all forms of Puerto Rican music, including exhibitions of drums used in the island's music—an enthusiastic employee will play each for you. There are photos and memorabilia of the island's famous musicians, album covers, posters, and a collection of priceless stringed instruments.

Each room of the museum is devoted to a different musical tradition, from the most formal and classical to the most spontaneous and experimental salsa. In addition to an array of *cuatros* (inspired by, but distinct from, Spanish classical guitars), there are Arawak gourds, African percussion instruments, famous microphones that recorded concerts by major musicians, radios from the 1940s, and even a 1959-era neon-lit jukebox.

The Museum of Puerto Rican Music is one of only two such institutions in the Caribbean—the other is in Cuba.

Admission: $1 adults, 50¢ children under 12, students, and senior citizens over 65.

Open: Wed–Sun 9am–noon and 1–5:30pm.

PARQUE DE BOMBAS, Plaza de Las Delicias. Tel. 840-4146, ext. 342.

Built in 1882 as the centerpiece of a 12-day agricultural fair intended at the time to promote the civic charms of Ponce, the building was designated a year later as the island's first permanent headquarters for a volunteer firefighting brigade. It has an unusual appearance—it's painted black, red, green, and yellow. The building today houses a branch office of the Ponce Municipal Tourist Office (this is *not* the same as the Puerto Rico Tourism Company, which maintains an office in the Casa Armstrong-Poventud). A tourist information kiosk is situated inside the building; if you find it temporarily unstaffed, go across the street to the second floor of the Citibank Building, where administrative offices are located.

Admission: Free.

Open: Wed–Mon 9:30am–6pm.

EL VIGÍA HILL, at the north end of Ponce.

The city's tallest geologic feature, El Vigía Hill dominates Ponce's northern skyline. Its base and steep slopes have been covered with a maze of 19th- and early 20th-century urban development. Once you reach the summit, you'll see the soaring Cruz del Vigía (Virgin's Cross). Built in 1984 of reinforced concrete to replace a 19th-century wooden cross in poor repair, this modern 100-foot structure bears lateral arms measuring 70 feet long and an observation tower (accessible by elevator), from which one can see all of the natural beauty that surrounds Ponce.

The cross commemorates Vigía Hill's colonial role as a deterrent to contraband smuggling. In 1801, on orders from Spain, a garrison was established atop the hill to detect any ships that might try to unload their cargoes tax-free along Puerto Rico's southern coastline. To get there, take a taxi. From Plaza de Las Delicias, the ride will cost about $3.

NEARBY SIGHTS

The oldest cemetery in the Antilles, excavated in 1975, is on Route 503 at km 2.7. The **Tibes Indian Ceremonial Center** (tel. 840-2255) contains some 186 skeletons, dating from A.D. 300, as well as pre-Taíno plazas from A.D. 700. Bordered by the

Portugues River, the museum is open Tuesday through Sunday from 9am to 4:30pm. Admission is $2 for adults, $1 for children. Guided tours in English and Spanish are conducted through the grounds. Shaded by such trees as the calabash, seven rectangular ballcourts and two dance grounds can be viewed. The arrangement of stone points on the dance grounds, in line with the solstices and equinoxes, suggests a pre-Columbian Stonehenge. A re-created Taíno village includes not only the museum but an exhibition hall that presents a documentary about Tibes, a cafeteria where you can find refreshments, and a souvenir shop.

Built in 1833, **Hacienda Buena Vista** preserves an old way of life, with its whirring waterwheels and artifacts of 19th-century farm production. Once it was one of the most successful plantations on Puerto Rico, producing coffee, corn, and citrus. It was a working coffee plantation until the 1950s. Some 80 of the original 500 acres are still part of the estate. The rooms of the hacienda have been furnished with authentic pieces from the 1850s. Tours are conducted Friday through Sunday at 8:30am, 10:30am, 1:30pm, and 3:30pm. Reservations are required and may be made by contacting the Conservation Trust of Puerto Rico (tel. 722-5882). Tours cost $5 for adults, $2 for children. The hacienda is situated in the small town of Barrio Magueyes, on Route 10 from Ponce to Adjuntas.

Carite is easily reached from the Ponce Expressway near Cayey. This 6,000-acre reserve has a dwarf forest, which was produced by the region's high humidity and its moist soil. From several peaks there are panoramic views of Ponce and the Caribbean Sea. On one peak is Nuestra Madre, a Catholic spiritual meditation center that permits visitors to stroll the grounds. Fifty species of birds live in the Carite Forest Reserve, which also has a large natural pool called Charco Azul. A picnic area and campgrounds are shaded by eucalyptus and royal palms.

WALKING TOUR — PONCE

Start: Plaza de Las Delicias.
Finish: Plaza de Las Delicias.
Time: 90 minutes, excluding coffee breaks, museum visits, and shopping stops.
Best Times: During daylight hours.
Worst Times: Any rainy day.

The downtown revitalization of Ponce has probably required more money and generated more publicity than that of any other city (after San Juan) on Puerto Rico. Your tour of this Caribbean showplace begins on the eastern edge of the town's main square, Plaza de Las Delicias (also known as Plaza Muñoz Rivera). Within the symmetrical borders of this main square, you'll see the red-and-black-striped clapboard facade of the town's most frequently photographed building. (Red and black, incidentally, are the colors of the city's flag.) Note the Victorian gingerbread and the deliberately garish colors of the:

1. **Parque de Bombas** (Old Municipal Fire House). The fire department has moved into more modern quarters in another part of the city, but you can still see a handful of bright-red fire engines parked inside.
   On the plaza's opposite side, adjacent to calle Concordia/calle Union is the:
2. **Cathedral of Our Lady of Guadalupe.** This is probably the best-known church in southern Puerto Rico. Its trio of alabaster altars were commissioned by an ex-governor of Puerto Rico in the late 1960s in Burgos, Spain; there will almost certainly be parishioners at prayer inside.
   Notice, as you leave the cathedral, the many impeccably clipped trees ringing the perimeter of the plaza. Identified as Indian laurels, they were planted between 1906 and 1908 and are considered one of the botanical triumphs of Ponce. Clipped with manually operated shears into their carefully groomed topiary

forms at frequent intervals by a master gardener, they are well worth a second or third glance. Even the gracefully elaborate iron lampposts illuminating them date from 1916.

Across calle Concordia from the main entrance to the cathedral is one of Ponce's most famous houses, the:

3. Casa Armstrong-Poventud. This paneled and ornately crafted building was once the home of a wealthy Scottish-born banker. Today, in addition to other offices, it houses a tourist information center (open Monday through Friday from 8am to 4:30pm).

Note that at this western border of the Plaza de Las Delicias, street signs might identify it as Plaza de Getou. Regardless of what the plaza is called, turn right on exiting from the Casa Armstrong-Poventud and walk southward beneath the Indian laurels. On the square's southern edge, you'll see one of the most historic buildings of Ponce, carefully restored to reflect its original function during Spanish colonial days, the:

4. Casa Alcaldía (City Hall). On the site of an 18th-century monastery, this building was erected in 1840 as a general assembly, and then served (until 1905) as the civic jail. Speeches by Theodore Roosevelt (in 1906), Herbert Hoover (in 1931), and Franklin D. Roosevelt (in 1934) were delivered from its central second-floor balcony to crowds assembled below. In 1987 the building was visited by George Bush. The clock set into the tower was imported from London in 1877, and a tour of the baronial street-level interior reveals a memorial plaque dedicated to the fallen American dead (Second Wisconsin Regiment) during the Spanish-American War. A few paces farther on you'll see a galleried courtyard that formerly served as prisoners' cells. The building's main courtyard was used for public executions. In City Hall, other plaques make clear that the city of Ponce was named not after the first European to explore Florida (Ponce de León), but rather after de León's great-grandson, Loíza Ponce de León, one of the town's early civic leaders.

Note across from the entrance to City Hall (in the town's main square) one of the most beautiful fountains of Puerto Rico, the:

5. Lion Fountain. Crafted from marble and bronze and modeled after a famous fountain in Barcelona (Spain), it was made for the 1939 New York World's Fair and later purchased and erected in Ponce by its mayor.

Continue your walk along the southern edge of the square. Note the way the plaza has "chopped corners" (broadly rounded 45° corners rather than 90° perpendicular corners). They were designed this way for increased visibility by the Spanish armies as a deterrent to civil unrest and the contraband trade that flourished here during their regime. Ponce is said to have the only large square on Puerto Rico equipped with this military-inspired feature.

As you cross calle Marina/calle Commercio, which borders the southeastern edge of the square, look to your right to the faraway beaux-arts–inspired building painted a creamy shade of white. Originally built in 1922, it served as the town's casino until it was closed during the mid-1960s. Today it houses government agencies and is not open to the public. Nearer and perhaps more spectacular are the pair of banks flanking the southeastern edge of the square, the:

6. Banco de Santander (built in 1895) and the **Scotia Bank** (built in 1917). Both are adorned with intricate stained-glass windows, art nouveau detailing, and dozens of unusual architectural features. The alleyway separating the two banks, callejon Amor, is lined with African tulip trees which are believed to evoke the romantic spirit of any couple in love. (This alleyway is also the site of public and very popular concerts held every Sunday between 8 and 9pm by one of the town's classical orchestras or dance bands.)

Proceed eastward along calle Cristina, which funnels into the main square directly opposite the red-and-black-sided fire station. Within less than a block, the pink-and-white neoclassical villa you'll see on your left is the:

7. Museo de la Música Puertorriqueña. Established in 1990, this is one of only two such museums in the Caribbean—the other is in Cuba.

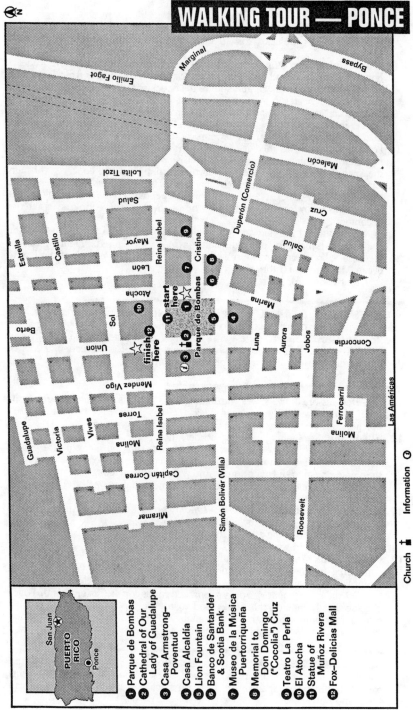

WALKING TOUR — PONCE

N

Marginal
Emilio Fagot
Bypass
Malecón
Lolita Tizol
Duperón (Comercio)
Cruz
Salud
Salud
Castillo
Estrella
Mayor
Reina Isabel
León
Cristina
Atocha
Berlo
Sol
Marina
Union
Méndez Vigo
Torres
Vives
Guadalupe
Victoria
Molina
Reina Isabel
Capitán Correa
Miramar
Simón Bolívar (Villa)
Roosevelt
Molina
Ferrocarril
Concordia
Jobos
Aurora
Luna
Las Américas

Parque de Bombas

start here ★ ①
finish here ★ ②
⑩
⑨
⑦
⑧
⑥
⑤
④
① ⑪
✝②
ⓘ③

Church ✝   **Information** ⓘ

PUERTO RICO
San Juan ★
Ponce ●

① Parque de Bombas
② Cathedral of Our Lady of Guadalupe
③ Casa Armstrong–Poventud
④ Casa Alcaldía
⑤ Lion Fountain
⑥ Banco de Santander & Scotia Bank
⑦ Museo de la Música Puertorriqueña
⑧ Memorial to Don Domingo ("Cocolia") Cruz
⑨ Teatro La Perla
⑩ El Atocha
⑪ Statue of Muñoz Rivera
⑫ Fox–Delicias Mall

6538

After your visit, leave the museum and continue your walk eastward along calle Cristina. At the next cross street, diagonal to where you're standing, you'll see the:

8. Memorial to Don Domingo ("Cocolia") Cruz (d. 1934), longtime leader of Ponce's municipal band and one of the best-known musicians from Ponce.

Turn left at calle Mayor and admire the neoclassical facade of the largest and most historic theater in the Caribbean, the:

9. Teatro La Perla. Originally built in 1862 to display the newfound prosperity of Ponce, it collapsed during an earthquake in 1918. For about 20 years only the massive Corinthian columns of its portico remained in place. In 1940 architect Porrato D'Oria redesigned it (retaining the original columns). After a radical restoration completed in 1990, the theater is now the largest and most historic in the Spanish-speaking Caribbean. Everything from plays and concerts to beauty pageants take place here; the excellent acoustics were designed along lines similar to those of New York City's Carnegie Hall. Depending on the time of day and the season, the lobby of this theater may be open for a quick look at its interior decoration.

Now continue walking northward along calle Mayor to the first intersection (calle Reina Isabel). To your right stands a Moorish-inspired building known as the Casa Salazar (Salazar House), which accommodates a branch of the Puerto Rican Museum of History.

It's now time for your:

REFUELING STOP Copious cups of coffee, assorted ice creams, and sandwiches are offered to tired pedestrians and talkative neighbors at the **Café Tomas/Café Tompy,** calle Reina Isabel at the corner of the calle Mayor (tel. 840-1965). Divided into a less formal and a more formal section, it is open daily from 7am to midnight. For more information, see "Where to Dine," below.

After this break, walk westward along calle Reina Isabel until you reach the edge of the previously explored Plaza de Las Delicias. From the square's northeastern corner stretches the city's main shopping street:

10. El Atocha. Stroll along its broad borders, noting the Spanish-inspired turn-of-the-century architecture, the cast-iron benches, and the many police guards ensuring one of the most tranquil urban streets of Puerto Rico. After your shopping, return to the main square and walk westward along its northern edge. Note, within the confines of the square, the memorial to one of Puerto Rico's best-known politicians, the:

11. Statue of Muñoz Rivera (1898–1980), who helped Puerto Ricans become U.S. citizens after a career of political lobbying.

Proceeding along the edge of the square, note one of the city's most alluring watering holes and shopping enclaves, the:

12. Fox-Delicias Mall. Originally built in 1931 as a movie theater, its pink walls are considered excellent examples of art deco architecture on Puerto Rico. In crumbling disrepair, the theater was transformed into a disco during the 1960s. In 1989 the government of Spain earmarked funds for the restoration of Ponce but specifically insisted that it be used to restore this building to its original celluloid glamour. Today this mall contains an array of shops, nightclubs, and cafés—any of which would be appropriate for a final:

REFUELING STOP Within the soaring confines of **Fox-Delicias Plaza** you'll find at least 25 different bars and cafés. Choose from establishments specializing in tacos, Spanish omelets, sandwiches, stuffed potatoes, Mexican food, and burgers.

WHERE TO STAY

DAYS INN, Rte. 1 km 123.5, Mercedita, Ponce, PR 00715. Tel. 809/ 841-1000. Fax 809/841-2560. 115 rms, 2 suites. A/C TV TEL

$ Rates: Year-round, $80 single; $90 double; $137.50 suite. Breakfast from $8 extra. AE, DC, MC, V. **Parking:** Free.

Located a 15-minute drive east of Ponce on Highway 52, opposite the Interamerican University, this hotel dates from 1989. Its two-story hacienda-inspired architecture sits in a garden-style setting; the bedrooms are conservatively modern and comfortable, equipped with pleasantly contemporary furnishings and receive plenty of sunlight. The prices appeal to families with children. Facilities include a courtyard swimming pool, a children's wading pool, a Jacuzzi, a coin-operated laundry, an international restaurant, a bar/disco, and ice and vending machines for sodas and snacks.

MELÍA, calle Cristina 2, Ponce, PR 00731. Tel. 809/842-0260. Fax 809/841-3602. 74 rms. TV TEL

$ Rates (including continental breakfast): Year-round, $65–$80 single; $70–$85 double. AE, DC, MC, V. **Parking:** $3.

A city hotel with southern hospitality, the Melía—which has no connection with other chain hotels in the world bearing the same name—often attracts businesspeople. The location is a few steps away from Our Lady of Guadalupe Cathedral and from the Parque de Bombas (the red-and-black firehouse). The lobby floor and all stairs are covered with Spanish tiles of Moorish design. The desk clerks, often family members, are courteous and speak excellent English. The rooms, comfortably furnished, are pleasant enough, and most have a balcony facing either busy calle Cristina or the old plaza. Breakfast is served on a rooftop terrace with a good view of Ponce, and the hotel's dining room provides some of the best cuisine in town. You can park your car in the lot nearby.

PONCE HILTON AND CASINO, avenida Santiago de los Caballeros 14 (P.O. Box 7419), Ponce, PR 00732. Tel. 809/259-7676, or toll free 800/HILTONS in the U.S., 800/268-9275 in Canada. Fax 809/259-7674. 148 rms, 8 suites. A/C MINIBAR TV TEL

$ Rates: Year-round, $140 single; $160 double; $300 suite. Extra person $25. Breakfast $9–$11 extra. AE, DC, MC, V. **Parking:** $4.50.

Opened in 1993 on an 80-acre tract of land, about a five-minute drive (7 miles) from the center of Ponce, this is the newest, best-accessorized, and most glamorous hotel in the area. Designed like a miniature village, with turquoise-blue roofs, white walls, and lots of open-sided exposure to tropical plants, ornamental waterfalls, and gardens, it welcomes conventioneers and individual tourists alike. The accommodations are equipped with tropically inspired furnishings, ceiling fans, terraces or balconies, and several luxurious amenities.

Dining/Entertainment: The most elegant of the hotel's three restaurants is La Hacienda (recommended separately in "Where to Dine," below). Other choices include Los Balcones, overlooking the sea, and a less formal place for hamburgers and snacks, El Bohío. There's also a casino, which is open daily from noon to 4am. Breakfasts, served from an elaborate buffet, are the best in Ponce.

Services: Room service, laundry, babysitting (if arranged in advance).

Facilities: Lagoon-shaped pool ringed with gardens, business center with a supply of personal computers, large convention center, fitness center, video arcade, summer camp for children. Water sports are also available.

NEARBY PLACES TO STAY

COPAMARINA BEACH RESORT, Rte. 333 km 6.5, Caña Gorda (P.O. Box 805), Guánica, PR 00653-0805. Tel. 809/821-0505, or toll free 800/468-4553 in the U.S. 69 rms, 1 suite. A/C TV TEL **Directions:** From Ponce, head west along Route 2 to Route 116 and go south; follow 116 until you reach Route 333, at which point head east.

$ Rates: Year-round, $128 single or double; $150 suite. Breakfast $10 extra. AE, DC, MC, V. **Parking:** Free.

Charming, low-key, and well maintained, this resort was originally built in the 1950s as the private vacation retreat of the de Castro family, the cement barons of Puerto Rico. In 1991 it was enlarged, upgraded, and opened to the European and North American tourist trade. It is situated beside a public beach, amid an attractively landscaped palm grove.

The bedrooms are in wood-sided one- and two-story wings that radiate out from the resort's central core. Each is decorated with lots of varnished pine (similar to what you might encounter in the Adirondack Mountains) and is outfitted with rattan and pinewood furniture.

Dining/Entertainment: The resort houses two restaurants, Ballena's (an elegant indoor restaurant for dinner only) and Las Palmas, which is set in the open air beneath a heavily trussed canopy. Service is slow but the food is well prepared.

Services: Babysitting, laundry.

Facilities: Swimming pool for adults, wading pool for children, two tennis courts, program of water sports (including snorkeling and scuba diving).

MARY LEE'S BY THE SEA, Rte. 333 km 6.7 (P.O. Box 394), Guánica, PR 00653. Tel. 809/821-3600. 8 units. A/C

$ Rates: $90–$120 unit for one couple; $120–$160 unit for two couples; $140–$160 unit for three couples. Taxes extra. Extra person $10. No credit cards. **Parking:** Free.

Owned and operated by Michigan-born Mary Lee Alvarez, a former resident of Cuba and a self-described "compulsive decorator," this is an informal collection of cottages, seafront houses, and apartments located beside the coastal highway, 4 miles east of Guánica. Designed in a modern, flat-roofed format of five California-style houses subdivided into eight different living units suitable for one to three couples, the entire compound is landscaped with flowering shrubs, trees, and vines.

To the north is the Guánica National Forest, a well-known sanctuary for birds and wildlife, recently designated an International Biosphere Reserve. Picnic areas, trails, and campsites are found throughout the reserve. The hotel sits next to sandy beaches and a handful of uninhabited offshore cays. For the benefit of its nature-watching guests, the hotel maintains about half a dozen rental boats with putt-putt motors, two different waterside sun decks, and several kayaks. A single visit by a maid per week is included in the price, although for an extra fee guests can arrange to have a maid come in every day. Each unit includes a modern kitchen, an outdoor barbecue pit, and a sense of privacy.

Don't come here looking for nighttime activities or enforced conviviality: The place is quiet, secluded, and appropriate only for low-key vacationers looking for privacy and isolation with a companion and/or with nature. There isn't a bar or restaurant here, and there aren't any formally organized activities on the premises.

WHERE TO DINE

EXPENSIVE

LA HACIENDA/LA CAVA DE LA HACIENDA, in the Ponce Hilton, avenida Santiago de los Caballeros 14. Tel. 259-7676.

Cuisine: INTERNATIONAL. **Reservations:** Recommended.

$ Prices: Appetizers $6–$7; main courses $19–$22. AE, DC, MC, V.

Open: Dinner only, daily 6:30–10:30pm.

These interconnected restaurants in the Ponce Hilton are the most elegant and stylish dining rooms in Ponce, evoking the traditions of Puerto Rico's colonial age. Designed as a network of rooms in a 19th-century coffee plantation, they offer impeccable service and a dignified sense of formality. The menu at both restaurants is the same—only the ambience differs. La Hacienda is a high-ceilinged octagon, with plenty of room between tables, lots of exposed paneling, and a dignified sense of calm. La Cava de la Hacienda resembles an underground wine cellar lined with wine racks and filled with rustic antiques and farm implements. There are also two private dining rooms for groups of 6 to 10 diners.

The menu changes every two weeks, but it might include seafood pot pie with shrimp and scallops, snails in a pinot noir sauce, cheese fondue for two, sushi rolls of salmon with a soy-wasabi sauce, a paillard of salmon with sorrel sauce, veal medallions with sautéed sweetbreads and apples, grilled skewers of lamb with almond rice, minted lamb chops, and lobster-stuffed ravioli with cream sauce. Typical desserts include flamed baked Alaska, crème brûlée, and apple beignets with honey-vanilla sauce.

MODERATE

EL ANCLA, avenida Hostos Final, Playa Ponce. Tel. 840-2450.
   Cuisine: PUERTO RICAN/SEAFOOD. **Reservations:** Not required.
$ **Prices:** Appetizers $2–$10; main courses $8–$22. AE, DC, MC, V.
   Open: Daily 11am–10pm (last order).
Established by members of the Lugo family in 1978, this restaurant, located south of the city on the beach, is among the best in Ponce. Much of its attraction is due to its position on soaring piers that extend from the rocky coastline out over the surf. As you dine, the sound of the sea rises literally from beneath your feet, an effect that somehow seems to improve both the view and the flavor of the fish.

Fresh fish is the specialty here, and typical dishes include red snapper served with a pumpkin flan, dorado in a tomato-and-brandy sauce, seafood casserole and seafood paella (prepared only for two or more diners), and several preparations of broiled lobster. Steak, veal, and chicken dishes are also available.

LA MONTSERRATE, Sea Port Sector Las Cucharas, Rte. 82. Tel. 841-2740.
   Cuisine: PUERTO RICAN/SEAFOOD. **Reservations:** Not required.
$ **Prices:** Appetizers $1.50–$6.95; main courses $13.95–$19.95. AE, DC, MC, V.
   Open: Daily 10:30am–11pm.
This restaurant is located about 4 miles west of the town center, right beside the sea. It attracts a loyal clientele from the surrounding area. Considered a culinary institution among Ponceros, it occupies a large, airy, modern building whose public areas are divided into two different dining areas. The first of these is slightly more formal than the other. Most visitors, however, head immediately for the large, grangelike room in back, where windows on three sides overlook some offshore islands. Nobody will mind if you roll up your sleeves and spend a leisurely afternoon over food and wine.

Dishes, prepared with whatever fish is freshest on the day of your arrival, might include octopus salad, a platter with seven different kinds of seafood in butter sauce, four kinds of asopao, or a whole red snapper in Créole sauce. For diners who have already had their fill of seafood, a selection of steaks and grills is available. The Velásquez family are the congenial owners.

INEXPENSIVE

CAFÉ TOMAS/CAFÉ TOMPY, calle Reina Isabel at calle Mayor. Tel. 840-1965.
   Cuisine: PUERTO RICAN. **Reservations:** Not required.
$ **Prices:** Appetizers $3.75–$5.50; main courses $8–$16. AE, DC, MC, V.
   Open: Lunch daily 11am–3pm; dinner daily 6–11pm. Café, daily 7am–midnight.
The more visible and busier section of this establishment functions as a simple café for neighbors and local merchants. On plastic tables flooded with sunlight from the big windows, you can order coffee, sandwiches, or cold beer, perhaps while relaxing after a walking tour of the city.

More formal, and more tuned in to the respectable and hardworking ethic of this old neighborhood, is the family-run restaurant. The discreet entrance is adjacent to the café on calle Reina Isabel. There, amid a decor reminiscent of a Spanish *tasca,* you can enjoy such dishes as salted fillet of beef, beefsteak with onions, four different kinds of asopao, buttered eggs, octopus salads, and *yuca* (similar to cassava) croquettes.

EL RESTAURANT, in the Melía Hotel, calle Cristina 2. Tel. 842-0260, ext. 516.

   Cuisine: PUERTO RICAN/INTERNATIONAL. **Reservations:** Not required.
$ **Prices:** Appetizers $2.50–$7; main dishes $6–$20. AE, DC, MC, V.
   Open: Lunch Mon–Sat 11:30am–2:30pm; dinner daily 5:30–10pm.
Located a few steps from Ponce's main square, on the street level of the Melía Hotel, this restaurant is run by a likeable and hardworking local family. The decor is solid, unpretentious, and filled with artists' depictions and old photographs of Ponce. The food is flavorful and plentiful, served with good cheer in simple surroundings. Menu offerings include octopus salads, guava shells filled with cheese, chicken Cordon Bleu, T-bone steaks, and broiled fillets of fish.

LUPITA'S MEXICAN RESTAURANTE, calle Reina Isabel 60. Tel. 848-8808.

   Cuisine: MEXICAN. **Reservations:** Required on weekends.
$ **Prices:** Appetizers $3–$9; main courses $7–$26. AE, DC, MC, V.
   Open: Mon–Wed 10am–10pm, Thurs–Sat 10am–2am, Sun 10am–midnight.
Established with fanfare in 1993, and adding a note of lighthearted fun to the city, this is the first (and only) Mexican restaurant in Ponce. Set in a 19th-century building and its adjoining courtyard, a short walk from Ponce's main square, it's the creative statement of Hector de Castro, who traveled throughout Mexico to find the elaborate fountains and the dozens of chairs and decorative accessories that fill these premises. The trompe l'oeil murals on the inside (featuring desert scenes in an amusing surrealism) were painted by the owner's sister, Flor de Maria de Castro.

A well-trained staff serves blue and green margaritas (frozen or unfrozen) and a wide array of other tropical drinks. Any of these might be followed by Mexican dishes cooked in cholesterol-free vegetable oil. Specialties include tortilla soup, taco salads, grilled lobster tail with tostones, seafood fajitas, and burritos, tacos, and enchiladas with a wide choice of fillings. Thursday through Saturday from 8pm to midnight, a mariachi band will probably provide musical entertainment. Lupita is an affectionate nickname for Guadalupe, the patron saint both of Mexico and the city of Ponce.

2. MAYAGÜEZ

98 miles W of San Juan, 15 miles S of Aguadilla

GETTING THERE   By Plane   American Eagle (tel. toll free 800/433-7300) flies five times daily from San Juan to Mayagüez (flying time: 30 min). Depending on restrictions, round-trip passage ranges from $70 to $90 per person.

By Car   Drive either west from San Juan on Route 2 (trip time: 2½ hours) or south from San Juan on the scenic Route 52 (trip time: 3 hours). Route 52 offers easier travel.

ESSENTIALS   Mayagüez doesn't have a tourist information office. Inquire in San Juan before going there (see "Tourist Information" in "Orientation," Chapter 4).

   If you fly into Mayagüez airport, taxis meet arriving planes. If you take a taxi, negotiate the fare with the driver first—cabs are unmetered here. You may wish to rent a car. There are branches of Avis (tel. 832-0460), Budget (tel. 831-4570), and Hertz (tel. 832-3314) at the Mayagüez airport.

The largest city on the island's west coast, Mayagüez is a port whose elegance and charm probably reached their zenith during the mercantile and agricultural prosperity of the 19th century. Most of the town's stately buildings were destroyed in a horrific earthquake in 1918, and today the town is noted more for its industry than its aesthetic appeal.

Despite the absence of grand architecture, Mayagüez is still identified as the honeymoon capital of Puerto Rico, partly because of the lush and beautiful vegetation that grows here and partly because of a peculiarly romantic 16th-century legend. It is said that local farmers often kidnapped young Spanish sailors en route to South America who had stopped at Mayagüez for provisions. However, it's anyone's guess whether this was good or bad luck: There was a scarcity of eligible bachelors in Mayagüez, and the farmers kidnapped the young sailors in hopes of providing their daughters with husbands and their farms with overseers.

Although the town dates from the mid-18th century, the area has figured in European history since the time of Christopher Columbus, who landed nearby when he discovered Puerto Rico in 1493. Today a bronze statue of Columbus stands atop a metallic globe of the world. Both are poised above the gracious plaza in the center of Mayagüez.

Famed for the size and depth of its harbor (the second largest on the island), Mayagüez was built to control the **Mona Passage,** a route considered essential to the Spanish Empire when Puerto Rico and the nearby Dominican Republic were vital trade and defensive jewels in the Spanish crown. (Today the Mona Passage is notorious for the destructiveness of its currents, the ferocity of its sharks, and the thousands of boat people who arrive illegally on Puerto Rico from either Haiti or the Dominican Republic on the adjacent island of Hispaniola.) Queen Isabel II of Spain recognized Mayagüez's status as a town in 1836. Her son, Alfonso XII, granted it a city charter in 1877. Permanently isolated from the major commercial developments of the island's leading city, San Juan, Mayagüez, like Ponce, has always retained its own distinct identity.

Today the town's major industry is tuna packing; 60% of the tuna consumed in the United States is packed here. It is also an important departure point for deep-sea fishing and is the bustling port for exporting the agricultural produce from the surrounding hillsides. Once considered the needlework capital of Puerto Rico, it still has women who create fine embroidery and drawn-thread work, industries that were brought to Puerto Rico centuries ago from Spain and Hapsburg-controlled Holland and Belgium.

WHAT TO SEE & DO

The chief attraction is the **Tropical Agriculture Research Station** (tel. 831-3435). It's located on Route 65, between Post Street and Route 108, adjacent to the University of Puerto Rico at Mayagüez campus and across the street from the **Parque de los Próceres** (Patriots' Park). At the administration office, ask for a free map of the tropical gardens, which have one of the largest collections of tropical plant species that are useful to people, including cacao, fruit trees, spices, timbers, and ornamentals. The grounds are open Monday through Friday from 7am to 4pm, charging no admission.

The **Puerto Rico Zoological Garden,** Route 108 (tel. 834-8110), houses birds, reptiles, and mammals, plus a South American exhibit—all within a tropical environment. Hours year-round are Tuesday through Sunday from 9am to 5pm; admission is $1 for adults, 50¢ for children, plus $1 for parking.

Mayagüez might also be the jumping-off point for a visit to **Mona Island,** the "Galápagos of the Caribbean," which enjoys many legends of pirate treasure and is known for its white sand beaches and marine life. Accessible only by private boat or plane, the island is virtually uninhabited, except for two policemen and a director of the Institute of Natural Resources. The island attracts hunters seeking pigs and wild goats, along with big-game fishers. Mostly it's intriguing to anyone who wants to escape civilization. Playa Sardinera on Mona Island was a pirates' lair. On one side of the island, Playa de Pajaros, there are caves where the Taíno peoples left their mysterious hieroglyphs.

Not far from Mayagüez is **Maricao.** You can reach it by taking Route 105 west and then driving north on Route 120. The town is colorful and rather small. On the outskirts look for a sign that reads **"Los Viveros"** (The Hatcheries); then take Route 410. Here, the Commonwealth Department of Agriculture hatches as many as 25,000 fish for stocking Puerto Rican freshwater lakes and streams.

Go back to Maricao to Route 120 south up to km 13.8 until you reach the **Maricao State Forest** picnic area, located 2,900 feet above sea level. The observation tower provides a splendid view across the green mountains up to the coastal plains. Continue on Route 120 across the forest to the town of Sabana Grande (Great Plain). Route 2 will then take you to the town of San Germán.

WHERE TO STAY

Staying overnight in Puerto Rico's "third city" offers these interesting possibilities:

MAYAGÜEZ HILTON AND CASINO, Rte. 104 (P.O. Box 3629), Mayagüez, PR 00709. Tel. 809/831-7575, or toll free 800/HILTONS in the U.S., 800/268-9275 in Canada. Fax 809/834-3475. 141 rms, 4 suites. A/C MINIBAR TV TEL

$ Rates: Year-round, $140–$180 single; $150–$190 double; from $300 suite. Breakfast $11.25 extra. AE, DC, MC, V. **Parking:** $4.

This country club–style hotel is situated on 20 acres of tropical gardens. Its grounds have been designated as an adjunct to the nearby Mayagüez Institute of Tropical Agriculture by the U.S. Department of Agriculture. No fewer than five species of palm trees grow here, including the royal palm (native to Puerto Rico); there are eight kinds of bougainvillea and numerous species of rare flora. If you want to get deep into botany, the institute has the largest collection of tropical plants in the western hemisphere.

The hotel, at the northern edge of the city, was built in 1964, and it has been completely refurbished. The well-appointed rooms open onto the swimming pool, and many have private balconies. Year-round rates depend on whether you take a standard, superior, or deluxe accommodation.

Dining/Entertainment: The Rôtisserie Dining Room serves a blend of Puerto Rican and international specialties. Buffets are presented four times a week. In the corner of the restaurant is the Chef's Corner, a small gourmet restaurant. The Hilton is also the entertainment center of the city. There's a casino, established in 1987, which has no entrance fee and is open daily from noon to 4am. In addition, you can dance to the latest hits at the Baccus Music Club, which is free to residents; others pay an entrance fee of $8.

Services: Room service, laundry, babysitting.

Facilities: Olympic-size swimming pool, Jacuzzi, minigym, three tennis courts, physical-fitness trails. Deep-sea fishing, skin diving, surfing, and scuba diving can be arranged. An 18-hole golf course lies at Borinquén Field, a former SAC airbase, about 30 minutes from the Hilton.

HOLIDAY INN, 2701 Rte. 2 (km 149.9), Mayagüez, PR 00680-6328. Tel. 809/833-1100, or toll free 800/HOLIDAY in the U.S. and Canada. Fax 809/833-1300. 148 rms, 4 suites. A/C TV TEL

$ Rates: $100–$130 single; $110–$140 double; $170 suite. Breakfast $8 extra. AE, DC, MC, V. **Parking:** Free.

Set beside Route 2 a couple of miles north of the city center, behind a parking lot and a well-maintained lawn, this six-story hotel opened in 1993. Clean, contemporary, and comfortable, it has a marble-floored, high-ceilinged lobby and a small swimming pool, which offer a bit of breathing space for motorists traveling through Mayagüez. The bedrooms are functionally furnished in an international style, and there's a bar and restaurant on the premises.

HOTEL PARADOR EL SOL, calle Santiago Riera Palmer, 9 Este, Mayagüez, PR 00680. Tel. 809/834-0303. Fax 809/265-7567. 52 rms (all with bath). A/C TV TEL
$ Rates: Year-round, $45–$55 single; $55–$65 double. Breakfast $6 extra. AE, MC, V. **Parking:** Free.
Located two blocks from the landmark Plaza del Mercado in the center of town, this modern concrete building provides some of the most reasonable and hospitable accommodations in this part of Puerto Rico. Central to the shopping district and to all western-region transportation and highways, the restored seven-floor hotel offers up-to-date facilities that include cable TV, a restaurant, and a swimming pool.

NEARBY PLACES TO STAY

HOTEL JOYUDA BEACH, Rte. 102 km 11.7, Cabo Rojo, PR 00623. Tel. 809/851-5650. Fax 809/265-6940. 41 rms. A/C TV TEL **Directions:** Follow Route 102 south of Mayagüez to Joyuda.
$ Rates: Year-round, $65–$85 single or double. Two children under 12 stay free in parents' room. Breakfast $8 extra. AE, MC, V. **Parking:** Free.
On the beach in scenic Cabo Rojo, this 1989 hotel offers comfortably furnished and air-conditioned bedrooms, with such amenities as private baths and room service. It's a good center for touring such attractions as El Combate Beach and the Cabo Rojo Wildlife Refuge. Tennis and golf are just five minutes away, and sport-fishing charters can also be arranged, as well as windsurfing and canoeing. The hotel is often a favorite of Puerto Rican honeymooners. Its restaurant is open for lunch only on Saturday and Sunday from noon to 2pm, although dinner is offered daily from 5:30 to 10:30pm.

PARADOR HACIENDA JUANITA, Rte. 105 km 23.5 (P.O. Box 777), Maricao, PR 00606. Tel. 809/838-2550, or toll free 800/443-0266 (for reservations only) in the U.S. Fax 809/838-2551. 21 rms (all with bath).
$ Rates: $60 single; $70 double. Children under 12 stay free in their parents' room. Breakfast $7 extra. AE, MC, V. **Parking:** Free.
Named after one of its long-ago owners, a matriarch named Juanita, the building was originally constructed in 1836 as part of a coffee plantation. Situated 2 miles west of the village of Maricao, beside Route 105 heading to Mayagüez, in relative isolation, surrounded by only a few neighboring buildings and the jungle, it's a pink stucco house with a long veranda and a living room that's decorated with a large-screen TV and the antique tools and artifacts of the coffee industry. The Luís Rivera family welcomes visitors and serves drinks and meals in their restaurant. There's a swimming pool, billiards table, and ping-pong table on the premises. The bedrooms are simple and rural, with ceiling fans, rocking chairs, and rustic furniture. None has a phone, TV, or air conditioning; with the cool temperatures in this high-altitude place, no one really needs air conditioning.

WHERE TO DINE

THE CHEF'S CORNER, in the Mayagüez Hilton and Casino, Rte. 104. Tel. 831-7575.
Cuisine: INTERNATIONAL. **Reservations:** Required.
$ Prices: Fixed-price five-course dinner $45 per person. AE, DC, MC, V.
Open: Dinner only, daily 7–10:30pm.
The Mayagüez Hilton has reached a laudable culinary achievement with this restaurant. A severely modern dining room whose main decor relies on the tropical gardens that can be seen through the huge windows, it contains only 20 seats. Varying with the season, the availability of ingredients, and the inspiration of the chef, the menu might offer such dishes as a paupiette of sole with a burgundy- and saffron-flavored butter sauce, a timbale of avocado and asparagus with a fresh basil-and-tomato coulis, veal sweetbreads in puff pastry, and a mango-and-strawberry

Bavarian cream with soft fruits of the season. Meals here, designed as culinary events, are usually presented with pride and a certain fanfare.

LA ROTISSERIE, in the Mayagüez Hilton and Casino, Rte. 104. Tel. 831-7575.
   Cuisine: INTERNATIONAL. **Reservations:** Recommended.
$ **Prices:** Appetizers $3.50–$10.50; main courses $14.95–$32.50; Wed-night all-you-can-eat Italian buffet $21.50; Fri-night seafood buffet $25.50; Sat-night Chinese buffet $26; lunch buffet $14.95; Sun brunch $21. AE, DC, MC, V.
   Open: Lunch Mon–Sat 11:30am–2:30pm; dinner daily 6:30–10:30pm; brunch Sun noon–4pm.

Considered the most sophisticated and elegant dining room in Mayagüez, it contains all the accoutrements (richly grained paneling, a formally dressed staff, and silver trolleys wheeled with main courses and desserts to your table) of a fine European restaurant. Menu specialties, changing with the seasons, might include such dishes as spinach tortellini with smoked salmon and cream sauce, asopao of shrimp; several kinds of steaks and grilled meats, fish such as salmon or red snapper, and a trio of dishes prepared flambé style at your table from steak, shrimp, or lobster. Desserts are appropriately dramatic and caloric, and a full array of wines are available to complement your meal.

A PLACE TO DINE IN NEARBY CABO ROJO

CASONA DE SERAFIN, Punta Arena Joyuda, Rte. 102 km 9. Tel. 851-0066.
   Cuisine: PUERTO RICAN. **Reservations:** Not required, except for Sun meals.
   Directions: Drive 3 miles south on Route 102; the restaurant lies beside the highway.
$ **Prices:** Appetizers $3–$10.50; main courses $16.50–$30. AE, MC, V.
   Open: Daily 11:30am–11pm.

Set in a modest concrete-sided building beside the highway and sporting a clean stucco-and-tile interior that's kept immaculately clean, this restaurant is owned by six members of the Ramírez family. Named after their youngest son, Serafin, whose birth coincided with the establishment of this place, it offers fresh seafood and well-prepared Puerto Rican platters. Seafood, brought in fresh every day, is served in such concoctions as lobster parmigiana, red snapper in Spanish sauce, a zarzuela of shellfish, three versions of asopao, and a number of shrimp preparations. There also are filet mignons and flank steaks from a charcoal brazier.

EVENING ENTERTAINMENT

THE CASINO, at the Mayagüez Hilton and Casino, Rte. 104. Tel. 831-7575.
   The completely remodeled casino with an adjoining Player's Bar is the only casino in Mayagüez. Try your luck at blackjack, dice, slot machines, roulette, and minibaccarat. It's open daily from noon to 4am.
   Admission: Free.

DISCO BACCUS, in the Mayagüez Hilton and Casino, Rte. 104. Tel. 831-7575.
   The music originates in New York, Los Angeles, London, or San Juan—the drinks are cold, the salsa's hot, and people dance, dance, dance. You'll find it in the city's most famous hotel. Open Wednesday through Friday from 8pm to 2:30am and on Saturday from 9pm to 3:30pm. Drinks begin at $4 each, and there's a two-drink minimum.
   Admission: Free for hotel guests, $5 for others.

VISTA TERRACE, in the Mayagüez Hilton and Casino, Rte. 104. Tel. 831-7575.

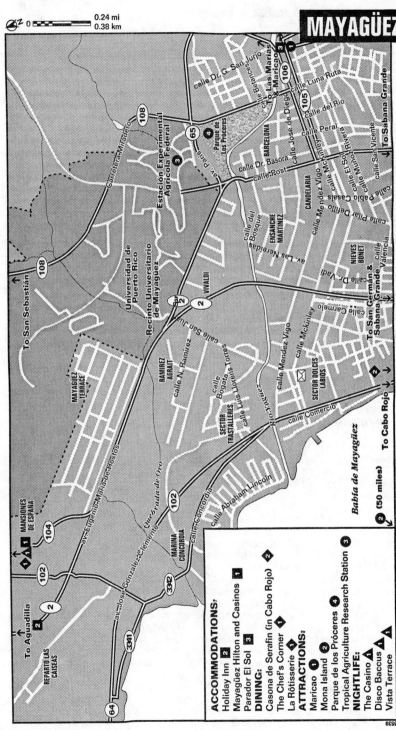

MAYAGÜEZ

0.24 mi
0.38 km

ACCOMMODATIONS:
Holiday Inn **2**
Mayagüez Hilton and Casinos **1**
Parador El Sol **3**

DINING:
Casona de Serafin (in Cabo Rojo) **2**
The Chef's Corner **1**
La Rôtisserie **1**

ATTRACTIONS:
Maricao **1**
Mona Island **2**
Parque de los Próceres **4**
Tropical Agriculture Research Station **3**

NIGHTLIFE:
The Casino **△**
Disco Baccus **△△**
Vista Terrace **△**

Post Office ☒

6539

On a large and airy covered terrace whose side is open to an eagle's-eye view of a manicured tropical garden, this is a relaxing and soothing place for a cocktail. The bartenders specialize in pastel-colored rum-based concoctions that seem to go well with the hibiscus-scented air. Open Sunday through Thursday from 5pm to midnight and on Friday and Saturday from 5pm to 2am. Drinks cost $4 and up.

3. RINCÓN

100 miles W of San Juan, 6 miles N of Mayagüez

GETTING THERE   By Plane   American Eagle (tel. toll free 800/433-7300) flies 15 times daily from San Juan to Mayagüez (flying time: 30 min.).

By Car   Travel either west from San Juan on Route 2 (trip time: 2 hours) or south from San Juan on the scenic Route 52 (trip time: 3½ hours). I recommend Route 52.

ESSENTIALS   There is no tourist information office in Rincón. Inquire in San Juan before going there (see "Tourist Information" in "Orientation," Chapter 4).

Taxis meet planes arriving from San Juan, but they're unmetered—negotiate the fare at the outset with your driver. For car rentals at Mayagüez, see "Essentials" under that city.

On the westernmost point of the island, Rincón, north of Mayagüez, has an exotic beach that draws surfers from around the world. In and around this small fishing village are some unique accommodations.

WHERE TO STAY

HORNED DORSET PRIMAVERA HOTEL, P.O. Box 1132, Rincón, PR 00743. Tel. 809/823-4030. Fax 809/823-5580. 24 suites. A/C. **Directions:** From the Mayagüez Airport, take Route 2 north half a mile to the Anasco intersection; turn left onto Route 115 toward Rincón and travel for four miles. After passing El Coche Restaurant, take a sharp left onto Route 429 and go about a mile. The hotel is on the left, at distance marker km 3.

$ Rates: Winter, $245 suite for one; $325–$345 suite for two. Off-season, $135 suite for one; $190–$210 suite for two. Third person $50 extra. Breakfast $10 extra. AE, MC, V. **Parking:** Free.

Many Caribbean aficionados consider this the most sophisticated hotel on Puerto Rico, and one of the most exclusive and elegant small hotels anywhere in the Caribbean. Established in 1987 and a member of Relais & Châteaux, its gracefully rambling headquarters have the class of a much older building—an effect carefully created by the owners and architects who assembled it. It was built on the massive breakwaters and seawalls erected for a local railroad many years ago and was named after a successful hotel—the Horned Dorset—which its owners still maintain successfully in upstate New York.

The hacienda evokes an aristocratic Spanish villa; there are hand-painted tiles, ceiling fans, seaside terraces, cascades of flowers spilling over the sides of earthenware pots, and the requisite number of wicker armchairs. Management does not allow children under 12, most pets, radios, or TVs. Accommodations are in a series of suites rambling uphill amid lush gardens. The decoration is tasteful, with four-poster beds and brass-footed tubs in marble-sheathed bathrooms.

Dining/Entertainment: The hotel's restaurant is one of the finest in the Caribbean (see "Where to Dine," below). There's a bar open throughout the day serving some of the most delectable rum punches on the island. Guitarists and singers often perform during cocktail and dinner hours.

Services: Room service, laundry, massage, limousine and touring services, a capable concierge.

Facilities: What may be the best hotel library in Puerto Rico contains books on art, music, comparative literature, and poetry. A pool stands near the neoclassical columns of a gazebo entwined with flowering vines. There are also a secluded, semiprivate beach; tennis courts; and deep-sea fishing, golf, and scuba diving are available nearby.

PARADOR VILLA ANTONIO, Rte. 115 km 12.3 (P.O. Box 68), Rincón, PR 00743. Tel. 809/823-2645, or toll free 800/443-0266. Fax 809/823-3380. 55 apartments. A/C TV **Directions:** Head north from Mayagüez along Route 2; then turn left (west) at the junction with Route 115.

$ Rates: Year-round, $69.55–$101.65 one-bedroom apartment; $90.95–$107 two-bedroom apartment. AE, DC, MC, V. **Parking:** Free.

Ilia and Hector Ruíz offer apartments by the sea with sand at your doorstep, privacy, and tropical beauty around you. The best way to get here is by way of Mayagüez Airport, just 25 minutes by car from Villa Antonio. Facilities at this guest complex include a children's playground, two tennis courts, and a swimming pool. Surfing and fishing can be enjoyed just outside your front door, and you can bring your catch right into your cottage and prepare a fresh seafood dinner in your own kitchenette. There is no restaurant.

WHERE TO DINE

HORNED DORSET PRIMAVERA, Rincón. Tel. 823-4030.
   Cuisine: CLASSICAL FRENCH. **Reservations:** Recommended.
$ Prices: Appetizers $11–$19.50; main courses $18–$24; fixed-price dinner $40; lunch from $15. AE, MC, V.
   Open: Lunch daily noon–2:30pm; dinner daily, with seatings at 7, 8, and 9pm.

It reigns without equal as the finest restaurant in western Puerto Rico and is so alluring that diners sometimes journey out from San Juan for an intimate dinner. It's the Caribbean counterpart of an award-winning hotel and restaurant in Leonardsville, New York—the Horned Dorset. It serves the kind of cuisine whose excellence can be maintained only through the constant, hands-on supervision of a demanding team of owners.

Meals are served beneath the soaring ceilings of what could easily be mistaken as the dining room of an aristocratic Spanish home. A masonry staircase sweeps from the garden to reach the second-floor precincts.

Menu specialties, changing with the availability of the ingredients, might include such dishes as medallions of lobster in an orange-flavored beurre-blanc sauce, grilled breast of duckling with bay leaves and raspberry sauce, piñon (a traditional Puerto Rican dish of sautéed plantains filled with seasoned ground meat and covered with a light mornay sauce), yellowfin tuna (hauled directly from the local piers within hours of being caught) grilled and served with a hot mustard/horseradish/cream sauce, and dorado (mahi-mahi) grilled and served with a ginger-cream sauce on a bed of braised Chinese cabbage. One of this establishment's many famous desserts is Martinique cake, a light-green confection made from sweet potatoes and coconuts, covered with chocolate and rum-flavored frosting, and served over a bed of strawberry sauce.

WHERE TO STAY & DINE IN NEARBY AGUADA

J.B. HIDDEN VILLAGE HOTEL, Bo. Piedras Blancas, Sector Villarrubia, Aguada, PR 00602. Tel. 809/868-8686. Fax 809/868-3442. 24 rms, 1 suite. A/C TV TEL
$ Rates: Year-round, $57 single; $74 double; $129 suite. Breakfast $8 extra. AE, MC, V. **Parking:** Free.

Named after the initials of its owners (Julio Bonilla, his wife Jinnie, and their son, Julio, Jr.), this clean and isolated hotel opened in 1990. Half a mile east of Aguada, on a side street running off Route 4414, nestled into a valley between three forested hillsides and almost invisible from the road outside, it offers a quiet and simple refuge to vacationers who enjoy exploring the area's many different beaches. There are two restaurants on the premises (one with a view looking out over a neighboring ravine), a small swimming pool, and a bar. Each bedroom is equipped with pastel-colored contemporary furniture and offers views of the pool.

CHAPTER 11

VIEQUES & CULEBRA

1. VIEQUES
- **WHAT'S SPECIAL ABOUT VIEQUES & CULEBRA**
2. CULEBRA

Virtually unknown to most visitors to Puerto Rico, the offshore islands of Vieques and Culebra are places that many knowledgeable Puerto Ricans go for their own vacations. Sandy beaches and low prices are a potent lure to both islands.

Culebra, 14 miles west of St. Thomas and 18 miles east of the Puerto Rican "mainland," is surrounded by coral reefs and edged with nearly deserted, powdery white sand beaches. Much of the island has been designated a wildlife preserve by the U.S. Fish and Wildlife Service.

Vieques, with more tourist facilities than Culebra, lies 7 miles off the eastern coast of Puerto Rico. The island had been occupied at various times by both the French and the British before Puerto Rico acquired it in 1854. The ruins of many sugar and pineapple plantations testify to its once-flourishing agricultural economy. The U.S. military, which took control of two-thirds of the island's 26,000 acres in 1941, has largely refrained from using this part as a bombing range, but it is still an important military training area. Today Vieques is visited for its 40-odd white-sand beaches.

---

1. VIEQUES

41 miles E of San Juan, 7 miles SE of Fajardo

GETTING THERE   By Plane   Sunaire Express (tel. toll free 800/524-2094 in the U.S., 800/595-9501 in Puerto Rico) flies to Vieques in 30 minutes from Terminal A at San Juan's international airport. **Vieques Air Link** (tel. 809/723-9882) also operates flights from San Juan's local airport.

By Ferry   The Puerto Rico Port Authority operates two ferryboats a day from the eastern port of Fajardo to Vieques; the trip takes about an hour. The round-trip fare is $4 for adults, $2 for children 14 and under. Tickets on the morning ferry leaving Saturday and Sunday sell out quickly, so passengers should be in line at the ticket window in Fajardo before 8am to be certain of a seat on the 9:30am boat. Otherwise, they'll have to wait until the 3pm ferry.

About 7 miles east of the big island of Puerto Rico lies Vieques (Bee-*ay*-kase), an island about twice as large as Manhattan with about 8,000 inhabitants and some 40 palm-lined white sand beaches. Since World War II about two-thirds of the 21-mile-long island has been controlled by the U.S. military forces. Much of the government-owned land is now leased for cattle grazing, and when there are no

WHAT'S SPECIAL ABOUT VIEQUES & CULEBRA

Beaches
- ☐ The beaches of Vieques, some 40 in all, most of them unnamed, although U.S. sailors have nicknamed their favorites—everything from Green Beach to Orchid.
- ☐ The beaches of Culebra, white sandy strips studding the island and opening onto coral reefs and clear waters—Flamenco Beach is the best.
- ☐ Sun Bay (Sombe), a public beach on Vieques, a splendid crescent of sand, with picnic tables and a bathhouse.

Ace Attractions
- ☐ Culebrita, a mile-long coral isle satellite of Culebra, with a hilltop lighthouse and crescent beaches.

- ☐ Punta Mula Lighthouse, north of Isabel Segunda on Vieques, providing panoramic views of land and sea.
- ☐ Mosquito Bay, home of the "fire gods," eerily glowing waters produced by tiny bioluminescent organisms that live near the surface.

Great Towns and Villages
- ☐ Isabel Segunda, on the north shore of Vieques, the island's capital and site of the last Spanish fort to be built in the New World, dating from 1843.
- ☐ Dewey, Culebra's only town, named for Admiral George Dewey, an American hero, although the islanders defiantly call it Puebla.

---

military maneuvers the public can visit the beaches, although you might be asked to produce some form of photo ID. Freedom to use the land has not, however, totally defused local discontent at the presence of navy and marine corps personnel on the island.

The Spanish conquistadores didn't think much of Vieques. They came here in the 16th century but didn't stay long, reporting that the island and neighboring bits of land held no gold and were therefore "las islas inutiles" (the useless islands). The name Vieques comes from a native Amerindian word for small island, *bieques*.

Later Spanish occupation is attested to by the main town, **Isabel Segunda,** on the northern shore. Construction on the last Spanish fort built in the New World began around 1843 during the reign of the Queen Isabella II, for whom the town was named. The fort, never completed, is not of any special interest. The **Punta Mula lighthouse,** north of Isabel Segunda, provides panoramic views of the land and sea. The island's fishermen and farmers conduct much of their business in Isabel Segunda.

On the south coast, **Esperanza,** once a center for the island's sugarcane industry and now a pretty little fishing village, lies near **Sun Bay (Sombe) public beach.** Sun Bay is a government-run, magnificent crescent of sand. The fenced area has picnic tables, a bathhouse, and a parking lot. A recently built resort, marina, and other facilities add to the allure of the many scalloped stretches of sandy waterfront along the south coast.

Few of the island's beaches have been named, but most have their loyal supporters—loyal, that is, until too many people learn about them, in which case the devotees can always find another good spot. The U.S. Navy named some of the beaches, such as **Green Beach,** a beautiful clean stretch at the island's west end. **Red and Blue Beaches,** also with navy nomenclature, are great jumping-off points for snorkelers. Other popular beaches are **Navia, Half Moon, Orchid,** and **Silver,** but if you continue along the water, you may find your own nameless secluded cove with a fine strip of sand.

One of the major attractions on the island is ✪ **Mosquito Bay,** also called

Phosphorescent Bay, with its glowing waters produced by tiny bioluminescent organisms that live near the surface. These organisms dart away from boats, leaving eerie blue-white trails of phosphorescence. *The Vieques Times* wrote: "By any name the bay can be a magical, psychedelic experience and few places in the world can even come close to the intensity of concentration of the dinoflagellates called pyrodiniums (whirling fire). They are tiny (⅟₅₀₀ inch) swimming creatures that light up like fireflies when disturbed but nowhere are there so many fireflies. Here a gallon of bay water may contain almost three-quarters of a million." The ideal time to tour is on a cloudy, moonless night, and you should wear a bathing suit since it's possible to swim in these glowing waters. **18° North** (tel. 741-8600) runs tours on powerboats from Esperanza, and **Sharon Grasso** (tel. 741-3751), aboard her *Luminosa,* operates trips leaving from La Casa del Francés (see "Where to Stay," below). These trips are not offered around the time of the full moon.

GETTING AROUND Public cabs or vans called *públicos* transport people around the island. **Island Car Rental,** Highway 201, Florida (tel. 809/741-1666), is one of the two largest car-rental companies on the island, with an inventory of stripped-down Suzukis which usually offer dependable, bare-boned transportation to many of the island's beautiful but hard-to-reach beaches. Jeep-like Samurais, with or without a "bikini top," are available as well. Regardless of the model, cars rent for $40 per day ($35 per day for rentals of a week or more). Collision-damage insurance costs $10 per day extra. AE, MC, and V are accepted. The establishment lies in the hamlet of Florida, about a 12-minute drive southwest of Isabel Segunda.

WHERE TO STAY

BANANAS, Barrio Esperanza (P.O. Box 1300), Vieques, PR 00765. Tel. 809/741-8700. 7 rms (all with bath), 1 suite.
$ Rates: Year-round, $40–$55 single or double; $60 suite. MC, V. **Parking:** Free.
While filming *Heartbreak Ridge* in 1986, the actors and crew transformed this establishment's windswept porch into their second home. Located on the south shore (east of the U.S. Naval Reservation) and best known for its bar and restaurant, this guesthouse also has seven simple, clean, and comfortable rooms, some recently renovated. Each has a ceiling fan; however, three rooms and the suite are air-conditioned, with their own screened-in porches.

The real heart of Bananas, however, is the pleasant veranda restaurant, which serves meals and potent rum punch to anyone who arrives. You can choose from deli sandwiches, burgers, grilled Caribbean lobster, local fish such as snapper and grouper, and filet mignon, plus homemade desserts. Lunches cost $6 to $10, and dinners go for $15 to $20. Meals are served from 11:30am to 10pm Sunday through Thursday and from 11:30am to 11pm on Friday and Saturday. Breakfast isn't served, although you can order food at other places nearby. The bar is extremely popular.

LA CASA DEL FRANCÉS, Barrio Esperanza, (P.O. Box 458), Vieques, PR 00765. Tel. 809/741-3751. Fax 809/741-2330. 18 rms (all with bath).
$ Rates: Winter, $99 single or double. Off-season, $75 single or double. MAP (in winter only) $20 per person extra. AE, MC, V. **Parking:** Free.
La Casa del Francés is about a 15-minute drive southeast of Isabel Segunda, just north of the center of Esperanza. Set in a field near the southern coastline, its columns and imposing facade rise from the lush surrounding landscape. It was built in 1905 by a retired French general as the headquarters for his working sugar plantation. In the 1950s it was acquired by Irving Greenblatt, who installed a swimming pool and, with his partner, Frank Celeste, transformed 18 of its high-ceilinged bedrooms into old-fashioned hotel accommodations as an oasis for his executives. Many rooms enjoy access to the sweeping two-story verandas ringing the white facade.

Scattered throughout the dozen acres attached to the main house are century-old tropical trees. The estate's architectural highlight is the two-story interior courtyard whose center is lush with bamboo, palms, philodendron, and well-chosen examples of Haitian art. The fixed-price dinners, which cost $15 each, attract many island residents who partake of Italian, barbecue, or Puerto Rican buffets which the staff spreads out beneath a 200-year-old mahogany tree.

NEW DAWN'S CARIBBEAN RETREAT AND GUEST HOUSE, Rte. 995 km 1.2 (P.O. Box 1512), Vieques, PR 00765. Tel. 809/741-0495. 6 rms (none with bath), 6 dormitory-style bunks.

$ Rates: Year-round, $35 single; $45 double; $15 per person for a bunk in a coed bunkhouse. Discounts available for stays of one week or more, especially for groups. No credit cards. **Parking:** Free.

Situated on a forested hillside 3 miles from Sun Bay in the center of the island, north of Esperanza and southwest of Isabel Segunda, this barebone establishment caters to budget-conscious campers as well as youthful adventurers. Its centerpiece is a plywood-sided house originally built by Gail Burchard (an Indiana-born nurse) and her students in 1986 when she was teaching a course in carpentry for women. Today, the guesthouse enjoys a spacious porch outfitted with hammocks and swinging chairs. A series of outbuildings contain a bath house, communal kitchen, and camp-style bunkhouse with six beds. The half-dozen conventional bedrooms, on the guest-house's second floor, are rustic and simple, usually with sleeping lofts and few (if any) extra amenities. Despite the simplicity of the setting, Ms. Burchard offers, for an extra fee, the use of a washing machine and rentals of snorkeling gear, bicycles, and air mattresses for campers. Also available, through referrals, are palm-weaving lessons, horseback riding, guided historical tours of Vieques, night swims and kayak trips through Phosphorescent Bay, and guided nature hikes. Between May and December the 5-acre site is often rented as a conference center to church groups, schools, and women's groups from North America.

TRADE WINDS GUESTHOUSE, 107C Flamboyan, Barrio Esperanza (P.O. Box 1012), Vieques, PR 00765. Tel. 809/741-8666. 9 rms (all with bath), 1 studio.

$ Rates: Year-round, $35 single; $45-$60 double; $90 studio. Breakfast $3 extra. Three-night deposit by check or money order required. MC, V. **Parking:** Free.

Along the shore on the south side of the island, in the fishing village of Esperanza, this oceanside guesthouse offers nine units, four of them air-conditioned and with terraces. The others have ceiling fans, and some also have terraces. The establishment is well known for its open-air restaurant overlooking the ocean and its hospitable atmosphere.

VIEQUES OCEAN VIEW HOTEL, Isabel Segunda (P.O. Box 124), Vieques, PR 00765. Tel. 809/741-3696. Fax 809/741-3696. 35 rms (all with bath). A/C TV

$ Rates: Winter, $35 single; $45 double. Off-season, $50 single; $55 double. Breakfast $5 extra. AE, MC, V. **Parking:** Free.

Situated in the heart of Isabel Segunda, directly on the coast and a block from the wharf where the ferryboat lands, this three-story building is one of the tallest on Vieques. Built in the early 1980s, it offers simple rooms with uncomplicated furniture and balconies overlooking either the sea or the town. There's a bar on the premises and a Chinese restaurant in the basement. The hotel charges higher rates in summer than in winter, partly to profit from the many families who come over on the ferryboat from the Puerto Rican mainland during warm-weather months. None of the rooms has a phone.

WHERE TO DINE

LA CAMPESINA, La Hueca. Tel. 741-1239.
   Cuisine: INTERNATIONAL. **Reservations:** Recommended.
$ Prices: Appetizers $3-$6; main courses $9-$17. MC, V.
   Open: Dinner only, Wed-Sun 6:30-9pm. **Closed:** Oct.

Consciously designed to reflect indigenous dwellings, this unusual and excellent restaurant was built just a short distance from one of the richest archeological deposits of Taíno artifacts in the Caribbean. It's located on the southwestern end of the island (follow the coast road from Esperanza) in the unspoiled fishing village of La Hueca.

Surrounded by baskets and weavings amid trailing vines of jasmine and flickering candles, you can enjoy a cuisine of distinctly tropical or uniquely Puerto Rican flare. Fresh herbs, such as cilantro, or the "sofrito" it embodies, tasty local vegetables, and fruits of the season (such as papaya, mango, and tamarind) served in sauces or relishes, in pastries and sorbets, complement the menu. Nightly specials might include shrimp coco, avocado remoûlade, conch fritters, lobster ravioli, piñon (a savory Puerto Rican casserole), yellowtail snapper en papillote, a chocolate pot de la crème, and for those who can't be without it, a great steak. Occasionally a potent type of cocktail is available—the traditional "coquito" made of coconut milk and rum, or a "Bili" made with local "quenepa," rum, and cognac. Wandering minstrels, jazz musicians escaping New York snow, and local guitar trios occasionally enliven the after-dinner hours with impromptu entertainment.

RICHARD'S CAFE, calle Antonio Mellado, Isabel Segunda. Tel. 741-5242.
  Cuisine: PUERTO RICAN/VIEQUES. **Reservations:** Not required.
  $ Prices: Appetizers $2–$3; main courses $3–$20. AE, MC, V.
  Open: Lunch Mon–Sat 11:30am–2:30pm; dinner Mon–Sat 6:30–10:30pm.

Its oilcloth decor and low-slung facade might remind you of an unpretentious roadside coffee shop, but this is actually a substantial restaurant, serving the freshest seafood on the island. It specializes in both Puerto Rican and Vieques cuisine, and offers air-conditioned comfort. You can order a snail or octopus salad, pork chops, or perhaps a savory version of asopao made from well-spiced hunks of lobster or shrimp. Or you can have a less expensive meal: Try one of the well-stuffed sandwiches or a special of the day, which includes fried chicken (or some other main dish), rice, beans, salad, and bread. Daily specials begin at $4.50, and many patrons consider this a meal unto itself.

TRADE WINDS, Barrio Esperanza. Tel. 741-8666.
  Cuisine: STEAK/SEAFOOD. **Reservations:** Recommended.
  $ Prices: Appetizers $2.50–$5.95; main courses $9.50–$16.95. MC, V.
  Open: Lunch daily 11:30am–2pm; dinner daily 6:30–9pm. (Bar, year-round, daily 5pm–midnight.) **Closed:** Off-season.

You'll find this restaurant at the ocean esplanade on the south side of the island in the fishing village of Esperanza (see "Where to Stay," above, for its guesthouse). It features the Topside Bar for relaxing drinks, with a view of the water, and the Upper Deck for open-air dining. Menu choices include several shrimp dishes and fresh fish daily. The chef's specialty is Carmen's piñon, made with layers of sweet plantains, tomato sauce, green beans, spiced beef, and mozzarella. A pasta of the day is also featured, served with a house or Caesar salad. Included in the price of a main dish are bread and butter, a salad, two fresh vegetables, and a choice of rice or potato.

2. CULEBRA

52 miles E of San Juan; 18 miles E of Fajardo

GETTING THERE   By Plane   Flamenco Airways, Inc. (tel. 809/725-7707 in San Juan), flies to Culebra four times daily from both San Juan and Fajardo.

By Ferry   From the port of Fajardo, the Puerto Rico Port Authority operates one or two ferryboats a day (depending on the day of the week) from the Puerto Rican mainland to Culebra; the trip takes about an hour. The round-trip fare is $4.50 for adults, $2.25 for children 14 and under. For information and reservations, call 809/863-0705, or toll free 800/981-2005 on Puerto Rico.

A tranquil, inviting little island, Culebra lies in a mini-archipelago of 24 chunks of land, rocks, and cays in the sea—halfway between Puerto Rico and St. Thomas, U.S. Virgin Islands. Just 7 miles long and 3 miles wide, with nearly 2,000 residents, the island is in U.S. territorial waters belonging to Puerto Rico, 18 miles away. This little-known, year-round vacation spot in what was once called the Spanish Virgin Islands was settled as a Spanish colony in 1886, but like Puerto Rico and Vieques, it became part of the United States after the Spanish-American War in 1898. In fact Culebra's only town, a fishing village called **Dewey,** was named for Adm. George Dewey, an American hero of that war, although the locals know it as **Puebla.**

For a long time, beginning in 1909, Culebra was used by the U.S. Navy as a gunnery range, even becoming a practice bomb site in World War II. In 1975, after years of protest over military abuse of the island's environment, the navy withdrew from Culebra, with the understanding that the island be kept as a nature preserve and habitat for the many rare species of birds, turtles, and fish that abound there. The four tracts of the Culebra Wildlife Refuge, plus 23 other offshore islands, are managed by the U.S. Fish and Wildlife Service. Culebra is one of the most important turtle-nesting sites in the Caribbean. Large seabird colonies, notably terns and boobies, can be seen.

Today vacationers and boating people can explore the island's beauties, both on land and under water. (There's even a sailing school; see below.) Culebra's white sand beaches—especially Flamenco Beach—the clear waters, and long coral reefs invite swimmers, snorkelers, and scuba divers. The flora ranges from scrub and cactus to poincianas, frangipanis, and coconut palms.

Culebrita, a mile-long coral-isle satellite of Culebra, has a hilltop lighthouse and crescent beaches.

SAILING The **Culebra School of Sailing,** Bahía Mosquito or Mosquito Bay (tel. 742-3136), is owned and operated by Hugh and Diane Callum, who come from Indiana and Québec, respectively. Daily sails cost $50 per person and include lunch. At the school's disposal is a fleet of boats, including a windsurfer, kayak, sloop, and ketch. Currently the only sailing school/rental on the island, it operates out of the Callums' home on Mosquito Bay, and they are happy to pick up their guests in town.

WHERE TO STAY

BAYVIEW VILLAS, Punta Aloe (P.O. Box 775), Culebra, PR 00775. Tel. 809/742-3392. 2 villas. TV
$ Rates: Year-round, $1,000–$1,300 per week villa. No credit cards. **Parking:** Free.

Located on a hillside above Ensenada Honda a mile east of Dewey, at the end of a privately maintained road, this compound consists of two separate villas, each of which overlooks the sea and has two floors and comfortably solid pinewood furniture. Some visitors claim that they are the finest accommodations on the island. Each has a kitchen and two bedrooms, suitable for housing four occupants and, under cramped conditions, up to six occupants. Each unit has ceiling fans, washing machines, high peaked ceilings, and sliding glass doors leading onto terraces. The villas are rented for periods of a week or more, although under certain circumstances daily rentals are available.

CLUB SEABOURNE, Fulladosa Rd. (P.O. Box 357), Culebra, PR 00775. Tel. 809/742-3169. Fax 809/742-3176. 15 units (all with bath). A/C **Directions:** From Puebla, follow Fulladosa Road along the south side of the bay for 1½ miles.
$ Rates (including continental breakfast): Year-round, $65–$75 double in the clubhouse; $110 double in a villa or the Crow's Nest. AE, MC, V. **Parking:** Free.

Across the road from an inlet of the sea, about an eight-minute drive from the center

VIEQUES & CULEBRA

⊕N

CULEBRA

Atlantic Ocean

Pasaje de la Virgen

CULEBRITA

CAYO NORTE

Canal de Cayo Norte

Cabeza de Perro

Culebra Airport

✈ Dewey (Pueblo)

250

251

CAYO LOBITO

CAYO LOBO

CAYO DE LUIS PEÑA

Puerto de Culebra

Sonda de Vieques

0 — 2 mi.
0 — 3.2 km.

Culebra

Vieques

Puerto Rico

VIEQUES

Accommodations
Bananas **2**
La Casa del Francés **2**
New Dawn's Caribbean
Retreat and Guest House **1**
Trade Winds Guesthouse **2**
Vieques Ocean View Hotel **3**

Dining
La Campesina ◆**2**
Richard's Café ◆**3**
Trade Winds ◆**4**

CULEBRA

Accommodations
Bayview Villas **2**
Club Seabourne **1**
Culebra Island Villas **3**
Flamenco Resort & Fishing Club **4**

Dining
El Batey ◆**3**
Marta's Al Fresco ◆**2**

Punta Mula Lighthouse

Santa María

989

Isabel Segunda

Barriada Monte Santo

✈ Puerto de Vieques

200

Proyecto Barracón

Colonia Luján

997

997

996

Sun Bay

Puerto Ferro

Punta Negra

CAYO DE AFUERA

Esperanza

201

Colonia Puerto Real

995

996

YALIS

Laguna Anones

Punta Jalova

200

Punta Conejo

CHIVA

Caribbean Sea

VIEQUES

✈ Vieques Airport **1**

U.S. Naval Res.

Mosquito Bay

Mesquite Bay

Laguna Kiani

Punta Arenas

Punta Boca Quebrada

Punta Goleta

Pasaje Vieques

0 — 4 mi.
0 — 6.4 km.

Airport ✈   Lighthouse ⚐   Ferry routes ·····

6540

of town, is this concrete-and-wood structure set in a garden of crotons and palms, lying at the mouth of one of the island's best harbors, Ensenada Honda. It offers 10 villas and four rooms inside the clubhouse. All villas and the Crow's Nest are equipped with small refrigerators, and all facilities are air-conditioned. Dive packages and day sails can be arranged at the office.

Overlooking Fulladosa Bay, the club's dining room offers some of the best food on Culebra, with fresh lobster, shrimp, snapper, grouper, and conch, as well as steaks and other specialty dishes, served nightly from 6 to 10pm. The hotel also has a large patio bar with a nightly happy hour, plus the only freshwater swimming pool on the island.

CULEBRA ISLAND VILLAS, Punta Aloe (P.O. Box 596), Culebra, PR 00775. Tel. 809/742-0333. 10 units (all with bath).

$ Rates (per week): Winter, $475–$595 studio or one-bedroom suite; $725–$895 two-bedroom suite. Off-season, $350–$475 studio or one-bedroom suite; $595–$725 two-bedroom suite. No credit cards. **Parking:** Free.

Located to the south of Ensenada Honda, half a mile south of Dewey, and separated from the Culebran "mainland" by a canal with a drawbridge, lies Punta Aloe, whose forested hillsides shelter about 15 privately owned houses. Each floor of four of these houses, which were built by different owners between 1980 and around 1990, are available for weekly rentals. Each offers views of the bay, wood-sided construction, simple kitchens, and accommodations suitable for one to three occupants (the studios and one-bedroom suites) or two to six occupants (the two-bedroom suites). None of the units has a phone, TV, or air conditioning, although many visitors prefer direct access to the trade winds anyway. No meals are available (most visitors prefer to cook their own meals anyway), and maid service is provided only once a week.

FLAMENCO RESORT & FISHING CLUB, 10 Pedro Marquez, Flamenco Beach (P.O. Box 183), Culebra, PR 00645. Tel. 809/742-3144. 29 units (all with bath). A/C

$ Rates: Winter, $85 studio; $115 one-bedroom suite; $160 two-bedroom suite; $175 three-bedroom suite. Off-season, $75 studio; $105 one-bedroom suite; $150 two-bedroom suite; $165 three-bedroom suite. Breakfast from $3.50 extra. MC, V. **Parking:** Free.

This is the only guesthouse or hotel near the white sands of one of the best beaches in the region—Flamenco Beach. Each unit has its own kitchen. This establishment would really be ideal for a group of friends or an extended family, since the accommodations are situated around spacious sitting rooms much like those in an informal beach house. The owner has studio apartments suitable for two, one-bedroom apartments also suitable for two, and three-bedroom bungalows suitable for six. All units are air-conditioned. Varied activities are available, including day trips on a sailboat to one of the nearby islands, snorkeling, and fishing expeditions. Evening meals are served at Marta's Al Fresco (see "Where to Dine," below).

WHERE TO DINE

Consider the Club Seabourne, listed above in "Where to Stay."

EL BATEY, 250 Carretera. Tel. 742-3828.
Cuisine: DELI. **Reservations:** Not required.
$ Prices: Appetizers $1.50–$2, sandwiches $2–$4; main courses $6–$14. MC, V. **Open:** Sandwiches, daily 8am–2pm; dinner daily 6:30–9:30pm. **Closed:** Dinner May–Nov.

Across from the harbor is a large, clean establishment that maintains a full bar and prepares an array of deli-style sandwiches, served until 2pm. Coffee and doughnuts are also offered every morning. Beer is a popular drink, and the pool tables make the place lively, especially on weekends when many locals are there. Weekdays, it's much calmer. The owners, Digna Feliciano and Tomás Ayala, have many fans on the island. Breezes from the harbor cool the place. In the evening El Batey provides full meals, including many fresh fish dishes.

MARTA'S AL FRESCO, 10 Pedro Marquez. Tel. 742-3575.
    Cuisine: AMERICAN/PUERTO RICAN. **Reservations:** Not accepted.
$ Prices: Sandwiches $3–$4.25; appetizers $3.50–$5.50; main courses $6.75–
$14. MC, V.
    Open: Lunch daily 11am–1pm; dinner daily 6–10pm.

In a simple building near the wharf where the ferryboats from Puerto Rico's mainland arrive and depart, this restaurant is named after its owner's wife, Marta. The space is divided into two sections: a deli on one side and a more formal *comedor* (dining room) on the other. The furniture is made of rattan and the view, through big windows, is of the sea. In addition to the deli-style sandwiches, the menu lists a wide range of fresh seafood, as well as steaks, asopaos, burgers, and pork chops with rice and beans.

AN EASY EXCURSION TO ST. THOMAS

St. Thomas is the most-visited excursion spot from Puerto Rico—it's just a short hop from San Juan for those who want to take advantage of the $1,200 duty-free shopping limit available to Americans. Although San Juan has bargains galore, the duty-free shopping of St. Thomas is extremely appealing.

This incentive, combined with the fact that many planes, especially those of American Airlines, often stop in San Juan before continuing on to St. Thomas, make this U.S. Virgin Island an interesting and fairly easy day trip. Some passengers visit just for an afternoon, whereas others settle in for overnight stays. If you're contemplating a serious shopping trip to St. Thomas, see my comments on Customs in Chapter 2. I've also included some restaurants and a few hotels for those who'd like to stay a little bit longer.

Sometimes a plane ticket to St. Thomas—where you fly from mainland U.S. cities to San Juan changing planes there—is actually cheaper than the APEX nonstop fare to Puerto Rico. Therefore, you may want to include both Puerto Rico and the U.S. Virgin Islands in one vacation. See *Frommer's The Virgin Islands* for more details, and also call American Airlines (tel. toll free at 800/433-7300) to get the current fares for a combined Puerto Rico–St. Thomas trip.

1. ORIENTATION TO ST. THOMAS

The busiest cruise-ship harbor in the West Indies, St. Thomas is the second largest of the U.S. Virgin Islands and lies about 40 miles north of the larger island of St. Croix. St. Thomas is about 12 miles long and 3 miles wide; its north shore faces the Atlantic Ocean, and the calmer Caribbean washes the island's south side. It's not unheard of to find the sun shining in the south while the north experiences showers.

Holiday makers discovered St. Thomas after World War II and they've been flocking to the island in increasing numbers ever since. Shopping, sun, and sights have proved to be a potent lure, and tourism has made the standard of living here one of the highest in the Caribbean.

The island is the seat of the capital of the U.S. Virgins, Charlotte Amalie, which may also be the greatest shopping center of the Caribbean. The island is indeed a boon for cruise-ship shoppers, who frequently flood Main Street, where dozens of shops are located within a three- or four-block radius. This area can get very crowded, but it's away from the beaches, major hotels, most restaurants, and entertainment facilities.

WHAT'S SPECIAL ABOUT ST. THOMAS

Beaches

- ☐ Magens Bay, 3 miles north of Charlotte Amalie, one of the most beautiful beaches in the world.
- ☐ Stouffer Grand Beach, one of the island's most stunning, with many water sports available.
- ☐ Sapphire Beach, with its luxury hotel complexes in the background, one of the finest on the island, and a favorite of windsurfers.

Ace Attractions

- ☐ Coral World, a marine complex featuring a three-story underwater observation tower 100 feet offshore.
- ☐ Jim Tillet's Art Gallery and Boutique, built around an old plantation-era sugar mill.

Great Towns and Villages

- ☐ Charlotte Amalie, the capital of St. Thomas, one of the most beautiful port cities in the Caribbean.
- ☐ Frenchtown, settled by the descendants of immigrants from the French islands, famous for its "cha-chas," or straw hats.

Historic Buildings

- ☐ The St. Thomas Synagogue, second oldest in America, built by Sephardic Jews in 1833.
- ☐ Government House, at Government Hill in Charlotte Amalie, residence of the U.S. Virgin Islands governor.
- ☐ Fort Christian, constructed by the Danes in 1671 and named for King Christian V.

One important note: If you're visiting in August, bring along some mosquito repellent.

TOURIST INFORMATION On St. Thomas, the Visitors Center is at Emancipation Square (tel. 774-8784). Much useful information is dispensed from here, and you can pick up a copy of *St. Thomas This Week,* which includes maps of St. Thomas and St. John as well as descriptions of the vast array of shopping possibilities.

The telephone area code for St. Thomas is 809, as it is for Puerto Rico.

MAIN STREETS & ARTERIES The capital, Charlotte Amalie, is the only town on St. Thomas. Bordering the waterfront, its seaside promenade is called **Waterfront Highway,** or just the Waterfront. Its old Danish name is Kyst Vejen. From the Waterfront, you can take any number of streets or alleyways leading back into town to the **Main Street,** or Dronningens Gade. Principal links between Main Street and the Waterfront include **Raadets Gade, Tolbod Gade, Storetvaer Gade,** and **Strand Gade.**

Main Street is aptly named, since it is the center of the capital and the site of the major shops. The western part of Main Street is **Market Square,** which was once the site of the biggest slave market auctions in the Caribbean Basin. It lies near the intersection with Strand Gade. Today it's an open-air block of stalls where island gardeners sell their produce, particularly on Saturday (closed Sunday). Go early in the morning to see the market at its best.

Running parallel to Main Street and lying north of it is **Back Street,** or Vimmelskaft Gade, which has many stores, including some of the less expensive ones. Quite dangerous to walk along at night, it's reasonably safe for daytime shopping.

In the eastern part of town, midway between Talbod Gade and Fort Pladsen, is **Emancipation Park,** northwest of Fort Christian, commemorating the liberation of the slaves in 1848. Most of the major historical buildings, including the Legislative Building, Fort Christian, and Government House, are within a short walk of this park.

Southeast of the park looms **Fort Christian,** crowned by a clock tower and painted a rusty red, constructed by the Danes in 1671. The **Legislative Building,** seat of the elected government of the U.S. Virgin Islands, is on the harbor side of the fort.

Kongens Gade (King's Street) leads to Government House on **Government Hill,** which overlooks the town and the harbor. Here stands a white-brick building, Government House, dating from 1867.

Between **Hotel 1829,** a former mansion constructed that year by a French sea captain, and Government House is a staircase known as the **Street of 99 Steps.** Actually, someone miscounted: It should be called the Street of 103 Steps. These steps lead to the summit of Government Hill.

Nearby are the remains of the 17th-century **Fort Skytsborg,** or Blackbeard's Tower, a reference to the notorious pirate Edward Teach, who is said to have spied on treasure galleons entering the harbor in the 1700s from here. Today an 11-room hotel, Blackbeard's Castle, stands here.

This should not be confused with **Bluebeard's Tower,** which crowns a 300-foot hill at the eastern edge of town. This is the site of what is perhaps the best known (but not the best) hotel in the Virgin Islands—Bluebeard's Castle.

GETTING AROUND   By Bus   St. Thomas has the best public transportation of any island in the U.S. chain. Administered by the government, **Vitran buses** service Charlotte Amalie, its outlying neighborhoods, and the countryside as far away as Red Hook. Vitran stops are found at reasonable intervals beside each of the most important traffic arteries on St. Thomas. Among the most visible are those along the edges of Veterans Drive on Charlotte Amalie. Buses run daily between 5:35am and 10:25pm. A one-way ride costs 75¢ within Charlotte Amalie, $1 for rides from Charlotte Amalie into its outer neighborhoods, and $3 for rides from Charlotte Amalie to such other communities as Red Hook, site of ferryboat departures for St. John. For information about Vitran buses, their stops and schedules, call 774-5678.

2. WHERE TO SHOP

Shoppers have not only the benefits of St. Thomas's liberal duty-free allowances, but also the opportunity to buy well-known brand names that may be on sale at 40% below Stateside prices. However, that doesn't happen every day. To find true value, you may have to plow through a lot of junk. Many items offered for sale—binoculars, stereos, watches, and cameras—can be matched in price at your hometown discount store. Therefore, you need to know an item's price back home to determine if you are in fact saving money. Having sounded that warning, I'll survey some St. Thomas shops where I have personally found good buys. There are lots more you can discover on your own.

Most of the shops, some of which occupy former pirate warehouses, are open from 9am to 5pm, and some stay open later. Nearly all stores close on Sunday and major holidays—that is, unless a cruise ship is in port. Few shopkeepers can stand the prospect of hundreds of potential customers, their purses full, wandering by their padlocked doors. Therefore, those gates are likely to swing open, at least for half a day on Sunday. Friday is the biggest cruise-ship visiting day at Charlotte Amalie (one day I counted eight ships at one time)—so try to avoid shopping then.

If you want to combine a little history with shopping, you might go into the courtyard of the old **Pissarro Building,** entered through an archway off Main Street. The impressionist painter lived here as a child. The old apartments have been turned into a warren of interesting shops.

A. H. RIISE GIFT & LIQUOR STORES, 37 Main St., at A. H. Riise Gift & Liquor Mall. Tel. 776-2303.
A wide selection of imported merchandise is displayed in a restored 18th-century

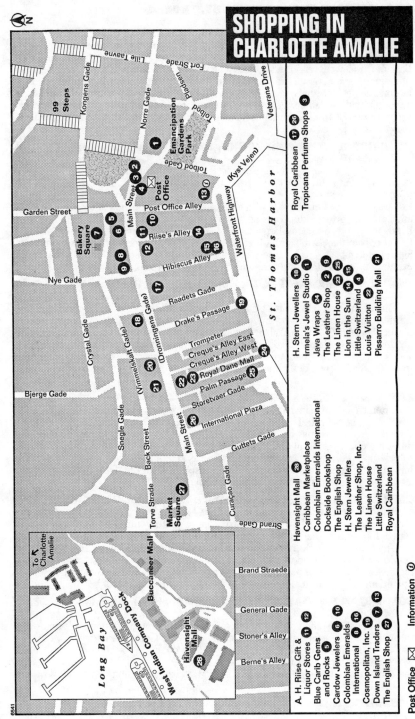

SHOPPING IN CHARLOTTE AMALIE

99 Steps

Kongens Gade

Lille Taarne

Norre Gade

Fort Strade

Veterans Drive

Emancipation Gardens Park

Tolbod Gade

Tolbod Gade

Kyst Vejen)

Waterfront Highway (Kyst Vejen)

Post Office

Post Office Alley

Garden Street

Bakery Square

Main Street

Riise's Alley

Hibiscus Alley

Nye Gade

Raadets Gade

Crystal Gade

Drake's Passage

Vimmelskaft Gade

(Dronningens Gade)

Trompeter

Creque's Alley East

Creque's Alley West

Royal Dane Mall

Bjerge Gade

Palm Passage

Snegle Gade

Storetvaer Gade

Back Street

International Plaza

Main Street

Guttets Gade

Market Square

Curaçao Gade

Torve Strade

Strand Gade

St. Thomas Harbor

Royal Caribbean

Tropicana Perfume Shops

H. Stern Jewellers 18
Irmela's Jewel Studio 1
Java Wraps 24
The Leather Shop 2
The Linen House 9
Lion in the Sun 14
Little Switzerland 4
Louis Vuitton 22
Pissarro Building Mall 21

Havensight Mall 28
Caribbean Marketplace
Colombian Emeralds International
Dockside Bookshop
The English Shop
H. Stern Jewellers
The Leather Shop, Inc.
The Linen House
Little Switzerland
Royal Caribbean

A. H. Riise Gift & Liquor Stores 11 12
Blue Carib Gems and Rocks 5
Cardow Jewelers 6 10
Colombian Emeralds International 8 16
Cosmopolitan, Inc. 19
Down Island Traders 7 13
The English Shop 27

To Charlotte Amalie

Long Bay

Buccaneer Mall

West Indian Company Dock

Havensight Mall

Brand Straede

General Gade

Stoner's Alley

Berne's Alley

Post Office ⊠   Information ℹ

Danish warehouse that extends from Main Street to the Waterfront. Special attention is paid to the collection of jewelry and watches from Europe. Featured among the many name brands in the china and crystal department are Waterford, Lalique, Daum, Baccarat, and Wedgwood. A. H. Riise Gift & Liquor Stores also has a large selection of fragrances and cosmetics for men and women, and carries a large selection of liquors, wines, cordials, and tobacco. Every purchase is backed by a 60-day unconditional guarantee. For a brochure and toll-free shop-by-phone service, call 800/524-2037 Monday through Saturday from 9am to 5pm Atlantic Standard Time; closed major holidays.

BLUE CARIB GEMS AND ROCKS, Bakery Square Shopping Mall. Tel. 774-8525.

For a decade the owners prospected for gemstones in the Caribbean, and these stones have been brought direct from the mine to you, in this store behind Little Switzerland. The raw stones are cut and polished, then fashioned into jewelry by the lost-wax process. On one side of the premises you can see the craftspeople at work, and on the other side you can view their finished products—including such handsomely set stones as larimar, the sea/sky-blue-patterned variety of pectolite found only in the Caribbean. A lifetime guarantee is given on all handcrafted jewelry. Since the items are locally made, they are duty-free and not included in the $1,200 exemption. Incidentally, this establishment also provides emergency eyeglass repair.

CARIBBEAN MARKETPLACE, Havensight Mall (Building III). Tel. 776-5400.

One of the best selections of Caribbean handcrafts is found here, including Sunny Caribbee products—a vast array of condiments (ranging from spicy peppercorns to nutmeg mustard). There's also a wide selection of Sunny Caribbee's botanical products such as foaming rosemary bath gel plus natural beauty soaps made from such concoctions as chamomile or coconut. Other items range from steel-pan drums from Trinidad to wooden Jamaican jigsaw puzzles, from St. Lucia batiks to Cayman Islands' bikinis.

CARDOW JEWELERS, 39 Main St. Tel. 774-1140.

Often called the Tiffany's of the Caribbean, it boasts the largest selection of fine jewelry in the world. This fabulous shop, which has more than 20,000 rings on display, provides savings because of its worldwide direct buying, large turnover, and duty-free prices. Unusual and traditional designs are offered in diamonds, emeralds, rubies, sapphires, and Brazilian stones, as well as in pearls. Cardow has a whole wall of Italian gold chains. Antique-coin jewelery is also featured. The Treasure Cove has case after case of fine gold jewelry, all priced under $200.

COKI OF ST. THOMAS, Compass Point Marina. Tel. 775-6560.

Just outside Charlotte Amalie in the East End, Coki is situated in the midst of a little "restaurant row," so you can combine a gastronomic tour with a shopping expedition. From the store's expansive cutting boards come some of the best easy-to-wear cotton clothes in the Virgin Islands. An American, George McBride, employs a bevy of island women who sew pieces of hand-woven Madras cotton into resortwear suitable for yachting, beaching, or "hanging out." In winter the shop is open daily from 9am to 9pm; its off-season hours are shortened.

COLOMBIAN EMERALDS INTERNATIONAL, Havensight Mall. Tel. 774-2442.

With another branch on Main Street, at the waterfront, this company is renowned throughout the Caribbean for the finest collection of Colombian emeralds, both set and unset. Each Colombian Emeralds store has a complete selection of loose stones, which are duty free for those returning to the U.S. mainland. In addition to jewelry, the shop stocks some of the world's finest watches, including Raymond Weil and Seiko.

COSMOPOLITAN, INC., Drakes Passage and the Waterfront. Tel. 776-2040.

Since 1973 this store has drawn a lot of repeat business. Its shoe salon features Bally of Switzerland and handmade A. Testoni of Bologna, Italy. In swimwear, it provides one of the best selections of Gottex of Israel for women and Gottex, Hom, Lahco of Switzerland, and Fila for men. A men's wear section offers Paul & Shark from Italy, Metzger shirts from Switzerland, and Burma Bibas sports shirts. Tenniswear is also featured.

DOWN ISLAND TRADERS, at the Waterfront. Tel. 776-4641.

The aroma of spices will lead you to this original native market. These outlets have an attractive display of spices, teas, seasonings, jams, and condiments, most of which are prepared from natural Caribbean products. The owner also carries candies and jellies, a line of local cookbooks, silk-screened island designs on T-shirts and bags, Haitian metal sculpture, and children's gifts. Caribbean art and jewelry are also sold.

There's a second Down Island Traders in Bakery Square on Back Street (tel. 774-4265).

THE ENGLISH SHOP, Main St. at Market Sq. Tel. 774-3495.

This store, along with a branch at Havensight Mall (tel. 776-3776), has a wide selection of china, crystal, and figurines from the world's top makers.

H. STERN JEWELLERS, Havensight Mall and Main St. Tel. 776-1939.

You'll find colorful gem and jewel creations at five locations on St. Thomas—two on Main Street; one in Havensight Mall; and one each at Bluebeard's Castle and Frenchman's Reef Hotel—as well as in a store on St. Maarten, Netherlands Antilles. Every shop has the same duty-free prices, a considerable savings for visiting shoppers. Stern gives worldwide guaranteed service, including a one-year exchange privilege.

IRMELA'S JEWEL STUDIO, in the Old Grand Hotel, at the beginning of Main St. Tel. 774-5875, or toll free 800/524-2047.

Irmela's has made a name for itself in the highly competitive jewelry business on St. Thomas. Here the jewelry is unique, custom-designed by Irmela and handmade by her studio or imported from around the world. Irmela has the largest selection of cultured pearls in the Caribbean, including freshwater Biwa, South Sea, and natural-color black Tahitian pearls. Choose from hundreds of clasps and pearl shorteners. Irmela has a large selection of unset stones, such as rubies, sapphires, emeralds, and unusual ones including tanzanite and alexandrite. Diamonds range from pear-shaped to emerald cut, marquis, and even heart-shaped, in sizes from tiny two-pointers to several carats.

JAVA WRAPS, 24 Palm Passage, on the waterfront. Tel. 774-3700.

With its distinctive brown tiles, this store is decorated with traditional Javanese matting and has exotic Balinese wood carvings on the walls. Locals and tourists alike buy the hand-batiked resortwear line, especially shorts, shirts, sundresses, and children's clothing. Java Wraps is known for its sarong pieces and demonstrates how to tie them in at least 15 different ways.

JIM TILLETT GALLERY, Tillett Gardens, Tutu. Tel. 775-1929.

A visit to the art gallery and craft studios of Jim Tillett is a sightseeing expedition. The Tillett compound was converted from a Danish farm called Tutu. The Tillett name conjures up high-fashion silk-screen printing by the famous Tillett brothers, whose exquisite fabrics were used for years by top designers and featured in such magazines as *Vogue* and *Harper's Bazaar*. Jim Tillett settled on St. Thomas, after creating a big splash in Mexico, where his work was featured in *Life* magazine. At his compound you can casually visit the adjoining workshops, where you can see silk-screening in progress.

Upstairs is an art gallery with an abundance of maps, paintings, sculpture, and graphics by local artists. Mr. Tillett created a series of maps on fine cotton canvas that are best-selling items. Arts Alive Fairs are held there three times a year—in spring, summer, and fall. These fairs give local artists a showcase for their work and offer crafts demonstrations and special features including puppet shows for children; folk dancers; other dancing, such as tap, ballet, and modern; steel bands; and calypso music.

THE LEATHER SHOP, INC., 1 Main St. and Havensight Mall. Tel. 776-0290.

Many handbags here are from chic Italian designers: Fendi, Bottega Veneta, Michel Clo, Furla, Prada, and Il Bisonte. You'll find a wide assortment of belts, sized to order with your choice of buckle. There are many styles of wallets, briefcases, and attaché cases, as well as all-leather luggage from Land.

THE LINEN HOUSE, 7A Royal Dane Mall. Tel. 774-8117.

The Linen House is considered one of the best stores for linens in the West Indies. It has another location at Havensight Mall (tel. 774-0868). You'll find a wide selection of placemats, decorative tablecloths, and many hand-embroidered goods. There are many high-fashion styles.

LION IN THE SUN, Riise's Alley. Tel. 776-4203.

It's one of the most expensive clothing stores on the island, but patrons go here for its collection of designer chic casual apparel. Whether it's tanks, Ts, shorts, pants, or skirts, this store is likely to have what you're looking for, including clothes by such designers as Sonia Rykiel. But because of the prices, it's better to start your shopping first at the sales rack, looking for some discounts. Otherwise, the owner is firm about prices as marked—no bargaining here.

LITTLE SWITZERLAND, 5 Main St. Tel. 776-2010.

Little Switzerland, with a branch on the dock at Havensight Mall, sells fine watches, a wide selection of jewelry from Europe and Asia, and the best in crystal and china. They also maintain the official outlets for Hummel, Lladró, and Swarovski figurines.

LOUIS VUITTON, 24 Main St., at Palm Passage. Tel. 774-3644.

For fine leather goods, you can't beat Louis Vuitton, where the complete line by the world-famous French designer is available: suitcases, handbags, wallets, and other accessories.

ROYAL CARIBBEAN, 33 Main St. Tel. 776-4110.

With additional branches at 23 Main St. (tel. 776-5449) and Havensight Mall (tel. 776-8890), this is the largest camera and electronics store in the Caribbean. Since 1977 it has offered good values in top-brand cameras and electronic equipment, including all accessories. Royal Caribbean is the authorized Sony dealer, with a complete selection of its products. It also has good buys in famous-name watches, Mikimoto pearls, Dupont and Dunhill lighters, jewelry for both men and women, and gift items.

TROPICANA PERFUME SHOPPES, 2 and 14 Main St. Tel. 774-0010, or toll free 800/233-7948.

These two stores stand at the beginning of Main Street near the Emancipation Gardens Post Office. The first is billed as the largest parfumerie in the world. Behind its rose-colored facade, it offers all the famous names in perfumes and cosmetics, including Nina Ricci and Chanel for women and men. Men will also find Europe's best colognes and aftershave lotions here. When you return home, you can mail-order all these fragrances by taking advantage of Tropicana's toll-free number.

3. WHERE TO DINE

Even if you're over just for the day from San Juan, chances are you'll be on St. Thomas for lunch. The island offers a wide selection of restaurants, but I'll review only a few choice ones.

IN CHARLOTTE AMALIE

BLACKBEARD'S CASTLE, 38-39 Dronningens Gade. Tel. 776-4321.
 Cuisine: AMERICAN/CARIBBEAN. **Reservations:** Recommended for dinner.

$ Prices: Appetizers $4.75–$9.75; main courses $17.50–$27.50. AE, MC, V.
Open: Lunch Mon–Fri 11:30am–2:30pm; dinner daily 6:30–9:30pm; brunch Sun
11am–3pm.

This hotel at the east end of town offers an elegant and ambitious dining room
featuring contemporary American cuisine with a Caribbean flair. Awarded three gold
medals for ambience, Caribbean dishes, and overall food in local contests, owners
Bob Harrington and Henrique Konzen offer one of the best Sunday brunches on the
island. Dinners include frequently changing specials. Guests have a wide choice of
appetizers, including sautéed escargots with sun-dried tomatoes and pan-seared
langostino cakes with a roasted red-pepper sauce. There is also the chef's daily
selection of hot or chilled soups, plus an array of salads, including the classic Caesar's.
Pastas, such as cheese tortellini with smoked chicken breast, are available in half
portions as appetizers. Main courses are likely to feature veal chop stuffed with fresh
vegetables; Black Forest ham and mozzarella; grilled swordfish steak with a tropical
salsa; or pan-seared red snapper filet with a fresh-fruit butter sauce. The dessert menu,
a treat unto itself, is likely to include everything from Bailey's Irish Cream cheesecake
to frozen peanut butter pie with chocolate drizzle. Lunches, which are slightly less
elaborate and about one-third the price, focus on salads, delicately seasoned platters, and
frothy rum-based drinks. In winter, live jazz is presented Tuesday through
Saturday from 8pm to midnight.

FIDDLE LEAF, 31 Kongens Gade, Government Hill. Tel. 775-2810.
Cuisine: MODERN CARIBBEAN. **Reservations:** Recommended.
$ Prices: Appetizers $6–$9; main courses $18–$27. AE, MC, V.
Open: Dinner only, Tues–Sun 6–10pm.

Decorated in an open, contemporary Caribbean style and with lush plants and
lattices, this restaurant serves some of the most creative food on the island. In what
had been a private house during the island's Danish occupation, nestled on a historic
hillside next to the Hotel 1829 (east of Main Street), it offers a menu by a chef (Robert
Oliver) who was born in New Zealand and has lived in both Fiji and New York City.
It includes such dishes as chilled tomato-and-mint soup with a peppered granita, roast
duck and mango salad with ginger-flavored vinaigrette, Caribbean bouillabaisse with
Jamaican curry and coconut sauce, swordfish roasted in a banana leaf served with
grilled pineapple and papaya salsa, ginger-crusted wahoo with fresh-fruit chutney and
grilled plantains, and such desserts as coconut shortcake with caramelized bananas
and a Myers rum crème caramel with clove-flavored cookies.

**HARD ROCK CAFE, International Plaza, The Waterfront, Queen's Quar-
ter. Tel. 777-5555.**
Cuisine: AMERICAN. **Reservations:** Not accepted.
$ Prices: Appetizers $4.25–$7; main courses $7.25–$16. AE, MC, V.
Open: Daily 11am–midnight. (Bar, daily 11am–2am.)

Occupying the second floor of a pink-sided mall whose big windows overlook the
ships moored in Charlotte Amalie's harbor, this restaurant is a member of the
international chain that calls itself the "Smithsonian of rock 'n' roll." Entire walls
are devoted to the memorabilia of such artists as John Lennon, Eric Clapton, and
Bob Marley. Throughout most of the day the place functions as a restaurant,
serving barbecued meats, salads, sandwiches, burgers (including a well-flavored
veggie burger), fresh fish, steaks, and what are said to be the best fajitas in the Virgin Islands. Tuesday through Saturday from 10:30pm to 2am a live band provides
music, at which time a small dance floor gets busy and the bar trade picks up considerably.

HOTEL 1829, Kongens Gade. Tel. 776-1829.
Cuisine: CONTINENTAL. **Reservations:** Required.
$ Prices: Appetizers $5.50–$12.50; main courses $22.50–$32.50. AE, MC, V.
Open: Dinner only, daily 6–10pm. **Closed:** Sun May–Nov.

The Hotel 1829 building is graceful and historic, and its restaurant serves some of the
finest food on St. Thomas. For carefully prepared food and drink with a distinctive

European flavor, guests walk up the hill at the east end of Main Street and climb the stairs of this old structure, heading for the attractive bar for a before-dinner drink. You can have a cocktail on a terrace, or you can be cooled by ceiling fans if you choose the main room, whose walls were made from ships' ballast. The floor consists of Moroccan tiles, two centuries old. For an appetizer, you might select escargots maître d'hôtel or perhaps one of the velvety smooth soups, such as cold cucumber. Also try the lobster bisque, which is made here fresh daily. The fish and meat dishes are usually excellent, as are the many grill dishes. The specialty of the house is the award-winning soufflés, such as chocolate, Amaretto, or raspberry.

VIRGILIO'S, 18 Dronningens Gade. Tel. 776-4920.

Cuisine: ITALIAN. **Reservations:** Recommended.

$ Prices: Appetizers $6–$8.25 at lunch, $8–$12 at dinner; main courses $12–$23 at lunch, $16–$39 at dinner. AE, MC, V.

Open: Lunch Mon–Sat 11:30am–4pm; dinner Mon–Sat 4–10:30pm.

Among the best Italian eateries in the Virgin Islands, this restaurant is sheltered with heavy ceiling beams and brick vaulting which remains exactly as it was designed 200 years ago. Be on the lookout for its entrance, which is located on a narrow alleyway running between Main Street and Back Street. With only 12 tables, this is one of the smallest and most intimate restaurants on St. Thomas; the staff is exceptionally well trained. Menu specialties include the full repertoire of northern Italy, including homemade pastas, elegant salads, seafood dishes such as red snapper l'amatriciana, cioppino (a savory seafood stew), and veal chop celestino (stuffed with prosciutto, mozzarella, and mushrooms), and an extensive array of desserts, many of them flambéed.

AT FRENCHTOWN

ALEXANDER'S, rue de St. Barthélemy. Tel. 774-4349.

Cuisine: CONTINENTAL. **Reservations:** Recommended. **Transportation:** Vitran bus.

$ Prices: Appetizers $5.25–$8.50; main courses $12–$20. AE, MC, V.

Open: Lunch Mon–Sat 11:30am–5pm; dinner Mon–Sat 5:30–10pm.

Alexander's will accommodate you in air-conditioned comfort with picture windows overlooking the harbor. It's named for its Austrian-born owner, Alexander Treml. There are only 12 tables, enabling Austrian cooking to be served with a flair. There's a heavy emphasis on seafood specialties, including conch schnitzel. Other dishes include a mouth-watering wienerschnitzel, Nürnberger rostbraten, goulash, and homemade pâté. For dessert, you might try the homemade strudel (either apple or cheese) or the Schwartzwalder torte. Lunch consists of a variety of crêpes, quiches, and a daily chef's special.

CAFE NORMANDIE, rue de St. Barthélemy. Tel. 774-1622.

Cuisine: FRENCH. **Reservations:** Recommended. **Transportation:** Vitran bus.

$ Prices: Appetizers $5.50–$14.50; fixed-price dinner $29.50–$38.50. AE, DC, MC, V.

Open: Dinner only, daily 6–10pm. **Closed:** Mon off-season.

The fixed-price meals offered here are one of the best dining values on the island. Although there's a selection of à la carte hors d'oeuvres, the price of the fixed-price dinners includes soup, a fresh garden salad, and an individually prepared main dish. Predominantly French, dinner begins with hors d'oeuvres, perhaps made with seafood, plus soup, often French onion. Then you're served a salad and sorbet (to clear your palate) before your main course, which you select from specialties ranging from langouste to beef Wellington or chicken breast with champagne sauce. The dessert special (not featured on the fixed-price meal) is their original chocolate-fudge pie. The restaurant is air-conditioned, and the glow of candlelight makes it quite elegant. It's beautifully run, and the service is excellent. There's a relaxed informality about the dress code, but you shouldn't show up in a bathing suit.

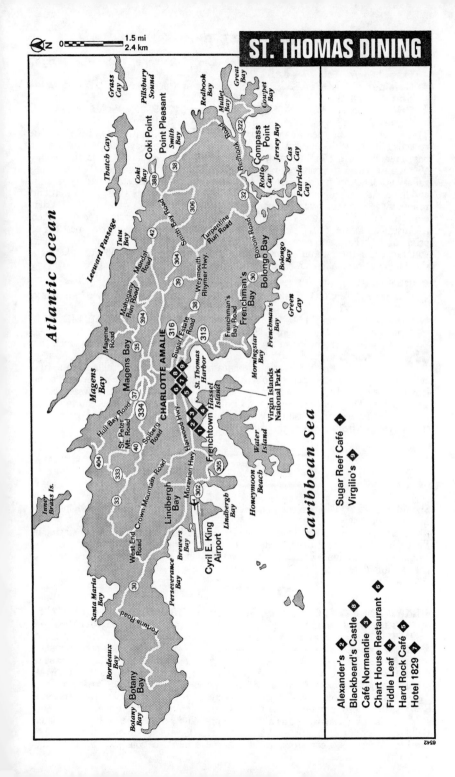

ST. THOMAS DINING

0 ——— 1.5 mi
——— 2.4 km

Sugar Reef Café ◆1
Virgilio's ◆9

Alexander's ◆2
Blackbeard's Castle ◆8
Café Normandie ◆3
Chart House Restaurant ◆6
Fiddle Leaf ◆4
Hard Rock Café ◆5
Hotel 1829 ◆7

6542

CHART HOUSE RESTAURANT, at the Admiral's Inn, Villa Olga, Frenchtown. Tel. 774-4262.
Cuisine: STEAK/SEAFOOD. **Reservations:** Recommended. **Transportation:** Vitran bus.
$ Prices: Appetizers $4.95–$8.95; main courses $12.95–$29.95. AE, DC, MC, V.
Open: Dinner only, Sun–Thurs 5–10pm, Fri–Sat 5–11pm.

This restaurant is on the same property as the Admiral's Inn (the site of the Russian consulate in the 19th century), but it's run separately. You may want to journey out past Frenchtown for dinner in this tranquil spot. The restaurant is in the rebuilt Victorian villa. In the bar area you can listen to divers' "bull sessions." The dining gallery is a large open terrace fronting the sea. Cocktail service starts nightly at 5pm, and the bartender will make you his special drink called a Bailey's banana colada. The restaurant features the best salad bar on the island, with a choice of 30 to 40 items that come with the dinner. Steaks are a specialty, but menu offers everything from chicken to Australian lobster tail. Of course, this chain is known for serving the finest cut of prime rib anywhere, and here it comes loading down a plate at 22 ounces. For dessert, you can order the famous Chart House "mud pie" which, despite its name, is a shockingly calorie-laden ice-cream concoction.

SUGAR REEF CAFE, 17 Crown Bay. Tel. 776-4466.
Cuisine: SEAFOOD. **Reservations:** Not required. **Transportation:** Vitran bus.
$ Prices: Appetizers $4.50–$9.50; main courses $12.50–$29.50. AE, MC, V.
Open: Lunch daily 11:30am–2:30pm; dinner daily 6–10pm.

Just west of Frenchtown on the waterfront, off East Gregerie Channel, this restaurant is a good choice for a quiet afternoon of boat watching. Guests anchor in at the mahogany bar beneath mulberry-colored ceiling beams and swirling fans in a breezy open-sided pavilion. Drinks are served here all day and often late into the night. Lunch is likely to include a choice of deli sandwiches, veal piccata, and omelets. The dinner menu features grilled yellowtail tuna, Caribbean lobster (a different recipe every day), sautéed veal medallions with dry vermouth and capers, and the Sugar Reef fresh catch of the day.

4. WHERE TO STAY

Should you like St. Thomas, you may decide to stay over for the night or perhaps settle in for a longer stay.

Nearly every beach has its own hostelry. You're faced with a choice of staying in the capital, Charlotte Amalie, or at any of the far points of St. Thomas. Perhaps St. Thomas has more inns of character than anyplace else in the Caribbean. I've included only a limited selection.

VERY EXPENSIVE

GRAND PALAZZO, Great Bay, St. Thomas, USVI 00802. Tel. 809/775-3333, or toll free 800/283-8666. Fax 809/775-4444. 152 suites. A/C MINIBAR TV TEL **Transportation:** Vitran bus.
$ Rates: Winter, $450–$495 junior suite for two; $785–$865 one-bedroom suite for two; $1,125–$1,235 two-bedroom suite for four. Off-season, $335 junior suite for two; $575 one-bedroom suite for two; $895 two-bedroom suite for four. MAP $65 per person extra in winter, $55 off-season. AE, DC, MC, V. **Parking:** Free.

The acquisition several years ago of one of the few remaining large tracts of seafront property on the island (15 acres of sloping land with a spectacular view of St. John) was viewed as a minor triumph in its own right. A short time later, the developers of this luxury hotel, the Pemberton Group of Barbados, hired some of the best architects, decorators, and landscape experts to construct what is today probably the most upscale and desirable hotel on St. Thomas. Set near Red Hook, it lies about 4½ miles southeast of Charlotte Amalie.

Opened in August 1992, the hotel comprises half a dozen three-story villas designed with Italian Renaissance motifs and pastel versions of such Mediterranean colors as ocher yellow and burnt sienna. The villas encircle a freshwater pond (home to a colony of Bahamian ducks) whose boundaries were retained as part of the ecology-conscious theme. Guests register in the "reception palazzo," whose arches and accessories were inspired by a Venetian palace, before heading to bedrooms with European themes. They are equipped with all the electronic amenities you'd expect (including a digital safe) and marble bathrooms. The public rooms are decorated with nautical themes.

Dining/Entertainment: The Palm Terrace, set beneath rows of arcades, is the more formal of the hotel's two restaurants. Equally appealing, though, is the Café Vecchio, whose murals depict the botanical diversity of a latter-day garden of Babylon. The hotel also has three bars, one of which has live piano music in winter.

Services: Concierge, 24-hour room service, top-notch tennis instructors, massage.

Facilities: Air-conditioned health club/gym, free use of Hobie cats and Sunfish, a 53-foot catamaran (*The Lady Lynsey*) for cocktail sails, four tennis courts, a swimming pool designed so that its water looks like an extension of the sea stretching toward St. John.

MARRIOTT'S FRENCHMAN'S REEF BEACH RESORT, Flamboyant Point (P.O. Box 7100), Charlotte Amalie, St. Thomas, USVI 00801. Tel. 809/776-8500, or toll free 800/524-2000 in the U.S. Fax 809/774-6249. 421 rms, 18 suites. A/C MINIBAR TV TEL **Transportation:** Water or land taxi from Charlotte Amalie.

$ Rates: Winter, $260–$295 single or double; from $443 suite. Off-season, $165 single or double; from $315 suite. MAP $52 per person extra. AE, DC, MC, V. **Parking:** Free.

Frenchman's Reef has a winning southern position on a projection of land overlooking both the harbor at Charlotte Amalie and the Caribbean. Everywhere you look are facilities devoted to the good life. Whatever your holiday needs, chances are you'll find them at "The Reef." To reach the private beach, you take a glass-enclosed elevator. The bedrooms vary greatly but are generally furnished in traditional good taste.

Dining/Entertainment: Seafood with a continental flair is served at Windows on the Harbour, which resembles the inside of a cruise ship and offers a view of the harbor, as promised by its name. You can also eat at the Lighthouse Bar, once an actual lighthouse. In addition, Caesar's offers an Italian cuisine at surfside. In the evening, the Top of the Reef, a supper club, provides entertainment, or you can go to La Terraza lounge.

Services: Room service (7am to 10:30pm daily), laundry, babysitting.

Facilities: Two giant swimming pools, suntanning areas, a poolside bar, tennis courts, many kinds of water sports (snorkeling, scuba diving, sailing, deep-sea fishing).

SAPPHIRE BEACH RESORT & MARINA, Rte. 38, Smith Bay Rd. (P.O. Box 8088), St. Thomas, USVI 00801. Tel. 809/775-6100, or toll free 800/524-2090 in the U.S. Fax 809/775-4024. 171 suites and villas. A/C MINIBAR TV TEL **Transportation:** Vitran bus.

$ Rates: Winter, $265–$335 suite for two; $330–$450 villa for two. Off-season, $175–$210 suite for two; $220–$250 villa for two. Children 12 and under stay free in parents' room. MAP $50 per person extra. AE, DC, MC, V. **Parking:** Free.

One of the finest modern luxury resorts in the Caribbean, this secluded retreat in the East End merits an extended stay. Guests can arrive by yacht and occupy a berth in the 67-slip marina or stay at a superb suite or villa. The casually elegant accommodations open onto a horseshoe bay, with one of St. Thomas's most spectacular beaches. The beaches are actually two ivory-sand crescents broken by the coral-reef peninsula of Prettyklip Point. The one-bedroom suites have fully equipped kitchens and microwaves, bedroom areas, living/dining rooms with queen-size sofa beds, and large, fully tiled outdoor galleries with lounge furniture. The villas are on two levels—the main one containing the same amenities as the suites, the upper level including a second full bath, a bedroom and sitting area with a queen-size sofa bed, and a sun deck with outdoor furniture. The suites accommodate one to four guests, whereas the villas are suitable for up to six.

Dining/Entertainment: Meals are served at the beach bar, and at night you can dine at the Seagrape, along the seashore, one of the island's finest eating places. Sometimes a 10-piece band is brought in for dancing under the stars.

Services: Beach towels, daily chamber service, guest-services desk, babysitting.

Facilities: Snorkeling equipment, Sunfish sailboats, windsurfing boards, four all-weather tennis courts—all free. The resort offers a quarter-acre freshwater pool and waterfront pavilion with a snack bar, plus one other big swimming pool. A complete diving center is right on the grounds.

STOUFFER GRAND BEACH RESORT, Rte. 38, Smith Bay Rd. (P.O. Box 8267), St. Thomas, USVI 00801. Tel. 809/775-1510, or toll free 800/HOTELS in the U.S. Fax 809/775-2185. 254 rms, 36 suites. A/C MINIBAR TV TEL **Transportation:** Take a taxi.

$ Rates: Winter, $315–$435 single or double; from $595 suite. Off-season, $215–$355 single or double; from $450 suite. MAP $65 per person extra. AE, DC, MC, V. **Parking:** Free.

Seven miles northeast of Charlotte Amalie, perched on a steep hillside above a 1,000-square-foot white sand beach, this resort occupies 34 acres on the northeast shore of St. Thomas. The accommodations are in two separate areas, poolside and hillside. The two-story townhouse suites and one-bedroom suites have Jacuzzis, and all units are decorated in shades of rose and mauve; the rooms are built at quirky acute angles, with fan-shaped windows, open balconies, and lighting. Each accommodation has a cable color TV with HBO and a hairdryer.

Dining/Entertainment: You can enjoy beachfront breakfast, lunch, and dinner at Bay Winds, featuring continental and authentic Caribbean cuisine. Breakfast buffets, mesquite-grilled dishes, and late-night desserts are served at Smugglers. Lighter fare is offered at the poolside snack bar. For drinks, live entertainment, and nightly dancing, there's the Smugglers Lounge.

Services: Daily children's program, round-the-clock babysitting, laundry service, 24-hour room service, twice-daily chamber service, guest-services desk/concierge, newspaper and coffee with wakeup call, newsstand.

Facilities: On the premises is one of the most innovative swimming pools on the island, with zigzag edges that provide a high-tech version of an Aztec ritual bath, plus another pool, a collection of boutiques, and a water-sports desk where you can rent sailboats or snorkeling equipment. Guests also can go scuba diving, windsurfing, and deep-sea fishing, and there are six lit tennis courts and an exercise facility. An 18-hole golf course is just 10 minutes away.

EXPENSIVE

BLUEBEARD'S CASTLE, Bluebeard's Hill (P.O. Box 7480), Charlotte Amalie, St. Thomas, USVI 00801. Tel. 809/744-1600, or toll free 800/524-6599 in the U.S. Fax 809/774-5134. 170 rms. A/C TV TEL

$ Rates: Winter, $195–$235 single or double. Off-season, $150–$185 single or double. Extra guest $30. MAP $50 per person extra. AE, DC, MC, V. **Parking:** Free.

Bluebeard's is almost a monument on St. Thomas, a popular, all-around resort on one side of the bay overlooking Charlotte Amalie. The history of this spot, at the east end of Main Street, goes back to 1665. The U.S. government turned what had been a private home into a hotel in the 1930s, and one of its guests was Franklin D. Roosevelt. Over the years Bluebeard's has built many additions and extensions to accommodate the ever increasing throng of holiday makers. The hotel has a

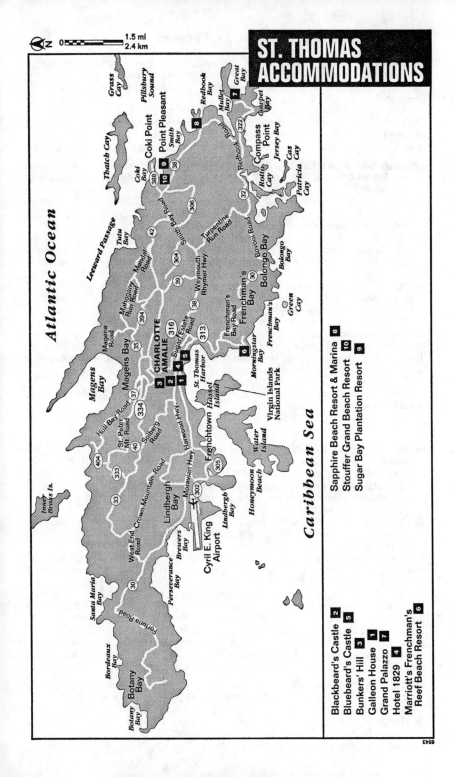

ST. THOMAS ACCOMMODATIONS

N

0   1.5 mi
     2.4 km

Atlantic Ocean

Caribbean Sea

Grass Cay
Pillsbury Sound
Point Pleasant
Coki Point
Redhook Bay
Great Bay
Mullet Bay
Campet Bay
Thatcb Cay
Coki Bay
Smitb Bay
322
Redhook Rd
Compass Point
Rotto Cay
Jersey Bay
Cas Patricia Cay
388
38
32
Leeward Passage
Smith Bay Road
306
42
Tutu Bay
Turpentine Run Road
Bovon Road
Bolongo Bay
304
Mandal Road
39
Weymouth Rhymer Hwy
Frenchman's Bay Road
Frenchman's Bay
Bolongo Bay
394
Mahogany Run Road
38
Green Cay
316
Sugar Estate Road
313
Magens Road
35
CHARLOTTE AMALIE
Morningstar Bay
Magens Bay
37
Magens Bay
St. Thomas Harbor
Hassel Island
Virgin Islands National Park
334
St. Peter Mt. Road
Solber'g Road
Harwood Hwy
Frenchtown
Water Island
40
Hull Bay Road
333
404
Crown Mountain Road
Moravian Hwy
Frenchtown Hwy
Honeymoon Beacb
Inner Brass Is.
West End Road
Lindbergh Bay
Brewers Bay
305
302
Lindbergb Bay
33
Santa Maria Bay
Perseverance Bay
Cyril E. King Airport
30
Fortuna Road
Bordeaux Bay
Botany Bay

Sapphire Beach Resort & Marina 8
Stouffer Grand Beach Resort 10
Sugar Bay Plantation Resort 9

Blackbeard's Castle 2
Bluebeard's Castle 5
Bunkers' Hill 3
Galleon House 1
Grand Palazzo 7
Hotel 1829 4
Marriott's Frenchman's Reef Beach Resort 6

6543

freshwater swimming pool and two whirlpools, but guests are also given free transportation to famous Magens Bay Beach. Championship tennis courts are on the premises. Bedchambers come in a wide variety of shapes and sizes—all pleasantly decorated.

The Sunset View Restaurant commands a panoramic view and offers many American and Caribbean specialties for open-air brunching, lunching, or late-night dining. Entre Nous, with views of the harbor, serves a continental cuisine, beginning with Caesar salad and going on to such dishes as rack of lamb and chateaubriand.

SUGAR BAY PLANTATION RESORT, 6500 Estate Smith Bay, St. Thomas, USVI 00802. Tel. 809/777-7100, or toll free 800/927-7100 in the U.S. Fax 809/777-7200. 294 rms, 6 suites. A/C TV TEL

$ Rates: Winter, $245–$295 single or double; from $595 suite. Off-season, $165–$215 single or double; from $450 suite. MAP $30 per person extra. AE, DC, MC, V. **Parking:** Free.

Located on the East End, a five-minute ride from Red Hook and adjacent to the Stouffer Grand Beach Resort, this hotel was built in 1992 as an upscale branch of the Holiday Inn chain. It has a central core where visitors register plus at least six pale-green/white-sided buildings of three to five stories for the accommodations. About 90% of these accommodations have balconies and ocean views, and all are equipped with a wall safe, a coffee maker, a hairdryer, and an unstocked refrigerator. The decor includes rattan furniture and pastel color schemes inspired by the tropics.

Dining/Entertainment: The resort has three food and beverage outlets, the most glamorous of which is the Manor, serving international food in a re-creation of a colonial plantation house. Another choice is the Ocean Club, near the hotel lobby. Its bar brings to mind a lounge on a cruise ship, complete with big windows and a sweeping view over the sea. Also available is a poolside bar and snack bar.

Services: Room service, babysitting, tour desk.

Facilities: Three swimming pools, a sandy beach, health club, five tennis courts, availability of snorkeling equipment.

MODERATE

BLACKBEARD'S CASTLE, Blackbeard's Hill (P.O. Box 6041), Charlotte Amalie, St. Thomas, USVI 00804. Tel. 809/776-1234, or toll free 800/344-5771 in the U.S. Fax 809/776-4321. 19 rms, 3 suites. A/C TV TEL

Directions: From the airport, turn right onto Highway 30, which you take to Highway 35, where you make a left turn; travel for half a mile until you see the sign pointing left to the hotel.

$ Rates (including continental breakfast): Winter, $110 single; $145 double; from $190 suite. Off-season, $75 single; $95 double; from $145 suite. AE, MC, V. **Parking:** Free.

It took the inspiration of an Illinois businessman to transform what had been a private residence into a genuinely charming inn. Owned by Bob Harrington, it enjoys one of the finest views of Charlotte Amalie and its harbor, thanks to its perch high on a hillside above the town. In 1679, the Danish governor erected a soaring tower of chiseled stone here as a lookout for unfriendly ships. According to legend, Blackbeard himself lived in the tower half a century later. Each bedroom has some type of semisecluded lattice-enclosed veranda, a flat-weave Turkish kilim, cable TV, terra-cotta floors, and simple furniture, along with a private bath. Guests enjoy use of a swimming pool whose waters almost lap the edge of the famous tower. The establishment's social center is within a stylish bar and restaurant.

HOTEL 1829, Kongens Gade (P.O. Box 1567), Charlotte Amalie, St. Thomas, USVI 00804. Tel. 809/776-1829, or toll free 800/524-2002 in the U.S. Fax 809/776-4313. 12 rms, 3 suites. A/C MINIBAR TV TEL

$ Rates (including continental breakfast): Winter, $70–$160 single; $80–$170 double; $280 suite. Off-season, $50–$110 single; $120 double; $155–$190 suite. Children under 12 not accepted. AE, MC, V. **Parking:** Free.

Erected by a French sea captain for his bride, this building was designed by an Italian architect in a Spanish motif. Danish and African workers completed the structure in 1829—hence the name. After a major renovation, this once-decaying historical site has become one of the leading small hotels of character in the Caribbean. Right in the heart of town, it is located about three minutes from Government House, built on a hillside with many levels and many steps (no elevator)—it's reached by a climb. The 1829 has actually been a hotel since the 19th century, welcoming such celebrated guests as King Carol of Romania (and his mistress, Madame Lupescu), Edna St. Vincent Millay, and Mikhail Baryshnikov.

Amid a cascade of flowering bougainvillea, you can reach the upper rooms, which overlook a central courtyard with a miniature swimming pool. The units, some of which are small, are beautifully designed, comfortable, and attractive. All have private baths and cable TVs, and most face the sea. During the hotel's restoration, old features were preserved whenever possible. A few rooms have antiques, such as four-poster beds.

INEXPENSIVE

BUNKERS' HILL, Bunkers' Hill, 7 Commandant Gade, Charlotte Amalie, St. Thomas, USVI 00802. Tel. 809/774-8056. Fax 809/774-3172. 11 rms (all with bath), 4 suites. A/C TV TEL

$ Rates (including continental breakfast): Winter, $80 single; $90 double; from $100 suite. Off-season, $60 single; $70 double; from $80 suite. AE, MC, V. **Parking:** Free.

This clean and centrally situated guest lodge would be suitable for students and others on a strict budget who don't want to sacrifice comfort and safety. Bunkers' Hill is situated right in the heart of town, across from the post office and just a short walk from Main Street and all the major restaurants of Charlotte Amalie.

GALLEON HOUSE, Government Hill (P.O. Box 6577), Charlotte Amalie, St. Thomas, USVI 00804. Tel. 809/774-6952, or toll free 800/524-2052 in the U.S. Fax 809/774-6952. 14 rms (12 with bath). A/C TV TEL

$ Rates (including continental breakfast): Winter, $59 single without bath, $109 single with bath; $69 double without bath, $119 double with bath. Off-season, $49 single without bath, $69 single with bath; $59 double without bath, $79 double with bath. AE, MC, V. **Parking:** Free.

The main attraction of this place is its location, next to the Hotel 1829 on Government Hill, at the east end of Main Street, about one block from the main shopping section of St. Thomas. To get there, walk up a long flight of stairs past a neighboring restaurant's veranda to reach the concrete terrace that doubles as this hotel's reception area. The rooms are scattered in several hillside buildings, and each has either a ceiling fan or air conditioning. There's even a small pool on the grounds. The home-cooked continental breakfast, consisting of fresh-baked goods, juice, and coffee, is served on the veranda overlooking the harbor.

APPENDIX

A. BASIC PHRASES & VOCABULARY

ENGLISH	SPANISH	PRONUNCIATION
Hello	**Buenos días**	*bway*-noss *dee*-ahss
How are you?	**Como está usted?**	koh-*moh* ess-*tah* oo-*steth*?
Very well	**Muy bien**	*mwee* byen
Thank you	**Gracias**	*gra*-thee-ahss
Good-bye	**Adiós**	ad-*dyohss*
Please	**Por favór**	pohr fah-*bohr*
Yes	**Sí**	see
No	**No**	noh
Excuse me	**Perdóneme**	pehr-*doh*-neh-may
Give me	**Deme**	*day*-may
Where is . . . ?	**Donde está . . . ?**	*dohn*-day ess-*tah* . . . ?
the station	**la estación**	la ess-*tah*-thyohn
a hotel	**un hotel**	oon oh-*tel*
a restaurant	**un restaurante**	oon res-tow-*rahn*-tay
the toilet	**el servicio**	el ser-*vee*-the-o
To the right	**A la derecha**	ah lah day-*ray*-chuh
To the left	**A la izquierda**	ah lah eeth-*kyayr*-duh
Straight ahead	**Adelante**	ah-day-*lahn*-tay
I would like . . .	**Quiero . . .**	*kyehr*-oh . . .
to eat	**comer**	ko-*mayr*
a room	**una habitación**	oo-nah ah-bee-tah-*thyon*
How much is it?	**Cuánto?**	*kwahn*-toh?
The check	**La cuenta**	la *kwen*-tah
When?	**Cuándo?**	*kwan*-doh
Yesterday	**Ayer**	ah-*yayr*
Today	**Hoy**	oy
Tomorrow	**Mañana**	mahn-*yah*-nah
Breakfast	**Desayuno**	deh-sai-*yoo*-noh
Lunch	**Comida**	co-*mee*-dah
Dinner	**Cena**	*thay*-nah

NUMBERS

1 **uno** (*oo*-noh)	11 **once** (*ohn*-thay)	18 **dieciocho** (dyeth-ee-*oh*-choh)
2 **dos** (dose)	12 **doce** (*doh*-thay)	19 **diecinueve** (dyeth-ee-*nyway*-bay)
3 **tres** (trayss)	13 **trece** (*tray*-thay)	20 **veinte** (*bayn*-tay)
4 **cuatro** (*kwah*-troh)	14 **catorce** (kah-*tor*-thay)	30 **trienta** (*trayn*-tah)
5 **cinco** (*theen*-koh)	15 **quince** (*keen*-thay)	40 **cuarenta** (kwah-*ren*-tah)
6 **seis** (sayss)	16 **dieciseis** (dyeth-ee-*sayss*)	50 **cincuenta** (theen-*kween*-tah)
7 **siete** (*syeh*-tay)	17 **diecisiete** (dyeth-ee-*sye*-tay)	
8 **ocho** (*oh*-choh)		
9 **nueve** (*nway*-bay)		
10 **diez** (dyeth)		

60 **sesenta**	80 **ochenta**	100 **cien** (thyen)
(say-*sen*-tah)	(oh-*chen*-tah)	1000 **mil** (mil)
70 **setenta**	90 **noventa**	
(say-*ten*-tah)	(noh-*ben*-tah)	

B. MENU TERMS

SOUPS

caldo gallego Galician broth
caldo de gallina chicken soup
sopa de ajo garlic soup
sopa de cebolla onion soup
sopa clara consommé
sopa espesa thick soup

sopa de fideos noodle soup
sopa de guisantes pea soup
sopa de lentejas lentil soup
sopa de pescado fish soup
sopa de tomate tomato soup
sopa de verduras vegetable soup

EGGS

huevos escaltados poached eggs
huevos fritos fried eggs
huevos duros hard-boiled eggs

huevos revueltos scrambled eggs
huevos por agua soft-boiled eggs
tortilla omelet

FISH

almejas clams
anchoas anchovies
anguilas eels
arenque herring
atún tuna
bacalao cod
calamares squid
cangrejo crab
caracoles snails
centollo sea urchin
chocos large squid
cigalas small lobsters
gambas shrimp
langosta lobster

langostinos prawns
lenguado sole
mejillones mussels
merluza hake
necoras spider crabs
ostras oysters
pescadilla whiting
pijotas small whiting
pulpo octopus
rodaballo turbot
salmonete mullet
sardinas sardines
trucha trout
vieiras scallops

MEATS

albondigas meatballs
bistec beefsteak
callos tripe
cerdo pork
chuleta cutlet
cocido stew
conejo rabbit
cordero lamb
costillas chops
gallina fowl
ganso goose
higado liver
jamón ham

lengua tongue
paloma pigeon
pato duck
pavo turkey
perdiz partridge
pollo chicken
riñón kidney
rosbif roast beef
solomillo loin
ternera veal
tocino bacon
vaca beef

VEGETABLES

aceitunas olives
alcachofa artichoke
arroz rice
berenjena eggplant
cebolla onion
col cabbage
coliflor cauliflower
esparragos asparagus
espinacas spinach

guisantes peas
judías verdes string beans
nabo turnip
patata potato
pepino cucumber
remolachas beets
setas mushrooms
tomate tomato
zanahorias carrots

SALADS

ensalada mixta mixed salad
ensalada de pepinos cucumber
  salad

ensalada verde green salad
lechuga lettuce

FRUITS

albaricoque apricot
aquacate avocado
cerezas cherries
ciruela plum
datil date
frambuesa raspberry
fresa strawberry
granada pomegranate
higo fig

limón lemon
manzana apple
melocoton peach
naranja orange
pera pear
piña pineapple
plátano banana
toronja grapefruit
uvas grapes

DESSERTS

buñuelos fritters
compota stewed fruit
flan caramel custard
fruta fruit

galletas tea cakes
helado ice cream
pasteles pastries
torta cake

BEVERAGES

agua water
agua mineral mineral water
café coffee
cerveza beer
ginebra gin
jerez sherry
jugo de naranjas orange juice
jugo de tomate tomato juice

leche milk
sangría red wine, fruit juice, and soda
sidra cider
sifon soda
té tea
vino blancho white wine
vino tinto red wine

BASICS

aceite oil
ajo garlic
azucar sugar
hielo ice
mantequilla butter
miel honey

mostaza mustard
pan bread
pimienta pepper
queso cheese
sal salt
vinagre vinegar

COOKING TERMS

asado roast
cocido broiled
empanado breaded
frito fried

muy hecho well done
poco hecho rare
tostado toast

C. THE METRIC SYSTEM

LENGTH

1 millimeter (mm)	=	.04 inches (*or* less than 1/16 in.)
1 centimeter (cm)	=	.39 inches (*or* just under 1/2 in.)
1 meter (m)	=	39 inches (*or* about 1.1 yards)
1 kilometer (km)	=	.62 miles (*or* about 2/3 of a mile)

To convert kilometers to miles, multiply the number of kilometers by .62. Also use to convert kilometers per hour (kmph) to miles per hour (m.p.h.).

To convert miles to kilometers, multiply the number of miles by 1.61. Also use to convert m.p.h. to kmph.

CAPACITY

1 liter (l)	=	33.92 fluid ounces	=	2.1 pints	=	1.06 quarts
	=	.26 U.S. gallons				
1 Imperial gallon	=	1.2 U.S. gallons				

To convert liters to U.S. gallons, multiply the number of liters by .26.

To convert U.S. gallons to liters, multiply the number of gallons by 3.79.

To convert Imperial gallons to U.S. gallons, multiply the number of Imperial gallons by 1.2.

To convert U.S. gallons to Imperial gallons, multiply the number of U.S. gallons by .83.

WEIGHT

1 gram (g)	=	.035 ounces (*or* about a paperclip's weight)
1 kilogram (kg)	=	35.2 ounces
	=	2.2 pounds
1 metric ton	=	2,205 pounds (1.1 short ton)

To convert kilograms to pounds, multiply the number of kilograms by 2.2.

To convert pounds to kilograms, multiply the number of pounds by .45.

AREA

1 hectare (ha)	=	2.47 acres		
1 square kilometer (km²)	=	247 acres	=	.39 square miles

To convert hectares to acres, multiply the number of hectares by 2.47.

To convert acres to hectares, multiply the number of acres by .41.

To convert square kilometers to square miles, multiply the number of square kilometers by .39.

To convert square miles to square kilometers, multiply the number of square miles by 2.6.

TEMPERATURE

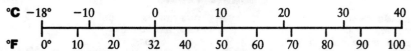

°C −18°   −10   0   10   20   30   40

°F 0° 10 20 32 40 50 60 70 80 90 100

To convert degrees Celsius to degrees Fahrenheit, multiply °C by 9, divide by 5, and add 32 (example: 20°C × 9 ÷ 5 + 32 = 68°F).

To convert degrees Fahrenheit to degrees Celsius, subtract 32 from °F, multiply by 5, then divide by 9 (example: 85°F − 32 × 5 ÷ 9 = 29.4°C).

D. MILEAGE CHART

	Utuado	San Sebastián	San Juan	San Germán	Ponce	Mayagüez	Humacao	Guayama	Fajardo	Coamo	Cayey	Caguas	Bayamón	Arecibo	Aguadilla
Aguadilla	42	16	81	31	63	15	107	101	113	84	103	91	74	33	—
Arecibo	20	28	48	62	52	49	74	89	81	73	72	59	41	—	33
Bayamón	61	69	8	105	69	90	33	48	38	43	29	16	—	41	74
Caguas	77	85	17	87	53	100	18	30	37	35	13	—	16	59	91
Cayey	63	87	30	74	40	87	31	17	50	23	—	13	29	72	103
Coamo	45	68	59	55	21	68	51	27	72	—	23	35	43	73	84
Fajardo	99	107	34	130	90	130	22	58	—	72	50	37	38	81	113
Guayama	69	83	44	73	38	84	36	—	58	27	17	30	48	89	101
Humacao	94	102	34	108	71	117	—	36	22	51	31	18	33	74	107
Mayagüez	47	21	98	14	46	—	117	84	130	68	87	100	90	49	15
Ponce	32	47	70	34	—	46	71	38	90	21	40	53	69	52	63
San Germán	66	31	105	—	34	14	108	73	130	55	74	87	105	62	31
San Juan	68	76	—	105	70	98	34	44	34	59	30	17	8	48	81
San Sebastián	27	—	76	31	47	21	102	83	107	68	87	85	69	28	16
Utuado	—	27	68	66	32	47	94	69	99	45	63	77	61	20	42

INDEX

226 • INDEX

Please Send Me the Books Checked Below:

FROMMER'S COMPREHENSIVE GUIDES
(Guides listing facilities from budget to deluxe,
with emphasis on the medium-priced)

	Retail Price	Code		Retail Price	Code
☐ Acapulco/Ixtapa/Taxco 1993–94	$15.00	C120	☐ Japan 1994–95 (Avail. 3/94)	$19.00	C144
☐ Alaska 1994–95	$17.00	C131	☐ Morocco 1992–93	$18.00	C021
☐ Arizona 1993–94	$18.00	C101	☐ Nepal 1994–95	$18.00	C126
☐ Australia 1992–93	$18.00	C002	☐ New England 1994 (Avail. 1/94)	$16.00	C137
☐ Austria 1993–94	$19.00	C119	☐ New Mexico 1993–94	$15.00	C117
☐ Bahamas 1994–95	$17.00	C121	☐ New York State 1994–95	$19.00	C133
☐ Belgium/Holland/ Luxembourg 1993–94	$18.00	C106	☐ Northwest 1994–95 (Avail. 2/94)	$17.00	C140
☐ Bermuda 1994–95	$15.00	C122	☐ Portugal 1994–95 (Avail. 2/94)	$17.00	C141
☐ Brazil 1993–94	$20.00	C111	☐ Puerto Rico 1993–94	$15.00	C103
☐ California 1994	$15.00	C134	☐ Puerto Vallarta/Manzanillo/ Guadalajara 1994–95 (Avail. 1/94)	$14.00	C028
☐ Canada 1994–95 (Avail. 4/94)	$19.00	C145	☐ Scandinavia 1993–94	$19.00	C135
☐ Caribbean 1994	$18.00	C123	☐ Scotland 1994–95 (Avail. 4/94)	$17.00	C146
☐ Carolinas/Georgia 1994–95	$17.00	C128	☐ South Pacific 1994–95 (Avail. 1/94)	$20.00	C138
☐ Colorado 1994–95 (Avail. 3/94)	$16.00	C143	☐ Spain 1993–94	$19.00	C115
☐ Cruises 1993–94	$19.00	C107	☐ Switzerland/Liechtenstein 1994–95 (Avail. 1/94)	$19.00	C139
☐ Delaware/Maryland 1994–95 (Avail. 1/94)	$15.00	C136	☐ Thailand 1992–93	$20.00	C033
☐ England 1994	$18.00	C129	☐ U.S.A. 1993–94	$19.00	C116
☐ Florida 1994	$18.00	C124	☐ Virgin Islands 1994–95	$13.00	C127
☐ France 1994–95	$20.00	C132	☐ Virginia 1994–95 (Avail. 2/94)	$14.00	C142
☐ Germany 1994	$19.00	C125	☐ Yucatán 1993–94	$18.00	C110
☐ Italy 1994	$19.00	C130			
☐ Jamaica/Barbados 1993–94	$15.00	C105			

FROMMER'S $-A-DAY GUIDES
(Guides to low-cost tourist accommodations and facilities)

	Retail Price	Code		Retail Price	Code
☐ Australia on $45 1993–94	$18.00	D102	☐ Israel on $45 1993–94	$18.00	D101
☐ Costa Rica/Guatemala/ Belize on $35 1993–94	$17.00	D108	☐ Mexico on $45 1994	$19.00	D116
☐ Eastern Europe on $30 1993–94	$18.00	D110	☐ New York on $70 1994–95 (Avail. 4/94)	$16.00	D120
☐ England on $60 1994	$18.00	D112	☐ New Zealand on $45 1993–94	$18.00	D103
☐ Europe on $50 1994	$19.00	D115	☐ Scotland/Wales on $50 1992–93	$18.00	D019
☐ Greece on $45 1993–94	$19.00	D100	☐ South America on $40 1993–94	$19.00	D109
☐ Hawaii on $75 1994	$19.00	D113	☐ Turkey on $40 1992–93	$22.00	D023
☐ India on $40 1992–93	$20.00	D010	☐ Washington, D.C. on $40 1994–95 (Avail. 2/94)	$17.00	D119
☐ Ireland on $45 1994–95 (Avail. 1/94)	$17.00	D117			

FROMMER'S CITY $-A-DAY GUIDES
(Pocket-size guides to low-cost tourist accommodations
and facilities)

	Retail Price	Code		Retail Price	Code
☐ Berlin on $40 1994–95	$12.00	D111	☐ Madrid on $50 1994–95 (Avail. 1/94)	$13.00	D118
☐ Copenhagen on $50 1992–93	$12.00	D003	☐ Paris on $50 1994–95	$12.00	D117
☐ London on $45 1994–95	$12.00	D114	☐ Stockholm on $50 1992–93	$13.00	D022

FROMMER'S WALKING TOURS
(With routes and detailed maps, these companion guides point out
the places and pleasures that make a city unique)

	Retail Price	Code		Retail Price	Code
☐ Berlin	$12.00	W100	☐ Paris	$12.00	W103
☐ London	$12.00	W101	☐ San Francisco	$12.00	W104
☐ New York	$12.00	W102	☐ Washington, D.C.	$12.00	W105

FROMMER'S TOURING GUIDES
(Color-illustrated guides that include walking tours, cultural and historic
sights, and practical information)

	Retail Price	Code		Retail Price	Code
☐ Amsterdam	$11.00	T001	☐ New York	$11.00	T008
☐ Barcelona	$14.00	T015	☐ Rome	$11.00	T010
☐ Brazil	$11.00	T003	☐ Scotland	$10.00	T011
☐ Florence	$ 9.00	T005	☐ Sicily	$15.00	T017
☐ Hong Kong/Singapore/			☐ Tokyo	$15.00	T016
Macau	$11.00	T006	☐ Turkey	$11.00	T013
☐ Kenya	$14.00	T018	☐ Venice	$ 9.00	T014
☐ London	$13.00	T007			

FROMMER'S FAMILY GUIDES

	Retail Price	Code		Retail Price	Code
☐ California with Kids	$18.00	F100	☐ San Francisco with Kids		
☐ Los Angeles with Kids			(Avail. 4/94)	$17.00	F104
(Avail. 4/94)	$17.00	F103	☐ Washington, D.C. with Kids		
☐ New York City with Kids			(Avail. 2/94)	$17.00	F102
(Avail. 2/94)	$18.00	F101			

FROMMER'S CITY GUIDES
(Pocket-size guides to sightseeing and tourist accommodations and
facilities in all price ranges)

	Retail Price	Code		Retail Price	Code
☐ Amsterdam 1993–94	$13.00	S110	☐ Montréal/Québec		
☐ Athens 1993–94	$13.00	S114	City 1993–94	$13.00	S125
☐ Atlanta 1993–94	$13.00	S112	☐ Nashville/Memphis		
☐ Atlantic City/Cape			1994–95 (Avail. 4/94)	$13.00	S141
May 1993–94	$13.00	S130	☐ New Orleans 1993–94	$13.00	S103
☐ Bangkok 1992–93	$13.00	S005	☐ New York 1994 (Avail.		
☐ Barcelona/Majorca/Minorca/			1/94)	$13.00	S138
Ibiza 1993–94	$13.00	S115	☐ Orlando 1994	$13.00	S135
☐ Berlin 1993–94	$13.00	S116	☐ Paris 1993–94	$13.00	S109
☐ Boston 1993–94	$13.00	S117	☐ Philadelphia 1993–94	$13.00	S113
☐ Budapest 1994–95 (Avail.			☐ San Diego 1993–94	$13.00	S107
2/94)	$13.00	S139	☐ San Francisco 1994	$13.00	S133
☐ Chicago 1993–94	$13.00	S122	☐ Santa Fe/Taos/		
☐ Denver/Boulder/Colorado			Albuquerque 1993–94	$13.00	S108
Springs 1993–94	$13.00	S131	☐ Seattle/Portland 1994–95	$13.00	S137
☐ Dublin 1993–94	$13.00	S128	☐ St. Louis/Kansas		
☐ Hong Kong 1994–95			City 1993–94	$13.00	S127
(Avail. 4/94)	$13.00	S140	☐ Sydney 1993–94	$13.00	S129
☐ Honolulu/Oahu 1994	$13.00	S134	☐ Tampa/St.		
☐ Las Vegas 1993–94	$13.00	S121	Petersburg 1993–94	$13.00	S105
☐ London 1994	$13.00	S132	☐ Tokyo 1992–93	$13.00	S039
☐ Los Angeles 1993–94	$13.00	S123	☐ Toronto 1993–94	$13.00	S126
☐ Madrid/Costa del			☐ Vancouver/Victoria 1994–		
Sol 1993–94	$13.00	S124	95 (Avail. 1/94)	$13.00	S142
☐ Miami 1993–94	$13.00	S118	☐ Washington, D.C. 1994		
☐ Minneapolis/St.			(Avail. 1/94)	$13.00	S136
Paul 1993–94	$13.00	S119			

SPECIAL EDITIONS

	Retail Price	Code		Retail Price	Code
☐ Bed & Breakfast Southwest	$16.00	P100	☐ Caribbean Hideaways	$16.00	P103
☐ Bed & Breakfast Great American Cities (Avail. 1/94)	$16.00	P104	☐ National Park Guide 1994 (avail. 3/94)	$16.00	P105
			☐ Where to Stay U.S.A.	$15.00	P102

Please note: if the availability of a book is several months away, we may have back issues of guides to that particular destination. Call customer service at (815) 734-1104.